Demography
of Indonesia's
Ethnicity

The **Institute of Southeast Asian Studies (ISEAS)** was established as an autonomous organization in 1968. It is a regional centre dedicated to the study of socio-political, security and economic trends and developments in Southeast Asia and its wider geostrategic and economic environment. The Institute's research programmes are the Regional Economic Studies (RES, including ASEAN and APEC), Regional Strategic and Political Studies (RSPS), and Regional Social and Cultural Studies (RSCS).

ISEAS Publishing, an established academic press, has issued more than 2,000 books and journals. It is the largest scholarly publisher of research about Southeast Asia from within the region. ISEAS Publishing works with many other academic and trade publishers and distributors to disseminate important research and analyses from and about Southeast Asia to the rest of the world.

Demography of Indonesia's Ethnicity

Aris Ananta
Evi Nurvidya Arifin
M. Sairi Hasbullah
Nur Budi Handayani
Agus Pramono

ISEAS

INSTITUTE OF SOUTHEAST ASIAN STUDIES
Singapore

First published in Singapore in 2015 by
ISEAS Publishing
Institute of Southeast Asian Studies
30 Heng Mui Keng Terrace
Pasir Panjang
Singapore 119614

E-mail: publish@iseas.edu.sg
Website: <http://bookshop.iseas.edu.sg>

The responsibility for facts and opinions in this publication rests exclusively with the authors and their interpretations do not necessarily reflect the views or the policy of the publishers or their supporters.

Ananta, Aris, 1954–
  Demography of Indonesia's Ethnicity / Aris Ananta, Evi Nurvidya Arifin,
  M. Sairi Hasbullah, Nur Budi Handayani, Agus Pramono.
  1. Ethnic groups—Indonesia.
  2. Names, Ethnological—Indonesia.
  3. Indonesia—Religion.
  4. Indonesia—Languages.
  5. Indonesia—Population.
  I. Arifin, Evi Nurvidya.
  II. Hasbullah, M. Sairi.
  III. Handayani, Nur Budi.
  IV. Pramono, Agus, 1955–
  V. Title.
DS631 A53   2015

ISBN 978-981-4519-87-8 (soft cover)
ISBN 978-981-4519-88-5 (e-book, PDF)

Typeset by Superskill Graphics Pte Ltd
Printed in Singapore by Markono Print Media Pte Ltd

CONTENTS

TABLES

FIGURES

FOREWORD

It is a great pleasure for me to write this foreword. Firstly because I have known Evi and Aris for many years and regard them as dear friends as well as important and gifted Indonesian scholars. However, the ethnic diversity of Indonesia has always been part of my research in the country. Ever since I found the treasure trove of ethnicity data in the 1930 Dutch-applied Volkstelling, I was hooked on following the important interactions between ethnicity and politics and the threats to it of attempts to rationalize Indonesian "culture", language etc. As a geographer, too, the spatial complexity of the heartlands of the various ethnolinguistic groups was fascinating. One of my great disappointments with the censuses of 1961, 1971, 1980 and 1990 was that they did not include an ethnicity question because of its sensitivity during a period when governments encouraged national Indonesian identification over ethnic-regional associations. However, this has fortunately changed. The 2000 census data was excellently analysed by Evi, Aris and Leo Suryadinata. As Professor Widjojo Nitisastro, one of Independent Indonesia's greatest economists and social scientists, said in his foreword to the volume, this study will see a flourishing of more ethnicity-based studies in Indonesia, and it certainly has.

Turning to the new study based on the 2010 census, Evi and Aris have been joined by three new co-authors — M. Sairi Hasbullah, Nur Budi Handayani and Agus Pramono — all from the BPS (Badan Pusat Statistik/Statistics – Indonesia). The latter have certainly added a significant understanding of the measurement of ethnicity in Indonesia and the ways in which they have been classified and the methods used to meaningfully aggregate small-sized groups into ethnic and sub-ethnic groups. A distinctive feature of the book is the development a new classification of ethnicity in Indonesia which reclassifies the 1,331 coded separate ethnicities into 600 ethnic groups and two excellent recommendations have been made to BPS to refine this further for the next census. The book contains the most detailed account of concepts, collection methods, data definition and methods of analysis that has yet been written and is to be highly recommended to scholars in this area.

The new classification will excite much discussion among scholars in this area. The choices are justified in Chapter 3. The new classification is tabled alongside the equivalent initial classification group for each province. The authors argue that the new approach has brought to light new evidence of increasing diversity within Indonesia. Particularly interesting is a spatial analysis of the ethnic diversity in each of the thirty-three provinces and a special analysis of foreigners in Indonesia. There is then a focus on the fifteen largest ethnic groups' demography and distribution, which is useful to read together with the equivalent chapter in the volume based on the 2000 census. In Chapter 7 there is a very interesting discussion on *Religion and Language* as two key ethnic dimensions in Indonesia.

Given the predominance of demographers and statisticians among the authors, it is not surprising that this is a very data-rich book which makes it extremely useful to scholars. However, there is a great deal more within the covers. Providing a full understanding of the way ethnicity was measured, but more importantly providing so many culturally based insights, which help us understand what is happening to Indonesia's languages and those who speak them. The book is presented in an excellent, accessible and readable style which makes it an essential read, not just for scholars focusing on ethnicity. It is crucial to those studying in other areas where the dynamic variable of ethnicity is playing an important role. Moreover, it is a very interesting "story" for those who love Indonesia.

The five authors are to be highly congratulated, as is the BPS for its continued emphasis and openness in making data available and in this case sharing their expertise with academic authors. Secondly, as with the first volume in this series, the Institute of Southeast Asian Studies (ISEAS) has done us a great service in publishing the book.

I thoroughly recommend this volume to all readers.

Graeme Hugo
Adelaide
17 December 2014

ACKNOWLEDGEMENTS

This is a very cohesive and engaging research collaboration between ISEAS (Institute of Southeast Asian Studies) and BPS (Badan Pusat Statistik; Statistics-Indonesia). The team consists of five researchers: two from ISEAS: Evi Nurvidya Arifin, a statistician-demographer, with intensive statistical experience involving large data sets, and Aris Ananta, an economist-demographer, with expertise on development issues. The three researchers from BPS are statisticians: M. Sairi Hasbullah, a senior researcher at BPS and the Head of Statistik-Indonesia in the Province of East Java, has the administrative capacity to manage the analysis of the very large and complex data set with a huge number of categories. Agus Pramono and Nur Budi Handayani, two researchers at BPS, are some of the people at BPS who were deeply involved in the field during the census. Not only did they gain statistical information, but they also obtained invaluable qualitative information on the various communities, enriching the statistics produced in this project.

We have also obtained information from our nationwide network. Our colleagues all over Indonesia have been willing to share their local expertise on ethnicity, religion, and language. We contacted the regional informants by email or telephone. We virtually travelled to all parts, including the remote areas, of Indonesia from our respective offices. Our study has also been much facilitated by the excellent collection on Indonesia's ethnicity in both ISEAS's and the University of Indonesia's libraries.

This study has been considerably sharpened by comments and questions from Prof. Charles Hirschman, a sociologist-demographer from the University of Washington, Washington State, and Prof Geoffrey Benjamin, an anthropologist-sociologist from Nanyang Technological University, Singapore.

We would also like to acknowledge critical questions and comments from ISEAS colleagues during the ISEAS internal seminar discussing the preliminary finding of this study. We are also indebted to important inputs from participants of the 27th IUSSP International Population Conference in South Korea, 2013, where we presented a poster on some results of our study, as well as participants of the Indonesian seminar series on 19 November 2013, when we shared the findings with members of the public in Singapore. We greatly appreciate the detailed comments from two anonymous referees.

This work has been made possible because of the continued openness in Indonesian politics, particularly on ethnicity. BPS also made an invaluable breakthrough by collecting information on ethnicity from the 2000 population census as well as the 2010 census.

The book would have never been realized without important contributions from many parties. First of all, we would like to convey our appreciation to Dr Suryamin, MSc, Chief Statistician of BPS, for supporting and providing tabulations based on the coded raw data set of the Indonesia 2010 population census. The strong encouragement from Bapak Wynandin Himawan, MSc, Deputy Chief Statistician for Social Statistics, BPS, has been very influential for the implementation of this study. We owe much to Bapak Sumarwanto, Dip. REIS, Chief of Sub-Directorate for Politics and Security Statistics, and Bapak Ano Herwana, SE, MM, Chief of Sub-Directorate for Environment Statistics, for their continuous support to this research.

Second, we are grateful to ISEAS for assigning us and providing a conducive environment in which to conduct this study. Our sincere thanks go to Ambassador Tan Chin Tiong, Director and Dr Ooi Kee Beng, Deputy Director for their strong support. Dr Hui Yew-Foong, coordinator of the Indonesian Studies Programme in ISEAS, has been highly instrumental in initiating and facilitating this study.

As usual, however, all remaining errors should be acknowledged by the authors themselves.

1

CHANGING INDONESIA:
An Introduction

Indonesia, the largest country in Southeast Asia, has as its national motto "Unity in Diversity." In 2010, Indonesia stood as the world's fourth most populous country after China, India and the United States, with 237.6 million people. This archipelagic country contributed 3.5 per cent to the world's population in the same year. Its relative contribution to the world population will be stable at around 3.4–3.5 per cent until 2050. According to the median variant of the United Nations estimate (2013), Indonesia's population will continue to grow, reaching 300 million in 2033.

The future demographics of Indonesia are likely to be very different from today's pattern, just as the current situation varies markedly from the past. Indonesians are increasingly living longer and having fewer children. Benefiting from the ease and advancement of transportation and information technology, Indonesians are increasingly more mobile, venturing into a wider labour market both within and outside Indonesia.

Indonesia has nearly completed its first demographic transition, from both high fertility and mortality to low fertility and mortality rates. The end of the first demographic transition is marked by the "replacement" level of fertility, which is the number of children a couple has that are needed to replace themselves. Population experts believe that the replacement level is reached when the fertility rate is about 2.1. However, Espenshade, Guzman and Westoff (2003) argue that the replacement rate does not occur at that rate, but relates instead to the mortality rate.[1]

The onset of the replacement level of fertility has further implications for the ethnic composition of a population. If the replacement level can be maintained for about forty years, the population will stabilize with zero growth. However, in many cases, this is not a reality. Some regions can easily fall into below replacement fertility for so long as to threaten the population with extinction. For instance, Japan and Germany are depopulating in this way.

Some provinces in Indonesia such as Jakarta, Yogyakarta and Bali have already completed their first demographic and are now in the second demographic transition, where the fertility rate is below the replacement level. As Lesthaeghe (1991) argues, under the regime of the second demographic transition, marriage is no longer universal, occurs at older ages and can be childless. There are higher-order needs on individualization, self-actualization and a rising awareness of human rights. An ageing population and a shortage of young workers are two other features in the second demographic transition.

In the meantime, a rising population mobility, with its varying patterns and levels of intensity, means that there are and will increasingly be greater interaction amongst peoples of different backgrounds such as ethnic and racial groups, religious groups, nationalities and languages. As a result, marriages involving peoples of different backgrounds will be likely to occur more often in Indonesia. Cultural assimilation amongst these different backgrounds will also create new group identities for people.

Alongside a persistent below-replacement level of fertility and acceleration in population mobility, Coleman (2006) examined what he called the third demographic transition: the transformation of ethnic composition. Indonesia has also experienced this third transition, especially at sub-national levels, and has witnessed how it can change quickly. At the same time, the democratization process and decentralization that started in 1998 in Indonesia has brought rising ethnic awareness and ethno-based politics in many parts of Indonesia.

Therefore, these demographic and political transitions have resulted in an emerging need to better understand the ethnic composition of Indonesia. This book aims to contribute to that need.

CONTINUATION AND DEEPER EXPANSION

The study of Indonesian ethno-demographic data sets began with *Indonesia's Population: Ethnicity and Religion in a Changing Political Landscape* (Suryadinata, Arifin and Ananta 2003), a pioneering work on ethno-demography (demography of ethnicity) in Indonesia. This pioneering work was the first publication on the demography of ethnic groups in Indonesia after the removal of a political taboo that restricted the collection and analysis of data on ethnicity in Indonesia in 2000. Although Indonesia is one of the world's most ethnically diverse nations, the recognition of ethnic groups used to be de-emphasized for the sake of nation building and identity. That book was written based on the publication of ethnic information from the 2000 population census by the Badan Pusat Statistik, Indonesia (hereafter the BPS) in 2001.

The book was prepared in a user-friendly manner, making statistics on ethnicity easily accessible to all. It outlined and described Indonesia's ethnic composition both as a whole country and within each of its provinces. The study succeeded in presenting a more comprehensive picture of all ethnic groups. It also discussed an important "foreign" minority, the ethnic Chinese in Indonesia. Therefore, Hugo (2003) commented that this book has long been awaited by many Indonesianists. The book was later translated into Bahasa Indonesia and published by the LP3ES in the same year.

Furthermore, the calculation and description of ethnicity at district levels were made available to the public and presented as part of the analysis in *Indonesian Electoral Behaviour: A Statistical Perspective* (Ananta, Arifin and Suryadinata 2004). The delineation of ethnic groups was limited to the Javanese vs. the non-Javanese, showing the number and percentage of Javanese in each district in Indonesia, as well as the geographical distribution of the Javanese at the district level. The Javanese group is the largest ethnic group in Indonesia, comprising about 40 per cent of Indonesia's population.

The book also contributed to statistics on religion at the district level. Because Islam has the largest number of followers in Indonesia, comprising about 86 per cent of Indonesia's population, the analysis was limited to Muslims versus non-Muslims. Similar to the way ethnic groups were defined, the book also presented the number and percentage of Muslims in each district, as well as the geographical distribution of Muslims by district in Indonesia.

Along with other social and economic variables such as GDP per capita, education, migration and urbanization, the statistics obtained on ethnicity and religion were used as predictors of electoral behaviour in 1999. The book was also the first to depict such a regression analysis of ethnicity and religion on electoral behaviour controlled by certain social and economic variables.

The three authors and many others have acknowledged some caveats concerning the 2000 population census (Hull 2001; Suryadinata, Arifin and Ananta 2003, and McDonald 2014). However, despite its limitations, the 2000 population census has provided a significant breakthrough for the understanding of ethnicity in Indonesia. Therefore, after the two aforementioned publications, two of the authors (Ananta and Arifin) continued their study of ethnicity in Indonesia using the 2000 population census. Ananta, Arifin and Bakhtiar (2005) examined the ageing population, fertility and mortality amongst the five largest ethnic groups in Indonesia. They also revised their calculation of the Malay population from their pioneering work of 2003. As a consequence, the second work had a different rank for Malays as is later discussed in this present book for comparison with the 2010 result.

Furthermore, Ananta (2006) related population mobility with changing ethnic composition and conflicts, particularly for the Province of the Riau Archipelago. The statistics on ethnic composition at the provincial level was also carried out in the Province of Aceh, taking into account the variation amongst districts (Ananta, Arifin and Hadumoan 2007). Using the 2005 Intercensal Population Survey, Ananta, Arifin and Bakhtiar (2008) updated the statistics on the ethnic Chinese in Indonesia and also compiled the statistics for two other "foreign" minorities, the Indian and the Arab groups. They also examined certain socio-economic conditions amongst the Chinese Indonesians and compared these to other ethnic groups in the Province of the Riau Archipelago.

Since then, opportunities to understand ethnicity in Indonesia have been greatly widened as the 2010 population census continued to collect information on ethnicity. This current book is a demographic study on ethnicity, mostly relying on the tabulation provided by the BPS based on the complete data set of the 2010 population census, which makes the statistics more reliable than the use of the subset data.[2] As detailed in Chapter 2, the information on ethnicity was collected for 236,728,379 individuals, a huge data set.

To some extent, the present study is a continuation from the earlier pioneering work and its subsequent studies using the 2000 population census. It is also an expansion of the analysis of ethnicity in the archipelago, taking into account a more comprehensive ethnic classification. The coded data set of ethnicity in the 2010 population census is still relatively raw, giving freedom to researchers to make their own classification of ethnic groups. This freedom for researchers to work on the coded data sets is one of the rich qualities of the Indonesian population census, particularly with respect to its statistics on ethnicity.

As religion and language are two of the ethnic markers, this book expands its analysis to include these as well. It attempts to answer the question on the pattern of religions of a particular ethnic group and the languages spoken daily at home. Such analyses are two other novelties of the present book.

OBJECTIVES

This book has four objectives. The first is to produce a new comprehensive classification of ethnic groups, what we like to call the "New Classification". This New Classification is expected to better capture the rich diversity of ethnicity in Indonesia, especially at the provincial and district levels, although the present book limits itself to the provincial level. It also seeks to improve the classification so that it will be a better, more useful and easier foundation for anybody who wants to understand statistics on ethnicity in Indonesia from the published data and/or raw coded data set. The New Classification is thus an important prerequisite for any study on ethnicity using the statistics from the 2010 census. It will also be useful for future data collection on ethnicity, including the 2015 intercensal population survey (SUPAS) and 2020 Population Census. The coding scheme of the New Classification could also be applied to other national surveys, such as the Indonesia Demographic and Health Survey (SDKI) and the annual National Social and Economic Survey (SUSENAS). Furthermore, looking just at the New Classification alone, the reader can already glimpse something of the richness of Indonesia's ethnic diversity.

The second objective is to report on the ethnic composition in Indonesia and in each of the thirty-three provinces using the New Classification. A more in-depth study is focused on the fifteen largest ethnic groups in Indonesia, already covering 84.9 per cent of the total number of Indonesian citizens living in Indonesia in 2010.

The third is to evaluate the dynamics of the fifteen largest ethnic groups in Indonesia during 2000–2010, and the fourth is to examine the religions and languages of each of the fifteen largest ethnic groups.

With these objectives, the book is structured as follows. Chapter 2 deals with the concept of ethnicity, the quantitative measurement of ethnicity, the data we are using and the problems we face in classifying the ethnic groups. In Chapter 3 we discuss the New Classification, including the way we produce it and its significance. The list of ethnic groups in the New Classification itself is expected to be able to provide some information on Indonesia's ethnic diversity. It is supplemented by the code for each group to facilitate easy reference for whoever wants to study ethnicity from the coded raw data set. The discussions in Chapter 3 and end of Chapter 2 are also expected to contribute some new insights on Indonesia's ethnicity.

With the New Classification, we have created and examined the ranking of ethnic groups in Indonesia as a whole and in each of the thirty-three provinces in Chapter 4. The provincial ethnic compositions are to show the multi-ethnicity of Indonesia's population across the provinces. We present the provinces according to the extent of their ethnic homogeneity.

We further elaborate each of the fifteen largest ethnic groups in Chapter 5. Amongst other things, we focus the discussion on the age-sex structure of each ethnic group and where they live. Chapter 6 analyses the dynamics of ethnic composition during 2000–2010, with some references to the 1930 census. The statistics for the 2000 and 1930 censuses are based on the pioneering work in 2003 of Ananta, Arifin and Bakhtiar (2005).

The religions and languages of each of the fifteen largest ethnic groups are discussed in Chapter 7. These new statistics on the religions and languages of each ethnic group are expected to provide the first quantitative information on religion and language of ethnic groups in Indonesia.

Finally, the present book is very timely, because of both the rising importance of ethnicity in Indonesia's social, economic and political development as well as the availability of the rich data set from the 2010 population census. This book is also expected to trigger further studies, using the rich raw data set of the 2000 and 2010 population censuses. Amongst the many possible important studies, we recommend more in-depth studies on the relationship between ethnic groups, religious followers and groups of language speakers. These studies can also be expanded to understand their educational, employment and urban-rural patterns.

This book should also be beneficial for policymakers, helping to make them aware that Indonesia has a large number of ethnic groups that will interact more frequently with one another. On one hand, this great diversity can be used to trigger social and political instability. Therefore, wise policies should be made to minimize unnecessary conflicts and make the huge variety of ethnic groups with their different religions and languages one of the elements that makes Indonesia so culturally rich.

The following sections in this chapter elaborate on the concept of the third demographic transition, which will help to place the discussion on ethnicity in the overall theoretical context of demographic changes. It is followed by a section describing recent and future challenges for Indonesia's population, providing a background in understanding ethnicity in Indonesia. Finally, it discusses the role of politics in providing data on ethnicity in Indonesia.

THE THIRD DEMOGRAPHIC TRANSITION

Initially, this feature was called the "demographic revolution", coined by French demographer Adolphe Landry in the seminal publication *La Revolution Demographique*, published in Paris in 1934. It was then reformulated as the "demographic transition" by American demographer Frank W. Notestein (1945). Kingsley Davis (1963) joined this work in establishing the foundation of the theory of demographic transition.

In essence, the theory of demographic transition attempts to describe a general pattern of demographic changes a country may experience. It states that initially a country experiences a level of demographic equilibrium (with very low population growth or no growth at all) because of both high fertility and mortality rates. Then, a decline in mortality precedes that in fertility, contributing to a high population growth rate. Ultimately, the fertility rate declines. Finally, both mortality and fertility are very low. Again, at this stage, population growth is very low. This process, from high fertility and mortality rates to low fertility and mortality rates, was called the demographic transition.

The real process may not be as smooth as is depicted by this theory. Nevertheless, it is a way to describe demographic changes caused by declining fertility and mortality rates.

One weakness of this "demographic transition" was that it did not take into account changes in population mobility, one of the three components of demographic change. Then, in the 1970s, Wilbur Zelinsky (1971) examined stages of internal population mobility (mobility within a country). In the 1990s, Ronald Skeldon (1990) improved Zelinsky's concept. However, both Zelinsky and Skeldon only briefly examined international population mobility and its connection with the stages of internal population mobility. Others, such as C.W. Stahl and R.T. Appleyard (1992) developed a separate theory of stages of international population mobility. Their framework related changes in international population mobility to the international movement of capital. It is disappointing that there has been no attempt to combine the demographic transition, internal population mobility transition and international population mobility transition into one unifying framework.

Meanwhile, in the 1980s, Van de Kaa (2002) created another term, the "second demographic transition". He refers to the demographic transition pioneered by Landry and reformulated by Notestein and Davis as the "first demographic transition". Van de Kaa described replacement-level fertility as the end of the first demographic transition. After that, when fertility and mortality levels are below the replacement level, the population is in the second demographic transition. The fertility level is usually fluctuating. During this period, there will be new norms regarding individual behaviour and the family, with a rising appreciation of individual aspirations and needs. At this stage, it is not easy to bring about social engineering.

Then, David Coleman (2006) argued that what he called the "third demographic transition" had emerged. During the second demographic transition, with an intense interrelationship between ageing and migration, we have another demographic transition. This is related to a fast change in ethnic composition because of rising population mobility, particularly the inflow of population with different ethnic and religious groups. The rapid change in ethnic composition in a given population can create potential social, economic and political conflicts.

Indonesia has seen all of these transitions too in their demographic trajectories. At the national level, Indonesia has almost completed its first demographic transition. Moreover, some provinces have completed their first demographic transition and are now in their second demographic transition. The patterns of internal and international population mobility have also become more complex.

As a result, Indonesia may also experience the third demographic transition, when changing ethnic composition becomes an increasingly important demographic phenomenon in Indonesia. Although the change will have wide social, economic and political implications, few studies have been done on the ethnic composition of population and its possible changes in Indonesia.

CHALLENGES FROM INDONESIA'S POPULATION

The fertility rate has declined from around six children per woman in the 1960s to about 2.4 in 2010. In some regions, the fertility rate has been even below the replacement level. Mortality has also declined. Life expectancy rose from around forty-five in the 1960s to around seventy in 2010. The Indonesian population has also been more mobile since the 1960s and travelling greater distances. A much greater number of foreigners has also come to reside in or visit Indonesia too, either for work, studies or tourism.

Indonesia faces three mega-demographic trends.[3] The first is that Indonesia's huge population will continue to grow, although the fertility rate as one of the key drivers of the population growth declined rapidly before 2000 and remained stable after that. The continued population growth is the so-called "population momentum", a result of the rise in the size of the reproductive-age population, although with each woman bearing fewer children, between two and three only. With the smaller number of children, a woman may have more opportunities to increase the quality of both hers and her children's lives. She can also have more time to pursue a career outside the household. The quality of life of the population may then continue to grow.

Recently, Indonesia's population size has been seen as contributing to a large lucrative market and strong production base in Southeast Asia. With the fact that its economy has been rising fast too, Indonesia is tipped to be one of the global economic powerhouses in the near future.

The second mega-demographic trend is the ageing population. As fertility has been relatively low, the ageing population will soon become a very important development issue in Indonesia. Indeed in some regions in Indonesia, the ageing population has become a serious issue. As is shown later in Chapter 5, some ethnic groups such as the Javanese, Madurese, Balinese and Chinese have been ageing faster than other ethnic groups.

The third mega-demographic trend is the changing pattern of population mobility in Indonesia. More mobile Indonesians equipped with better transportation and high technology will make Indonesians more connected to one another and to other people from outside Indonesia. Indonesians will increasingly be meeting more people from other ethnic groups, other religions, cultural backgrounds, and people speaking other languages, including people from other countries. There have been and will be more marriages between people from different groups and cultural assimilation in Indonesia. Thus, Indonesia is joining the globalization process. Another important factor is that since 1998, Indonesia has decentralized the country by giving district leaders more power, resulting in local ethnic politics becoming more prominent.

These demographic shifts are occurring alongside many other rapid social and economic changes, including changes in ethnic composition, transforming the lives of Indonesians. As Indonesia is a country with a huge number of ethnic groups, spread unevenly, the rising contact of people from different groups may create social and political conflicts. However, wisely managed, this contact will become an asset for Indonesia, enriching the culture and maturing Indonesian democracy.

Nevertheless, despite its richness, Indonesia's multi-ethnicity is still not well understood, partly due to the lack of statistics on ethnicity. The mapping of ethnicity in Indonesia is still limited and to some extent distorted when it comes to the estimates of particular ethnic groups, such as the Chinese.[4] Therefore, ethnic composition in Indonesia becomes an important aspect to better understand Indonesia's economic, social and political dynamics.

POLITICS AND STATISTICS ON ETHNICITY

The limited availability of statistics on ethnicity in Indonesia has mostly been because of former political policies in Indonesia. The governments in both the Old Order era (1945–67) and the New Order era (1967–98) held the view that knowing the "truth" about ethnic composition could result in social and political instability. Therefore, no data on ethnicity were collected during these two eras. The only statistics on ethnicity came from the 1930 population census, conducted during the colonial era. Many analyses at the national level taking into account ethnic composition were simply based on extrapolation from the 1930 data and, at best, were educated guesstimates. These analyses were often influenced by the bias of the analysts themselves. Some tried to understand ethnicity by using language as a proxy. For instance, in the 1980 and 1990 population censuses, the information on ethnicity included questions on language, both the mother tongue and languages spoken daily at home.

On the other hand, the government's attitude to ethnicity was different from its views of religion. The government was not afraid to know the truth about the composition of followers of the various religions. The question of which religion a person belongs to has been included in all population censuses, although this is only limited to the six officially recognized religions.[5] This is in contrast to what happens in some countries with the world's most advanced and modern statistical systems. As described by Eberstadt and Shah (2012), the American government explicitly forbids the US Bureau of Census from collecting data on religion. A similar situation is found in much of the European Union, the Russian Federation and other more developed regions.

With the change into a reforming, democratzing era since 1998, the government's attitude towards the truth about ethnic composition has also changed. It encourages knowledge of the actual ethnic composition of the country and is not afraid of possible social and political instability ensuing therefrom. During the government of Abdurrahman Wahid (Gus Dur), the BPS made a breakthrough by inserting a question on ethnicity in its 2000 population census. Therefore, after a break of seventy years, Indonesia began to collect statistics on ethnicity. The 2000 population census deleted the question on language and continued collecting data on religion.

With the 2000 census, Indonesia was only nine years behind the United Kingdom with regard to the census question on ethnic groups. The 1991 population census saw the first census question on ethnicity in the United Kingdom. This ethnic question was first proposed in 1981 but was not allowed on the basis of political security (Akinwale 2005).

The 2010 population census continued to collect data on ethnicity and religion. A new feature in the 2010 population was the inclusion of a question on language daily spoken at home. As a result, in addition to religion, the 2010 population census is endowed with very rich information linking ethnicity on one hand and religion and language on the other. Furthermore, the 2010 population census collected many more questions than the 2000 population census did, allowing much richer analyses of ethnic identities as related to many variables such as education, health and employment.

When the statistics on ethnicity based on the 2000 population census were published, they triggered unhappiness amongst the Dayak community as the size of the Dayak population seemed to be highly underestimated. The group felt that their true proportion had not been recognized by the state. In fact, this was due to the way the ethnic group was presented, without making an aggregation of the Dayak sub-ethnic groups. For instance, the publication of ethnic groups in West Kalimantan in 2000 presented the Kendayan, Darat and Pesaguan Dayak ethnic groups as the fourth, sixth and eighth largest ethnic groups (BPS, 2001a), and these numbers were lower than that of the ethnic Javanese migrants who were reported as the third largest in the province. But, when combined, the Dayak groups together formed the largest ethnic group in West Kalimantan. This percentage could actually have been larger if all other sub-groups of Dayak in addition to these three named had been combined. In fact, the same caveat of the 2000 publication on ethnic groups was applied to other ethnic groups with a number of sub-groups such as the Malays, Batak, Javanese and Sundanese, amongst others. The 2000 data opened up new opportunities to study and understand ethnicity in Indonesia.

The unhappiness of the Dayak over their statistics has been wisely managed. Their objections brought about a valuable lesson to help improve the publication on ethnic composition in the latest 2010 population census.

As with the 2000 population census, the BPS also published the data on ethnicity, shown on "Tabel Jenis Suku Bangsa Indonesia/Table of Ethnic Groups in Indonesia" (BPS, 2011a). It is what we call the "Initial Classification" of ethnic categories based on the 2010 census. All ethnic response categories were aggregated into thirty-one smaller groups (BPS 2011a). Amongst these, some categories have been put in a group. An example is "Ethnic Groups from East Nusa Tenggara", which lumps all ethnic groups in the Province of East Nusa Tenggara into one group, whereas in fact the province has many distinctive ethnic groups. Due to this grouping, the ethnic composition in the Province of East Nusa Tenggara only differentiates the population amongst ethnic migrants and "local ethnic groups". The local multi-ethnicity was hidden under the group of "Ethnic Groups from East Nusa Tenggara".

Moreover, the Initial Classification has many other issues that need to be improved to make the statistics on ethnicity more meaningful and accessible at the regional level. Therefore, a revision of the Initial Classification is needed to enrich our understanding of ethnicity in Indonesia and anticipate the rising ethnic politics in this period of decentralization in Indonesia.

Therefore, we need the New Classification to achieve a more comprehensive and accurate delineation of ethnic groups in Indonesia.

TWO RECOMMENDATIONS FOR STATISTICS IN INDONESIA

The first recommendation is on the coding of ethnic categories. The study in this book has reclassified the 1,331 coded categories into more than six hundred ethnic groups in the New Classification as presented in Appendix 1. The classification was created from a combination of a thorough examination of statistics on ethnicity collected by the BPS, literature review and local expertise. Importantly, the classification does not change the original coded raw data set at all, preserving the freedom for other users to work with alternative classifications. This work is possible because the BPS has minimized its effort to group the ethnic categories found from the field.

However, during the coding, the BPS combined several categories into one coded category. Examples are two complicated cases of Ayfat versus Arfak (both with origins in Papua) and Toraja versus Kaili (both with origins in Sulawesi). Ayfat and Arfak are actually two different ethnic groups that have been wrongly lumped under one category. Similarly, Toraja and Kaili are two separate ethnic groups, but both come under the same code. Consequently, we cannot separate the number of population of the Ayfat from the Arfak or the Toraja from the Kaili.

Therefore, the BPS is recommended to continue collecting ethnic categories without trying to amalgamate the existing categories. Moreover, they should envision revising and disaggregating them to make more opportunities to classify them.

The BPS expands users' freedom by not making any grouping of ethnic categories at all and letting the researchers make their own groupings. The freedom given to researchers will make the subsequent data much more meaningful.

The second recommendation is on future data collection. As there will be more interaction of peoples from different backgrounds, there will be an increasing number of people who may identify themselves with more than one ethnic group. Consequently, future data collection on ethnicity should allow a respondent to mention more than one ethnic group. Furthermore, the censuses/surveys should also put "Indonesian" as one of the options to answer the question on ethnicity. The term "Indonesian" provides an answer for those who are "confused" about their ethnic identities.

In the current question on religion, one of the options to answer is "others". Nevertheless, there is no information what "others" means. Future censuses/surveys should record what "others" means. It is perhaps a local religion, another world religion or no religion at all. As a democratizing country, Indonesia should not be afraid to know the truth about religions in Indonesia, although Indonesia officially only recognizes six distinct religions.

If social science is to deal effectively with the actual beliefs and behaviours of citizens, future censuses/surveys will need to include more specific questions on belief, including more detailed codes on the *aliran* (sect) and the rich variety of animistic, spiritualistic and sectarian groups found across Indonesia. The respondent should be encouraged to record whatever *aliran* he/she believes in, whether as a manifestation of an "official religion" or an expression of spirituality irrespective of deity. The availability of such information will enrich our understanding of the spread of religious persuasions in Indonesia, although it also means another big challenge for demographers and other social scientists to classify religions and their *aliran*.

These two lessons will also be beneficial for whoever collects and codes information on ethnicity in Indonesia.

A MAJOR AND SIGNIFICANT ETHNO-DEMOGRAPHIC STUDY IN INDONESIA

This book is expected to make a major and important contribution to ethno-demography (demography on ethnicity) in Indonesia, mostly based on the raw data of the 2010 population census. The information provided in this book is crucial and up to date and is not available elsewhere. Therefore, the statistics produced and presented in this book can be an important reference for whoever needs information on demography, ethnicity, religion or languages in Indonesia.

This work on ethno-demography is also aimed at enriching anthropological and sociological studies on ethnicity in Indonesia. All future analyses on Indonesia's ethnicity, both quantitative and qualitative, can further improve the quality of ethno-demographic studies of Indonesia.

Finally, the BPS should continue conducting its population census with 100 per cent enumeration, as it will provide a much more accurate set of statistics on Indonesia's population, particularly at lower administrative levels, such as the district. Information on ethnicity, along with religion and language, should continue to be collected in the population censuses/surveys, as Indonesia is already in the process of the third demographic transition — a process towards a rapid change in ethnic composition of population, especially at sub-national levels. Yet, we still need to further improve the questionnaire and coding, as recommended earlier.

Notes

1. Espenshade, Guzman and Westoff (2003) argued that the replacement level of fertility cannot be assumed to always occur when the TFR equals to 2.1. Their study found that the replacement level of fertility ranges from as low as 2.05 for Réunion to as high as 3.43 in Sierra Leone. The range is also different between developed and developing countries, where in developed countries the replacement level of fertility ranges between 1.4 and 2.1; and in developing countries, the rates are higher than 2.2 but below 3.5.

2. Therefore, the coverage of the data is different from that of the IPUMS's data collection. The IPUMS has a collection of micro-data of a series of population censuses from many countries, but the data is only a subset with a 10 per cent sample from the original data.

3. A detailed discussion on Indonesia's mega-demographic trends is available in Arifin and Ananta (2013).

4. See discussion on this issue in Skinner (1963) and Suryadinata (2005).

5. The 1961 population census was the first census after Indonesian independence (1949). It collected information on religion, with the following options to answer the question: Islam, Catholicism, Protestantism and other Christianity, Hinduism and Buddhism, Confucianism and Others (including those with no religion). Yet the statistics on religion were not published for the public until 1971. Before the 2010 population census, there were only five official religions, as is later discussed in Chapter 7.

2

COMPLEXITY OF STATISTICS ON ETHNICITY: Concept, Data and Method of Analysis

CONCEPT OF ETHNICITY

As elaborated by Baumann (2004), it is not easy to define ethnicity. It is a much debated topic, though best defined in cultural anthropology. There is no consensus on how to define ethnicity and how ethnic groups are created. This chapter does not aim to elaborate on the debate. Rather, it focuses on the concept used in the demographic analysis on Indonesia's ethnicity, the theme of this book.

Ethnicity is not "culture". It is related to a particular kind of identity, imposed or otherwise. It is a result of self and group identity that is created within extrinsic and intrinsic contexts as well as social interaction.

Ethnicity is generally defined as a sense of group belonging, with the core characteristics of common origin, history, culture, language, experience and values (Baumann 2004; Radcliffe 2010). Bulmer (1996) defined an ethnic group as follows:

> An ethnic group is a collectivity within a larger population having real
> or putative common ancestry, memories of a shared past and a cultural
> focus upon one or more symbolic elements which define the group's
> identity, such as kinship, religion, language, shared territory, nationality
> or physical appearance. Members of an ethnic group are conscious of
> belonging to the group.[1]

Ethnicity is different from race. Racial stratification is related to birth-ascribed status based on physical and cultural characteristics imposed by outsiders. A person cannot change his/her race. On the other hand, although also ascribed at birth, ethnic groups usually can define their own cultural characteristics themselves.

Ethnic identity may be dynamic, not static over time, and dependent upon context, as people inhabit a more complex world in which they interact with more than one ethnic group. An ethnicity of a person is voluntary, meaning that an individual may change his/her ethnic identity if s/he feels that s/he is closer to his/her new ethnic group. Through intermarriage, cultural exchange, political change, migration and assimilation, some individuals may change their ethnic identities and affiliation (Baumann 2004; Radcliffe 2010).

People may change their identities because of political reasons. An example is a Chinese person who was born and grew up in a Javanese community. He does not speak any Chinese, but speaks Javanese fluently. During the Soeharto New Order era, he hid his Chinese identity and identified himself as a Javanese person. With the openness towards ethnic identity in the reform era, he can now openly say that he is Chinese or Javanese-Chinese.

People can also change their identities because of the pride of belonging to a particular ethnic group. Thung, Maunati and Kedit (2004) elaborated on the fact that for centuries the term Dayak was used to imply a humiliation or insult. The primary identity was with a tribal group, such as Kenyah, Benuaq, Tunjung or Kayan. However, currently, they are now known as the Dayak, an ethnic group, mostly referring to the non-Muslim, non-Malay natives of the island of Borneo (in the provinces of Kalimantan in Indonesia and the state of Sarawak in Malaysia). The Dayak identity has since been enhanced and is now a term seen as a symbol of unity and pride.

Others change their identities because of changes in the communities in which they live. For example, the Dayak who become Muslim may then identify themselves as Malay. A girl from a Javanese couple born and growing up in Papua may have been recorded as Javanese by her parents in the 2000 population census as she was still fifteen years old. However, when she was twenty-five years old in the 2010 population census and she answered the question on ethnicity by herself, she may not have felt that she was Javanese, because she has lived all her life in Papua.

Ethnicity can also be related to occupation. Traditionally, people of different ethnic groups tended to specialize in certain occupations. For example, Buginese and Makassarese are well known in Indonesia as seafarers, having maintained inter-island contacts for centuries and established a reputation outside their homelands, such as in other parts of Sulawesi, Kalimantan and Java, as well as in Singapore. Their livelihood was in coastal economies.

The people of Sangir and Bajo from Sulawesi, Bawean from North of Java and some Malay are also well known for their coastal economies. On the other hand, the people of Pasemah and Komering from South Sumatra, Gayo from Aceh, Tengger from East Java, Dayak from Kalimantan and Toraja from South Sulawesi have been associated with livelihoods mainly in the hinterlands.

However, these occupational differences may have disappeared along with economic integration and urbanization. Indeed, Indonesia's economy has been shifting away from the primary sector and towards industrialization and service sectors. In addition, the rate of urbanization in Indonesia has been increasing rapidly from 14.9 per cent in 1961 to 49.8 per cent in 2010. Therefore, ethnic-based traditional occupations may have disappeared and been replaced by new ethnic-based occupations. More studies should be done to understand this issue.

Finally, in Indonesia, ethnicity is "nowhere, but everywhere". It is nowhere, as only at the turn of the twenty-first century did modern Indonesia follow the global trend in its decennial census. It is everywhere, as is stated in Indonesia's constitutional motto, *Bhinneka Tunggal Ika*, which basically means "Unity in Diversity", or an acceptance of its pluralistic society in both ethnic and religious multiplicity. This "everywhere" diversity has also been used in marketing campaigns to promote the tourist industry, which always promotes the cultural mosaic of Indonesian ethnicity.[2] (Klinken 2003)

MEASUREMENT OF ETHNIC GROUPS

Consistent and Reproducible

Defining ethnicity is the concern and expertise of anthropologists, sociologists and political scientists. On the other hand, demographers are concerned with how people identify themselves and how they are regarded by their peers. They provide demographic and geographic mappings of ethnic groups — with the statistics of ethnicity — as well as its dynamics.

Demographers produce simpler classifications, combining statistics with results of studies by sociologists and anthropologists on ethnicity. They pay much attention to the collection, accuracy and presentation of the statistics. The results should be consistent and reproducible. That is, with agreed techniques and assumptions, whoever interviews a respondent should get the same results. These precise and detailed statistics on ethnicity can be meaningful for social, economic, political policies/planning (Shryock and Siegel 1976).

Note that the words "consistent and reproducible" are very important features of ethno-demographic studies, as in other demographic analyses. In demographic studies, and also ethno-demographic studies, if the results are not "consistent and reproducible" — for example if more than one interviewer obtains different answers from one respondent — then there must be something wrong with the methods of collecting this information.

Demographers study ethnicity through population censuses/surveys or registration data. For example, in the Netherlands, they rely on national registration data, while in the United Kingdom, the United State of America and Canada, they rely on data collected from national censuses (Radcliffe 2010). Morning (2008) found that eighty-seven out of 138 countries in the world collected ethnicity information through their population censuses.

Self-identification

The most common method used in censuses/surveys is self-identification, according to how the respondents define themselves. With self-identification, the name of an ethnic group is recorded according to the perception of the respondent. The Badan Pusat Statistik, Statistics Indonesia (hereafter the BPS) applies the concept of self-identification. However, when needed, the enumerator helped the respondents to answer the question on ethnicity with the enumerator's observation and judgement of the respondents' ethnicity. The respondents are free to mention whatever ethnic group they want to identify themselves with. They did not choose from a list of ethnic groups. It was then possible that the respondents mentioned ethnic groups which were not in the list of the BPS.[3] In other words, it is possible to find new ethnic groups — groups that had not been known in earlier sociological and anthropological studies. In other words, the ethno-demographic relies on the respondent's statement about who they are, rather than the interpretation of the researchers.

With the rising mobility and contact with other groups, the complexity of measuring ethnicity will increase in the future. The rising population mobility within Indonesia and worldwide, as well as an increasing flow of foreigners into Indonesia will quickly increase the opportunities for Indonesians to interact with people from various backgrounds, ethnicities, races, religions and cultures. Different experiences, including mixed marriages, may result in changing perceptions of people's own identity, including their ethnicity. Probably, a growing number of individuals will identify themselves with more than one ethnic group. Future censuses/ surveys will have to accommodate these trends.

Questionnaires

The way in which ethnicity is determined, and the terms of ethnicity themselves in population censuses, varies from country to country. As discussed in Morning (2008), there are many ways to address "ethnicity" in censuses worldwide: ethnicity, race, nationality, indigenous/tribal, ancestry/descent/origin, cultural group, community/population, caste and colour/phenotype. Morning found that four terms (ethnicity, nationality, indigenous/tribe and race) were the most frequently used. Yet, she found that there was some ambiguity surrounding the meaning of these terms. For example, "race" in a country could be labelled as "ethnicity" in another country. Meanwhile, nationality considered as ancestry in one country could be citizens in others. Nationality can also mean citizenship or citizens with foreign origins.

Furthermore, Morning found that the terms "ethnicity" or "ethnic" were mostly used throughout the censuses, or forty-nine out of eighty-seven cases (56 per cent). Ethnicity was mostly used in Asia and Oceania. "Nationality" was the second most frequently used term, mostly in Europe and Asia. Two other terms generally used were "indigenous/tribe" and "race". The term "indigenous/tribe" was mainly used in South America and Oceania and "race" was used in North America and Oceania.[4]

In Indonesia's 2000 and 2010 population censuses, as well as in the 2005 Intercensal Population Survey, *suku bangsa* (ethnic group) and *kewarganegaraan* (citizenship) were used to reveal information on ethnicity. The question on ethnicity was only asked amongst the citizens of Indonesia. The censuses asked for information on the country of citizenship for non-Indonesian citizens. Amongst the ethnic groups, the censuses also identified *Asing/Luar Negeri* (foreign origins) for Indonesian citizens with origins from foreign countries, such as from China, the Arab states, India, Japan, the United States and Australia. This may mean "nationality" in some censuses outside Indonesia. Indonesian censuses also allow users to trace indigenous groups/tribes in the data sets, by combining the statistical data with anthropological studies.

In 2010, Indonesia used a single, simple, direct question, combining ethnicity and citizenship. Ethnicity is recorded in Question no 208. It is written as *Apakah kewarganegaraan dan sukubangsa (NAMA)?* (What is the citizenship and ethnic group of [NAME]?)

The answer can be one of the following options:

a.   *WNI (Warga Negara Indonesia,* Indonesian citizen), *tuliskan suku bangsa* (write in the ethnic group)
b.   *WNA (Warga Negara Asing,* non-Indonesian citizen), *tuliskan kewarganegaraan* (write in the citizenship)

Around the globe, there are three formats of response category in a questionnaire: closed-ended responses, closed-ended responses with an open-ended "Other" option and an open-ended response. The closed-ended responses take two forms: that is when the respondents check the available box of ethnic category they belong to or they check the code list of ethnic groups. Sometimes this format also permits the respondents not to identify with any one of the stated groups in the questionnaire, by providing "none" as one of the options. The second format is the extension from the closed-ended format while permitting the respondents to write in an ethnic group name that is not listed. The last one is when the respondents have to write in their ethnic group in the blank space available in the questionnaire (Morning 2008). The last format has the most freedom for the respondents to mention their ethnic groups.

The early censuses in the United States, which has been collecting information on ethnicity since 1790, followed the first format. Initially it recorded Americans in only two groups: White and Black. Over time, more categories have been included. The ethnicity question was revised and expanded. Since 2000, the U.S. Census allowed the respondents to provide up to three answers for the three questions on ethnicity (Morning 2008). The response category utilizes a combination of three response formats for the answers. First, a closed-ended format is applied for the first question, such as for "Is this person Spanish/Hispanic/Latino?" Second, a combination of a closed-ended with an open-ended response is used for the second question, "What is this person's race?", with eleven choices and four open-ended responses for those who belong to American-Indian or Alaska native, Other Asian, Other Pacific Islander or some other race. In addition, the open-ended response format is used for the last question, "What is the person's ancestry or ethnic origin?"

Meanwhile, in Asian countries, such as in Singapore, the second format is used, providing more alternatives for an answer, with an additional open-ended list for "Other" category. The question on ethnicity lists fifteen possible responses for "ethnic/dialect group", namely, Hokkien, Teochew, Cantonese, Hakka (Khek), Hainanese, Malay, Javanese, Boyanese, Tamil, Sikh, Caucasian, Filipino, Eurasian, Vietnamese and Japanese. If a respondent cannot identify her/himself with one of the groups, s/he can write any other group s/he likes (Singapore Department of Statistics 2011, p. 99).

The Indonesian ethnicity question takes the third format, an open-ended option. As found by Morning (2008), about two thirds of Asian censuses employ the open-ended format for their ethnicity questions. Thus, the Indonesian method is a common feature of other Asian countries' censuses. With the open-ended response format, the Indonesian census recorded more than 1,300 response categories of ethnic, sub-ethnic and sub-sub-ethnic groups, including several categories of foreigners living in Indonesia. To distinguish from Indonesian citizens with foreign descent, the foreigners were coded separately.[5]

In each of the three formats, only one answer is allowed. A respondent can only have one ethnic group. However, as intercultural interaction is increasing, with mixed marriages and geographical mobility, it can become increasingly difficult for a respondent to identify with just one ethnic group. Therefore, the United States started allowing the respondents to choose more than one race in its 2000 population census.

In the case of Indonesia, respondents are only allowed to have one ethnic group. This can cause difficulty and confusion in certain circumstances. If a respondent comes from various cultural backgrounds, such as from a mixed marriage and/or living in regions with different cultures from those in the respondent's place of birth, then s/he can answer whichever ethnic group s/he feels most close to. If the respondent still cannot decide which ethnic group s/he feels most comfortable with, the field enumerator may guide the respondent to follow the ethnicity of the respondent's father, grandfather and great-grandfather, and so on. This applies in patrilineal societies. In matrilineal societies, the interviewers follow the respondent's mother's line (BPS 2009b).

When a person is the child of an international marriage or of foreign origins due to migration, the census provides categories such as Chinese, Arabs, Indians, Americans and Australians.

Finally, it should be noted that the head of the household answered not only for him/herself, but also for the members of his/her household. In the case of ethnicity, the head identified his/her own ethnicity and provided his/her knowledge on the ethnicity of members of his/her household. It is also possible that the head of the households made the answers in consultation with the interviewers. This possible bias should be considered when analysing the data.

DATA SET

Brief Description of the 2010 Population Census

As detailed in *Buku 1* (BPS 2009a), the implementation of the 2010 population census was mandated in Law no 16/1997 on Statistics, in which the BPS should conduct a population census (Sensus Penduduk), an agricultural census (Sensus Pertanian) and an economic census (Sensus Ekonomi). The 2010 population census was the sixth population census conducted since Indonesia's independence, after the ones in 1961, 1971, 1980, 1990 and 2000. The 2010 population census was a massive and complex statistical undertaking in this huge archipelagic country, covering all thirty-three provinces[6] (as seen in Figure 2.1) and 497 districts scattered all over Indonesia, employing more than 650,000 field workers consisting mainly of enumerators, together with others such as team coordinators and field supervisors. Data collection was designed to be undertaken in groups, and each group (team) consisted of four persons, i.e., three numerators and one team coordinator. All field workers undertook a three-day training programme beforehand.

As in earlier censuses, population is defined following a *de jure* concept, meaning that they are recorded in their "usual residence", which term refers to the areas where people have lived for more than six months, the areas where people have lived for less than six months but where they intend to settle down in or the areas where people reside in order to work or study. The term "usual residence" also includes the areas where people travel to but do not intend to live in these destination areas, as well as diplomatic corps staff and their members of households who live overseas.

In addition, the census also enumerates population, using a *de facto* concept, recording people living in a place where the interview is undertaken. The *de facto* concept is used for those who are travelling or do not have a usual place of residence for six months or more or for those who have resided in an area for more than six months but do not intend to live there permanently. The *de facto* concept is applied to those who do not constitute a regular household and who belong to a more mobile population.

As Indonesian society has become more complex, four kinds of questionnaires were developed to reach different groups of the population for the 2010 population census. The first was C1, a complete questionnaire, containing forty-two questions, including ethnicity. It was used to enumerate permanent (*de jure*) households who live in a "conventional building". The second was C2. It is simpler, containing fourteen questions to enumerate permanent households that are not covered in C1. The households in C2 include populations living in remote areas, those living under bridges and in slums and aboard-ship populations. The third kind of questionnaire was C2*, similar to C2, covering people living in apartments and diplomatic corps staff, including their household members. The last was L2. This was a much simpler questionnaire, only counting the number and sex amongst non-permanent households and more mobile (*de facto*) populations such as the homeless, sailors and nomadic tribes, as well as people living in large institutions with at least one hundred persons, such as prisons, mental hospitals, military barracks, student dormitories, Islamic boarding houses (*pesantrens*) and displaced persons living in tents/barracks. C2 and L2 did not have an ethnicity question, but the C2* Apartment questionnaire collected ethnicity information, including foreigners living in Indonesia. Thus, the analysis in this book mostly relates to the population recorded under C1, for regular households, and C2* Apartment, only for Indonesian citizens.

As presented in Table 2.1, the recorded population of Indonesia in this census was 237.64 million, placing Indonesia as the fourth most populous country in the world. Its permanent population, the population recorded under C1, numbers 236.72 million, or 99.6 per cent of the recorded

Figure 2.1
2010: Map of Indonesia's Population

> 40,000,000

13,000,000 - 39,999,999

6,000,000 - 12,999,999

3,000,000 - 5,999,999

3,000,000 - 5,999,999

Notes: The number refers to the provincial code. All numbers contain two digits. One and two tens refer to provinces on the island of Sumatra, three tens are provinces on the island of Java, five tens on the islands of Bali and Nusa Tenggara, six tens on the island of Kalimantan, seven tens on the island of Sulawesi, eight tens in Maluku and nine tens in the Indonesian portion of New Guinea, 11 = Aceh, 12 = North Sumatra, 13 = West Sumatra, 14 = Riau, 15 = Jambi, 16 = Bengkulu, 17 = South Sumatra, 18 = Lampung, 19 = Bangka Belitung, 21 = Riau Archipelago, 31 = Jakarta, 32 = West Java, 33 = Central Java, 34 = Yogyakarta, 35 = East Java, 36 = Banten, 51 = Bali, 52 = West Nusa Tenggara, 53 = East Nusa Tenggara, 61 = West Kalimantan, 62 = Central Kalimantan, 63 = South Kalimantan, 64 = East Kalimantan, 71 = North Sulawesi, 72 = Central Sulawesi, 73 = South Sulawesi, 74 = Southeast Sulawesi, 75 = Gorontalo, 76 = West Sulawesi, 81 = North Maluku, 82 = Maluku, 91 = West Papua and 94 = Papua.
Source: Drawn by the authors.

Table 2.1
Number of Population based on the Types of Questionnaires: Indonesia, 2010

Type of Questionnaires	Population	Percentage
C1	236,715,601	99.61
C2 General	82,612	0.03
C2* Apartment	85,995	0.04
C2* Diplomat	3,458	0.00
L2	753,660	0.32
Total	237,641,326	100.00

Notes: Diplomatic corps is mentioned under L2 in the source below. It should have been under C2, according to BPS (2009a). Therefore, we have placed it under C2.
Source: Compiled and calculated from http://sp2010.bps.go.id/index.php/site/tabel?tid=337&wid=0.

population, and the C2* accounted for only less than 0.1 per cent. Therefore, the population for the data on ethnicity covers almost all the recorded population in the census. The selected population for the analysis on ethnicity includes the population recorded under C1 and C2* Apartment only for Indonesian citizens. Specifically, the analysis related to ethnic groups only relies on 236,728,379 respondents. We should expect to have smaller numbers of respondents when the information on ethnicity is crossed with other information. It is not clear how the missing information on ethnicity from the groups enumerated under C2 and L2 will affect the whole ethnic composition, especially to those of small ethnic groups outside the fifteen largest ethnic groups in Indonesia.

Coded Raw Data Set

The opportunity to understand ethnicity in Indonesia is widened in the 2010 census as the census continued collecting information on ethnicity. The 2010 population census together with the 2000 one has led to significant progress in understanding Indonesia's population, particularly with respect to its ethnic composition.

The information on ethnicity collected from respondents was "coded" by *kortim*s (team coordinators) in the field, by following a list of codes already prepared by the staff of the BPS in Jakarta. A *kortim* is a coordinator/supervisor of a team consisting of field interviewers. A *kortim* is selected from the best *mitra statistik* (non-permanent staff of the regional statistical office to conduct surveys/censuses), who know the census area very well. Amongst other things, a *kortim* is tasked to fill in the codes to the information on administrative areas of place of birth and place of residence five years earlier, language spoken daily at home and ethnicity, collected by his/her field enumerators (BPS 2009).

The coded information was further modified in the BPS central office, in Jakarta, where the information was entered into the database. One of the features of this coded data set is that it is still relatively raw, allowing freedom for researchers to make their own groupings on ethnicity. In the 2010 raw coded data set, there are 1,331 categories consisting of ethnic, sub-ethnic and sub-sub-ethnic groups, making a very rich and complicated data set. Furthermore, different names and spellings amongst these categories have increased the complexity of the statistics on Indonesia's ethnicity.

Each of the 1,331 categories has a code, the smallest (0001) to the highest (1331). The list of the codes includes "9999" for "not in the universe" or the "don't know" answer. In addition to these four-digit codes, BPS (2009c) added one more digit to the first four digits to make each of them unique. The response categories are listed in alphabetical order as presented in *Buku 7* on *Pedoman Kode Provinsi dan Kabupaten/Kota, Negara, Suku Bangsa, Kewarganegaraan, Bahasa dan Lapangan Usaha pada Sensus Penduduk 2010* (BPS 2009c). For those with no access to that book, they can refer to Appendix 1 of this book.

Therefore, the coded information is still very raw and untrained eyes may not be able to read the information properly. Moreover, the long list of ethnic categories is not workable unless it is classified into more simple and meaningful ethnic groups. BPS (2011a) made another important contribution by making a classification of the large number of ethnic groups. It classified the information into thirty-one groups and quickly made the classification available worldwide as it is published online[7] under the title of *Kewarganegaraan, Suku Bangsa, Agama dan Bahasa Sehari hari Penduduk Indonesia: Hasil Sensus Penduduk Indonesia 2010* [Citizenship, ethnicity, religion and languages spoken of Indonesian population: Results of 2010 Population Census] (BPS 2011a). The report also produced ethnic statistics based on the thirty-one groups, which hereafter throughout the book we refer to as the "Initial Classification".

This Initial Classification is intended to help users better understand the mapping of ethnicity in Indonesia. In that report, BPS (2011a) described the members of each of the thirty-one groups as seen in *Tabel Jenis Suku Bangsa di Indonesia* [Table for ethnic groups in Indonesia] (pp. 23–27). Table 4.3 of this book depicts the ethnic composition based on the Initial Classification.

This table has a longer list of ethnic categories than the earlier 2000 census publication, which only published the eight largest ethnic categories out of more than 1,300 categories at both the national level and for each of the thirty provinces. By presenting only the eight largest ethnic categories, many smaller ethnic categories which belong to a particular ethnic group cannot be presented in the 2000 census publication.

However, the Initial Classification is a quick and simple reference. It does not deal with problems associated with the coding of the raw data. It also has problems in classifying the ethnic categories. Therefore, it needs to be further improved. The next section deals with the problems and the way we make a new classification — hereafter referred to as the "New Classification".

CLASSIFYING ETHNIC GROUPS

Problems with the Coded Raw Data

Two problematic cases are to be found in the coded raw data. The first occurred in the field when an interviewer and/or *kortim* made a mistake in choosing a code. Moreover, because the data includes some open questions, it is also possible that there are some answers without any codes. Another explanation might be that those answers are names of ethnic groups that have not been recognized in anthropological/sociological references. In this case, the interviewer and *kortim* had to make a decision and this decision could be open to error. We cannot do anything with this error and simply need to be aware of such possible errors.

The second is found when one coded category has more than one label, indicated with a slash sign (/). It is not clear whether the labels refer to several different names/spelling of one ethnic or sub-ethnic group or separate ethnic or sub-ethnic groups. If they are different names/spellings or sub-ethnic groups of an ethnic group, we do not lack any information on the number of population in the ethnic group, although we do lack the information about the population size of the sub-ethnic groups. However, if the labels are names of separate ethnic groups or sub-ethnic groups, then we lack important information on each of the ethnic or sub-ethnic groups.

For instance, the ethnic group Pamona with its origin on the island of Sulawesi, an island taking a K-shape as seen in Figure 2.1, has several sub-ethnic groups, one of which is the sub-group Pada, also called "Topada" (0726). However, the sub-group Pada is combined together with other labels into one code number, 0659, and is written as "Pada/Pakambia/Palende/Payapi/Pebato". As mentioned in Melalatoa (1996, p. 212), Pada, Pakambia, Palende, Payapi and Pebato are separate sub-ethnic groups of the ethnic group Pamona. Therefore, because they have been grouped into one code, we cannot separate information for each of the five sub-ethnic groups. If we are only interested in the ethnic group, in this case Pamona, then this case is irrelevant. If we want to examine the sub-ethnic groups of Pamona, then this way of coding the data does not allow us to know separate information about each of the five sub-ethnic groups. Future censuses/surveys should give one code separately for each of these five sub-ethnic groups.

A similar case occurs for the ethnic group of Alor, which is also the name of an island in the province of East Nusa Tenggara, and which has several sub-ethnic groups. Hidayah (1996, p. 9) mentioned that Alor consists of sixteen sub-ethnic groups, namely, Abui, Alor, Belagar, Deing, Kabola, Kawel, Kelong, Kemang, Kramang, Kui, Lemma, Maneta, Mauta, Seboda, Wersin and Wuwuli. However, Wuwuli is not available in the 2010 population census. Several of them are coded into one group, that is 0133 for "Alor/Belagar/Kelong/Manete/Mauta/Seboda/Wersin". As a result, we lack the individual information about each of the seven sub-ethnic groups identified in the anthropological literature.

This problem can also occur with an ethnic group. This can result in an overestimation of an ethnic group and an underestimation of another ethnic group. An example is the code number 0665 for "Raranggonau/Sibalaya/Sidondo/Toraja". According to Melalatoa (1995) and Hidayah (1996) as well as the earlier study by Nooy-Palm (1975), these groups used to be called Alfuru, before they became Muslims or Christians. The name Toraja appeared by the end of the nineteenth century, and was later divided into West, East and South Toraja. But the people in South Toraja then became Christians and said that they were the Torajans. Researchers then named the people from East Toraja the Pamona and from West Toraja the Kaili.

However, code 0665 put the two different ethnic groups together — Raranggonau, Sibalaya and Sidondo as sub-ethnic groups of the Kaili on the one hand and the Toraja ethnic group on the other — into one category. If we consider this code as part of the Kaili, then the population size of the Kaili would be overestimated, as it would include the Toraja, and the number of Toraja would thereby be underestimated.

We then tried to find a way to break this coded category (0665) into the Kaili and Toraja. From Melalatoa (1995), we know that the Kaili are mostly Muslims and the Toraja mostly Christians. Therefore, if the population in 0665 were Muslims, we would put them under the Kaili; if they were not Muslims, we would put them under the Toraja. Thus, the classification of Toraja could be solved, stopping it from becoming a sub-group of the Kaili.

However, we cannot use this approach to solve the problem we face for "Arfak/Ayfat" (coded number 1002). The Arfak and Ayfat are actually two different ethnic groups. They should not be put in one code. Unfortunately, there is no information that can be used to separate them. Their religions/beliefs are the same, Christian and local tradition. Therefore, we decided to put "Arfak/Ayfat" (code 1002) under the Arfak ethnic group with a note explaining that the number of Arfak may be overestimated because it may have included some Ayfat. On the other hand, the number of Afyat in Afyat/Mey Brat/Ayamuru may have been underestimated. Fortunately, this is the only such case found in this study.

Problems with the Initial Classification

The Initial Classification has two main problems: aggregating ethnic categories into regional categories and misplacing ethnic and sub-ethnic groups.

Aggregation into Regional Groups

This is an aggregation of several ethnic categories into a single regional category such as "Other ethnic groups from the island of Sulawesi". This category hides the richness of ethnic diversity on the island of Sulawesi and therefore this category needs to be disaggregated into more meaningful ethnic groups. In the Initial Classification, using such an aggregation, the "Other ethnic groups from the island of Sulawesi" appears to be the fourth largest ethnic group at the national level after Javanese, Sundanese and Batak. However, this category clearly cannot be said to constitute an ethnic 'group'. The label does not show important features as it comprises so many different ethnic groups originating in the island of Sulawesi. Therefore, the New Classification decomposes the group "Other ethnic groups from the island of Sulawesi" into several ethnic groups, to reflect the richness of the ethnic composition in Sulawesi. Just to mention some of them, they are Bajao, Buol, Mongondow, Minahasa, Mamasa, Mamuju,

Mandar, Pamona, Kaili, Tolaki, Tomini and Toraja. This grouping in the Initial Classification may become more problematic as we examine ethnicity at lower administrative levels — province and district.

The issue is more apparent when the group of "Ethnic groups from ..." has a high percentage. For instance, "Ethnic groups from the province of Aceh" contributes 85.38 per cent, a large majority of the total population in the province of Aceh, and yet this group consists of twelve ethnic categories. The remaining groups of about 15 per cent consist of ethnic groups originating from outside Aceh. Therefore, we need to disaggregate "Ethnic groups from the province of Aceh" to make the statistics more meaningful.

In the New Classification, we have disaggregated this group into the following ethnic groups separately: "Aceh/Achin/Akhir/Asji/A-Tse/ Ureueng Aceh" combined with Lambai/Lamari — the so called Acehnese, separated from the Alas, Aneuk Jamee, Singkil, Tamiang, Gayo, Simeulue and Kluet. Gayo itself consists of Gayo, Gayo Lut, Gayo Luwes and Gayo Serbe Jadi. Sigulai is part of Simeulue. In other words, there are eight ethnic groups in the province of Aceh, existing with some other ethnic groups originating from other parts of Indonesia.

East Nusa Tenggara is another example of a province with a large percentage falling under "Ethnic groups from...". The group of "Ethnic groups from the province of East Nusa Tenggara" accounts for a very large 81.2 per cent of this province's population. It actually consists of the Atoni, Manggarai, Lamahot, Ngada, Rote, Lio, Alor and some other smaller ethnic groups. Therefore, in the New Classification, we present all of these ethnic groups to show the richness of ethnic groups in East Nusa Tenggara.

Misplaced Ethnic Groups[8]

In the Initial Classification we find cases where ethnic groups originating from Province A, for example, have been misplaced as originating from Province B. Therefore, in the New Classification, we return them to their origins. Gumba Cadek/Muslim Gunung Ko was initially put under a code for "Other ethnic groups from the island of Sumatra". This ethnic group actually originated in the province of Aceh, on the same island of Sumatra. Gumbak Cadek has an alias of Muslim Gunung Ko, or *Orang Cumbok*, considered as a mix between Acehnese and Gayo. They live as a tribe in a remote area of the province of Aceh (Hidayah 1996, p. 94). We then return Gumba Cadek to the province of Aceh. As a result, the New Classification has an "unusual" code in the province of Aceh. The code for Gumba Cadek/Muslim Gunung Ko is 0103, outside the range of codes of other ethnic groups in Aceh, which range from 0001 to 0010.

Another "unusual" code is found for Lambai/Lamuri with code 0105. In the raw data set this ethnic group was coded differently from that of the Acehnese. Actually, Lam Muri (recorded in the census as Lamuri) and Lambri (recorded in the census as Lambai) are two aliases for Acehnese, not separate ethnic groups from the Acehnese. The Lamuri originated from the Regency of Aceh Besar, province of Aceh. Therefore, we classify "Lambai/Lamuri" (code 0105) along with the Acehnese ("Orang Aceh", code 001).

Nagarigung is moved from "Ethnic groups from the province of South Sumatra", and classified as a sub-ethnic group of the Javanese in the New Classification. See further discussion on this under Javanese, in Chapter 3.

"Marobo" (0653) was misplaced under "Ethnic groups from the island of Sulawesi" in the Initial Classification. However, it is a sub-ethnic group of "Kemak" (0160), an ethnic group originating in the province of East Nusa Tenggara. Thus, Marobo has then been reclassified under Kemak in the New Classification.

Pasir Adang, Pasir Balik, Pasir Burat Mato, Pasir Keteban, Pasir Laburan, Pasir Misi, Pasir Pematang, Pasir Pembesi, Pasir Saing Bewei, Pasir Tajur and Pasir Telake were listed under "Other ethnic groups from the island of Sulawesi" in the Initial Classification. Actually, they are sub-ethnic groups of Pasir, originating on the island of Kalimantan, not from the island of Sulawesi. In the New Classification, they are grouped as sub-ethnic groups of Pasir on the island of Kalimantan.

"Boano/Buano" (0898) was put under "Ethnic groups from Maluku" in the Initial Classification. However, this was a sub-ethnic group of the Tomini, originating on the island of Sulawesi. In the New Classification, Boano/Buano is included under Tomini in Sulawesi, rather than Maluku.

There are several ethnic groups originating from the province of East Nusa Tenggara that were misplaced into other regions. The following are cases of misplaced ethnic groups originating in East Nusa Tenggara. Orang Gunung and Dawam/Rawan, with the code of 0578 and 0561, respectively, have been reclassified as aliases of the Atoni ethnic group in the province of East Nusa Tenggara. In the Initial Classification, these were recorded under

"Other ethnic groups from the island of Kalimantan". In addition, "Ata Kiwan" (0552) is now classified as an alias of the Lamahot ethnic group in the province of East Nusa Tenggara, rather than part of "Other ethnic groups from the island of Kalimantan". Furthermore, "Anas/Toi" (0550) is just another name for "Toi Anas" (0195), an ethnic group originating in the province of East Nusa Tenggara. It was misplaced under "Other ethnic groups from the island of Kalimantan".

"Rai Hawu/Savu/Sawu" (0580) is the alias for the Sawu or Sabu ethnic group from East Nusa Tenggara. It is not part of "Other ethnic groups from the island of Kalimantan". Similarly, Humba/Sumba/Tau Humba with code 0563 was initially found in "Other ethnic groups from the island of Kalimantan", but is now under East Nusa Tenggara. Humba and Tau Huma are aliases for Sumba ethnic groups. They originate from Sumba Island in this province.

The last case of misplaced ethnic group in East Nusa Tenggara is "Fataluku" (0148), which is also known as "Dagada" (0834). This was misplaced under "Ethnic groups from Maluku". Thus, Fataluku or Dagada has been listed as one of the ethnic groups from the province of East Nusa Tenggara in the New Classification.

"Trunyan" (0208) is another name for Bali Aga, in the province of Bali, and therefore it does not belong to the category "Ethnic groups from the province of East Nusa Tenggara". In the New Classification, "Baliaga" (0197) is another spelling of "Bali Aga" (0126), in Bali.

"Manyuke" (1144) was misplaced under "Ethnic groups from the island of Papua" in the Initial Classification. Based on Melalatoa, it is actually a sub-ethnic group of the Dayak in Kalimantan. It is an alias of Dayak Menyuke. Other sub-ethnic groups of Dayak have also been misplaced on other islands. For example, Dayak Tagelan, Kenyah Lo Bakung, Pinihing, Punan Badeng and Putuk were part of "Other ethnic groups from the island of Sulawesi" in the Initial Classification. The New Classification reclassified them as sub-ethnic groups of the Dayak. Furthermore, many sub- or sub-sub-ethnic groups of Dayak without the term Dayak were misplaced under "Other ethnic groups from the island of Kalimantan" in the Initial Classification.

Four Main Issues in Classifying the Ethnic Groups

The first issue is when there are no published references or local expertise for an ethnic group. Indeed, during the 2010 census, we found some categories without any references at all. For instance, we find the "Lha" ethnic group with code 1134 from the island of Papua, but we do not have any references for this ethnic group. At the same time, we have "Iha/Kapaur" with code 0952. As mentioned in Melalatoa (1995, p. 310), Iha or Kapaur is an ethnic group originating in Papua. Therefore, we guess that Lha is actually only a misspelling for Iha. Therefore, in the New Classification, Lha is put as an alias of Lha or Kapaur.

We then have "Saqi" (0585) in Kalimantan, but we do not know whether Saqi is a sub-ethnic group of Dayak, a separate ethnic group or originating from outside Kalimantan. On the other hand, under "Others with origins on the island of Sulawesi", we have "Wang Saq" (code 0817). Is Saqi a misspelling or another name for Wang Saq and should therefore be put under "Other groups with origins in Sulawesi"? As there is no reference for this group, we keep Saqi as a separate ethnic group in Kalimantan. Similarly, we have "Remucles" with code 0582, but there is no reference for this group, and we keep Remucles as a separate ethnic group in Nusa Tenggara. Hopefully, some studies will find out who Saqi and Remucles are and then the classification can be revised accordingly.

The second issue is that there are some ethnic groups with more than one different spelling. This may be because there are different ways to spell the names of the ethnic groups or because it is a different way the interviewer interprets what the respondents pronounced. Therefore, two different spellings may have been considered as two separate responses and interpreted as two different ethnic groups, when in fact they are one ethnic group. Yet, we must be careful in grouping them, as slightly different spellings may actually indicate an authentic difference of more than one ethnic group.

The New Classification puts an ethnic group with more than one spelling into one group. Here are some examples. "Tauraf" (1255) is similar to "Taurap" (1256) on the island of Papua. "Loun" (0680) is similar to "Lo'on" (0758) on the island of Sulawesi. "Dayak Aoheng" (0469), "Auheng" (0553), "Oheng" (0575) and "Ohong" (0536) are also just different spellings for one ethnic group on the island of Kalimantan. "Barangas" (0500) is also spelled differently from "Berangas" (0501) in Kalimantan.

"Naulu, Nuahunai or Nuaulu" (0867) is a sub-ethnic group from the ethnic Seram in the Maluku archipelago. "Huaulu" (0850) is coded as a separate ethnic group from Nuaulu. However, "Huaulu" is just a different way of spelling "Nuaulu". Therefore, we put Huaulu as an alias for Nuaulu.

The third issue is that some ethnic groups have more than one name. As each of them is coded separately, we may get the impression that they are more than one ethnic group. Therefore, we classify them into one ethnic group. For example, the Airoran, Adora, Iriemkena and Sasawa on the island of Papua are coded as four different categories. Actually, they are one ethnic group with four different names. In the New Classification we have Airoran as an ethnic group with three aliases, Adora, Iriemkena and Sasawa.

Other examples are Banda and Eli Elat in Maluku, Fataluku and Dagada in East Nusa Tenggara and Suwawa and Bune in Gorontalo. Many others have also been classified and presented in Appendix 1.

The fourth issue is when there is no consensus amongst anthropologists on how to classify an ethnic group. An example is the ethnic group Wawonii, originating on the island of Wawonii in the province of Southeast Sulawesi. As mentioned by Melalatoa (1995), some experts have argued that Wawonii is a sub-ethnic group of Tolaki. Others say that it is a separate ethnic group. Some linguistic experts maintain that they have their own language, the Wawonii or Kalisusu. However, others have shown that it is just a dialect of Tolaki. We had to make a decision. We decided to put Wawonii as a sub-ethnic group of Tolaki. The number of Wawonii people is so very small that it may not affect the number of Tolaki significantly. Nevertheless, further information is needed to justify or revise this grouping.

Aggregating Ethnic Categories into Ethnic and Sub-Ethnic Groups

This involves deciding whether several ethnic categories can be combined into one ethnic or sub-ethnic group. We start by grouping some ethnic groups into single groups based on what the respondents reported, particularly the first word of their ethnic groups. For example, all ethnic groups starting with the term Malay are grouped under Malay: with Dayak, under Dayak; and with Batak, under Batak. With this rule, for example, under Malay we have Melayu Asahan, Melayu Deli, Melayu Lahat, Melayu Riau, Langkat/Melayu Langkat, Melayu Banyu Asin, Melayu and Melayu Semendo. Combined with Asahan, these categories were also classified as Malay under the Initial Classification.

An exception to this rule is when we consider Dayak Melayu Pontianak and Dayak Melayu Sambas. We classify these groups under Malay rather than Dayak. Melalatoa (1995) showed that the Malay peoples identify themselves with Islam, and therefore those Dayak who convert to Islam are regarded as "becoming Malay" (*masuk Melayu*).

We also check whether there is any coded ethnic group that is not included in the first stage. For example, is there any ethnic group that does not start with Malay, but should have been included under Malay? Following Hidayah (1996), we put Jambi[9] under Malay because it is Melayu Jambi. Similarly, Bengkulu[10] is under Malay because it is Melayu Bengkulu. Furthermore, based on local expertise, we put Asahan, Semendo and Serawai under Malay.[11]

Next is to find whether there are sub-sub-ethnic groups of Malay. For instance, based on anthropological literature, the Melayu Lahat sub-ethnic group has some sub-sub-ethnic groups such as Melayu Lahat, Kikim, Lematang, Lintang and Pasemah. Furthermore, the Pasemah sub-sub-ethnic group consists of two sub-sub-sub-ethnic groups: Gumai and Kisam. Thus, we have a new group for Malay. The Malay in the New Classification has a larger number of ethnic groups than that in the Initial Classification. See Appendix 1.

It should be borne in mind here that it is not easy to define who the Malay are.[12] Melalatoa (1995) states that Malay is the name for a number of ethnic groups spreading through many regions in Indonesia and even into other Southeast Asian countries, such as Malaysia, Thailand and the Philippines. One opinion has it that all ethnic groups in Indonesia are Malay. The second opinion argues that all of these "Malay" have developed into many separate identities and ethnic groups, according to where they live, such that they cannot be said to belong to one ethnic group of "Malay". Melalatoa followed this second opinion, that many originally Malay ethnic groups have developed into distinct ethnic groups in Indonesia. In other words, many of them no longer consider themselves as Malay, but as other ethnic groups such as Javanese, Sundanese, Minang, Banjarese and Buginese. The remaining, who still consider themselves as Malay, are what we call Malay in Indonesia.[13]

We follow this second opinion, also followed by Melalatoa. A respondent is called Malay if s/he says that s/he is Malay. The Malay is an ethnic group, originating from several provinces on the island of Sumatra: Riau, the Riau Archipelago, Jambi, Bengkulu, Bangka-Belitung and South Sumatra.

It is possible that other researchers may have their own groupings for Malay. Appendix 1 facilitates the producing of different definitions of Malay by others, as the list fully provides the code of each category. Different ways of grouping ethnic groups such as Malay may result in a different number of ethnic groups.

Another example is the classification of Dayak. The New Classification has included many more sub-groups under Dayak. The Initial Classification only includes those ethnic groups starting with the term *Dayak*. The groups carrying the term of Dayak make a long list, consisting of 264 categories. After adding other Dayak categories, we finally have 375 categories of Dayak as presented in Appendix 1. Some of them may be aliases or sub-sub- or sub-sub-sub-ethnic groups of Dayak. The additional 111 sub-ethnic groups in the New Classification were initially classified under "Other ethnic groups from the island of Kalimantan" in the Initial Classification. Further discussion on the classification of the Dayak can be referred to Chapter 3.

Notes

1. It should be borne in mind that this "group" is an imagined one, and not necessarily sociologically a real group. Moreover, we use "ethnic group" as a translation from *suku bangsa*, the official term used in Indonesia. Other opinions are welcome and may be recommended to the BPS.
2. As is often shown in television programmes, each province in Indonesia can be portrayed as the stereotypical homeland of a distinctive named ethnicity, with costume, music and architecture etc. to match. The reality is, as this publication makes abundantly clear, much more complex.
3. In Indonesia, the state does not define ethnic groups.
4. An "indigenous" group may not be an ethnic group, but it can be reshaped into an ethnic group, as is the case of the *Bumiputera* ("sons of the soil") concept in Malaysia. "Tribe" can have even more meanings. In modern Africa it is fully synonymous with an "ethnic" group and in West Asia it refers to a "clan". In South and Southeast Asia, tribe is associated with many state-avoiding social formations, including the traditional ways of life of various *Orang Asli* or *Suku Terasing*.
5. As an illustration, the Chinese Indonesians (Indonesian citizens) have a code in the list of coded ethnic groups. On the other hand, the Chinese (non-Indonesian citizens) have their own codes, showing that they are foreigners.
6. Up until 1999, Indonesia had twenty-seven provinces. Since the enactment of the law on regional autonomy in 1999, several provinces were created from the existing ones. This began with the independence of East Timor in 1999, when Indonesia lost a province. However, several provinces were created and,

by 2000, the census covered thirty provinces. Between 2000 and 2010, a few more were created. By 2010 Indonesia had a total of thirty-three provinces. In 2012 another one was created and thus, as of 2014, Indonesia has thirty-four provinces. This changing administrative boundary should be taken into account in understanding population dynamics over time.

7. The publication of ethnic groups by the Badan Pusat Stastistik is under the title of *Kewarganegaraan, Suku Bangsa, Agama, dan Bahasa Sehari hari Penduduk Indonesia: Hasil Sensus Penduduk Indonesia 2010* <http://sp2010.bps.go.id/files/ebook/kewarganegaraan%20penduduk%20indonesia/index.html> (accessed December 2012).

8. Chapter 3 discusses more cases of misplaced ethnic groups.

9. Jambi is also the name of a province on the island of Sumatra.

10. Bengkulu is a name of a province on the island of Sumatra.

11. Readers should note that the respondents do not actually identify themselves as "Malay", but rather as Jambi, Bengkulu, Asahan, Semendo or Serawai. We put these categories under "Malay" because previous studies (mostly by Hidayah and Melalatoa) and local expertise have put them into groups as sub-ethnic groups of Malay.

12. In this book, we use the group name "Malay" in the singular form, which has usually been seen in the Indonesian literature. On the other hand, "Malays" (a plural) is usually used in Malaysia and Singapore. In these two countries, Malays are defined by the state. Therefore, we should be careful when comparing the term "Malay" in Indonesia on the one hand and "Malays" in Malaysia and Singapore on the other. More discussion on state-defined ethnic groups can be followed in Lai (2004).

13. This may be one reason why Malay is written in the singular in Indonesia.

3

THE NEW CLASSIFICATION:
Uncovering Diversity

Creating a new classification system for ethnic groups in Indonesia is not an easy task. The long list of ethnic categories, with its problems and issues as discussed in Chapter 2, coupled with limited or a complete absence of references (no published literature or local expertise) as well as certain political and social sensitivities, requires a thorough examination of each ethnic category. This is a time-consuming search. The published references used include Melalatoa (1995), Hidayah (1996), Koentjaraningrat (1994), Riwut (1958) and Riwut and Mantikei (2003).

Our New Classification is not an attempt to make a list of official ethnic groups. As discussed in Chapter 2, the peoples of Indonesia are free to determine their own ethnic groups. They may even change their ethnic groups as frequently as they wish, as the change does not have any consequences. This is different from some other countries such as China, whose government officially recognizes fifty-six ethnic groups, and Singapore, who categorizes its population into four major groups.

Therefore, the New Classification is not supposed to be fixed for a long time. Rather, the New Classification should be continuously improved as new data and references are available. Yet, this is the first comprehensive classification of ethnic groups based on the 2010 population census.

This chapter sets out the New Classification of ethnic groups based on the 2010 population census for Indonesia. It is new because our classification is different from the Initial Classification discussed in Chapter 2. To some extent it is also significantly different from the one resulting from the 2000 population census, although it has some similarities with that of 2000. This chapter discusses the significance of the New Classification and examines what new groups are revealed from the New Classification. To provide a better understanding of the New Classification, this chapter also presents three comparative case studies on ethnic composition based on the New and Initial Classifications at the provincial level. The selected case studies are on the provinces of Aceh, West Sulawesi and East Nusa Tenggara.

SIGNIFICANCE OF THE NEW CLASSIFICATION

The New Classification of ethnic groups is expected to capture the rich diversity of the ethnic composition of Indonesia as a whole and its provinces, particularly amongst those with many small ethnic groups in the eastern provinces of Indonesia. It is designed as a statistically robust classification, constructed based on the coded raw 1,331 ethnic categories, incorporating information from anthropological, sociological and demographic literature as well as local expertise.

The New Classification, as presented in Appendix 1, expands, details, regroups and redefines the recorded responses to the ethnicity question into four levels: ethnic group, sub-ethnic group, sub-sub-ethnic group and perhaps the sub of sub-sub-ethnic groups. In addition, the New Classification also provides aliases (different names or different spellings) of an ethnic or sub-ethnic group. This makes the New Classification significantly distinct from the existing limited information on ethnicity.

The New Classification is also presented in a user-friendly way. The ethnic groups are arranged in alphabetical order for each main region. We group them into six "main" islands/regions, namely, Sumatra, Java and Bali, Nusa Tenggara, Kalimantan, Sulawesi and Papua. Furthermore, we have an additional group for Indonesians of "foreign origins". This order of presentation simply follows the one employed by the BPS. The order here does not carry any meaning.

It should be noted that the regional groupings of the ethnic groups do not necessarily mean that the people belonging to these groups live in these respective regions. The list shows the regions of origin of the ethnic groups. The people themselves may very well live somewhere else within the country. They may, for example, have migrated from their home provinces.

As observed in Appendix 1, the variation in the numbers of ethnic groups originating on each island is very great. The long list of ethnic groups presented in Appendix 1 provides further indication of the richness and complexity of ethnic groups in Indonesia.

Furthermore, to facilitate easy reference to the data set for those who are studying Indonesia's ethnicity using the New Classification, Appendix 1 is equipped with the code for each ethnic and sub-ethnic group. Moreover, the New Classification lists members of each group. Importantly, the classification does not change the original coded raw data set, preserving the freedom for other users to work with alternative classifications. It should be noted that for the names of the ethnic groups we use the English spelling, but the names of the response categories (coded categories) remain in Bahasa Indonesia (Indonesian), exactly the same as in the coded data set.

We have also reclassified and disaggregated the aggregated groups to reveal many important ethnic groups that are not listed in the Initial Classification. For example, as explained in more detail later, the Initial Classification has a group labelled "Ethnic groups from the province of Aceh". The disaggregation of such a group into several different local ethnic groups is one of the significant features of the New Classification.

In a nutshell, we have classified the long list of ethnic responses of 1,331 coded categories into at least 609 ethnic groups as presented in Appendix 1. This number (609) does not include 21 groups of Indonesian citizens with "foreign origins". One of these groups is the Chinese. Nor does this number include "Others…." for each region/island, which may consist of several very small local ethnic groups.

HOW NEW IS "NEW"?

This section focuses on some of the "new things" provided by the New Classification, in particular related to groupings into an ethnic group or sub-ethnic group. We do not discuss the "simple" ethnic groups, those without any further grouping, as these can be easily understood from Appendix 1. They are ethnic groups without sub-ethnic groups or aliases.

As observed in Appendix 1, local ethnic groups are listed by "Island of Origin", revealing the richness of Indonesia's culture in terms of its large number of small ethnic groups, spreading throughout the whole country. At the end of the list of local ethnic groups in a region/island, there is always "Others in…". For example, in the list for Sumatra, the Table has "Others in Sumatra" at the end of the list. This "Others" may include many other small local ethnic groups originating in Sumatra. We cannot disaggregate this "Others", because the small groups under this "Others" section have been coded into one group. Therefore, the number of local ethnic groups shown in a region is simply the minimal, excluding the possible existence of very small local ethnic groups under "Others…". For the case of Sumatra, there are 55 local ethnic groups plus "Others", meaning that there are at least 55 local ethnic groups originating in Sumatra. For simplicity, in the subsequent discussions in this chapter, the term "ethnic groups" refers to "local ethnic groups", rather than "migrant ethnic groups".

Sumatra

As mentioned earlier, the New Classification in Sumatra produces 55 local ethnic groups plus "Others in Sumatra", much more than just the four groups (Batak, Malay, Minangkabau and Nias) defined in the Initial Classification. The classifications of Minangkabau, a matrilineal community originating in the province of West Sumatra and Nias, originally from the Nias Islands, a chain of islands located along the western coast of the province of North Sumatra, are "simple" cases. There was no reclassification for the ethnic groups of the Minangkabau and Nias. There are many other ethnic groups with such a simple classification, such as Alas, Kerinci and Lingga.

However, the classification of Batak, originating in the province of North Sumatra, is a little complicated. As shown in Appendix 1, Batak, also known as Tapanuli or Batak Tapanuli, consist of six sub-ethnic groups. One sub-ethnic group, the Dairi, has an alias, Batak Pakpak Dairi.

The classification of Malay is even more complicated. It has nine sub-ethnic groups: Melayu Asahan, Melayu Langkat, Melayu Riau, Melayu Banyu Asin, Melayu Lahat, Dayak Melayu Pontianak, Dayak Melayu Sambas, Jambi and Bengkulu. Two sub-ethnic groups of Malay have aliases: Melayu Asahan is also recorded as Asahan; and Melayu Langkat as Langkat as well as Melayu Deli. It should be noted that it is not easy to decide whether Melayu Deli is an alias of Melayu Langkat or a different sub-ethnic group of Malay. Hidayah (1996) mentioned that Melayu Langkat is also often known as Melayu Deli. However, Melalatoa (1995) argued that Melayu Langkat is different from Melayu Deli. Melayu Langkat originated from the regency of Langkat, but Melayu Deli from the regency of Deli Serdang and around the city of Medan. Both are in the province of North Sumatra. In this book, we treat Melayu Deli as another name for Melayu Langkat. Further studies should be carried out to better understand Melayu Langkat and Melayu Deli.

Melayu Lahat was recorded as having four sub-sub-ethnic groups of Malay: Kikim, Lematang, Lintang and Pasemah, each with a different code. Furthermore, the Pasemah, one of the sub-sub-ethnic groups, has five sub-sub-sub-ethnic groups of Malay: Gumai, Kisam, Serawai, Melayu Semendo or Semendo and Semidang. Melayu Semendo has the alias of Semendo.

It should be noted that Melayu Banyu Asin is a sub-ethnic group of Malay. It is different from Musi Banyuasin, a sub-ethnic group of Musi. Musi is an ethnic group originally living on the banks of the Musi River in the province of South Sumatra, with two sub-ethnic groups. Likewise, the people of Ogan are also those who originally lived alongside a river, the Ogan River, in the province of South Sumatra. Pegagan is its sub-ethnic group.

We do not classify Palembang as a sub-ethnic group of Malay, because the people of Palembang call themselves *Wong* Palembang, rather than Melayu Palembang (Palembang Malay). Belitung is not part of the Malay group, because the people of Belitung see themselves as "*Urang* Belitong". Bangka is also different from Malay. The people of Bangka are the "*Orang* Bangka*", who were living on the island of Bangka before the arrival of the Malay. Since 2000, the islands of Bangka and Belitung, together with several smaller islands, were separated from the province of South Sumatra to create an autonomous province called Bangka-Belitung.

Further discussion on the other five sub-ethnic groups of Malay can be found in the section "Aggregating Ethnic Groups into Ethnic and Sub-ethnic Groups" in Chapter 2.

Lampung is another very complicated ethnic group consisting of three lower layers (sub-ethnic, sub-sub-ethnic and sub-sub-sub-ethnic groups) also carrying different names. As described in Melalatoa (1995) and Hidayah (1996), Lampung is an ethnic group with origins in the province of Lampung, on the island of Sumatra. It has two sub-ethnic groups, the Lampung Papadun and Lampung Peminggir. In the population census, as shown in Appendix 1, Lampung Papadun was written as Pepaduan.

It is not clear whether there has been a renaming of the sub-ethnic group or if this is a matter of spelling by the interviewers and *kortims* (team coordinators) as discussed in Chapter 2. On the other hand, Peminggir or Lampung Peminggir was not recorded in the census. However, Lampung Peminggir is also known as Saibatin, Sebatin or Seibatin and the name Seibatin was recorded in the census. Therefore, in the New Classification, Lampung has two sub-ethnic groups: Seibatin and Pepaduan.

Each of these two sub-ethnic groups has many sub-sub-ethnic groups. The Pepaduan has four sub-sub-ethnic groups: Siwo Megou (also known as Sembilan Marga), Megau Pak Tulang Bawang, Buay Lima and Pubian (also known as Pubian Telu Suku). Pubian is also written Pubiyan in the census.

It can be noted here that Melalatoa and Hidayah put "Abung" in front of Siwo Megou and Sembilan Marga, becoming Abung Siwo Megou and Abung Sembilan Marga. Abung Siwo Megou has sub-sub-sub ethnic groups: the Buay Unyai, Buay Unyi, Buay Nuban, Buay Subing, Buay Beliuk, Buay Kunang, Buay Selagi and Buay Nyerupa — which are not recorded in the census. Furthermore, Melalatoa and Hidayah spelled "Megou Pak Tulang Bawang" for the name that was written in the census as "Megau Pak Tulang Bawang". It is likely that there was a misspelling in the field.

Seibatin (or Peminggir) has four sub-sub-ethnic groups: Peminggir Semangka, Peminggir Melinting Rajabasa, Peminggir Teluk and Peminggir Skala Brak. Peminggir Skala Brak has two sub-sub-sub-ethnic groups: Bunga Mayang and Abung. The census recorded "Peminggir Melinting Rajabasa" as "Melintang Rajabasa". "Melintang" in the census is perhaps a misspelling of "Melinting". Peminggir Teluk was recorded as Teluk; and Peminggir Skala Barak as Skala Brak.

Peminggir Semangka may include Komering. However, as some people of Komering do not want to say that they are a sub-sub-ethnic group of Lampung, the New Classification keeps Komering as a separate ethnic group, distinct from the Lampung.

In the New Classification, we also put "Belalau" and "Krui" as sub-sub-ethnic groups of Lampung, part of Seibatin. As the migrants to the province of Lampung may now call themselves Lampung, the Lampung in the New Classification may include these migrants, as long as they said they were Lampung. Hidayah (1996) argued that Belalau is perhaps part of the Lampung ethnic group, speaking Lampung with Belalau dialect. We rely on local expertise to treat Krui as part of Seibatin, a sub-sub-ethnic group of Lampung. Krui is an area located in the west coast of Lampung which is known for its damar agroforest, or *repong* damar (Budidarsono et al. 2000).

Simpler than Lampung, the ethnic group of Anak Dalam, originating in the province of Jambi, has four different names: Anak Rimbo, Lubu, Kubu and Ulu. However, each of these has a different code. Therefore, in the New Classification, these five categories are put under one group, labelled Anak Dalam.

Gayo is here defined as an aggregation from several sub-ethnic groups: Gayo, Gayo Lut, Gayo Luwes and Gayo Serbe Jadi. These are the peoples originally living in the highlands of the province of Aceh.

The Simeulue group originally lived on the island of Simeulue located along the western coast of this province, with Sigulai as its sub-ethnic group.

The Rejang people primarily lived in the province of Bengkulu, also called Keme or Lebong. Taba Saling, recorded in the census as Saling, is a sub-ethnic group of Rejang.

Mentawai is an ethnic group originally from the islands of Mentawai, part of the province of West Sumatra. These islands consist of four main islands: Siberut, Sipora, Pagai Utara and Pagai Selatan. The census only recorded "Mentawai" as one code (0031). However, we have "Pagai" (0108) and "Siberut" (0027) separately in the census. In the Initial Classification, these two groups were simply put under the category of "Other ethnic groups from the island of Sumatra". In the New Classification, these two groups are considered as sub-ethnic groups of the Mentawai.

Java and Bali

Java is a small yet densely inhabited island, but the census only recorded nine local ethnic groups from Java: the Badui/Baduy, Bantenese, Bawean/ Boyanese, Betawi, Cirebonese, Javanese, Madurese, Osing/Using and Sundanese. Another heavily populated island to the east of the island of Java is Bali. This island has four local ethnic groups. Perhaps there are some other smaller ethnic groups on these two islands but these were not recorded in the census.

The New Classification has five sub-ethnic groups (Jawa, Samin, Tengger, Nagaring and Nagarigung) under Javanese. This is smaller than the seven categories in the Initial Classification. In the New Classification,

Javanese does not include Osing or Using and Bawean or Boyan. These are distinctive ethnic groups, not sub-ethnic groups of the Javanese. The people of Osing claim that they are the *orang asli* (native people) of Banyuwangi in the eastern part of the province of East Java. Bawean is closer to Madurese than to Javanese. The Bawean originated from the island of Bawean located north of Surabaya, the capital city of the province of East Java. Their young men are well known for their migration culture, leaving their women behind on the island. Thus, the island is also known as *Pulau Putri*, Women's Island.

Nagarigung is problematic, as there is no clear anthropological reference for this ethnic group. It belongs to "ethnic groups from province of South Sumatra" in the Initial Classification. Nevertheless, we suspect that Nagarigung may come from the term Nagari or Nagara Agung. Traditionally, Javanese believe in four *Ranah Budaya* (centrifugal hierarchical social layers). The first and the most respected is *nagara*, the centre of the Javanese *ranah budaya*. Lifestyles and everything related to this community are seen as holy and sacred. The second, outside the *nagara*, is *nagara agung*, which is not as respected as the *nagara*. The next two *ranah budaya*s that are even lower in terms of status are *manca negara* and *pasisir* (Sairin 2002). Therefore, Nagarigung has been moved from "ethnic groups from the province of South Sumatra" and is treated as a sub-ethnic group of Javanese in the New Classification.

Nagaring is more problematic. This appears under the Javanese in both the Initial and New Classifications. Yet, we cannot find any information on Nagaring. However, based on the 2010 population census, they lived in the Javanese home provinces of East and Central Java. Therefore, we must assume that they are a sub-ethnic group of the Javanese. Perhaps it is just a misspelling of Nagarigung. Further studies should be done on the Nagaring.

Another ethnic group on the island of Java is the Sundanese. In the New Classification this includes "Sunda" (0113) and "Naga" (0117). Yet, in the Initial Classification, Naga was under Javanese. Naga is actually a small Sundanese community living in Naga village in Tasikmalaya in the province of West Java. Therefore, it is a sub-ethnic group of the Sundanese, speaking Sundanese, yet their belief system is different from that of the Sundanese majority.

Bantenese is an ethnic group which is distinct from its neighbouring ethnic groups of Javanese and Sundanese. Together with Badui/Baduy, it was categorized under "Ethnic groups from the province of Banten" in the Initial Classification. Thus, the New Classification disaggregates it to make the Bantenese a single ethnic group.

In the New Classification, the Bantenese is separated from the Badui/Baduy, a traditional community living on the Kendeng Mountain of the province of Banten. This small group is different from the majority Bantenese. The Badui people resist modern life, preserving their ancient way of life. They live in a sacred area of the mountain. They consist of two groups: Badui Dalam (Inner Badui) and Badui Luar (Outer Badui). The Badui Dalam are also called Baduy Jero, Urang Tangtu or Urang Girang. The Badui Luar also have different names, such as Urang Panamping and Urang Dangka (Ichwandi and Shinohara, 2007). Their clothing differentiates the social division, with the Badui Dalam wearing white and the Badui Luar wearing black or dark blue. However, the census data did not recode the Badui into these two groups. Although the Badui themselves claim that they are the "beginning" of the Sundanese and even mankind, we classify them as a separate ethnic group from the Sundanese, with Banten as their home province.

The Cirebonese group were originally located in the province of West Java, the home province of the Sundanese. Nevertheless, the Cirebonese are different from the majority of Sundanese. They are a mixture of Sundanese and Javanese.

We also have Betawi on the island of Java. These are natives of the capital city of Jakarta (derived from Batavia, the colonial name for Jakarta). They have a distinct culture, different from the neighbouring ethnic groups of Sundanese and Bantenese.

In the New Classification, Balinese consists of two categories: "Bali Hindu" (0124) and "Bali Majapahit" (0125). Both are aliases. Yet, Bali Aga, or Baliaga (a variant spelling), is considered a tribal group on the island of Bali. They are culturally and geographically different from the Majapahit/Hindu Balinese. The Baliaga live in remote areas of Mount Agung and many of them live in the village of Trunyan on the shores of Lake Batur (Susilo 1997). Thus, this group are also called by a different name, the Trunyan. Their traditional funeral ritual of not burying their dead is distinct from other Baliaga groups. Thus, the Balinese in the New Classification does not include "Bali Aga" (0126) "Baliaga" (0197) or "Trunyan" (0208).

Apart from these two, Nyama Selam and Loloan are two small ethnic groups on the island of Bali. These small groups are mostly the Muslim minority living amongst the Hindu Balinese majority, who have also adopted some traditional Balinese culture. Giving names for their children, they use Balinese names such as Wayan, Nengah, Nyoman and Ketut, in order to present the birth order, in combination with the Arabic names. For example, Wayan Abdullah is for the first born boy. Nyama Selam originated in the village of Pegayaman, on the Bukit Gigit Mountain, on the route to Singaraja in the province of Buleleng.[1] The Loloan group were located in Jembrana, originally migrating from the island of Sulawesi to escape from the Dutch in the seventeenth century.

Nusa Tenggara

Nusa Tenggara or the Lesser Sunda Islands is a group of islands administered into two provinces: West Nusa Tenggara in the west and East Nusa Tenggara in the east. West Nusa Tenggara consists of two main islands, Lombok and Sumbawa. East Nusa Tenggara contains many distinct islands, each with its own history and cultural make-up. It includes West Timor where Kupang, the capital of East Nusa Tenggara, is located. West Timor borders the Democratic Republic of Timor-Leste, formerly known as the province of East Timor under Indonesia.

"Ethnic groups from the province of East Nusa Tenggara" described in the Initial Classification has been split into several groups in the New Classification. Alor is a group of small islands in East Nusa Tenggara with Alor itself as one of them (Figure 3.2). Alor is also one of the largest local ethnic groups in East Nusa Tenggara. As mentioned in Chapter 2, this group includes sixteen sub-ethnic groups recorded in the census. Seven of these are recorded under one code (0133) covering the Alor, Belagar, Kelong, Maneta (recorded as Manete in the census), Mauta, Seboda and Wersin. Therefore, we do not have separate information about each of these sub-ethnic groups. The New Classification also uncovers different spellings for two sub-ethnic groups of Alor. The Kawel, a sub-ethnic group of Alor, was recorded as "Kawei" in the census with code 0158. Belagar was also spelled "Blagar" in the census with the code number of 0141. However, the census did not record three sub-ethnic groups of the Alor: the Ndebang, Malua and Wuwuli. Is this a matter of data collection or did the three sub-ethnic groups disappear? Further studies should be conducted on this question.

In the New Classification there are eight aliases for Atoni. Four aliases have been recorded in one code (0134): Atanfui, Atani, Atoni Meto and

Dawan. Atoni Meto is also called Atoni Pah Meto but this is not recorded in the census. Two aliases were coded 0561: Dawam and Rawan. "Dawam" in 0561 may be a misspelling of Dawan in 0134. Two other aliases were Gunung-Orang Gunung and Orang Gunung, each with a different code. These two codes may actually refer to one alias, Orang Gunung.

Atoni Meto means the people of the dry land. They originate from Timor Island in the province of East Nusa Tenggara. As mentioned by Cunningham (2007), the Indonesian-speaking people living in the city of Kupang, the capital city of the province, call the Atoni *orang gunung* (mountain people), *orang asli* (indigenous people) or simply *orang Timor* (Timorese).

Lamahot is another important ethnic group in East Nusa Tenggara that has several different names, such as Lamholot, Lamkolot, Larantuka, Solor, Solot, Ata Kiwan and Holo. However, Holo is not recorded in the census. Neighbouring with Alor, Solor is also a group of islands (Kepulauan Solor) with the island of Solor as part of it.

Ngada consists of six sub-ethnic groups. The sub-ethnic group of Ngada has other names, Nage and Bajawa. They are originally from the island of Flores, which means flowers in Portuguese.

Sumba is an island in the western part of East Nusa Tenggara, or south of Flores Island (Figure 3.2), and Sumbanese is an ethnic group there, where they are called Humba or Tau Humba. The Sawu Islands consist of three islands: Rai Hawu (or Savu), Rai Jua and Rai Dana, located between Sumba Island and West Timor. Sawu is another local ethnic group in East Nusa Tenggara, known as Rai Hawu, Savu, Hawu and Sabu. Another local ethnic group there is Toi Anas, with Anas/Toi as a variant spelling.

In short, we have listed 55 ethnic groups in Nusa Tenggara, and many of these are simple ethnic groups, without any sub-grouping. See Appendix 1.

Kalimantan

The smallest number of ethnic groups in the New Classification is found in Kalimantan, with only six local ethnic groups: Banjarese, Dayak, Kutai, Pasir, Saqi and Telaga. However, Dayak, one local ethnic group, has 375 sub-ethnic groups. It is possible that some of the 375 sub-ethnic groups are actually sub-sub-ethnic groups or even sub-sub-sub-ethnic groups of Dayak. However, as there is no consensus to classify the sub-sub-ethnic groups and sub-sub-sub-ethnic groups of Dayak, it is beyond the scope of this book to examine the possible sub-sub-ethnic or even sub-sub-sub-ethnic groups of the Dayak.[2] Deeper studies should improve the New Classification to show the sub-sub- and sub-sub-sub-ethnic groups of Dayak.

The term Dayak as mentioned by Klinken (2006) is a generic term employed by Western anthropologists in encompassing various non-Muslim indigenous people in Borneo. It is the most complex ethnic group. Several researchers have tried to classify the various groups of Dayak in Borneo based on various reasons. The earliest study was carried out in the early twentieth century by Mallinckrodt, whose work became a starting point for subsequent studies on Dayak classification. Mallinckrodt (1928) grouped the Dayak into six groups, called Stammenras, namely, Kenyah-Kayan-Bahau Stammenras, Ot Danum Stammenras, Iban Stammenras, Murut Stammenras, Klemantan Stammenras and Punan Stammenras. Furthermore, Danum Stammenras includes Ot Danum, Ngaju, Maanyan, Dusun and Luangan, while Punan Stammenras includes Basap, Punan, Ot and Bukat.

Later on, Stohr (1959) grouped the Dayak into six groups based on their distinctive funeral rituals. They are the Kenyah-Kayan-Bahau, Ot Danum (including Ot Danum-Ngaju and Maanyan-Lawangan), Iban, Murut (including Dusun-Murut-Kelabit), Klemantan (including Klemantan and Dayak Darat) and Punan. Riwut (1958), a Dayak himself, grouped the Dayak into seven groups with eigthteen sub-ethnic groups covering 405 sub-sub-ethnic groups for the whole of Kalimantan. Most of the categories in the 2010 population census are found in the list of Dayak proposed by Riwut (1958). Some were not mentioned by Riwut, perhaps reflecting new developments since 1958.

Although they are different in several respects, the Dayak share a similar collective identity, which is exemplified by longhouse living (called Lou, Lamin, Betang or Lewu Hante), using traditional weapons called Mandau and *sumpit* (blowpipe), making earthenware, *anyam-anyaman* (plaited materials), having *perladangan gilir balik* (lit. turn back cultivation), i.e., swidden farming, dancing and mostly following a patrilineal genealogic system.

Some of the Dayak groups have sub-ethnic groups and/or different names or different spellings. Sub-ethnic groups with more than one name or spelling include Empran also known as Ulu Batang Ali; Dayak Seru or Undup or Skrang or Serul or Srul; and Dayak Kriau or Karehan.

Banjarese is another ethnic group originating in South Kalimantan, often associated with the Barito River. This may be a mixture of four ethnic groups: the Buginese, Dayak, Javanese and Malay. The Banjarese are called Urang Banjar. However, the Dayak who convert to Islam are also known as Urang Banjar. It should be noted that "Urang Banjar" was not recorded in the census.

The Banjarese speak Banjarese with two dialects, Banjar Kuala and Banjar Hulu Sungai. The census has two codes for the Banjarese: the first is "Banjarese" (0520) and the second is "Banjar Kuala/Batang Bunyu/Pahuluan" (0499). These three names may refer to three sub-ethnic groups of Banjarese, but we cannot break them into three sub-ethnic groups, because they have been put under one code (0499).

Pasir is also a local ethnic group on the island of Kalimantan. It is different from Dayak Pasir, which is a sub-ethnic group of Dayak. According to Melalatoa (1995), Pasir has five sub-ethnic groups: Pasir Telake, Pasir Adang, Pasir Kendilo, Pasir Labuan and Pasir Tanjung Aru. There are two sub-ethnic groups which were not recorded in the census: Pasir Tanjung Aru and Pasir Kendilo. On the other hand, the census recorded several sub-ethnic groups of Pasir which were not mentioned in Melalatoa (1995). See Appendix 1. Two sub-ethnic groups had different spellings. The sub-ethnic group of Pasir Pematung was recorded as Pasir Pematang and Pasir Labuan as Pasir Laburan.

Another ethnic group originally from Kalimantan is Kutai. It is a historic name related to the Kutai Kingdom, the oldest Hindu Kingdom in Indonesia, located in East Kalimantan. Kutai used to be a sub-ethnic group of Dayak. However, when they became Muslim, they wanted to make their own identities, becoming a separate ethnic group, the Kutai.

In the New Classification, we also have two "unclear" ethnic groups in Kalimantan: "Saqi" (code 0585) and "Telaga" (0592). As discussed in the section "Four Main Issues in Classifying Ethnic Groups" in Chapter 2, we cannot find any literature on the Saqi. Nor have we found any literature on the Telaga. Further studies should be done to find out who the Saqi and Telaga are. Are they from Kalimantan, from other islands or simply a misspelling of other sub-ethnic groups?

Finally, perhaps, it would be more interesting if we would find out which groups are under "Other tribes with origins in Kalimantan". Nevertheless, there is no way to break down this category, as it has been coded under one code "5000" in the coded raw data set.

Sulawesi

The Initial Classification also has a grouping such as "Others from the island of Sulawesi". This is a category of all local ethnic groups from the island of Sulawesi, except for the Buginese, which is singled out from this group. The New Classification disaggregates this category into distinct local ethnic groups on the island of Sulawesi as seen in Appendix 1. Later in this chapter we elaborate further on the case of the province of West Sulawesi to compare the results between the Initial and New Classifications.

The Balantak people's homeland is the regency of Banggai, in the province of Central Sulawesi, mostly living in the hat-shaped end of the peninsula of the province. They have their own language, *bahasa Balantak*, an Austronesian language (Berg and Busenitz 2012). Balantak has the alias Mian Balantak, but this is not coded in the census. The census recorded three separate codes for "Balantak/Tanutor" (0626), "Dale-Dale" (0637) and "Tanoturan" (0791). However, as mentioned in Hidayah (1996, p. 35), Tanoturan and Dale-Dale are two different sub-ethnic groups of Balantak. "Tanutor" (0626), as recorded in the census, was perhaps a misspelling of Tanoturan. As Tanutor is considered as a sub-ethnic of Balantak, it should not be placed under the same code as Balantak, but should have its own code. Perhaps it should be in the same code as the Tanoturan. In the New Classification we have put the three codes under one group of Balantak.

The Bugis group is well known to have its homeland in the province of South Sulawesi. The Buginese have another name, Ugi (Hidayah 1996, p. 63). The group has three sub-ethnic groups: Tolotang (Hidayah 1996, p. 269), Amatoa (Hidayah 1996, p. 13) and Bugis Pagatan (Melalatoa 1995, p. 469). Ammatowa is a different spelling for Amatoa. Ammatowa are also called Orang Kajang (Hidayah 1996, p. 13). The group Bugis Pagatan or Pagatan is the name used for those Buginese who have migrated and reside in South Kalimantan, in the area called Pagatan.

Kaili, as described by Melalatoa (1995, p. 111) or Hidayah (1996), are also known as Toraja Barat, Toraja Palu, Toraja Parigi-Kaili or Toraja Sigi. The recorded aliases were put in one code (0660) in the raw data set, consisting of Palu, Parigi, Sigi, Tokaili and Toraja Barat, as well as Tamungkolowi, which is a sub-ethnic group of the Kaili. As mentioned in Melalatoa (1995), the Kaili group has many sub-ethnic groups, each group sometimes with a prefix of "To", meaning people (*orang*). For instance, Kaili is also called Tokaili or To Kaili. To these aliases, we add "Tosigi (0633)" as another alias for Kaili, referring to Toraja Sigi. However, in the raw data set, Tosigi was put together with two sub-ethnic groups of Kaili, Binimaru and Lindu, under one code (0633).

According to Melalatoa and Hidayah, sub-ethnic groups of the Kaili include *Baku*, Balinggi, Baluase, Bangga, Banggakoro, Kulawi, Susu,

Biromaru/Tobiromaru (recorded in the census as "Binimaru", 0633 and "Birumaru/Tobirumaru", 0734), *Dolago*, Dolo/Todolo (we recorded another alias, Toridolo), Lindu, *Pakuli*, Palu, Parigi, *Petimpe*, Raranggonau, Sibalaya, Sidondo, Sigi, Tamungkolowi and *Tawaeli (Payapi)*. The terms given in italics here are not available in the coded raw data set.

The census also recorded "Ledo" (0651). According to Hidayah, the language of the Kaili is called the language of Ledo (meaning "No"). Melalatoa (1995) mentioned that Ledo is a dialect of the Kaili language. It is not clear whether Ledo is also an alias of Kaili, but here we treat it as a sub-ethnic group of the Kaili.

As seen here, Raranggonau, Sibalaya and Sidondo are sub-ethnic groups of Kaili, yet in the coded raw data they are combined with Toraja in one coded group, "Raranggonau/Sibalaya/Sidondo/Toraja" (0665). As mentioned in Chapter 2, we have separated the Toraja from these three groups by division of their religions — the Muslims as Kaili and the non-Muslims as Toraja.

Minahasa has ten sub-ethnic groups, namely Bantik, Pasan or Ratahan, Ponosakan, Tombulu, Tonsawang, Tonsea, Totembuan, Toulour, Borgo and Babontehu. The sub-ethnic group Totemboan or Tonteboan was recorded with the code 0617. "Totembuan" (0618) was perhaps just a misspelling of "Totemboan". The two codes refer to one sub-ethnic group. One of the nine sub-ethnic groups is Borgo, an ethnic group resulting from intermarriages between the Minahasa with Europeans (Spanish, Portuguese and Dutch) in the sixteenth century. Nowadays, the people of Borgo consider themselves as Minahasa. We do not have any reference for Babontehu. However, according to local expertise, this is also a sub-ethnic group of the Minahasa. We decided to consider "Babontehu" (0599) as a sub-ethnic group of the Minahasa.

Mongondow is an ethnic group originating in North Sulawesi and consisting of five sub-groups (Appendix 1). One of these is "Kaidipang" (0606). The census also recorded "Kodipiang" in a separate code (0607). We assume that "Kodipiang" is just another spelling of "Kaidipang".

Pamona is also known as Toraja Poso-Tojo (recorded as Tojo in the census), Toraja Bare'e (recorded as Bare'e) or Toraja Timur. The sub-ethnic groups include four lists, depending on where they originally lived. The first is Lalaeo (recorded as Lalaleo or Tolalaeo in the census) Poso, Ra'u (recorded as Rau in the census) and Wana. The second is Bancea, Buyu, Kadambuku, Lage/Tolage, Lamusa, Longken (recorded as Longkea in the census), Payapi, Pebato, Pu'umboto, Unda'e and Wotu. The third list includes Kalae, Pada, Pakambia, Palende, Pu'umnana and Tanandoa. The fourth one is Laiwono (recorded as Laiwonu in the census), Lampu/ Tolampu, Tawi and Lembo. Thus, in the New Classification, Pamona includes all of these sub-ethnic groups.

Another important ethnic group in Sulawesi is the Tolaki, also called Laki-laki, Lolaki or Toke. Tolaki includes seven sub-ethnic groups: Tolaki Mekongga, Aserawanua, Labeau, Mowewe, Tamboki, Tolaki Konawe and Wawonii. Tolaki Mekongga is also called Mekongga or Wiwirano.

Tomini has several sub-ethnic groups such as Balaesang, Dampelas, Dondo, Kasimbar, Moutong, Patapa, Tinombo, Toli Toli, Tomenui or Tomini, Umalasa and Boano or Buano. However, the census recorded four sub-ethnic groups (Kasimbar, Moutong, Patapa and Tinombo) under one code (0645). The census also has "Mautong" (0709), which we consider to be the same as "Moutong" (0645). The census also recorded "Tajio/Ta'jio" (0669), a different code from "Kasimbar" (0645). Hidayah (1996, p. 252) mentioned that Tajio or Takjio is also called Kasimbar.

Altogether, there are at least 117 local ethnic groups in Sulawesi plus "Others in Sulawesi". A large majority of these are single ethnic groups, without any further grouping. Perhaps, with more information, some of these can be combined and the number of separate local ethnic groups will decline.

Maluku

The islands of Maluku have at least ninety-nine local ethnic groups, mostly simple ethnic groups. Only a few ethnic groups have sub-ethnic groups and a few others have aliases.

The Makian ethnic group originated from the island of Makian and the southern island of Halmahera. This group has two sub-ethnic groups. One is Makian Barat or Makian Luar. Their language is Jitine or Desite and this is often used as an alias of Makian Barat. The second is Makian Timur or Makian Dalam. Their language is Tabayama and therefore they are also called Tabayama.

The ethnic group of Seram is also known as Alifuru (recorded in the census as "Alfuru") or Ibu. They originated from a community on the island of Seram and claim that they are the beginning of mankind. This group has several sub-ethnic groups, such as Wemale, Orang Alune, Orang Nuaulu and Orang Lumoli (Melalatoa, 1996). The census recorded the four sub-ethnic groups: "Wemale" (0895), "Alune" (0819), "Lumoli" (0863) and "Nuaulu" (0867 and 0850). Nuaulu was recorded to have three aliases, Naulu, Nuahunai and Huaulu.

The Tanimbar are people originating in the Tanimbar Islands. The Tanimbar (Orang Tanimbar) themselves prefer to be called Orang Numbar. Others call themselves Orang Timur Laut. This last group has three sub-ethnic groups: Tomata Yamdena (recorded as Yamdena in the census), Tomata Laru (recorded as Laru-Tomata Laru in the census) and Tomata Nember (recorded as Nember in the census). However, the census put "Orang Timur Laut" in the same code as the Nember sub-ethnic group, 0868, rather than with the Tanimbar ethnic group, 0891.

There are four ethnic groups originating from the islands of Maluku, but these were misplaced into Sulawesi in the Initial Classification. The first is the Laloda/Loloda, an ethnic group originating in Laloda in the province of North Maluku. The second is the Mare, a native community on the island of Mare in the province of North Maluku. The third is the Moa, a community on the island of Moa in the province of Maluku. The fourth is the Modole, originating on the island of Halmahera in the province of North Maluku.

Papua

The land of Papua has the largest number of local ethnic groups. There are at least 261 local ethnic groups spread throughout the provinces of West Papua and Papua. Further studies should be done to examine whether some of these are simply aliases or sub-ethnic groups or sub-sub-ethnic groups.

Asmat is one of the best known of the ethnic groups in Papua. Descriptions of the Asmat can be found in much of the literature. The New Classification has many response categories for the Asmat, including "Asmat" itself. Based on Hidayah (1996, pp. 20–21, 57 and 75), Asmat has several different sub-ethnic groups such as Betch-Mbup, Bismam, Brazza, Cicak, Emari Ducur, Joerat, Kaimo, Safan, Simai and Unisirau. The way the census recorded these names was a little complicated but the codes do not affect the analysis of the overall Asmat. Some complication can arise when someone is interested in knowing the sub-ethnic groups of the Asmat. This is because the sub-ethnic group of Betch-Mbup is combined with Asmat into one code (1004). Cicak has two aliases, Citak Mitak and Kaunak, but "Cicak/Citak Mitak" (1034) has been coded differently from "Kaunak" (1101). On the other hand, Braza is different from Cicak/Citak

Mitak but it has been put in one code along with "Cicak/Citak Mitak" (1034). Another sub-ethnic group, Sawi, has two codes, 1221 for "Sawi" and 1123 for "Sawuy". Kayagar also has two codes, 1084 for Kaigir and Kayigi, as well as 1104 for "Kaygir". Unisirau, one of the sub-ethnic groups, was spelled as "Unisiarau" (1267) in the census. Awyu is a sub-ethnic group, having the alias Away, and both are coded 1008. Asmat actually has two other sub-ethnic groups, Keenok and Batia, but these were not recorded in the census. It is not clear why the census did not record Keenok and Batia, but perhaps this is a misspelling or the sub-ethnic groups have disappeared.

The ethnic group Arfak also illustrates the complexity of classification. There are sub-ethnic groups with more than one name and spelling as well as a misclassification due to two different groups being put under one code. Melalatoa (1995, p. 51) mentioned that the Arfak consists of four sub-ethnic groups, namely the Atam, Manikion, Meiyakh and Moire. Atam has four aliases — Hatam, Hattam, Tinam and Mire — each with their own separate code.

Meiyakh has two aliases, Meyah and Meyek, and the census classified the two into one code (0970). Another sub-ethnic group, the Moire, has no alias. Manikion has only one alias, Sough, but this has two different codes, 0966 and 0978.

As discussed in Chapter 2 under "Problems with the Coded Raw Data Set", we also have one code (1002) for "Arfak/Ayfat". Actually, Arfak and Ayfat are two different ethnic groups. We therefore put this code under Arfak and note that the number of Arfak may be overestimated and that of Ayfat underestimated.

Ayfat also faces issues with bearing more than one name. Hidayah (1996, p. 27) considered that the Ayfat may be in the same group with the Ayamaru or Meybarat. "Ayamaru" has one code, 1010. However, in the census, Meybrat has two codes. One is 1158, with a different spelling, "Mey Brat". Another one is 0967, with another different spelling, "Meibarat". As a result, as presented in Appendix 1, Ayfat consists of these three codes (0967, 1010 and 1158). As discussed in the sub-section "Problems with the Coded Raw Data" in Chapter 2, the number of Ayfat may be underestimated, as some of the group may fall under "Arfak/Ayfat" with the code number 1002.

We also have the Mintamani, Aiso, Kais and Atori as four separately coded ethnic groups. Actually, according to Hidayah (1996, p. 26), these are one ethnic group with four different names. In the New Classification we put them under one ethnic group, the Mintamani.

Peoples of Foreign Origins

These are Indonesian citizens living in Indonesia but with foreign descent. They can be the first generation, second generation or longer, even more than seventh generation Indonesians. They may have adapted to local cultures.

The census recorded three categories of Chinese. The first is the Cina, referring to those born in Indonesia, and with no knowledge of their descent. The second is the Cina PRC, indicating those Chinese who were not born in Indonesia and were originally citizens of the People's Republic of China (PRC). The third one is the Cina Taiwan, those Indonesians who were formerly citizens of the Republic of China (Taiwan). It should be noted that, following Presidential Decree No. 12/2014, the term "Cina" should be replaced by "Tionghoa" in Bahasa Indonesia in the next surveys/censuses.

The New Classification also classifies Indonesians with "Timor-Leste Origins". The people of East Timor had a referendum on seceding from Indonesia in 1999. It officially became an independent country in 2002. The people with Timor-Leste origins may be people who were already in Indonesian East Timor before 2002 but who decided to choose Indonesian citizenship or some people in East Timor (Timor-Leste) who, after 1999, migrated to Indonesia and became Indonesian citizens. This group consists of seven ethnic groups; each has with its own code.

The New Classification lists two other groups with foreign origins: the Arabs (originating in the Arab States) and Indonesians with Other Foreign Origins. As with those of Chinese and Timor-Leste origins, there is no indication whether they are the first generation or not.

With the anticipated rise in the flow of people from other countries into Indonesia, it is possible that the group of Indonesians with foreign origins will become larger and more important in the future.

ETHNIC GROUPS IN THREE SELECTED PROVINCES

This section discusses ethnic composition based on the New Classification in comparison with the Initial Classification in three selected provinces, namely Aceh, East Nusa Tenggara and West Sulawesi. The selection was made mainly on the basis of the significant existence of a category called "Ethnic groups originating in..." under the Initial Classification, hiding the diversity of local ethnic groups in a province. Therefore, the New Classification disaggregates this category, uncovering the rich diversity of local ethnic groups. This kind of disaggregation will become more relevant when we later examine statistics at the provincial and especially the district level.

The discussion in this section is limited to the ten largest ethnic groups in each of the three provinces. The ten ethnic groups in each province can be local or migrant ethnic groups. It is expected to exemplify the importance of the New Classification in bringing a better understanding of the ethno-demography of local ethnic groups. The discussion at the district level is beyond the scope of this book.

Province of Aceh

The 2010 population census is perhaps the most comprehensive census in the province of Aceh. The data is comparable with those in other provinces. Due to prolonged local conflicts between the Government of Indonesia and GAM (Gerakan Aceh Merdeka, Free Aceh Movement), the data in the 2000 population census for Aceh suffered from a significant undercounting. The western coast of this province was the most severely hit area. The census takers only managed to record less than half of the population. In 2005, Aceh was also missing from the comparative data across provinces under the Intercensal Population Survey (SUPAS), as Aceh had its own survey after the powerful earthquake-triggered deadly tsunami on 26 December 2004. This province had an Aceh-Nias population survey (SPAN) in 2005 to evaluate the rehabilitation process in the tsunami's aftermath. The Aceh-Nias survey was also regarded as a comprehensive survey for Aceh.

The people of Aceh started a new, peaceful, life after the signing of the Helsinki Peace Agreement on 15 August 2005, ending an approximately three-decade conflict. The 2010 population census was thus conducted in a much more peaceful environment.

As shown in Table 3.1, the Initial Classification differentiates local ethnic and migrant ethnic groups. The table shows that migrant ethnic groups[3] in the province of Aceh include the Javanese, Batak, Minangkabau,

Table 3.1
Ethnic Composition by the Two Classifications: Province of Aceh, 2010

	New Classification*			Initial Classification**		
Rank	Ethnic Group	Number	Per cent	Ethnic Group	Number	Per cent
1	Acehnese	3,160,728	70.65	Ethnic groups from Aceh	3,819,955	85.38
2	Javanese	399,976	8.94	Javanese	400,023	8.94
3	Gayo	322,996	7.22	Batak	147,295	3.29
4	Batak	147,295	3.29	Minangkabau	33,112	0.74
5	Alas	95,152	2.13	Malay	22,198	0.50
6	Simeulue	66,495	1.49	Sundanese	10,864	0.24
7	Aneuk Jamee	62,838	1.40	Chinese	9,620	0.22
8	Tamiang	49,580	1.11	Nias	9,366	0.21
9	Singkil	46,600	1.04	Ethnic groups from Papua	4,418	0.10
10	Minangkabau	33,112	0.74	Banjarese	2,734	0.06
	Others	89,172	1.99	Others	14,359	0.32
	Total	4,473,944	100.00	Total	4,473,944	100.00

Sources:* Authors' calculation.
** Badan Pusat Statistik (2011a).

Malay, Sundanese, Chinese, Nias and Banjarese, as well as those coming from as far as Papua under "All ethnic groups from Papua".

The Initial Classification shows that a group of local ethnic groups, put under "All ethnic groups originating in the province of Aceh", comprise a very large 85.4 per cent of the 4.5 million Indonesian citizens in the province. However, this information hides the diversity of the local ethnic groups in Aceh. This group actually consists of nine different local ethnic groups from the province, including Acehnese, Alas, Aneuk Jamee, Kluet,[4] Sigulai, Simeulue, Singkil, Tamiang and Gayo. Acehnese has different names such as Achin, Akhir, Asji, A-Tse and Ureung Aceh.

The disaggregation of the "Ethnic groups from the province of Aceh" has revealed that Acehnese are the predominant ethnic group in the province, accounting for 70.7 per cent, or a population of about 3.2 million in 2010.

In the undercounted data in 2000, the Acehnese also formed the majority but its percentage was significantly smaller, 50.3 per cent (BPS 2001a). The 2000 census only recorded less than a million Acehnese (872,000 only) and there was no record at all for the regency of Pidie, the stronghold of GAM and the Acehnese hometown.

With the New Classification, we can also see that Gayo, another ethnic group mainly living in the highlands of the central part of the province (Figure 3.1), is number 3 on the list, replacing the Batak (originating from outside the province of Aceh). Similarly, we observe other local ethnic groups appearing in the ten largest ethnic groups: Alas (number 5), Simuelue (number 6), Aneuk Jamee (number 7), Tamiang (number 8) and Singkil (number 9). The Aneuk Jamee are the descendants of Minangkabau migrants who have settled in the province (Schröter 2010). Some of the local ethnic groups have names that are similar to the names of districts, as seen in Figure 3.1. Furthermore, Schröter (2010) explains that Gayo and Alas are actually of Karo Batak origin from the neighbouring province of North Sumatra, but came to settle in the Barisan Mountains. Thus, they mostly live in the more sparsely populated mountain areas. Alas mainly live in the Alas river valley in the regency of Southeast Aceh (Aceh Tenggara). Aceh Tamiang is in the border between the provinces of Aceh and North Sumatra.

The New Classification uncovers that there are only three out of the ten largest ethnic groups that did not originate from the province of Aceh. They are the Javanese who are ranked the second largest ethnic group in the province. The Javanese was the most influential ethnic group from the island of Java. Their presence can be traced back to colonial times when they were needed to work on the damar pine estates in the Gayo hills. Between the 1960s and 1980s, they came to Aceh through the transmigration programme in the east coast areas and settled in central Aceh (Schröter 2010). The rank of the Javanese remained the same as in the 2000 census.

The Batak is the fourth largest ethnic group under the New Classification, down from the third under the Initial Classification. The Minangkabau was the tenth largest ethnic group, below the placing of fourth under the Initial Classification. The Batak and Minangkabau are two large ethnic groups originating in the same island of Sumatra, where Aceh is located.

Province of East Nusa Tenggara

Unlike in the province of Aceh, whose land is part of the larger island of Sumatra surrounded by only a few small islands in Western Indonesia, the province of East Nusa Tenggara is an archipelagic province consisting of about 500 islands in Eastern Indonesia. As seen in Figure 3.2, West

Figure 3.1
Geographical Population Density by Districts: Aceh, 2010

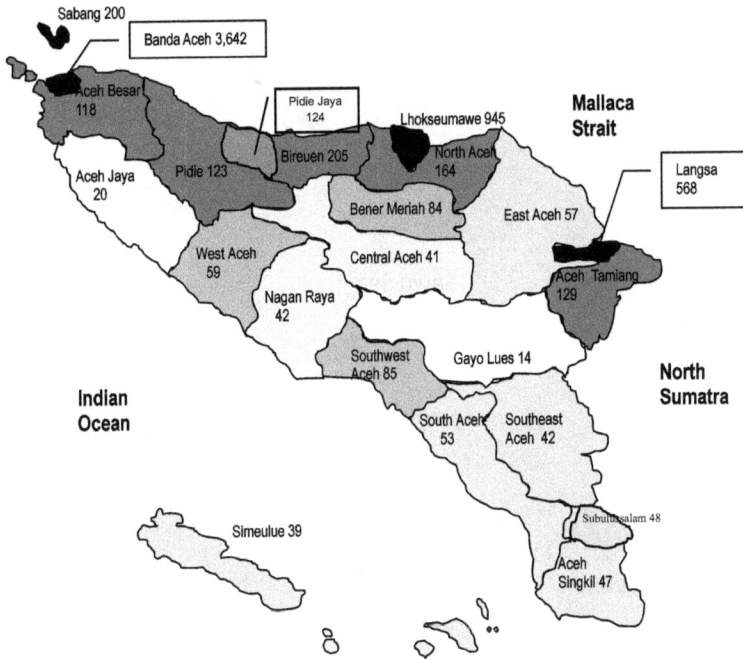

Sabang 200

Banda Aceh 3,642

Aceh Besar 118

Pidie Jaya 124

Lhokseumawe 945

Mallaca Strait

Pidie 123

Bireuen 205

North Aceh 164

Aceh Jaya 20

Langsa 568

Bener Meriah 84

East Aceh 57

West Aceh 59

Central Aceh 41

Aceh Tamiang 129

Nagan Raya 42

Southwest Aceh 85

Gayo Lues 14

North Sumatra

Indian Ocean

South Aceh 53

Southeast Aceh 42

Simeulue 39

Subulussalam 48

Aceh Singkil 47

Note: Numbers in brackets refer to number of population per km².
Source: Authors' cartography.

Timor in the province of East Nusa Tenggara has a land border with the Democratic Republic of Timor-Leste. Timor-Leste also has a landlocked area surrounded by West Timor. In 2010, about 5.3 per cent of the Indonesians in the province had origins from Timor-Leste. Going by many socio-economic indicators, the province of East Nusa Tenggara is relatively disadvantaged. It is considered a poor province with a high percentage of people in poverty.

To uncover the diversity of ethnic groups in East Nusa Tenggara, we have disaggregated two categories from the Initial Classification: "Ethnic groups from the province of East Nusa Tenggara" and "Other ethnic groups from the island of Kalimantan". The category of "Ethnic groups from the province of East Nusa Tenggara" consists of different

Figure 3.2
Map of East Nusa Tenggara

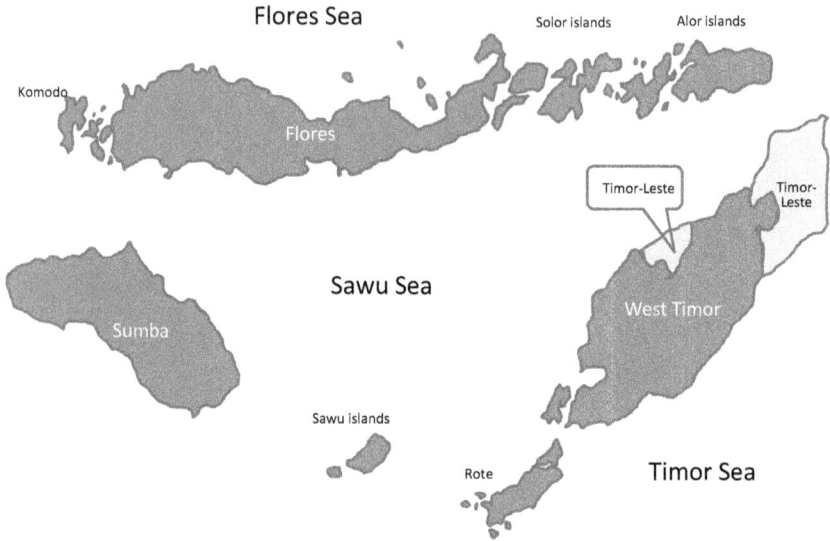

Source: Authors' cartography.

local ethnic groups from the province. This category forms 81.18 per cent of 4.7 million Indonesian citizens in the province, masking the richness of local ethnic diversity.

All remaining categories were very small, with each under 1 per cent, except the Javanese (1.17 per cent). This means that the Initial Classification has not presented the ethnic composition in this archipelagic province very accurately.

With the New Classification, we discovered that the Atoni, a local ethnic group, was in fact the largest one, contributing almost one fifth of the total population of the province. Unlike in the province of Aceh, where the Acehnese are the dominant people, there is no such dominant local ethnic group in the province of East Nusa Tenggara. See Table 3.2.

Atoni's share was not much larger than the second largest one, the ethnic Manggarai with 15.5 per cent. Sumba, with 13.8 per cent, ranked as the third largest group. The remaining seven ethnic groups ranged from 3.7 per cent to 6.1 per cent. All of the ten largest ethnic groups in

Table 3.2

Ethnic Composition by the Two Classifications: Province of East Nusa Tenggara, 2010

Rank	New Classification* Ethnic Group	Number	Per cent	Initial Classification** Ethnic Group	Number	Per cent
1	Atoni	927,753	19.85	Ethnic groups from East Nusa Tenggara	3,793,242	81.18
2	Manggarai	727,404	15.57	Other ethnic groups from the island of Kalimantan	678,090	14.51
3	Sumba	643,045	13.76	Javanese	54,511	1.17
4	Solor	284,105	6.08	Other ethnic groups from the island of Sulawesi	41,527	0.89
5	Ngada	274,870	5.88	Buginese	22,481	0.48
6	Timor-Leste origins	246,867	5.28	Other ethnic groups from the province of West Nusa Tenggara	18,798	0.40
7	Rote	232,104	4.97	Ethnic groups from Papua	14,218	0.30
8	Lio	183,479	3.93	Ethnic groups from Maluku	11,633	0.25
9	Alor	182,270	3.90	Chinese	8,039	0.17
10	Sawu	172,916	3.70	Balinese	6,567	0.14
11	Others	797,835	17.07	Others	23,542	0.50
	Total	4,672,648	100.00	Total	4,672,648	100.00

Sources: * Authors' calculation based on tabulations provided by the BPS.
** Badan Pusat Statistik (2011a).

East Nusa Tenggara are local ethnic groups. The only ethnic group from "outside" was one with origins from Timor-Leste. The nine largest local ethnic groups account for a very significant percentage of 87.7 per cent.

The second largest category in the Initial Classification was "Other ethnic groups from the island of Kalimantan", with a relatively large percentage, 14.51 per cent. However, we found that there was no ethnic group from the island of Kalimantan contributing to the ten largest ethnic groups in East Nusa Tenggara. That is because, as discussed in Chapter 2, there were many ethnic and sub-ethnic groups originating in East Nusa Tenggara which were misplaced under the category of "Other ethnic groups from the island of Kalimantan" in the Initial Classification.

The percentage of "Others" is relatively large, 17.1 per cent. Amongst these, we found the Javanese, Buginese, Chinese and Balinese migrant ethnic groups. Altogether, these four migrant ethnic groups comprised 2 per cent. Thus, the remaining others accounted for 15.1 per cent, or 706,000, indicating the existence of still many ethnic groups in the province. Some of them may be small local ethnic groups while others may be migrant ethnic groups.

The migrants may have come from ethnic groups that are large at the national level but are found in small numbers in East Nusa Tenggara. East Nusa Tenggara is the only province where the Javanese contribute less than 2 per cent and are not part of the ten largest ethnic groups. Yet, amongst the migrant ethnic groups, the Javanese are still considered the largest group in this province. On the other hand, as described in Ananta and Arifin (2008), East Nusa Tenggara is known as a source of labour, with people migrating to other provinces in Indonesia and overseas.

Province of West Sulawesi

West Sulawesi is the newest province created prior to 2010, in 2004 to be exact, as a separation from the province of South Sulawesi. An understanding of the reason behind this administrative separation is important, especially for a trend analysis of demographic parameters and other statistics across time. West Sulawesi consisted of five regencies in the 2010 population census, listed as Mamuju, North Mamuju, Majene, Mamasa and Polewali Mandar, as seen in Figure 3.3. In contrast, it consisted of only Polewali Mamasa, Mamuju and Majene in the 2000 population census, when they were still parts of the province of South Sulawesi. In 2002, when still under the province of South Sulawesi, the regency of Polewali

Figure 3.3
Geographical Population Density by District: West Sulawesi Province, 2010

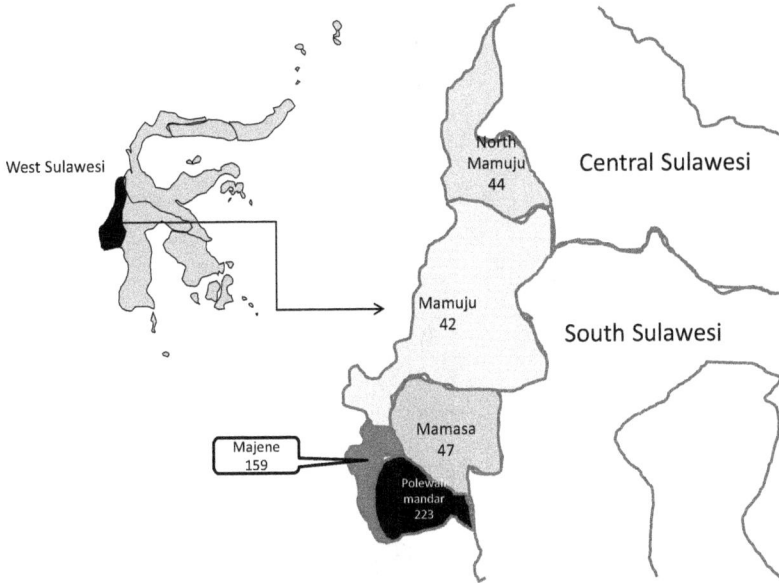

Note: Numbers refer to number of population per km².
Source: Authors' cartography.

Mamasa was split into two districts: Polewali Mamasa and Mamasa. In 2003, the regency of Mamuju became the regencies of Mamuju and North Mamuju. In 2006, after the province had been established, the regency of Polewali Mamasa was renamed Polewali Mandar.

The province of West Sulawesi in 2000 was inhabited by less than one million people, or about 864,000 as estimated from the three districts. The population increased to 1.16 million in 2010, or an increase of 3 per cent annually in the period of 2000–2010. Under the Initial Classification presented in Table 3.3, the largest category in West Sulawesi was "Other ethnic groups from Sulawesi", forming more than three quarters of the province's population. However, there are many important ethnic groups inside this category.

By disaggregating "Other ethnic groups from Sulawesi", we discovered that Mandar was the largest ethnic group in West Sulawesi. The split of the regency of Mamasa from the regency of Polewali Mandar may

Table 3.3
Ethnic Composition by the Two Classifications: Province of West Sulawesi, 2010

Rank	New Classification*	Number	Per cent	Initial Classification**	Number	Per cent
1	Mandar	525,762	45.42	Other ethnic groups from Sulawesi	896,597	77.46
2	Buginese	144,554	12.49	Buginese	144,533	12.49
3	Mamasa	126,299	10.91	Javanese	56,960	4.92
4	Mamuju	93,958	8.12	Makassarese	25,367	2.19
5	Javanese	56,955	4.92	Balinese	14,657	1.27
6	Kaili	50,724	4.38	Sasak	6,111	0.53
7	Pattae	30,260	2.61	Ethnic groups from NTT	5,106	0.44
8	Makassarese	25,367	2.19	Sundanese	1,800	0.16
9	Toraja	22,728	1.96	Other ethnic groups from Kalimantan	1,367	0.12
10	Galumpang	18,005	1.56	Chinese	660	0.06
	Others	62,953	5.44	Others	4,407	0.35
	Total	1,157,565	100.00	Total	1,157,565	100.00

Sources:* Authors' calculation based on tabulations provided by the BPS.
** Badan Pusat Statistik (2011a).

indicate that the people of Mamasa wanted to have their own identity, being Mamasa, rather than being Mandar. Therefore, the ethnic group of Mandar currently only includes those originally from the regencies of Majene and Polewali Mandar.

The 2010 census recorded these three ethnic groups separately, each with their own separate code. "Mamasa" (code 0809) was the third largest ethnic group and "Mamuju" (code 0810), the fourth. The split of the regency of Mamasa from the regency of Polewali Mandar and the rising identity of Mamuju may partly explain the decline of the percentage of the "Mandar" (code 0513), from 49.7 per cent in 2000 (BPS 2001) to 45.4 per cent in 2010.

Another local ethnic group is Pattae, the seventh largest ethnic group in the province. The Pattae used to live in the forests in West Sulawesi, but some have been settled in the regency of Majene. Galumpang, the tenth largest, is also a local ethnic group, originally from the regencies of Mamuju and North Mamuju. The people of Galumpang are also known as Kalumpang.

The five other largest ethnic groups are migrant groups. Only one, the Javanese, is from off the island of Sulawesi. The Buginese originated from the province of South Sulawesi; the Kaili from the province of Central Sulawesi; and the Makassarese and Toraja from the province of South Sulawesi.

With regard to the category of "Others", the province of West Sulawesi is also different from the province of Aceh, because the percentage of "Others" in West Sulawesi still comprises a relatively large percentage, 5.4 per cent, of the population. "Others" in Aceh was only 1.99 per cent. Therefore, the province of West Sulawesi may have more very small ethnic groups than the province of Aceh. In other words, the province of West Sulawesi is more multi-ethnic than the other two provinces discussed here.

Notes

1. http://www.beritabali.com/index.php/page/berita/bll/detail/09/08/2011/petNyama-Selampet-di-Pegayaman-Buleleng/201107020294. 'Nyama Selam' di Pegayaman Buleleng.
2. Readers may refer to Riwut (2007) for a description of sub-ethnic groups and sub-sub-ethnic groups of Dayak.
3. See Chapter 4 for a discussion on the concept of migrant ethnic groups versus local ethnic groups.
4. Kluet is an ethnic group generated through marriage between the descendants from Nias Island with the indigenous people of the province (Schröter 2010).

4

ETHNIC DIVERSITY:
New Demographic Evidence

This chapter uncovers new demographic evidence of ethnic diversity in Indonesia. As listed in Chapter 3, the 2010 population census recorded a very large number of ethnic categories and we reclassified them into a New Classification of ethnic groups. With this classification, this chapter presents and discusses the ethnic composition in Indonesia as a whole and within each province. First, it examines the ethnic composition at the national level by limiting itself to the fifteen largest ethnic groups in Indonesia. These fifteen ethnic groups already formed a very large portion of the total citizens in Indonesia, accounting for 84.9 per cent in 2010.

Second, it analyses the ethnic diversity in each of the 33 provinces. This discussion at the provincial level better shows Indonesia's ethnic diversity. It details various degrees of heterogeneity amongst provinces. It then provides an expanded list of ethnic groups to capture a more comprehensive view of Indonesia's ethnic spread as a whole, by combining all large ethnic groups within the provinces. Finally, this chapter reveals the degree of "ubiquity" of the ethnic groups amongst the various provinces in Indonesia.

Amongst other things, this chapter also discusses local ethnic groups versus migrant ethnic groups in each province to provide a glimpse into migration phenomena. Local ethnic groups are defined as the people who originate in a province although nowadays they may live in many other provinces in Indonesia or overseas. On the other hand, migrant ethnic groups are defined as those who did not identify themselves as one of the local ethnic groups in the provinces where they live. They may just have arrived in Province A some years earlier, they may not have been born in this province, but it is also possible that they were born in Province A and have been in Province A for many generations. As long as they identify themselves with an ethnic group originating from outside Province A, these respondents are called migrant ethnic groups.

Furthermore, although the number and percentage of foreigners are still small, the presence of foreigners is likely to increase and hence play an important role in future interaction with the people of Indonesia (Ananta and Arifin 2014). Therefore, this chapter discusses the demography of the foreigners before elaborating on the ethnic composition in each province. This is the first detailed demographic study on foreigners in Indonesia, another first for this book. To provide the context in understanding regional ethnic diversity in Indonesia, this chapter begins with a snapshot of Indonesia's demography in 2010. It describes the size of population in each province and its provincial distribution.

SIZE AND DISTRIBUTION OF INDONESIA'S POPULATION IN 2010

Based on the 2010 population census, Indonesia's population numbered 237.6 million, an increase from 205.8 million in 2000. Today (in 2014) Indonesia's population has passed the 250-million mark, with males outnumbering females (119.6 million versus 118.0 million, respectively). This is different from all censuses conducted prior to 2000, where females always outnumbered males. At the regional level, Indonesia has the largest population in Southeast Asia, followed by the Philippines, Vietnam and Thailand. This order will remain the same in the next few decades.

Ever since Indonesia gained its independence in 1945, the problem of development imbalances amongst regions has existed, especially between western and eastern parts of Indonesia or between the island of Java and the outer islands. The island of Java, with only seven per cent of

Indonesia's land area, is the most populous island, with more advanced infrastructure, manufacturing industries and services. This island had a population of 137.0 million in 2010, equal to twice the population of Thailand combined with Singapore in the same year. However, over a long period of time, the predominance of this island in terms of its contribution to Indonesia's total population has been slowly declining, from 63.8 per cent in 1971 to 57.5 per cent in 2010. By 2030, this island will contribute to 55.2 per cent of Indonesia's population (Bappenas, BPS and UNFPA 2013).

One of the reasons for the declining share was the effect of the transmigration programme in moving the population away from Java. Another reason was that the government strongly supported a family planning programme, which was first implemented on this island in 1970. As a result, provinces on the island of Java had lower fertility rates than elsewhere in Indonesia.

At the provincial level, the share of West Java increased steadily from 17.4 per cent in 2000 to 18.1 per cent in 2010, as did that of Banten from 3.9 per cent to 4.5 per cent in the respective years. As seen in Table 4.1, the province of West Java had the largest population with 43.1 million. It is followed by the provinces of East Java and Central Java. They are starkly in contrast with the province of West Papua with 0.7 million population only. The population in West Papua faced more challenging issues than those living on the island of Java, because of West Papua's geographical conditions in tandem with a less developed infrastructure. This unequal distribution of the population amongst provinces necessitates a different strategy in development planning. As elaborated later in this chapter, the degree of ethnic heterogeneity amongst these provinces varies from one province to another.

Table 4.1 not only provides the total population throughout the various provinces, but also presents the population with regard to their citizenship status, categorizing them into Indonesian citizens and foreign citizens as well as "not asked". The "not asked" category is the recorded population who were enumerated by the C2 and L2 types of questionnaires that did not ask the corresponding question.[1] They were more likely to be Indonesians rather than foreigners. However, as there is no way to find out the ethnic groups of those "not asked", the analysis for ethnicity in this book relies mostly on the answers from the citizens presented in the third column of Table 4.1.

Table 4.1
Population by Citizenship Status: Indonesia and Provinces, 2010

Code	Province	Citizenship				Distribution		
		Citizens	Foreigners	Not Asked	Total	Citizens	Foreigners	Total
11	Aceh	4,473,944	342	20,124	4,494,410	1.89	0.47	1.89
12	North Sumatra	12,930,319	772	51,113	12,982,204	5.46	1.05	5.46
13	Sumatera Barat	4,832,145	214	14,550	4,846,909	2.04	0.29	2.04
14	West Sumatra	5,507,842	521	30,004	5,538,367	2.33	0.71	2.33
15	Jambi	3,069,771	208	22,286	3,092,265	1.30	0.28	1.30
16	South Sumatra	7,434,042	1,163	15,189	7,450,394	3.14	1.59	3.14
17	Bengkulu	1,710,677	230	4,611	1,715,518	0.72	0.31	0.72
18	Lampung	7,581,948	356	26,101	7,608,405	3.20	0.49	3.20
19	Bangka Belitung	1,219,398	81	3,817	1,223,296	0.52	0.11	0.51
21	Riau Archipelago	1,671,891	3,486	3,786	1,679,163	0.71	4.76	0.71
32	Jakarta	9,547,541	27,882	32,364	9,607,787	4.03	38.08	4.04
32	West Java	42,982,078	11,410	60,244	43,053,732	18.16	15.58	18.12
33	Central Java	32,295,172	2,636	84,849	32,382,657	13.64	3.60	13.63
34	Yogyakarta	3,451,006	2,152	4,333	3,457,491	1.46	2.94	1.45
35	East Java	37,205,052	6,600	265,105	37,476,757	15.72	9.01	15.77
36	Banten	10,601,515	3,392	27,259	10,632,166	4.48	4.63	4.47
51	Bali	3,880,721	4,523	5,513	3,890,757	1.64	6.18	1.64
52	West Nusa Tenggara	4,489,281	462	10,469	4,500,212	1.90	0.63	1.89
53	East Nusa Tenggara	4,672,648	1,137	10,042	4,683,827	1.97	1.55	1.97
61	West Kalimantan	4,385,356	348	10,279	4,395,983	1.85	0.48	1.85
62	Central Kalimantan	2,207,367	483	4,239	2,212,089	0.93	0.66	0.93
63	South Kalimantan	3,613,992	219	12,405	3,626,616	1.53	0.30	1.53
64	East Kalimantan	3,536,503	1,062	15,578	3,553,143	1.49	1.45	1.50
71	North Sulawesi	2,263,463	514	6,619	2,270,596	0.96	0.70	0.96
72	Central Sulawesi	2,623,679	271	11,059	2,635,009	1.11	0.37	1.11
73	South Sulawesi	8,020,418	1,051	13,307	8,034,776	3.39	1.44	3.38
74	Southeast Sulawesi	2,227,937	146	4,503	2,232,586	0.94	0.20	0.94
75	Gorontalo	1,039,430	66	668	1,040,164	0.44	0.09	0.44
76	West Sulawesi	1,157,565	29	1,057	1,158,651	0.49	0.04	0.49
81	Maluku	1,526,710	195	6,601	1,533,506	0.64	0.27	0.65
82	North Maluku	1,035,425	35	2,627	1,038,087	0.44	0.05	0.44
91	West Papua	753,399	300	6,723	760,422	0.32	0.41	0.32
94	Papua	2,780,144	931	52,306	2,833,381	1.17	1.27	1.19
	Indonesia	236,728,379	73,217	839,730	237,641,326	100.00	100.00	100.00

Notes: As mentioned in Chapter 2, there were four types of questionnaires used to record the population living in Indonesia. As seen above, there were 839,730 people who were not asked about their citizenship. They were more likely to be Indonesians than foreigners.
Source: Calculated by the authors, based on tabulations provided by the BPS.

FOREIGNERS: RISING PRESENCE

The Need to Study the Demography of Foreigners

The large and ever rising size of the population has helped Indonesia to realize an emerging economic powerhouse status in the world. Its population has increased from 205.1 million at the turn of this century to 237.6 million in 2010. It is projected to reach 255.5 million in 2015 and will be 296.4 million in 2030 (Bappenas, BPS and UNFPA 2013). Indonesia is projected to be the seventh largest economy in the world by 2030 after China, the United States, India, Japan, Brazil and Russia, overtaking Germany and the United Kingdom (Oberman et al. 2012). Measured by GDP, Indonesia's economy has remained robust by growing 5–6 per cent on average since 2009. A large domestic consumption is one of the key drivers of the continuously strong GDP growth. Indeed, the reliance on domestic consumption is one of the reasons why Indonesia successfully steered through the 2008/09 financial crisis.

The trend towards a global economic powerhouse has brought the world's attention to Indonesia. World business interest to have trade with and invest in Indonesia will continue to rise. At the same time, the influx of foreigners working in Indonesia is more likely to increase as well (Ananta and Arifin 2014). Therefore, the rising presence of foreigners will have important economic, social and political effects, including on housing and labour markets in Indonesia.

As the foreigners are mostly from different ethnic groups and cultural backgrounds, understanding the demography of the foreigners can complement the richness of the demographic analysis of Indonesia's ethnicity. Furthermore, the need to study the foreigners is especially important since Indonesia is currently undergoing its third demographic transition, a transformation towards a rapid change in ethnic composition at the sub-national level.

Although the question on ethnicity was only asked to Indonesian citizens, the census recorded foreigners who had stayed or intended to stay in Indonesia for six months or more. They may be working or studying, they may be accompanying their spouses or parents or they may be living out their retirement in Indonesia. These foreigners may include the Chinese who were born in Indonesia and have been in Indonesia for many generations but who do not have Indonesian citizenship. On the other hand, the census did not record foreigners living temporarily. Thus, tourists and foreigners working on short contracts are not included. We neither know whether the recorded foreigners are mainly *orang bule*, the term used by Indonesians referring to those with fair skin such as Europeans or North Americans, or *orang asing* (foreign people) such as Malaysians, Bruneians, Singaporeans and Japanese.

Number of Foreigners

The number of resident foreigners recorded in the census was very small, only amounting to 73,217 and contributing 0.03 per cent to the total population of Indonesia in 2010. The 2010 census reveals an unexpected trend, as there were fewer foreigners living in Indonesia, just less than half of the number of foreigners in 2000 census (149,761 persons).[2]

However, it is possible that more foreigners were staying in Indonesia for a shorter duration, less than six months, and therefore were not recorded in the census. As shown by the data from the Minister of Manpower, the number of foreigners coming to work in Indonesia has risen tremendously from 24,319 in 2001 to 102,288 in 2010. It is not clear how many of them have stayed in Indonesia for more than six months. This pattern, staying for a shorter duration, may be in line with the tendency of Indonesians to be moving with a shorter duration but a higher frequency, as elaborated in Ananta and Arifin (2014).

It should be noted that the data from the Ministry of Manpower focuses on those who were working in Indonesia. This data set did not include those who stayed in Indonesia to study, to join their family, to visit as tourists or to spend their retirement in Indonesia. The data set records the number of foreign arrivals for work in Indonesia. These statistics therefore do not reveal the cumulative number of foreigners who have been working in Indonesia.

More data should be collected on foreigners and deeper studies should be conducted to examine whether other kinds of foreigners (who do not work) also stay in Indonesia for a shorter duration, less than six months.

Geographical Distribution of Foreigners

Table 4.1 shows that 73.4 per cent of foreigners were living on the island of Java with the province of Jakarta hosting the largest number of foreigners, contributing 38.08 per cent to total foreigners in Indonesia. This factor relates to the existence of facilities and branches of multinational companies, as well as embassies. West Java and East Java are two other host provinces for foreigners. About ten per cent lived on the island of Sumatra with the province of the Riau Archipelago as the most preferred province. This may be because of the existence of the Special Economic Zone in the Riau Archipelago. In the eastern part of Indonesia, Bali is the most popular province for foreigners. Yet, as seen in Table 4.1, foreigners were actually spreading across all provinces. It will be worth observing future patterns of foreigner distribution when Indonesia becomes more open to the globalization process.

Age-Sex Structure of Foreigners

To know better about the foreign residents who live in the country for more than six months, we need to examine the age-sex structure of the population of foreigners in Indonesia in 2010.

Figure 4.1 shows an unusual shape for the age-sex structure of the population of foreigners as compared to Figure 4.4 for Indonesians overall. As seeking jobs is one important reason for people migrating to other places, Figure 4.1 indicates that a high percentage (more than 10 per cent) of foreigners was seen in each of the age groups of 35–39 and 40–44. The third highest was at ages 45–49. Altogether, 29.44 per cent of the foreigners came from the mature prime-working-age population. This was larger than the corresponding percentage for Indonesians (20.65 per cent).

Amongst the foreigners of these mature ages, the sex ratios were very high. The highest was 2.27 for ages 45–49, meaning that there were at least two male foreigners aged 45–49 for every one female counterpart. The lowest was 1.73, although this is still considered high, at ages 35–39. This may mean that these male mature foreigners were in Indonesia without their spouses. They may also be single or their spouses chose not to join them in Indonesia.

However, as seen in Table 4.2, the high sex ratios were not only seen amongst the mature prime-working-age population, but also amongst all age groups except those older than 80 years old. The highest sex ratio was found amongst older persons aged 60–64. With a sex ratio at 2.85, there were almost three male foreign older persons aged 60–64 for every one female of that age group. On the other hand, there was an excess of females amongst foreign older persons aged 80 years and over.

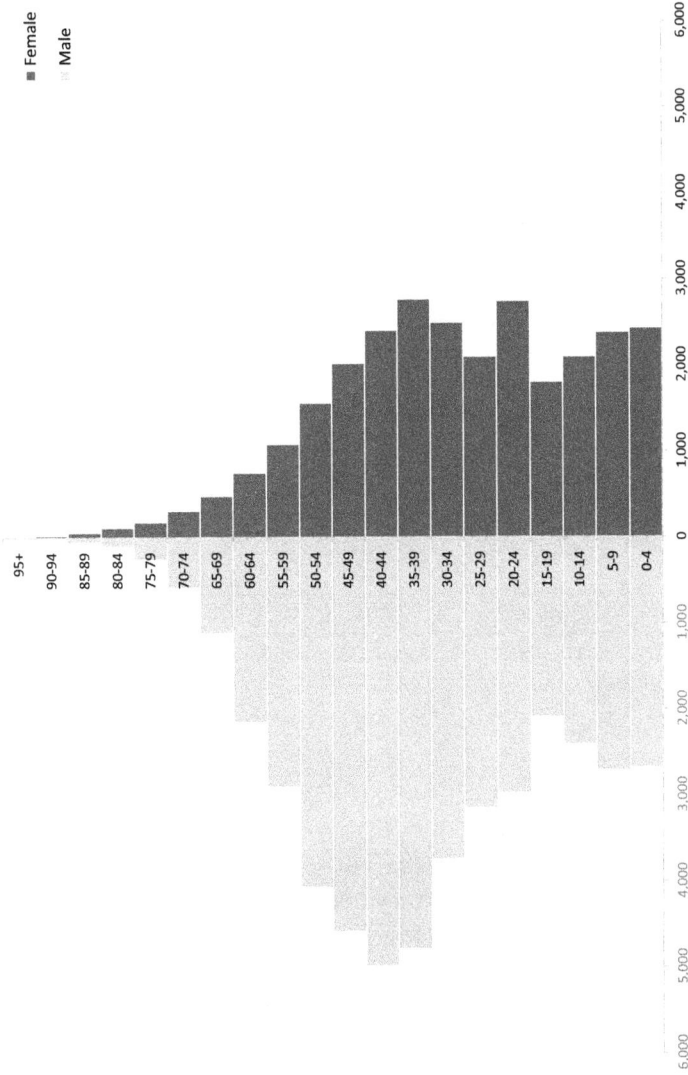

Figure 4.1
Age-Sex Structure of Foreigners: Indonesia, 2010

Source: Drawn from Table 4.1.

Table 4.2
Number and Percentage of Foreigners by Age and Sex: Indonesia, 2010

Age Group	Males	Females	Total	Per cent	Sex Ratio
0–4	2,678	2,432	5,110	6.98	1.101
5–9	2,708	2,387	5,095	6.96	1.134
10–14	2,411	2,103	4,514	6.17	1.146
15–19	2,091	1,803	3,894	5.32	1.160
20–24	2,978	2,747	5,725	7.82	1.084
25–29	3,151	2,104	5,255	7.18	1.498
30–34	3,744	2,497	6,241	8.52	1.499
35–39	4,784	2,769	7,553	10.32	1.728
40–44	4,983	2,409	7,392	10.10	2.068
45–49	4,583	2,018	6,601	9.02	2.271
50–54	4,064	1,564	5,628	7.69	2.598
55–59	2,903	1,084	3,987	5.45	2.678
60–64	2,144	752	2,896	3.96	2.851
65–69	1,111	486	1,597	2.18	2.286
70–74	580	311	891	1.22	1.865
75–79	254	182	436	0.60	1.396
80–84	107	118	225	0.31	0.907
85–89	53	62	115	0.16	0.855
90–94	19	26	45	0.06	0.731
95+	7	10	17	0.02	0.700
Total	45,353	27,864	73,217	100.00	1.628

Source: Calculated by the authors, based on tabulations provided by the BPS.

The foreign population was relatively old, with 8.51 per cent of them aged 60 years and over, higher than 7.6 per cent for the Indonesian population. These older persons may have come on their own, especially those under 70 years old or they may have come to Indonesia joining their children or grandchildren. It is also possible that some of them chose to spend their retirement in Indonesia with its pleasant weather and cheaper living costs.

It is also possible that some foreigners brought their children with them. About one fifth of the foreigners were below 15 years old. This is smaller than the percentage amongst the Indonesians. The Indonesians aged below 15 accounted for almost 29 per cent in 2010.

INDONESIA: ORDER OF ETHNIC GROUPS

Ranking of Ethnic Groups and Their Home Provinces

Table 4.3 (under "New Classification") and Figure 4.2 show the ranking of the fifteen largest ethnic groups in Indonesia. Figure 4.3 supplements both the tables and figures with information on the home provinces of each ethnic group, along with the code of each province.

As expected, Javanese were the largest ethnic group, forming 40.06 per cent of total Indonesian citizens living in Indonesia in 2010. As seen in Figure 4.3, the Javanese homeland covers the three adjacent provinces of Central Java (code 33), Yogyakarta (code 34) and East Java (code 35).

The Sundanese made up a much smaller percentage, 15.51 per cent, as the second largest group, with West Java (32) as their home province bordering Central Java, Jakarta and Banten. This was followed by the Malay with a still much smaller percentage, 3.70 per cent. The Malay home provinces were on the island of Sumatra, particularly the provinces of the Riau Archipelago (21), Riau (14) and Jambi (15).

The Malay were then followed by five ethnic groups (Batak, Madurese, Betawi, Minangkabau and Buginese) with a smaller variation in percentages, ranging between 3.70 per cent and 2.70 per cent. The home province of the Batak is North Sumatra (code 12), bordering Riau and West Sumatra in the south and Aceh in the north. The Madurese originated from the island of Madura, in the province of East Java (code 35), a home province of the Javanese. The home province of the Betawi is Jakarta (code 31), bordering Banten in the west and West Java in the south and east. The home province of the Minangkabau is West Sumatra (code 13); and the home province of the Buginese is South Sulawesi (code 73).

Geographically, the seven largest ethnic groups, not including the Buginese, were located on the islands of Java and Sumatra in Western Indonesia. Altogether, these groups already formed 71.49 per cent of Indonesia's total population of citizens.

The contribution of each of the remaining seven ethnic groups was between 1.20 per cent and 2 per cent. The Bantenese originating in the province of Banten (code 36), the Banjarese from South Kalimantan (code 63), the Balinese from Bali (code 51), the Acehnese from Aceh (code 11), the Dayak from the island of Kalimantan (codes 61, 62, 63 and 64) and

Table 4.3
Composition of Ethnic Groups in Indonesia: New and Initial Classifications, 2010

Ethnic group	New Classification*				Initial Classification**		
	Rank	Number	Percentage of total population	Percentage of all Indonesians	Rank	Number	Percentage of all Indonesians
Javanese	1	94,843,073	40.05	40.06	1	95,217,022	40.22
Sundanese	2	36,704,944	15.50	15.51	2	36,701,670	15.50
Malay	3	8,753,791	3.70	3.70	9	5,365,399	2.27
Batak	4	8,466,969	3.58	3.58	3	8,466,969	3.58
Madurese	5	7,179,356	3.03	3.03	5	7,179,356	3.03
Betawi	6	6,807,968	2.87	2.88	6	6,807,968	2.88
Minangkabau	7	6,462,713	2.73	2.73	7	6,462,713	2.73
Buginese	8	6,415,103	2.71	2.71	8	6,359,700	2.69
Bantenese	9	4,642,389	1.96	1.96		na	na
Banjarese	10	4,127,124	1.74	1.74	13	4,127,124	1.74
Balinese	11	3,924,908	1.66	1.66	15	3,946,416	1.67
Acehnese	12	3,404,109	1.44	1.44		na	na
Dayak	13	3,219,626	1.36	1.36	17	3,009,494	1.27
Sasak	14	3,175,006	1.34	1.34	16	3,173,127	1.34
Chinese	15	2,832,510	1.20	1.20	18	2,832,510	1.20
Others from Sulawesi Island		—	—	—	4	7,634,262	3.22
Ethnic groups from South Sumatera Province		—	—	—	10	5,119,581	2.16
Ethnic groups from Banten Province		—	—	—	11	4,657,784	1.97

Ethnic group						
Ethnic groups from East Nusa Tenggara Province			—	12	4,184,923	1.77
Ethnic groups from Aceh Province			—	14	4,091,451	1.73
Ethnic groups from Papua Province			—	19	2,693,630	1.14
Makassarese			—	20	2,672,590	1.13
Others from Sumatra Island			—	21	2,204,472	0.93
Ethnic groups from Maluku			—	22	2,203,415	0.93
Others from Kalimantan Island			—	23	1,968,620	0.83
Cirebonese			—	24	1,877,514	0.79
Ethnic groups from Jambi Province			—	25	1,415,547	0.60
Ethnic groups from Lampung Province			—	26	1,381,660	0.58
Others from West Nusa Tenggara Province			—	27	1,280,094	0.54
Gorontalo			—	28	1,251,494	0.53
Minahasa			—	29	1,237,177	0.52
Nias			—	30	1,041,925	0.44
Other foreign Indonesians			—	31	162,772	0.07
Other Indonesians	35,768,790	15.10	15.11		—	—
All Indonesians	236,728,379	99.97	100.00		236,728,379	100.00
Foreigners	73,217	0.03			73,217	
Total	236,801,596	100.00	100.00		236,801,596	

Source: * Authors' calculation, based on tabulations provided by the BPS.
**Badan Pusat Statistik 2011a.

Figure 4.2
Ethnic Composition: Indonesia, 2010

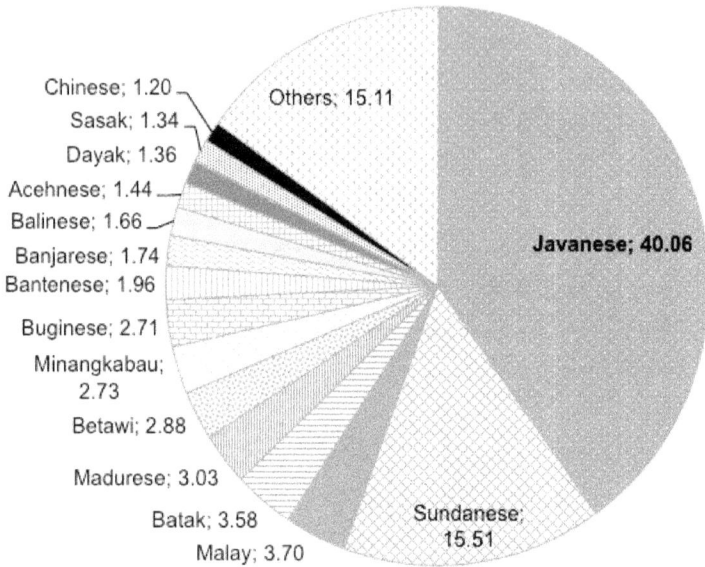

Chinese; 1.20
Sasak; 1.34
Dayak; 1.36
Acehnese; 1.44
Balinese; 1.66
Banjarese; 1.74
Bantenese; 1.96
Buginese; 2.71
Minangkabau; 2.73
Betawi; 2.88
Madurese; 3.03
Batak; 3.58
Malay; 3.70
Others; 15.11
Javanese; 40.06
Sundanese; 15.51

Source: Drawn from Table 4.3.

the Sasak from the island of Lombok, West Nusa Tenggara (code 52). The last group is the ethnic Chinese with foreign origins.

Figure 4.4 is the 2010 population pyramid, showing the age-sex structure of the 2010 population. Overall, this figure indicates a continuous change in the age structure of Indonesia's population. The percentage of young population, below 15 years old, in 2010 was 28.6 per cent, a decline from 30.4 per cent in 2000. Meanwhile, the percentage of older persons, aged 60 and above, is becoming more significant, accounting for 7.6 per cent in 2010, an increase from 7.2 per cent in 2000. At the same time, the proportion of the working-age population, aged 15–59, is increasing, gaining a favourable momentum for the economy.

In particular, Figure 4.4 shows the relative importance of ethnic groups in Indonesia. It focuses on just the five largest ethnic groups: the Javanese, Sundanese, Malay, Batak and Madurese, as the figure would have been too complicated if it had covered all of the fifteen ethnic groups.

Figure 4.3
Home Provinces of the Fifteen Largest Ethnic Groups: Indonesia, 2010

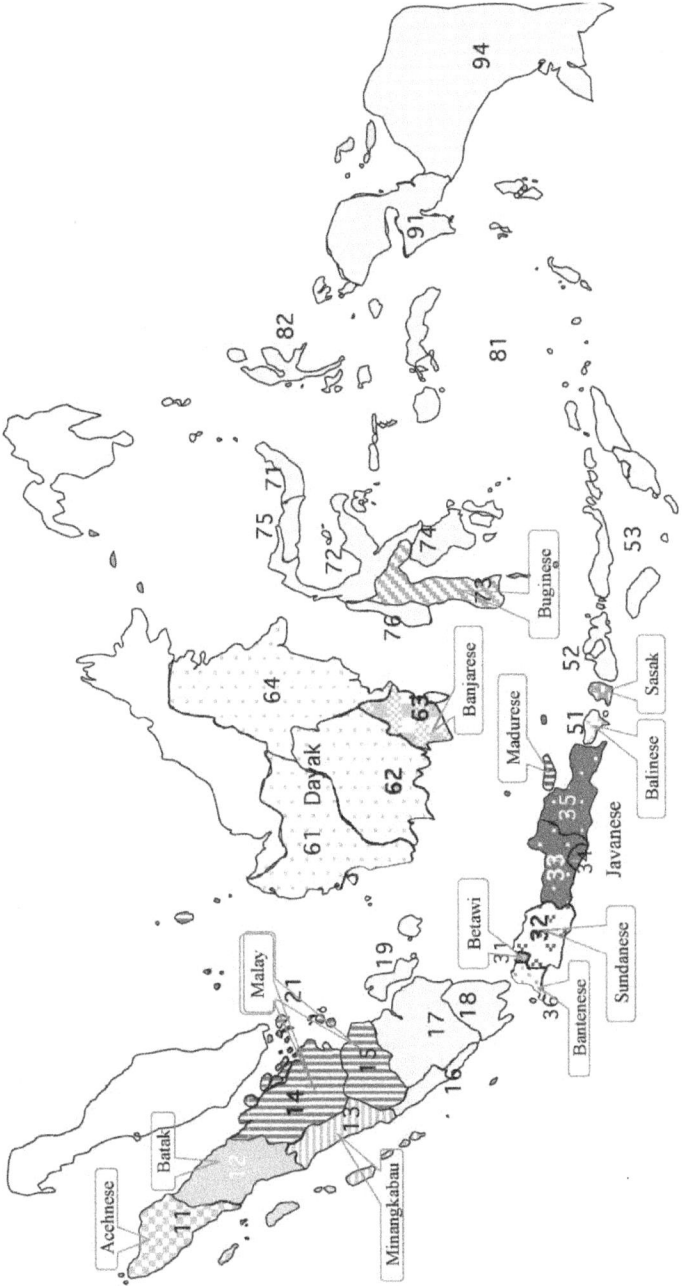

Notes: The labels for the above numbers refer to Figure 2.1.

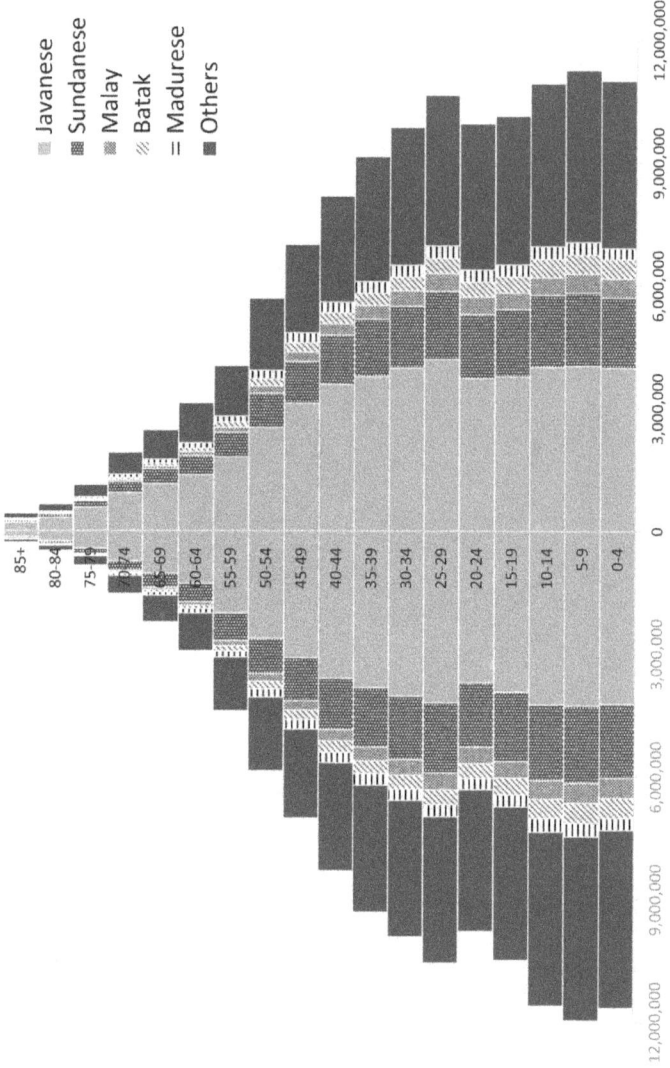

Figure 4.4
Age-Sex Structure of Population by Ethnic Group: Indonesia, 2010

Source: Drawn by the authors.

Figure 4.4 shows that not only were the Javanese the largest ethnic group but they were also the most dominant one. Their presence was dominant in each age group of the population. Shown by the solid, lightest colour in the middle of Figure 4.4, the contribution of Javanese to Indonesia's population is much larger than those contributed by each of the four other largest ethnic groups: the Sundanese, Malay, Batak and Madurese. The dominance of the Javanese would be even clearer if it were compared with the remaining ethnic groups, though this is not shown in this figure.

Although not as dominant as the Javanese, the Sundanese, shown by the patterned area on the left and right of the Javanese, was also relatively significant in each age group. The large solid darkest colour in the extreme right and left of the Figure 4.4 refers to "Others", representing all remaining ethnic groups made up of more than 600 groups. This figure clearly shows that, with the exception of the Javanese and Sundanese, all other ethnic groups accounted for much smaller percentages in each age group of the population.

The third demographic transition, a process of changing ethnic composition, can be seen from the composition of ethnic groups by age. Table 4.4 reveals the contrast in ethnic composition between the younger and older persons. The Javanese are proportionately more prevalent amongst the older persons, constituting about half of the number of all older persons. In contrast, amongst the toddlers, the Javanese only made up about one third. On the other hand, the "Others" (outside the five largest ethnic groups — the Javanese, Sundanese, Malay, Batak and Madurese) are predominant amongst the toddlers, aged 0–4; their number is larger than that of the Javanese toddlers.

Therefore, the future population of Indonesia will be characterized with a declining percentage of Javanese younger persons and a rising percentage of Javanese older persons. A similar pattern is found amongst the Madurese, which will also have a declining percentage of younger persons and a rising percentage of older persons. On the other hand, as also seen amongst the "Others", the Malay and Batak will be observed more amongst the younger persons than amongst the older persons. The contribution of the Sundanese will not change significantly amongst all ethnic groups. The percentage of Sundanese amongst older persons will also become smaller, but the change is insignificant.

Table 4.4
Simple Ethnic Composition by Broad Age Group: Indonesia, 2010

Age Groups	Javanese	Sundanese	Malay	Batak	Madurese	Others	Total
Number (in millions)							
0–4	8.22	3.52	0.95	0.96	0.58	8.44	22.66
5–14	16.58	7.26	1.83	1.88	1.30	16.93	45.78
15–24	15.16	6.46	1.64	1.53	1.16	14.41	40.36
25–59	46.44	16.78	3.88	3.64	3.45	35.79	109.97
60+	8.45	2.68	0.47	0.46	0.69	5.28	18.03
Total	94.84	36.70	8.75	8.47	7.18	80.85	236.80
Distribution (percentage)							
0–4	36.29	15.52	4.18	4.24	2.54	37.23	100.00
5–14	36.21	15.87	3.99	4.11	2.84	36.98	100.00
15–24	37.55	16.01	4.06	3.79	2.88	35.71	100.00
25–59	42.22	15.26	3.52	3.31	3.14	32.55	100.00
60+	46.88	14.87	2.59	2.54	3.85	29.27	100.00
Total	40.05	15.50	3.70	3.58	3.03	34.14	100.00

Source: Calculated from Tables 5.1, 5.3, 5.5, 5.7 and 5.9.

Comparison between the New and Initial Classifications of Ethnic Groups

Table 4.3 presents our findings on the number and percentage of ethnic groups under the New Classification in comparison with the Initial Classification. The New Classification has resulted in significant changes on the absolute and relative numbers of population in many ethnic groups as well as in their ranking. This section compares the results and shows some of the richness from the use of the New Classification.

From the fifteen largest ethnic groups, there are six groups (Javanese, Sundanese, Madurese, Betawi, Minangkabau and Buginese) with the same ranks in both classifications. There are two other ethnic groups (Malay and Dayak) which have major changes in their classifications. (Another ethnic group which moved up in ranking was the Dayak, mentioned earlier.) Two groups (Bantenese and Acehnese) are "new faces", appearing on the list of the fifteen largest groups based on the New Classification, but not listed in the Initial Classification. Sasak and Chinese are two other "new faces" that moved up to be part of the fifteen largest groups in the New Classification. They are listed in the Initial Classification but are not included in the fifteen largest categories. There are two groups (Balinese and Banjarese) in the fifteen largest ethnic groups which have moved up in ranking on the list. Finally, the Batak was the only ethnic group that moved down in ranking in the New Classification, from the third to the fourth.

Keeping their Positions: Javanese, Sundanese, Madurese, Betawi, Minangkabau and Buginese

These six ethnic groups (Javanese, Sundanese, Madurese, Betawi, Minangkabau and Buginese) do not see any significant changes in percentages and ranking. They keep their positions. The Madurese, Betawi and Minangkabau have similar classifications. Furthermore, the additions and deletions of ethnic categories within the Javanese, Sundanese or Buginese do not result in significant changes in their population. For example, the percentage of Javanese declined only 0.17 of a percentage point. This difference, about 374,000 individuals, was because of the exclusion of Bawean/Boyan, Osing/Using and Naga and the inclusion of Nagarigung.

There is no significant change for the Sundanese in the relative number, but there is a small increase in the absolute number of 3,274 individuals because of the inclusion of the sub-ethnic of Naga. In the Initial Classification, Naga was under Javanese. However, Naga is actually a Sundanese group living in Tasikmalaya in West Java Province. Therefore, the Naga are a sub-ethnic group of the Sundanese and speak Sundanese.

The Buginese have an addition of 0.02 per cent, or 55,403 individuals. This difference is due to the inclusion of five categories in the New Classification. One is Ugi as an alias of Buginese. Four others are sub-ethnic groups of Buginese and their aliases: Bugis Pagatan or Pagatan (two different codes), Amatoa or Ammatowa or Orang Kajang (one code) and Tolotang in the New Classification.

Significant Changes in Classification: Malay and Dayak

The groupings of Malay (originating on the island of Sumatra) and Dayak (originating on the island of Kalimantan) in the New Classification are very different from those in the Initial Classification. Table 4.3 demonstrates that there is a great difference in population sizes and percentages between these two groups in both classifications. The possible explanation is that the New Classification has discovered many more ethnic groups under the Malay and Dayak groups.

As a result, the percentage of Malay has changed significantly from 2.27 per cent in the Initial Classification to 3.70 per cent in the New Classification. The Malay numbered 8.75 million, instead of 5.37 million. In other words, there is an addition of 3.39 million to the Malay population brought about by the inclusion of several categories in the New Classification.

Meanwhile, the percentage of Dayak changed from 1.27 per cent under the Initial Classification to 1.36 per cent under the New Classification. The absolute number only changed from 3.01 million to 3.22 million after the reclassification, although there were many additional new sub-ethnic groups. This means that the new sub-ethnic groups belonging to the Dayak were mostly small groups, with the change of only 0.21 million people.

However, although small, this addition has moved the Dayak rank up to thirteenth place, while it appears in seventeenth place in the Initial Classification. The Initial Classification for Dayak only covers those names that start with the term Dayak (consisting of 264 categories). Yet, as discussed in Chapter 2, we discovered that many sub-ethnic groups of Dayak were not recorded using the term Dayak itself. Thus, the size of the overall Dayak population mentioned in this book is the first comprehensive number of the Dayak in the history of Indonesia.

New Faces: Bantenese and Acehnese

The New Classification also brings in the Bantenese and Acehnese as new faces included in the fifteen largest ethnic groups. The Initial Classification does not include these two groups as they are included under "Ethnic groups from the province of Aceh" and "Ethnic groups from the province of Banten". The Acehnese and Bantenese were the majority in the respective groups. As seen in Table 4.3, the Acehnese numbered 3.4 million out of a population of 4.1 million under the former "Ethnic groups from the province of Aceh". There were 4.6 million Bantenese out of 4.7 million population under the former "Ethnic groups from the province of Banten".

The Acehnese were originally from the province of Aceh located at the northern tip of Sumatra island. The Acehnese formed 83.2 per cent of the population under "Ethnic groups from the province of Aceh". The remaining 16.8 per cent consisted of many ethnic groups originating in the province of Aceh living all over Indonesia.

A similar case is seen for the Bantenese, who formed almost all (99.67 per cent) of the population under "Ethnic groups from the province of Banten" in the Initial Classification. The remaining 0.33 per cent, or 15,395 persons, were the Badui/Baduy, a very small local ethnic group from the province of Banten.

The province of Banten is located at the western tip of the island of Java. It is famous for its "debus" martial art as well as traditional demonstrations of strength. After the regional autonomy law was enacted in 1999, the province of Banten was created from the province of West Java, the home province of the Sundanese. Bantenese ethnic identity strengthened and they wanted to distinguish themselves from the Sundanese, yet they were categorized as Sundanese in the 1930 census (Suryadinata, Arifin and Ananta 2003).

Entering the Fifteen Largest Ethnic Groups: Sasak and Chinese

Unlike the Bantenese and Acehnese, the Sasak and Chinese were found in the Initial Classification but were not among the fifteen largest ethnic groups. Because of the disaggregation of five categories such as "All ethnic groups..." and "Other ethnic groups from...", the Sasak moved up from number 16 in the Initial Classification to number 14 in the New Classification and the Chinese moved from number 18 to number 15.

The Sasak accounted for 1.34 per cent, or 3.18 million. There was an additional 1,879 population in the New Classification, as compared to the Initial Classification. This difference is due to the inclusion of Bayan, originating at the foot of Mount Rinjani, as a sub-ethnic group of Sasak in the New Classification.

On the other hand, there is no different category for Chinese between the two classifications. The Chinese accounted for 1.20 per cent, or 2.83 million.

It should be noted that the Dayak, discussed earlier, can also be mentioned in this category, as they moved up to be included in the fifteen largest ethnic groups.

Moving Up within the Fifteen Largest Groups:
Banjarese and Balinese

The Banjarese did not change in number as there was no change in their classification, but their relative position moved from the thirteenth to the tenth. This change in ranking occured because we broke up groups of "Others from the island of Sulawesi", which was the fourth category in the Initial Classification, "Ethnic groups from the province of South Sumatra", the tenth, "Ethnic groups from the province of Banten", the eleventh and "Ethnic groups from the province of East Nusa Tenggara", the twelfth.

Likewise, the Balinese moved from fifteenth to eleventh place, although the number declined because of the disaggregation of Baliaga/Trunyan from the Initial Classification. The difference reflects the number of Baliaga (21,508 people). The Baliaga culture has its distinct character which is promoted as an attraction in tourism. Their belief is different from the Balinese. They lived in remote areas of Mount Agung.

Declining in Ranking: Batak

The Batak are the only ethnic group amongst the fifteen largest ethnic groups who moved down in ranking because of the New Classification. The change in the Malay classification has replaced the Batak position from its initial third position, now ranking fourth in the New Classification. In turn, the Batak, in fourth position, replaced "Other ethnic groups from the island of Sulawesi", which was in fourth position in the Initial Classification.

ETHNIC GROUPS IN THE PROVINCES: BETWEEN HOMOGENEITY AND HETEROGENEITY

The Expanded List of Ethnic Groups

Tables 4.5 up to 4.37 present another original idea in this book, detailing ethnic composition in each of the thirty-three provinces in Indonesia in 2010 using the New Classification. Because of the numerous ethnic groups in Indonesia, the discussion in this section is limited to the ten largest ethnic groups in each province. Although they were "the ten largest" in a province, some of them were actually "small" due to the presence of dominant ethnic groups. On the other hand, in some provinces the ten largest ethnic groups altogether can be relatively small, leaving a large proportion of "Others" at 20 per cent or more. Therefore, we have expanded the list of ethnic groups in five provinces: Central Sulawesi, Maluku, North Maluku, Papua and West Papua — all in Eastern Indonesia. The expansion is to reduce the proportion of "Others" to approximate 20 per cent, so as to accommodate the many ethnic groups in the respective five provinces, reflecting different degrees of multi-ethnicity amongst provinces. Then, we have the fifteen largest groups each for Central Sulawesi, North Maluku and Maluku; we include the largest twenty-five ethnic groups for West Papua and Papua.

The series of tables reveals that each province is different with regard to its ethnic composition. Some provinces show an ethnically homogenous population and some others indicate the opposite, an ethnically heterogeneous population. Others are somewhere between the two.

Tables 4.5 to 4.37 are not ordered based on geographical locations but on the percentage of the first largest ethnic group in a province so as to show the degree of ethnic homogeneity in the province. The higher the percentage of the largest ethnic group, the more homogeneous the province. We have six groups based on the percentage of the largest ethnic group: homogeneous provinces, with above 95 per cent, almost homogeneous provinces, between 80 and 94.99 per cent, less homogeneous provinces, between 60 and 79.99 per cent, less heterogeneous provinces, between 40 and 59.9 per cent, almost heterogeneous provinces, between 20 and 39.99 per cent and heterogeneous provinces, below 20 per cent.

Homogeneous Provinces

The group consists of two provinces with the largest ethnic groups contributing more than 95 per cent to the total population in the respective provinces, making the provinces ethnically homogeneous. They were Central Java and Yogyakarta, homes of the Javanese. Both were homogeneously Javanese provinces, where the Javanese contributed 97.32 per cent in Central Java and 96.53 per cent in Yogyakarta. The second largest group, the Sundanese, were very much below the Javanese, contributing only 1.40 per cent in Central Java and 0.69 per cent in Yogyakarta.

Because the Javanese are the only local ethnic group in both provinces, the other nine ethnic groups are migrant ethnic groups. The migrant ethnic groups in Central Java (Table 4.5) mostly originated from the islands of Java and Sumatra, but those in Yogyakarta (Table 4.6) also originated from the islands of Kalimantan (for the Dayak), Bali (for the Balinese) and Sulawesi (for the Buginese). Moreover, the contribution of each of the seven smallest ethnic groups was higher in Yogyakarta than in Central Java. Unlike in Central Java, no ethnic group in Yogyakarta contributed less than 0.10 per cent. The existence of the University of Gadjah Mada, a first tier university, and many other educational institutions in Yogyakarta may have resulted

Table 4.5
Ethnic Composition by Sex: Central Java, 2010

Rank	Ethnic Group	Males	Females	Total	Per cent	Sex Ratio
1	Javanese	15,665,118	15,895,252	31,560,370	97.72	0.986
2	Sundanese	226,262	225,128	451,390	1.40	1.005
3	Chinese	67,932	71,946	139,878	0.43	0.944
4	Batak	13,178	11,179	24,357	0.08	1.179
5	Arab	7,088	7,350	14,438	0.04	0.964
6	Madurese	7,263	5,657	12,920	0.04	1.284
7	Lampung	5,345	6,310	11,655	0.04	0.847
8	Malay	5,424	5,213	10,637	0.03	1.040
9	Betawi	4,899	4,620	9,519	0.03	1.060
10	Minangkabau	4,776	3,819	8,595	0.03	1.251
11	Others	27,369	24,044	51,413	0.16	1.138
	Total	16,034,654	16,260,518	32,295,172	100.00	0.986

Source: Calculated by the authors, based on tabulations provided by the BPS.

Table 4.6
Ethnic Composition by Sex: Yogyakarta, 2010

Rank	Ethnic Group	Males	Females	Total	Per cent	Sex Ratio
1	Javanese	1,638,007	1,693,296	3,331,303	96.53	0.967
2	Sundanese	13,020	10,749	23,769	0.69	1.211
3	Malay	9,463	7,322	16,785	0.49	1.292
4	Chinese	5,716	5,829	11,545	0.33	0.981
5	Batak	5,799	4,059	9,858	0.29	1.429
6	Madurese	2,986	2,303	5,289	0.15	1.297
7	Minangkabau	2,927	2,225	5,152	0.15	1.316
8	Dayak	2,520	2,097	4,617	0.13	1.202
9	Balinese	1,898	1,555	3,453	0.10	1.221
10	Buginese	1,927	1,434	3,361	0.10	1.344
11	Others	20,317	15,557	35,874	1.04	1.306
	Total	1,704,580	1,746,426	3,451,006	100.00	0.976

Source: Calculated by the authors, based on tabulations provided by the BPS.

in a relatively larger contribution from and more variation in the origins of the migrant ethnic groups.

Although homogeneously Javanese, Central Java was also characterized by its third largest, though small, ethnic group — the Chinese, one group of Indonesian citizens with foreign origins. Standing at 0.43 per cent or about

140,000 people, the long-term presence of the Chinese in this province can be illustrated by its famous Chinese heritage landmarks such as the Sam Po Kong and Tay Kak Sie temples, located in the capital city of Semarang. The Tay Kak Sie temple is located in the Chinatown area as a Confucian landmark. These temples have become landmarks of Semarang, together with the Pagoda Avalokitesvara.

In the province of Central Java we can also find another ethnic group with foreign origin, the Arabs, although this group only contributed 14,400 people, or 0.04 per cent of the population in Central Java. However, because of the very large dominance of the Javanese, the Arabs were the fifth largest ethnic group in the province, after the Batak.

Yogyakarta is also special because of the presence of a Javanese Sultan, who is formally recognized by the Government of Indonesia as the Governor of the province of Yogyakarta. The province is called Special Region of Yogyakarta (Daerah Istimewa Yogyakarta).

Almost Homogeneous Provinces

This second group consists of three provinces (Gorontalo, West Sumatra and Bali), each with a significantly dominant largest ethnic group, contributing between 80 and 94.99 per cent.

Gorontalo is a province created at the end of 2000, a split from the province of North Sulawesi. The province of Gorontalo is located in Sulawesi's northern arm, lying horizontally from west to east on the map. To the north is the Sulawesi Sea and to the east is the Gulf of Tomini, with several islands on both sides belonging to the province. Gorontalo, a local ethnic group, made up the predominant group accounting for 89.05 per cent of the population, with the existence of many other ethnic groups. The Suwawa and Atinggola were two other local ethnic groups from this province. However, the Suwawa or Bune contributed a small percentage of only 1.37 per cent, as the third largest ethnic group. Atinggola accounted for an even smaller percentage, 0.36 per cent, as the ninth largest ethnic group.

We also found that the Minahasa, Sangir and Mongondow were amongst the ten largest ethnic groups in this province. These three ethnic groups originated from the neighbouring province of North Sulawesi.

The remaining seven groups were migrant ethnic groups. The Javanese migrant ethnic group made up the second largest group with 3.39 per cent, or 35.2 thousand. The Balinese came last on the list (shown in Table 4.7) and the other migrant ethnic groups were mostly from the neighbouring provinces on the same island of Sulawesi.

West Sumatra is the home province of the Minangkabau, accounting for a predominant group (87.33 per cent) in its home. The Minangkabau are famous for their *merantau* tradition, a rite of passage where the young men must leave their homelands and return home only after they have become successful in their life outside their homelands. The word *merantau* was coined by Naim (1984). The *merantau* is now used to describe other ethnic groups with such a trait. The word *perantau* is used to describe the people who go out to *merantau*. This tradition can account for considerable numbers of Minangkabau found outside their traditional homeland.

The Batak as the second largest ethnic group in this province are a much smaller community. The Batak are a migrant ethnic group originating in the neighbouring province of North Sumatra. The third group were the Javanese, another migrant ethnic group. As presented in Table 4.8, the fourth group in this province was a local ethnic group, the Mentawai, at only 1.37 per cent. The Mentawai originate from the islands of Mentawai, a group of islands lying on the western coast of the province of West Sumatra.

Thus, the Minangkabau in this province live with many ethnic groups, especially the two migrant ethnic groups of Batak and Javanese, each

Table 4.7
Ethnic Composition by Sex: Gorontalo, 2010

Rank	Ethnic Group	Males	Females	Total	Per cent	Sex Ratio
1	Gorontalo	461,980	463,653	925,633	89.05	0.996
2	Javanese	18,599	16,679	35,278	3.39	1.115
3	Suwawa	7,289	6,968	14,257	1.37	1.046
4	Minahasa	4,637	4,607	9,244	0.89	1.007
5	Buginese	5,078	3,757	8,835	0.85	1.352
6	Sangir	4,155	3,869	8,024	0.77	1.074
7	Bajao	2,195	2,356	4,551	0.44	0.932
8	Mongondow	1,996	2,330	4,326	0.42	0.857
9	Atinggola	1,927	1,853	3,780	0.36	1.040
10	Balinese	1,918	1,774	3,692	0.36	1.081
11	Others	11,492	10,318	21,810	2.10	1.114
	Total	521,266	518,164	1,039,430	100.00	1.006

Source: Calculated by the authors, based on tabulations provided by the BPS.

Table 4.8
Ethnic Composition by Sex: West Sumatra, 2010

Rank	Ethnic Group	Males	Females	Total	Per cent	Sex Ratio
1	Minangkabau	2,078,142	2,141,587	4,219,729	87.33	0.970
2	Batak	111,140	111,409	222,549	4.61	0.998
3	Javanese	115,654	101,430	217,084	4.49	1.140
4	Mentawai	34,032	32,189	66,221	1.37	1.057
5	Malay	21,527	20,901	42,428	0.88	1.030
6	Nias	9,909	8,330	18,239	0.38	1.190
7	Sundanese	8,865	7,075	15,940	0.33	1.253
8	Chinese	5,340	5,459	10,799	0.22	0.978
9	Kerinci	1,530	1,265	2,795	0.06	1.209
10	Lampung	1,520	1,197	2,717	0.06	1.270
11	Others	7,505	6,139	13,644	0.28	1.223
	Total	2,395,164	2,436,981	4,832,145	100.00	0.983

Source: Calculated by the authors, based on tabulations provided by the BPS.

significantly contributing to the ethnic landscape in the province with 4.61 per cent and 4.49 per cent, respectively. The Malay, Batak and Javanese are culturally distinct. The proportion of "Others" was tiny, with 0.28 per cent or 13,600 people. This tiny portion indicates that the ethnic composition in West Sumatra can be explained by the ten largest ethnic groups only.

The province of Bali, the island itself encompassing the whole province together with some smaller islands, is well known globally for its tourist attractions. This province is different in many ways from other provinces. The Balinese form of Hinduism is recognized as an essential part of Balinese culture. The community is well organized under *banjar*, which is not the name of an ethnic group but a self-governing community that takes care of and looks after the community. The Balinese are also great farmers with their *subak* system. They have their own naming system for their children by providing four names representing their birth order. Today the Balinese form 85.50 per cent of 3.88 million people in the province. Although they have a unique culture, many other ethnic groups exist on the *Pulau Dewata*, a famous alias for the island of Bali. The Javanese, a migrant ethnic group, who are mostly Muslim, ranked second with almost 10 per cent. They may have moved there because they were attracted by economic opportunities in this province.

Each of the eight remaining ethnic groups contributed less than 1 per cent, indicating the presence of many ethnic groups with very small contributions to the total population in the province (Table 4.9). One of these was a local ethnic group, the Bali Aga. The people of Bali Aga (almost 20,000 people) claim that they were the original Balinese. Although small, each group of the Madurese, Malay and Sasak in Bali is larger than the population in each of a few districts in the province of Papua. For instance, the regency of Supiori had an even smaller number, only about 15,800. The regency of Tambrauw in the province of West Papua was inhabited by 6,000 people only, perhaps the least populous regency in Indonesia. As seen in Table 4.9, the Chinese in Bali were the seventh group, with almost 15,000 people, just slightly smaller than the local ethnic group of the Bali Aga. The Sundanese, Buginese and Flores peoples were the last three of the ten largest ethnic groups in Bali.

Less-Homogeneous Provinces

There were six provinces in this group, each with the largest ethnic group contributing between 60 to 79.9 per cent. These were East Java, South Kalimantan, West Java, Aceh, West Nusa Tenggara and Lampung, presented in Tables 4.10–4.15, respectively.

Table 4.9
Ethnic Composition by Sex: Bali, 2010

Rank	Ethnic Group	Males	Females	Total	Per cent	Sex Ratio
1	Balinese	1,655,358	1,662,707	3,318,065	85.50	0.996
2	Javanese	197,576	174,474	372,050	9.59	1.132
3	Madurese	15,853	14,011	29,864	0.77	1.131
4	Malay	11,706	11,415	23,121	0.60	1.025
5	Sasak	12,533	10,139	22,672	0.58	1.236
6	Bali Aga	10,139	9,860	19,999	0.52	1.028
7	Chinese	7,668	7,302	14,970	0.39	1.050
8	Sundanese	6,508	5,202	11,710	0.30	1.251
9	Buginese	4,806	4,486	9,292	0.24	1.071
10	Flores	3,972	2,859	6,831	0.18	1.389
11	Others	28,232	23,915	52,147	1.34	1.181
	Total	1,954,351	1,926,370	3,880,721	100.00	1.015

Source: Calculated by the authors, based on tabulations provided by the BPS.

East Java is located to the west of the province of Bali, separated by the Bali Strait. It is another home province for the Javanese. However, unlike Central Java and Yogyakarta, East Java is a less homogenous province. The Javanese only constituted 79.72 per cent of the population of East Java. The Madurese ranked second with 17.53 per cent, or 6.5 million. The third and fifth largest ethnic groups were two other local ethnic groups: the Osing or Using and the Bawean. Similar to Central Java, the Chinese and Arabs were amongst the ten largest ethnic groups in East Java (Table 4.10). Each of these groups had a larger population than that in Central Java. In the capital city of Surabaya, a Chinese landmark is seen from the existence of the Cheng Ho mosque, built in 2001–2 by the PITI (Indonesian Association of Chinese Muslims). In the city of Malang, the second largest city in East Java, we can find the Eng An Kiong Buddhist temple and Ma Chung University.

To the north of the province of East Java crossing the Java Sea is the province of South Kalimantan, the home of the Banjarese. The Banjarese only constituted 74.34 per cent (2.69 million) of the South Kalimantan population. The Banjarese shared this province with another local ethnic group, the Dayak, who were the fourth largest ethnic group. Other local ethnic groups, such as the Kutai, Saqi and Telaga were not amongst the

Table 4.10
Ethnic Composition by Sex: East Java, 2010

Rank	Ethnic Group	Males	Females	Total	Per cent	Sex Ratio
1	Javanese	14,669,780	14,990,795	29,660,575	79.72	0.979
2	Madurese	3,171,662	3,348,741	6,520,403	17.53	0.947
3	Osing/Using	139,991	145,257	285,248	0.77	0.964
4	Chinese	118,947	125,446	244,393	0.66	0.948
5	Bawean	33,746	38,011	71,757	0.19	0.888
6	Batak	28,302	28,037	56,339	0.15	1.009
7	Sundanese	25,753	21,900	47,653	0.13	1.176
8	Lampung	14,234	14,250	28,484	0.08	0.999
9	Arab	13,782	14,657	28,439	0.08	0.940
10	Bajao	12,903	13,719	26,622	0.07	0.941
11	Others	122,180	112,959	235,139	0.63	1.082
	Total	18,351,280	18,853,772	37,205,052	100.00	0.973

Source: Calculated by the authors, based on tabulations provided by the BPS.

ten largest ethnic groups in South Kalimantan. The Banjarese and Dayak shared the province with eight migrant ethnic groups. The Javanese were the second largest ethnic group, contributing 14.51 per cent and numbering 6.5 times the number of Dayak. The presence of the large number of Javanese is perhaps because of a long relationship between the people on the island of Java, particularly with the Javanese, and South Kalimantan. The remaining ethnic groups were relatively small (Table 4.11). The third largest, the Buginese, contributed only 2.81 per cent, much lower than the contribution of the second largest ethnic group.

West Java is the most populous province in Indonesia, a home for 30.9 million Sundanese or 71.87 per cent of the population of the province. In addition to the Sundanese, the largest ethnic group in West Java, there was only one local ethnic group, the Cirebonese, the fourth largest ethnic group in this province (Table 4.12). The Javanese were the second largest ethnic group in this province, as a migrant ethnic group originating from the neighbouring provinces in the east — Central Java, Yogyakarta and East Java. The Javanese numbered 5.71 million, larger than the Javanese presence in Lampung. The number of Betawi, the third largest ethnic group in the province, was almost the same number as those living in their home province of Jakarta. Betawi is a migrant ethnic group from the neighbouring

Table 4.11
Ethnic Composition by Sex: South Kalimantan, 2010

Rank	Ethnic Group	Males	Females	Total	Per cent	Sex Ratio
1	Banjarese	1,332,563	1,354,064	2,686,627	74.34	0.984
2	Javanese	283,883	240,393	524,276	14.51	1.181
3	Buginese	53,338	48,389	101,727	2.81	1.102
4	Dayak	39,849	40,859	80,708	2.23	0.975
5	Madurese	27,498	25,504	53,002	1.47	1.078
6	Mandar	20,254	19,587	39,841	1.10	1.034
7	Sundanese	13,462	11,130	24,592	0.68	1.210
8	Chinese	6,688	6,312	13,000	0.36	1.060
9	Batak	7,063	5,345	12,408	0.34	1.321
10	Balinese	6,300	5,666	11,966	0.33	1.112
11	Others	36,807	29,038	65,845	1.82	1.268
	Total	1,827,705	1,786,287	3,613,992	100.00	1.023

Source: Calculated by the authors, based on tabulations provided by the BPS.

Table 4.12
Ethnic Composition by Sex: West Java, 2010

Rank	Ethnic Group	Males	Females	Total	Per cent	Sex Ratio
1	Sundanese	15,621,893	15,268,609	30,890,502	71.87	1.023
2	Javanese	2,965,309	2,744,241	5,709,550	13.28	1.081
3	Betawi	1,348,166	1,315,977	2,664,143	6.20	1.024
4	Cirebonese	927,532	885,310	1,812,842	4.22	1.048
5	Batak	244,159	223,279	467,438	1.09	1.094
6	Chinese	127,063	127,857	254,920	0.59	0.994
7	Minangkabau	126,167	115,002	241,169	0.56	1.097
8	Malay	110,349	101,071	211,420	0.49	1.092
9	Lampung	44,515	47,881	92,396	0.21	0.930
10	Palembang	39,261	38,551	77,812	0.18	1.018
11	Others	301,830	258,056	559,886	1.30	1.170
	Total	21,856,244	21,125,834	42,982,078	100.00	1.035

Source: Calculated by the authors, based on tabulations provided by the BPS.

province of Jakarta. Interestingly, the Bantenese in West Java were not one of the ten largest ethnic groups, although there were some Bantenese living in West Java. Except for the Chinese, all other ethnic groups were migrant ethnic groups from the island of Sumatra. The Chinese only accounted for less than one per cent or, to be precise, 0.59 per cent only. Yet, the number of Chinese in West Java was larger than those living in each of the provinces of Central Java, Yogyakarta and East Java.

In the provinces of Aceh and West Nusa Tenggara, the respective local ethnic groups were also very significant. As seen in Table 4.13, the Acehnese in Aceh accounted for 70.65 per cent and, as seen in Table 4.14, the Sasak in the province of West Nusa Tenggara comprised 67.58 per cent. In Aceh, amongst the largest ten ethnic groups, only the Javanese and Minangkabau were migrant ethnic groups, the rest being local ethnic groups.

In West Nusa Tenggara, the four largest ethnic groups were local — the Sasak, Bima, Sumbawa and Mbojo. Two other local ethnic groups were also found amongst the ten largest ethnic groups in the province. They were the Dompu (seventh largest) and the Kore (tenth largest). There were four migrant ethnic groups: the Balinese, Javanese, Buginese and Bajo. The Balinese and Javanese are ethnic groups from the islands of Bali and Java, to the west of West Nusa Tenggara. The Buginese and Bajo originated from South Sulawesi, in the north of West Nusa Tenggara, crossing the Java Sea.

Table 4.13
Ethnic Composition by Sex: Aceh, 2010

Rank	Ethnic Group	Males	Females	Total	Per cent	Sex Ratio
1	Acehnese	1,574,245	1,586,483	3,160,728	70.65	0.992
2	Javanese	202,832	197,144	399,976	8.94	1.029
3	Gayo	161,019	161,977	322,996	7.22	0.994
4	Batak	74,367	72,928	147,295	3.29	1.020
5	Alas	47,460	47,692	95,152	2.13	0.995
6	Simeulue	33,744	32,751	66,495	1.49	1.030
7	Aneuk Jamee	30,425	32,413	62,838	1.40	0.939
8	Tamiang	25,038	24,542	49,580	1.11	1.020
9	Singkil	23,197	23,403	46,600	1.04	0.991
10	Minangkabau	16,962	16,150	33,112	0.74	1.050
11	Others	45,471	43,701	89,172	1.99	1.041
	Total	2,234,760	2,239,184	4,473,944	100.00	0.998

Source: Calculated by the authors, based on tabulations provided by the BPS.

Table 4.14
Ethnic Composition by Sex: West Nusa Tenggara, 2010

Rank	Ethnic Group	Males	Females	Total	Per cent	Sex Ratio
1	Sasak	1,443,226	1,590,436	3,033,662	67.58	0.907
2	Bima	283,079	286,995	570,074	12.70	0.986
3	Sumbawa	194,533	185,781	380,314	8.47	1.047
4	Mbojo	63,886	63,405	127,291	2.84	1.008
5	Balinese	60,236	58,591	118,827	2.65	1.028
6	Javanese	42,037	36,784	78,821	1.76	1.143
7	Dompu	29,361	29,858	59,219	1.32	0.983
8	Buginese	10,051	9,967	20,018	0.45	1.008
9	Bajao	9,082	8,872	17,954	0.40	1.024
10	Kore	6,449	7,245	13,694	0.31	0.890
11	Others	35,407	34,000	69,407	1.55	1.041
	Total	2,177,347	2,311,934	4,489,281	100.00	0.942

Source: Calculated by the authors, based on tabulations provided by the BPS.

The Lampung ethnic group is not the largest ethnic group in its own province, Lampung. The Javanese, with home provinces on the island of Java, were the largest ethnic group in Lampung, contributing 64.06 per cent. This may have been because Lampung was one of the first destination provinces for the transmigration programme in which people were moved away from the crowded islands of Java and Bali to people Indonesia's more "empty" islands. As seen in Table 4.15, the Lampung were only the second largest ethnic group, contributing a relatively small percentage, 13.54 per cent to the province of Lampung. The remaining eight ethnic groups were migrant ethnic groups. Three groups (the Sundanese, Bantenese and Balinese) were from outside Sumatra and five (the Malay, Palembang, Ogan, Minangkabau and Batak) were from Sumatra. By adding Sundanese and Bantenese (originally from the island of Java) to the Javanese, the ethnic groups originating on the island of Java formed more than three quarters of the total population in Lampung.

The plan to connect the two islands of Sumatra and Java by building the Sunda Straits Bridge for which the President of Indonesia signed the presidential decree for its construction in 2011 should be anticipated to have an impact on population mobility. The bridge will shorten the trip of crossing the Sunda Straits by 30 minutes, connecting the provinces of Lampung (in Sumatra) and Banten (in Java). The anticipated rising mobility within Lampung (Sumatra) and Banten (Java) may result in a quick change in the ethnic compositions of Java and Sumatra, especially in Banten and Lampung.

Table 4.15
Ethnic Composition by Sex: Lampung, 2010

Rank	Ethnic Group	Males	Females	Total	Per cent	Sex Ratio
1	Javanese	2,499,577	2,357,228	4,856,805	64.06	1.032
2	Lampung	524,323	502,369	1,026,692	13.54	1.239
3	Sundanese	376,338	352,377	728,715	9.61	1.036
4	Bantenese	90,541	81,830	172,371	2.27	1.045
5	Malay	81,033	79,997	161,030	2.12	1.077
6	Palembang	73,620	70,893	144,513	1.91	1.211
7	Ogan	54,416	52,253	106,669	1.41	1.192
8	Balinese	54,358	50,248	104,606	1.38	1.428
9	Minangkabau	35,932	33,720	69,652	0.92	1.629
10	Batak	28,007	24,304	52,311	0.69	1.176
11	Others	83,029	75,555	158,584	2.09	1.367
	Total	3,901,174	3,680,774	7,581,948	100.00	1.088

Source: Calculated by the authors, based on tabulations provided by the BPS.

Less-Heterogeneous Provinces

These provinces are less heterogeneous because their largest ethnic groups still form between 40 and 59.9 per cent, a relatively large percentage. There were eight provinces in this group: Bangka-Belitung, Central Kalimantan, West Sulawesi, North Sulawesi, South Sulawesi, North Sumatra, Banten and Jambi. Of these, only the province of Bangka-Belitung had the largest percentage of a single ethnic group above 50 per cent. The Bangka ethnic groups accounted for 52.73 per cent and the Belitung ethnic group, 16.14 per cent of the population of the province of Bangka-Belitung.

The Javanese and Chinese represent similar contributions to the population of Bangka-Belitung, with 8.19 per cent for the Javanese and 8.17 per cent for the Chinese. They were the third and fourth largest groups (Table 4.16) and may play important economic roles in the society of Bangka-Belitung.

Another example of a "less heterogeneous" province is the province of Central Kalimantan, with the Dayak as the largest ethnic group contributing 46.62 per cent and the second group (Javanese) and the third (Banjarese) each contributing just above 21 per cent. The fourth (Malay) had a much smaller percentage, forming just 3.96 per cent. As seen in Table 4.17, the migrant ethnic group of Madurese ranked fifth in this province, with

Table 4.16
Ethnic Composition by Sex: Bangka-Belitung, 2010

Rank	Ethnic Group	Males	Females	Total	Per cent	Sex Ratio
1	Bangka	325,089	317,875	642,964	52.73	1.023
2	Belitung	99,500	97,285	196,785	16.14	1.023
3	Javanese	57,501	42,379	99,880	8.19	1.357
4	Chinese	50,897	48,727	99,624	8.17	1.045
5	Palembang	22,165	18,778	40,943	3.36	1.180
6	Buginese	18,101	15,491	33,592	2.75	1.168
7	Malay	11,828	10,092	21,920	1.80	1.172
8	Sundanese	10,449	8,517	18,966	1.56	1.227
9	Madurese	8,302	7,127	15,429	1.27	1.165
10	Batak	5,225	4,227	9,452	0.78	1.236
11	Others	23,174	16,669	39,843	3.27	1.390
	Total	632,231	587,167	1,219,398	100.00	1.077

Source: Calculated by the authors, based on tabulations provided by the BPS.

Table 4.17
Ethnic Composition by Sex: Central Kalimantan, 2010

Rank	Ethnic Group	Males	Females	Total	Per cent	Sex Ratio
1	Dayak	522,618	506,564	1,029,182	46.62	1.032
2	Javanese	264,750	213,643	478,393	21.67	1.239
3	Banjarese	236,248	228,012	464,260	21.03	1.036
4	Malay	44,639	42,709	87,348	3.96	1.045
5	Madurese	22,121	20,547	42,668	1.93	1.077
6	Sundanese	15,651	12,929	28,580	1.29	1.211
7	Buginese	9,301	7,803	17,104	0.77	1.192
8	Batak	7,249	5,075	12,324	0.56	1.428
9	Flores	5,187	3,185	8,372	0.38	1.629
10	Balinese	3,971	3,377	7,348	0.33	1.176
11	Others	18,356	13,432	31,788	1.44	1.367
	Total	1,150,091	1,057,276	2,207,367	100.00	1.088

Source: Calculated by the authors, based on tabulations provided by the BPS.

only 1.9 per cent in 2010, which was much smaller than the 3.46 per cent in 2000 (Suryadinata, Arifin and Ananta 2003). The Sundanese is another migrant ethnic group constituting more than 1 per cent of the population in this province.

In West Sulawesi, the largest local ethnic group, the Mandar, accounted for 45.42 per cent of the population. As seen in Table 4.18, the second largest ethnic group was the Buginese, a migrant ethnic group from South Sulawesi. It can be noted here that the province of South Sulawesi was split into South Sulawesi and West Sulawesi in 2004. See Chapter 3 for a more detailed discussion of West Sulawesi.

In North Sulawesi, as presented in Table 4.19, the largest group was the Minahasa, the dominant local ethnic group, forming 45.16 per cent. The Sangir and Mongondow were two other local ethnic groups, making the second and third largest groups, respectively. The three local ethnic groups, which are the three largest groups, accounted for more than three quarters of the population. Adding the Talaud in fifth place, another local ethnic group, the total share of local ethnic groups increases to more than 80 per cent. The remaining groups were migrant ethnic groups. The Gorontalo were amongst these. Many of the Gorontalo in North Sulawesi may not be "migrants" in the sense that they or their descendants moved from Gorontalo to North Sulawesi. They may have been in their current

Table 4.18
Ethnic Composition by Sex: West Sulawesi, 2010

Rank	Ethnic Group	Males	Females	Total	Per cent	Sex Ratio
1	Mandar	257,314	268,448	525,762	45.42	0.959
2	Buginese	74,082	70,472	144,554	12.49	1.051
3	Mamasa	64,240	62,059	126,299	10.91	1.035
4	Mamuju	46,944	47,014	93,958	8.12	0.999
5	Javanese	29,340	27,615	56,955	4.92	1.062
6	Kaili	25,833	24,891	50,724	4.38	1.038
7	Pattae	14,920	15,340	30,260	2.61	0.973
8	Makassarese	13,702	11,665	25,367	2.19	1.175
9	Toraja	12,164	10,564	22,728	1.96	1.151
10	Galumpang	9,286	8,719	18,005	1.56	1.065
11	Others	32,856	30,097	62,953	5.44	1.092
	Total	580,681	576,884	1,157,565	100.00	1.007

Source: Calculated by the authors, based on tabulations provided by the BPS.

Table 4.19
Ethnic Composition by Sex: North Sulawesi, 2010

Rank	Ethnic Group	Males	Females	Total	Per cent	Sex Ratio
1	Minahasa	517,218	505,003	1,022,221	45.16	1.024
2	Sangir	231,010	227,770	458,780	20.27	1.014
3	Mongondow	149,032	144,450	293,482	12.97	1.032
4	Gorontalo	97,772	89,401	187,173	8.27	1.094
5	Talaud	44,885	43,765	88,650	3.92	1.026
6	Javanese	38,864	32,044	70,908	3.13	1.213
7	Buginese	12,103	9,936	22,039	0.97	1.218
8	Balinese	7,400	6,910	14,310	0.63	1.071
9	Ambonese	6,160	5,390	11,550	0.51	1.143
10	Makassarese	5,612	4,635	10,247	0.45	1.211
11	Others	44,852	39,251	84,103	3.72	1.143
	Total	1,154,908	1,108,555	2,263,463	100.00	1.042

Source: Calculated by the authors, based on tabulations provided by the BPS.

residence for a long time and they were considered to be a local ethnic group from North Sulawesi. After Gorontalo split administratively from North Sulawesi, those people from Gorontalo in North Sulawesi become a migrant ethnic group in the new province of North Sulawesi.

The Buginese in their home province only formed 45.12 per cent of the South Sulawesi population, living with other local ethnic groups such as the Makassarese in second place, the Toraja in third and the Luwu in fourth (Table 4.20). These four local ethnic groups accounted for 87.07 per cent. There were two other local ethnic groups seen amongst the ten largest ethnic groups in South Sulawesi: the Duri (the sixth largest) and Selayar (the seventh largest). It can be noted here that the Luwu can be seen as an ethnic group close to the Buginese, and the Selayar to the Makassarese.

The Javanese, a migrant ethnic group, ranked fifth, just about the same as the local ethnic group of the Duri. The Chinese and Dayak were two other migrant ethnic groups in South Sulawesi. The Mandar (the eighth largest) originated from the neighbouring province of West Sulawesi, a split from the province of South Sulawesi. It should be noted, however, that some Mandar might never change their place of residence, as the change was merely because of the change of the administrative boundary. Further studies should examine the possibility of the Mandar changing their place of residence.

The Batak in North Sumatra did not form a large majority in their home province (Table 4.21). Although they are the largest ethnic group, the Batak only constituted 44.75 per cent of the population in their home

Table 4.20
Ethnic Composition by Sex: South Sulawesi, 2010

Rank	Ethnic Group	Males	Females	Total	Per cent	Sex Ratio
1	Buginese	1,736,718	1,881,965	3,618,683	45.12	0.923
2	Makassarese	1,165,463	1,214,745	2,380,208	29.68	0.959
3	Toraja	296,009	292,656	588,665	7.34	1.011
4	Luwu	192,437	203,111	395,548	4.93	0.947
5	Javanese	120,852	108,159	229,011	2.86	1.117
6	Duri	111,803	113,159	224,962	2.80	0.988
7	Selayar	49,907	54,082	103,989	1.30	0.923
8	Mandar	25,598	26,756	52,354	0.65	0.957
9	Chinese	21,550	22,296	43,846	0.55	0.967
10	Dayak	13,967	15,287	29,254	0.36	0.914
11	Others	178,490	175,408	353,898	4.41	1.018
	Total	3,912,794	4,107,624	8,020,418	100.00	0.953

Source: Calculated by the authors, based on tabulations provided by the BPS.

Table 4.21
Ethnic Composition by Sex: North Sumatra, 2010

Rank	Ethnic Group	Males	Females	Total	Per cent	Sex Ratio
1	Batak	2,877,719	2,907,997	5,785,716	44.75	0.990
2	Javanese	2,159,926	2,158,830	4,318,756	33.40	1.001
3	Nias	455,873	455,947	911,820	7.05	1.000
4	Malay	383,443	389,752	773,195	5.98	0.984
5	Chinese	169,842	170,478	340,320	2.63	0.996
6	Minangkabau	169,914	163,327	333,241	2.58	1.040
7	Banjarese	63,997	61,710	125,707	0.97	1.037
8	Acehnese	64,127	60,399	124,526	0.96	1.062
9	Bantenese	24,168	22,453	46,621	0.36	1.076
10	Sundanese	18,054	17,535	35,589	0.28	1.030
11	Others	67,775	67,053	134,828	1.04	1.011
	Total	6,454,838	6,475,481	12,930,319	100.00	0.997

Source: Calculated by the authors, based on tabulations provided by the BPS.

province. They live side by side with the Javanese as the second largest group who made up 33.40 per cent of North Sumatra's population. Another local ethnic group, the Nias, were the third largest ethnic group, but contributing only 7.05 per cent. The Batak also live with the Malay, an ethnic group from neighbouring provinces. The province of North Sumatra also has a significant number of Chinese, the fifth largest ethnic group, contributing 2.63 per cent. The Chinese live mostly in Medan, the capital of the province.

In the province of Banten, as shown in Table 4.22, the Bantenese, the only local ethnic people, formed the largest group with 40.65 per cent of the province's population. The Badui, another local ethnic group, were too small in number to be in the ten largest ethnic groups. The other nine largest ethnic groups were migrant ones. The first three migrant ethnic groups were relatively large: the Sundanese, Javanese and Betawi who altogether formed a larger percentage, 51.17 per cent, than the Bantenese. The remaining ethnic groups were small, each with under 2 per cent and even 1 per cent.

As shown in Table 4.23, in Jambi, a Malay home province, the Malay formed 40.35 per cent as the largest group, and another local ethnic group, the Kerinci, contributed only 8.67 per cent as the third largest ethnic group. The Kerinci fell behind the Javanese, a migrant ethnic group,

Table 4.22
Ethnic Composition by Sex: Banten, 2010

Rank	Ethnic Group	Males	Females	Total	Per cent	Sex Ratio
1	Bantenese	2,197,303	2,112,355	4,309,658	40.65	1.040
2	Sundanese	1,230,751	1,171,622	2,402,373	22.66	1.050
3	Javanese	864,714	792,568	1,657,282	15.63	1.091
4	Betawi	691,064	674,550	1,365,614	12.88	1.024
5	Chinese	92,262	91,427	183,689	1.73	1.009
6	Batak	72,358	66,901	139,259	1.31	1.082
7	Malay	49,921	48,253	98,174	0.93	1.035
8	Minangkabau	49,788	46,057	95,845	0.90	1.081
9	Lampung	29,930	39,807	69,737	0.66	0.752
10	Palembang	25,597	27,817	53,414	0.50	0.920
11	Others	119,777	106,693	226,470	2.14	1.123
	Total	5,423,465	5,178,050	10,601,515	100.00	1.047

Source: Calculated by the authors, based on tabulations provided by the BPS.

Table 4.23
Ethnic Composition by Sex: Jambi, 2010

Rank	Ethnic Group	Males	Females	Total	Per cent	Sex Ratio
1	Malay	620,048	618,497	1,238,545	40.35	1.003
2	Javanese	469,257	423,876	893,133	29.09	1.107
3	Kerinci	131,972	134,162	266,134	8.67	0.984
4	Minangkabau	82,642	81,118	163,760	5.33	1.019
5	Batak	57,241	49,008	106,249	3.46	1.168
6	Banjarese	51,543	50,694	102,237	3.33	1.017
7	Buginese	48,380	47,766	96,146	3.13	1.013
8	Sundanese	41,196	38,016	79,212	2.58	1.084
9	Palembang	26,906	24,647	51,553	1.68	1.092
10	Chinese	19,160	18,086	37,246	1.21	1.059
11	Others	19,236	16,320	35,556	1.16	1.179
	Total	1,567,581	1,502,190	3,069,771	100.00	1.044

Source: Calculated by the authors, based on tabulations provided by the BPS.

which accounted for 29.09 per cent. The sum of Malay and Kerinci, two local ethnic groups, formed only about a half of the population (49.02 per cent) and the remaining eight groups were ethnic migrants accounting for a similar percentage (49.83 per cent).

Almost Heterogeneous Provinces

This group consisted of ten almost heterogeneous provinces, with the percentages of their largest ethnic groups falling between 20 and 40 per cent. The Javanese migrant ethnic group was the largest in three provinces: Jakarta, East Kalimantan and South Sumatra. In seven other provinces, the largest ethnic groups were the local ones — the Malay in the provinces of Riau, the Riau Archipelago and Bengkulu; the Dayak in West Kalimantan; the Kaili in Central Sulawesi; the Buton or Wolio in Southeast Sulawesi and the Dani in Papua.

The population of Jakarta, the capital city of Indonesia, is mainly dominated by Javanese migrant ethnic groups (36.16 per cent), with the local ethnic group the Betawi just behind with 28.29 per cent. As seen in Table 4.24, the third largest ethnic group was the Sundanese, originating in West Java, bordering the province to the south and west, with about a half the number of the Betawi. The Chinese come out in fourth place, contributing a relatively large 6.62 per cent. Another closest neighbouring ethnic group, the Bantenese, was not on the list of the ten largest ethnic groups in Jakarta. However, the Madurese, from far away across the Madura Strait, ranked eighth in 2010. The Minangkabau, Malay and Palembang

Table 4.24
Ethnic Composition by Sex: Jakarta, 2010

Rank	Ethnic Group	Males	Females	Total	Per cent	Sex Ratio
1	Javanese	1,742,759	1,709,409	3,452,168	36.16	1.020
2	Betawi	1,362,884	1,337,838	2,700,722	28.29	1.019
3	Sundanese	704,955	690,285	1,395,240	14.61	1.021
4	Chinese	311,848	320,524	632,372	6.62	0.973
5	Batak	167,173	159,472	326,645	3.42	1.048
6	Minangkabau	140,883	131,135	272,018	2.85	1.074
7	Malay	57,218	53,907	111,125	1.16	1.061
8	Madurese	42,697	37,228	79,925	0.84	1.147
9	Buginese	36,698	31,668	68,366	0.72	1.159
10	Palembang	31,821	31,512	63,333	0.66	1.010
11	Others	231,410	214,217	445,627	4.67	1.080
	Total	4,830,346	4,717,195	9,547,541	100.00	1.024

Source: Calculated by the authors, based on tabulations provided by the BPS.

from the island of Sumatra were three other important migrant ethnic groups in Jakarta, as well as the Buginese from the island of Sulawesi.

East Kalimantan is another almost heterogeneous province with the Javanese migrant ethnic group as the largest one in the province (Table 4.28). It contributed 30.24 per cent to the population of East Kalimantan. The second largest, 20.81 per cent, was also a migrant ethnic group, the Buginese. The next three largest ethnic groups were all originally from the island of Kalimantan: the Banjarese, Dayak and Kutai. Another ethnic group from Kalimantan was the Pasir, at seventh. Others were migrant ethnic groups: the Toraja from South Sulawesi, Sundanese from West Java, Madurese from East Java and Buton from Southeast Sulawesi.

The almost heterogeneous South Sumatra (Table 4.30) also has the Javanese as the largest ethnic group in the province. The second migrant ethnic group was the Sundanese, constituting only 2.19 per cent, being the eighth largest ethnic group. The other eight ethnic groups were local, with the Malay as the largest local ethnic group. The Malay were only the second largest group in South Sumatra, although South Sumatra is one of the Malay home provinces. Except for the Javanese and Sundanese, all the other largest ethnic groups were local ethnic groups, with none contributing less than 2 per cent. Rambang was an exception, with 1.94 per cent.

Other almost heterogeneous provinces have their local groups as the largest ones. Unlike East Kalimantan, the Dayak in West Kalimantan (Table 4.25) were the largest with 34.93 per cent; followed by the Malay, a migrant ethnic group, forming 33.84 per cent. The Javanese and Chinese came third and fourth, having almost the same percentage of 9.74 per cent and 8.17 per cent, respectively. Meanwhile, the Madurese, who were involved in the violent conflict in the early reform era, came out fifth in 2010 with 6.27 per cent, or 274,900. This number was larger than the Madurese in 2000, with 203,600 (Suryadinata, Arifin and Ananta 2003). The Buginese formed a significant portion with 3.13 per cent, ranking one above the Sundanese. The Banjarese in West Kalimantan came out as the last amongst the ten largest groups.

The largest ethnic group in almost heterogeneous Riau was a local group, the Malay. As seen in Table 4.26, the second largest group were the Javanese. The contributions of the first two largest groups were 33.28 per cent and 29.20 per cent, respectively. The Batak and Minangkabau as the third and fourth largest groups were far from the first two, but the difference between these two was very small. Therefore, the Malay there

Table 4.25
Ethnic Composition by Sex: West Kalimantan, 2010

Rank	Ethnic Group	Males	Females	Total	Per cent	Sex Ratio
1	Dayak	785,755	746,234	1,531,989	34.93	1.053
2	Malay	730,600	753,485	1,484,085	33.84	0.970
3	Javanese	231,280	195,958	427,238	9.74	1.180
4	Chinese	188,662	169,789	358,451	8.17	1.111
5	Madurese	139,815	135,054	274,869	6.27	1.035
6	Buginese	71,664	65,618	137,282	3.13	1.092
7	Sundanese	26,903	22,627	49,530	1.13	1.189
8	Batak	15,289	11,197	26,486	0.60	1.365
9	Daya	10,382	12,308	22,690	0.52	0.844
10	Banjarese	7,735	6,695	14,430	0.33	1.155
11	Others	32,002	26,304	58,306	1.33	1.217
	Total	2,240,087	2,145,269	4,385,356	100.00	1.044

Source: Calculated by the authors, based on tabulations provided by the BPS.

Table 4.26
Ethnic Composition by Sex: Riau, 2010

Rank	Ethnic Group	Males	Females	Total	Per cent	Sex Ratio
1	Malay	919,713	913,175	1,832,888	33.28	1.007
2	Javanese	846,325	761,858	1,608,183	29.20	1.111
3	Batak	361,796	329,603	691,399	12.55	1.098
4	Minangkabau	344,600	332,348	676,948	12.29	1.037
5	Banjarese	115,488	111,751	227,239	4.13	1.033
6	Buginese	54,941	52,256	107,197	1.95	1.051
7	Chinese	52,742	49,122	101,864	1.85	1.074
8	Sundanese	40,653	37,323	77,976	1.42	1.089
9	Nias	38,238	33,299	71.537	1.30	1.148
10	Akik/Akit	13,390	12,774	26,164	0.48	1.048
11	Others	46,271	40,176	86,447	1.57	1.152
	Total	2,834,157	2,673,685	5,507,842	100.00	1.060

Source: Calculated by the authors, based on tabulations provided by the BPS.

mostly lived and interacted with migrant ethnic groups. The only other local ethnic group were the Akik or Akit, the tenth largest ethnic group in the province.

The pair of the Malay as the first and Javanese as the second largest ethnic groups, with small differences, was also seen in the heterogeneous

Table 4.27
Ethnic Composition by Sex: Bengkulu, 2010

Rank	Ethnic Group	Males	Females	Total	Per cent	Sex Ratio
1	Malay	275,961	273,513	549,474	32.12	1.009
2	Javanese	204,382	182,893	387,275	22.64	1.117
3	Rejang	177,494	176,589	354,083	20.70	1.005
4	Lembak	44,091	43,263	87,354	5.11	1.019
5	Minangkabau	36,416	35,056	71,472	4.18	1.039
6	Sundanese	27,126	25,393	52,519	3.07	1.068
7	Muko-Muko	22,132	21,192	43,324	2.53	1.044
8	Kaur	20,299	19,835	40,134	2.35	1.023
9	Batak	18,135	14,837	32,972	1.93	1.222
10	Pekal	14,403	13,761	28,164	1.65	1.047
11	Others	33,595	30,311	63,906	3.74	1.108
	Total	874,034	836,643	1,710,677	100.00	1.045

Source: Calculated by the authors, based on tabulations provided by the BPS.

Table 4.28
Ethnic Composition by Sex: East Kalimantan, 2010

Rank	Ethnic Group	Males	Females	Total	Per cent	Sex Ratio
1	Javanese	568,815	500,790	1,069,605	30.24	1.136
2	Buginese	391,713	344,106	735,819	20.81	1.138
3	Banjarese	222,489	217,964	440,453	12.45	1.021
4	Dayak	178,624	172,813	351,437	9.94	1.034
5	Kutai	139,556	136,140	275,696	7.80	1.025
6	Toraja	41,023	37,228	78,251	2.21	1.102
7	Pasir	34,379	32,636	67,015	1.89	1.053
8	Sundanese	29,946	25,713	55,659	1.57	1.165
9	Madurese	25,303	21,520	46,823	1.32	1.176
10	Butonese	23,018	21,175	44,193	1.25	1.087
11	Others	203,906	167,646	371,552	10.51	1.216
	Total	1,858,772	1,677,731	3,536,503	100.00	1.108

Source: Calculated by the authors, based on tabulations provided by the BPS.

provinces of Bengkulu and the migrant province of the Riau Archipelago. The third largest ethnic group was a local one, the Rejang, contributing 20.70 per cent. This group is also known as the Taba Saling, the Keme or the Lebong. The province of Bengkulu has four other local ethnic groups: Lembak (the fourth largest group), Muko Muko (the seventh largest group),

Kaur (the eighth largest group) and Pekal (the tenth largest group). The Pekal is also known as the Anak Sungai, Orang Katau, Orang Seblat, Mekea or Orang Ipuh.

In the Riau Archipelago, as seen in Table 4.29, the Malay were the only local ethnic group, with only 30.23 per cent, sharing the islands with the majority migrant ethnic groups. The province's ethnic heterogeneity can be partly explained by the development of Batam Island as a part of a free trade zone of the Growth Triangle for Indonesia, Malaysia and Singapore, attracting people from many provinces in Indonesia as well as from other nations. As seen in Table 4.1, the presence of foreigners there was significant, 4.76 per cent of the total foreigners in Indonesia. The ethnic groups of Javanese and Sundanese (from the island of Java) stood in second and sixth places, respectively. The Javanese accounted for a significant share with a quarter of the population. The Batak, Minangkabau and Palembang were migrant ethnic groups from the island of Sumatra, the Flores from the islands of East Nusa Tenggara and the Buginese from the island of Sulawesi. The Chinese ranked fifth in the Riau Archipelago, with 7.70 per cent.

In the group of almost heterogeneous provinces, the province of Papua (Table 4.31) had the largest number of ethnic groups, each contributing little

Table 4.29
Ethnic Composition by Sex: Riau Archipelago, 2010

Rank	Ethnic Group	Males	Females	Total	Per cent	Sex Ratio
1	Malay	255,819	249,572	505,391	30.23	1.025
2	Javanese	213,667	196,761	410,428	24.55	1.086
3	Batak	99,420	109,258	208,678	12.48	0.910
4	Minangkabau	81,254	81,198	162,452	9.72	1.001
5	Chinese	66,890	61,814	128,704	7.70	1.082
6	Sundanese	25,266	24,173	49,439	2.96	1.045
7	Buginese	20,223	16,922	37,145	2.22	1.195
8	Flores	17,849	12,003	29,852	1.79	1.487
9	Palembang	14,450	14,924	29,374	1.76	0.968
10	Banjarese	6,279	5,532	11,811	0.71	1.135
11	Others	54,659	43,958	98,617	5.90	1.243
	Total	855,776	816,115	1,671,891	100.00	1.049

Source: Calculated by the authors, based on tabulations provided by the BPS.

Table 4.30
Ethnic Composition by Sex: South Sumatra, 2010

Rank	Ethnic Group	Males	Females	Total	Per cent	Sex Ratio
1	Javanese	1,062,149	975,362	2,037,511	27.41	1.089
2	Malay	769,478	757,717	1,527,195	20.54	1.016
3	Palembang	366,829	373,993	740,822	9.97	0.981
4	Musi	324,042	321,646	645,688	8.69	1.007
5	Ogan	299,825	297,753	597,578	8.04	1.007
6	Komering	172,707	167,221	339,928	4.57	1.033
7	Rawas	91,392	91,498	182,890	2.46	0.999
8	Sundanese	85,384	77,512	162,896	2.19	1.102
9	Enim	80,715	80,600	161,315	2.17	1.001
10	Rambang	72,189	71,724	143,913	1.94	1.006
11	Others	456,478	437,828	894,306	12.03	1.043
	Total	3,781,188	3,652,854	7,434,042	100.00	1.035

Source: Calculated by the authors, based on tabulations provided by the BPS.

to the population of the province. Most of these were local ethnic groups, originating from the land of Papua. Eight out of the twenty-five largest ethnic groups were migrant ethnic groups. Except for the Javanese (from the island of Java), Ambonese and Kei (from the islands of Maluku), all other migrant ethnic groups originated from the island of Sulawesi (the Buginese, Butonese, Makassarese, Minahasa and Toraja). In Papua, Dani, a local ethnic group, was the largest ethnic group, contributing only 23.32 per cent. The second largest group was also a local one, the Auwye/Mee, forming 11.32 per cent. The third was a migrant ethnic group, the Javanese. In addition to the Javanese, each of the next five largest groups contributed more than 3 per cent. Ten ethnic groups had contributions of more than 1 per cent each. With twenty-five ethnic groups on the list, the "Others" still comprised 15.39 per cent, reflecting the most heterogeneous province.

In Southeast Sulawesi (Table 4.32), the local ethnic group the Butonese or Wolio was the largest, contributing 22.80 per cent. The second ethnic group was almost as large as the first one. These were the Buginese, originating in South Sulawesi. The third, the Tolaki, also from South Sulawesi, were not far behind the second, contributing 18.47 per cent. The Javanese and Sundanese from the island of Java were listed as two of the ten largest groups there, with the Javanese ranking fifth and the Sundanese tenth. None of the ten ethnic groups contributed less than 1 per cent.

Table 4.31
Ethnic Composition by Sex: Papua, 2010

Rank	Ethnic Group	Males	Females	Total	Per cent	Sex Ratio
1	Dani	344,015	304,212	648,227	23.32	1.131
2	Auwye/Mee	161,875	152,707	314,582	11.32	1.060
3	Javanese	123,383	109,557	232,940	8.38	1.126
4	Biak-Numfor	75,388	70,514	145,902	5.25	1.069
5	Ngalik	71,065	62,497	133,562	4.80	1.137
6	Asmat	63,665	59,276	122,941	4.42	1.074
7	Dauwa	52,590	44,338	96,928	3.49	1.186
8	Buginese	49,182	39,809	88,991	3.20	1.235
9	Yapen	37,948	35,456	73,404	2.64	1.070
10	Toraja	25,891	22,138	48,029	1.73	1.170
11	Ketengban	22,285	19,316	41,601	1.50	1.154
12	Moni	21,337	20,109	41,446	1.49	1.061
13	Makassarese	22,807	18,432	41,239	1.48	1.237
14	Marind Anim	18,849	18,003	36,852	1.33	1.047
15	Ambonese	18,717	15,780	34,497	1.24	1.186
16	Butonese	16,951	13,494	30,445	1.10	1.256
17	Ngalum	15,553	13,563	29,116	1.05	1.147
18	Sentani	14,816	14,129	28,945	1.04	1.049
19	Hupla	14,069	13,254	27,323	0.98	1.061
20	Waropen	12,948	12,116	25,064	0.90	1.069
21	Mimika	12,113	11,164	23,277	0.84	1.085
22	Damal	11,842	10,567	22,409	0.81	1.121
23	Kei/Evav	11,906	10,228	22,134	0.80	1.164
24	Minahasa	10,633	10,762	21,395	0.77	0.988
25	Yaghay	10,751	10,274	21,025	0.76	1.046
26	Others	228,611	199,259	427,870	15.39	1.147
	Total	1,469,190	1,310,954	2,780,144	100.00	1.121

Source: Calculated by the authors, based on tabulations provided by the BPS.

Unlike Southeast Sulawesi, Central Sulawesi is more heterogeneous, with each of the fifteen ethnic groups representing more than one per cent (Table 4.33). Kaili, the largest and a local ethnic group, made up 21.45 per cent only. The other ethnic groups on the list were from the same island of Sulawesi, except for the Javanese and Balinese. The second largest group was the Buginese, a migrant ethnic group from the neighbouring province of South Sulawesi, contributing 15.62 per cent of the population

Table 4.32
Ethnic Composition by Sex: Southeast Sulawesi, 2010

Rank	Ethnic Group	Males	Females	Total	Per cent	Sex Ratio
1	Butonese	246,676	261,246	507,922	22.80	0.944
2	Buginese	255,460	240,972	496,432	22.28	1.060
3	Tolaki	206,622	204,976	411,598	18.47	1.008
4	Muna	149,335	159,302	308,637	13.85	0.937
5	Javanese	82,786	76,366	159,152	7.14	1.084
6	Makassarese	32,329	26,972	59,301	2.66	1.199
7	Bajao	25,144	26,718	51,862	2.33	0.941
8	Balinese	25,739	23,650	49,389	2.22	1.088
9	Moronene	18,793	20,151	38,944	1.75	0.933
10	Sundanese	13,056	12,357	25,413	1.14	1.057
11	Others	62,455	56,832	119,287	5.35	1.099
	Total	1,118,395	1,109,542	2,227,937	100.00	1.008

Source: Calculated by the authors, based on tabulations provided by the BPS.

Table 4.33
Ethnic Composition by Sex: Central Sulawesi, 2010

Rank	Ethnic Group	Males	Females	Total	Per cent	Sex Ratio
1	Kaili	283,821	278,872	562,693	21.45	1.018
2	Buginese	212,729	197,012	409,741	15.62	1.080
3	Javanese	115,349	105,617	220,966	8.42	1.092
4	Banggai	79,297	78,085	157,382	6.00	1.016
5	Pamona	62,426	60,928	123,354	4.70	1.025
6	Buol	58,858	57,784	116,642	4.45	1.019
7	Balinese	60,073	55,687	115,760	4.41	1.079
8	Gorontalo	54,691	50,461	105,152	4.01	1.084
9	Saluan	47,881	47,699	95,580	3.64	1.004
10	Tomini	38,786	38,421	77,207	3.64	1.010
11	Lauje	36,733	35,492	72,225	2.94	1.035
12	Bajao	27,835	28,407	56,242	2.75	0.980
13	Ta'a	22,264	22,084	44,348	2.14	1.008
14	Mariri	20,853	20,909	41,762	1.59	0.997
15	Tialo	20,739	20,529	41,268	1.57	1.010
16	Others	200,510	182,847	383,357	14.61	1.097
	Total	1,342,845	1,280,834	2,623,679	100.00	1.048

Source: Calculated by the authors, based on tabulations provided by the BPS.

in Central Sulawesi. The third largest was the Javanese, another migrant ethnic group from the island of Java.

Heterogeneous Provinces

This group consists of four heterogeneous provinces, all of them from the eastern part of Indonesia. The largest ethnic group contributed less than 20 per cent to each province's total population. There were no dominant ethnic groups and the contributions from many groups were almost the same.

As seen in Table 4.34, East Nusa Tenggara is a heterogeneous province, with all ten of the largest ethnic groups being of local origin. An exception was the ethnic group with Timor-Leste origins. The Democratic Republic of Timor-Leste used to be the province of East Timor, bordering East Nusa Tenggara.[3] The largest ethnic group in East Nusa Tenggara was the Atoni, contributing 19.85 per cent to the total population of this province. None contributed less than 3 per cent. For a more detailed discussion on this province, see Chapter 3.

In the heterogeneous province of West Papua, the largest ethnic group formed only 14.76 per cent of the total population in the province (Table 4.35). This migrant ethnic group, the Javanese, was the largest ethnic group in Indonesia as a whole. The Arfak, a local ethnic

Table 4.34
Ethnic Composition by Sex: East Nusa Tenggara, 2010

Rank	Ethnic Group	Males	Females	Total	Per cent	Sex Ratio
1	Atoni	465,063	462,690	927,753	19.85	1.005
2	Manggarai	358,768	368,636	727,404	15.57	0.973
3	Sumbanese	331,211	311,834	643,045	13.76	1.062
4	Solor	135,687	148,418	284,105	6.08	0.914
5	Ngada	134,637	140,233	274,870	5.88	0.960
6	Timor-Leste origins	120,899	125,968	246,867	5.28	0.960
7	Rote	117,161	114,943	232,104	4.97	1.019
8	Lio	86,598	96,881	183,479	3.93	0.894
9	Alor	91,122	91,148	182,270	3.90	1.000
10	Sawu	87,816	85,100	172,916	3.70	1.032
11	Others	389,819	408,016	797,835	17.07	0.955
	Total	2,318,781	2,353,867	4,672,648	100.00	0.985

Source: Calculated by the authors, based on tabulations provided by the BPS.

Table 4.35
Ethnic Composition by Sex: West Papua, 2010

Rank	Ethnic Group	Males	Females	Total	Per cent	Sex Ratio
1	Javanese	58,695	52,486	111,181	14.76	1.118
2	Arfak	35,613	33,569	69,182	9.18	1.061
3	Biak-Numfor	29,168	27,101	56,269	7.47	1.076
4	Ayfat	23,160	22,527	45,687	6.06	1.028
5	Buginese	21,770	18,317	40,087	5.32	1.189
6	Ambonese	17,382	15,539	32,921	4.37	1.119
7	Butonese	17,067	14,024	31,091	4.13	1.217
8	Baham	11,489	10,680	22,169	2.94	1.076
9	Yapen	9,821	8,948	18,769	2.49	1.098
10	Mooi	9,341	8,737	18,078	2.40	1.069
11	Makassarese	9,343	7,682	17,025	2.26	1.216
12	Kei/Evav	8,914	7,694	16,608	2.20	1.159
13	Tehit	8,063	7,899	15,962	2.12	1.021
14	Toraja	7,293	6,344	13,637	1.81	1.150
15	Minahasa	6,793	6,702	13,495	1.79	1.014
16	Wandamen	7,058	6,413	13,471	1.79	1.101
17	Irahutu	5,964	5,850	11,814	1.57	1.019
18	Kokoda	5,087	4,939	10,026	1.33	1.030
19	Seram	5,229	4,287	9,516	1.26	1.220
20	Inanwatan	4,573	4,348	8,921	1.18	1.052
21	Wamesa	4,490	4,244	8,734	1.16	1.058
22	Flores	4,523	2,982	7,505	1.00	1.517
23	Sundanese	4,027	3,167	7,194	0.95	1.272
24	Batak	3,908	3,278	7,186	0.95	1.192
25	Ternate	3,726	3,024	6,750	0.90	1.232
26	Others	74,010	66,111	140,121	18.60	1.119
	Total	396,507	356,892	753,399	100.00	1.111

Source: Calculated by the authors, based on tabulations provided by the BPS.

group, was the second largest, constituting 9.18 per cent, followed by the Biak-Numfor and Ayfat. West Papua has many ethnic groups, each with a very small population. They are also minor ethnic groups in the context of Indonesia as a whole.

It is also possible that some of the ethnic groups with small populations in West Papua belong to large ethnic groups nationally. The Sundanese were the second largest ethnic group in Indonesia, but only contributed 0.95 per cent to the population of West Papua. The Batak contributed 3.58 per cent to the total population of Indonesia, the fourth largest in Indonesia, but their presence in West Papua only formed 0.95 per cent. The last in the twenty-five largest ethnic groups in the province of West Papua was also a migrant ethnic group, the Ternate, originating in the province of North Maluku. However, their presence is tiny, only forming 0.90 per cent. Yet, the "Others" in West Papua still made up 18.60 per cent, implying that this province has many ethnic groups, each contributing very few people to the total population in the province. These may be local ethnic groups or migrant ethnic groups.

The province of Maluku is another heterogeneous province. Yet, like West Papua, the largest ethnic group was not a local one. The Butonese or Wolio, a migrant ethnic group originating in Southeast Sulawesi, formed the largest population in Maluku with 12.74 per cent, just slightly higher than the local Ambonese (12.13 per cent). As seen in Table 4.36, there were only two migrant ethnic groups amongst the remaining 13 largest ethnic groups in the province of Maluku: the Javanese as the seventh largest and the Buginese, the fourteenth. Because of the many small ethnic groups in Maluku, we have presented the 15 largest ethnic groups in the province. Yet, the "Others" still formed about one fifth of the population, meaning that there are still many other groups with smaller contributions.

The last heterogeneous province was North Maluku, with an even smaller percentage, 10.78, for its largest ethnic group, the Tobelo, a local ethnic group. The second group were the Galela, not much lower than the Tobelo, contributing 9.70 per cent. As seen in Table 4.37, there were many almost equally small ethnic groups in North Maluku. There were four migrant ethnic groups originating from the island of Sulawesi, to the west of North Maluku. The largest migrant ethnic group was the Buton or Wolio, originating in Southeast Sulawesi, but it was only the seventh largest one. Three other migrant ethnic groups from Sulawesi were the Sangir, from North Sulawesi, the Buginese, from South Sulawesi and the Bajao, another ethnic group from Southeast Sulawesi. The Javanese in this province is the only ethnic group from the island of Java included in the fifteen largest groups.

From Central Java to North Maluku

In conclusion, the thirty-three provinces vary in terms of their ethnic homogeneity. They range from Central Java as the most ethnically

Table 4.36
Ethnic Composition by Sex: Maluku, 2010

Rank	Ethnic Group	Males	Females	Total	Per cent	Sex Ratio
1	Butonese	97,570	96,986	194,556	12.74	1.006
2	Ambonese	91,078	94,163	185,241	12.13	0.967
3	Seram	89,970	87,025	176,995	11.59	1.034
4	Kei/Evav	83,600	83,983	167,583	10.98	0.995
5	Tanimbar	49,921	49,971	99,892	6.54	0.999
6	Saparua	43,236	43,844	87,080	5.70	0.986
7	Javanese	41,165	38,142	79,307	5.19	1.079
8	Buru	29,141	27,680	56,821	3.72	1.053
9	Geser-Gorom	16,549	15,884	32,433	2.12	1.042
10	Haruku	15,338	15,222	30,560	2.00	1.008
11	Aru	15,182	14,753	29,935	1.96	1.029
12	Babar	13,551	13,369	26,920	1.76	1.014
13	Kisar	12,949	12,684	25,633	1.68	1.021
14	Buginese	13,430	12,089	25,519	1.67	1.111
15	Banda	9,887	10,225	20,112	1.32	0.967
16	Others	157,009	151,226	308,235	20.19	1.038
	Total	769,689	757,021	1,526,710	100.00	1.017

Source: Calculated by the authors, based on tabulations provided by the BPS.

homogeneous province to North Maluku as the most heterogeneous province. The province of Central Java is homogeneously Javanese, with the Javanese forming 97.72 per cent of the total population in the province. In contrast, the largest ethnic group in North Maluku, the Tobelo, only contributed 10.78 per cent to the province's population. No ethnic group was dominant in North Maluku.

EXTENSION LIST OF ETHNIC COMPOSITION IN INDONESIA

Each of the fifteen largest ethnic groups in Indonesia can be found in any province, although the contribution of some of these to a province's total population may be small, even very small. Combining all ethnic groups in the thirty-three provinces presented in Tables 4.5–4.37, we have produced an extended list of the fifteen largest ethnic groups in Indonesia, as shown in Table 4.38.

Table 4.37
Ethnic Composition by Sex: North Maluku, 2010

Rank	Ethnic Group	Males	Females	Total	Per cent	Sex Ratio
1	Tobelo	56,562	55,007	111,569	10.78	1.028
2	Galela	50,819	49,641	100,460	9.70	1.024
3	Ternate	48,952	48,413	97,365	9.40	1.011
4	Makian	44,674	43,420	88,094	8.51	1.029
5	Tidore	40,399	39,902	80,301	7.76	1.012
6	Sula	36,629	35,592	72,221	6.98	1.029
7	Butonese	30,255	28,470	58,725	5.67	1.063
8	Javanese	23,302	19,400	42,702	4.12	1.201
9	Sangir	16,511	15,009	31,520	3.04	1.100
10	Laloda	13,777	13,267	27,044	2.61	1.038
11	Tobaru	11,956	11,255	23,211	2.24	1.062
12	Kau	11,180	11,039	22,219	2.15	1.013
13	Buginese	11,227	9,580	20,807	2.01	1.172
14	Patani	9,621	9,472	19,093	1.84	1.016
15	Bajao	9,079	8,852	17,931	1.73	1.026
16	Others	114,237	107,926	222,163	21.46	1.058
	Total	529,180	506,245	1,035,425	100.00	1.045

Source: Calculated by the authors, based on tabulations provided by the BPS.

This list depicts 145 ethnic groups in Indonesia, accounting for 99.07 per cent of the total population of the country. Outside this list, there were more than four hundred tiny ethnic groups, but they only formed 0.93 per cent or 2.2 million of the total population of Indonesia. Indeed, Indonesia is a country with a huge number of tiny ethnic groups. We are aware of the economic, social and political importance of all of these groups in Indonesian society, but a detailed analysis of these tiny groups is beyond the scope of this book. These minorities deserve further studies to understand the nature of their existence or perhaps extinction, as until today they are still understudied. These studies will enrich the knowledge of the landscapes of ethnicity in this huge archipelagic country.

The list shows a large range of sizes of populations for each ethnic group, from as huge as 94.8 million for the Javanese to as small as 6,000 for the Atinggola, contributing almost zero per cent to the total population of Indonesia. In addition to the Atinggola, which originated from Gorontalo, there were three other tiny ethnic groups, each with an almost zero percentage contribution to the whole population of Indonesia. They were

Table 4.38
The 145 Ethnic Groups: Indonesia, 2010

Rank	Ethnic Group	Males	Females	Total	Distribution %	Sex Ratio
1	Javanese	47,644,647	47,198,426	94,843,073	40.06	1.009
2	Sundanese	18,603,257	18,101,687	36,704,944	15.51	1.028
3	Malay	4,388,443	4,365,348	8,753,791	3.70	1.005
4	Batak	4,268,074	4,198,895	8,466,969	3.58	1.016
5	Madurese	3,518,361	3,660,995	7,179,356	3.03	0.961
6	Betawi	3,441,848	3,366,120	6,807,968	2.88	1.022
7	Minangkabau	3,228,346	3,234,367	6,462,713	2.73	0.998
8	Buginese	3,205,165	3,209,938	6,415,103	2.71	0.999
9	Bantenese	2,370,617	2,271,772	4,642,389	1.96	1.044
10	Banjarese	2,063,769	2,063,355	4,127,124	1.74	1.000
11	Balinese	1,972,299	1,952,609	3,924,908	1.66	1.010
12	Acehnese	1,704,138	1,699,971	3,404,109	1.44	1.002
13	Dayak	1,643,024	1,576,602	3,219,626	1.36	1.042
14	Sasak	1,522,636	1,652,370	3,175,006	1.34	0.921
15	Chinese	1,425,236	1,407,274	2,832,510	1.20	1.013
16	Makassarese	1,325,342	1,347,248	2,672,590	1.13	0.984
17	Cirebonese	961,406	916,108	1,877,514	0.79	1.049
18	Lampung	690,832	685,558	1,376,390	0.58	1.008
19	Palembang	627,063	625,195	1,252,258	0.53	1.003
20	Gorontalo	631,916	619,968	1,251,884	0.53	1.019
21	Minahasa	626,675	613,557	1,240,232	0.52	1.021
22	Nias	526,723	515,202	1,041,925	0.44	1.022
23	Butonese	470,425	467,336	937,761	0.40	1.007
24	Atoni	468,068	465,025	933,093	0.39	1.007
25	Toraja	438,757	418,493	857,250	0.36	1.048
26	Kaili	387,572	382,516	770,088	0.33	1.013
27	Manggarai	365,146	372,469	737,615	0.31	0.980
28	Ogan	363,158	358,455	721,613	0.30	1.013
29	Mandar	339,247	345,441	684,688	0.29	0.982
30	Bangka	344,958	338,235	683,193	0.29	1.020
31	Bima	335,281	330,102	665,383	0.28	1.016
32	Sumbanese	339,698	319,023	658,721	0.28	1.065
33	Musi	328,487	325,618	654,105	0.28	1.009
34	Dani	345,713	305,185	650,898	0.27	1.133
35	Sangir	280,654	273,199	553,853	0.23	1.027
36	Rejang	227,660	227,013	454,673	0.19	1.003

continued on next page

Table 4.38 — _cont'd_

Rank	Ethnic Group	Males	Females	Total	Distribution %	Sex Ratio
37	Ambonese	231,089	211,496	442,585	0.19	1.093
38	Tolaki	214,014	211,924	425,938	0.18	1.010
39	Luwu	205,167	214,950	420,117	0.18	0.954
40	Sumbawa	204,392	192,514	396,906	0.17	1.062
41	Komering	188,643	181,476	370,119	0.16	1.039
42	Gayo	167,958	168,898	336,856	0.14	0.994
43	Muna	162,300	170,137	332,437	0.14	0.954
44	Auwye/Mee	162,859	153,498	316,357	0.13	1.061
45	Mongondow	154,378	149,914	304,292	0.13	1.030
46	Kerinci	150,844	152,706	303,550	0.13	0.988
47	Lamahot	141,218	153,397	294,615	0.12	0.921
48	Ngada	142,406	147,544	289,950	0.12	0.965
49	Osing/Using	140,699	145,954	286,653	0.12	0.964
50	Kutai	141,210	137,845	279,055	0.12	1.024
51	Timor-Leste origins	133,091	136,277	269,368	0.11	0.977
52	Flores	150,799	109,270	260,069	0.11	1.380
53	Bajao	119,772	122,064	241,836	0.10	0.981
54	Rote	121,053	118,293	239,346	0.10	1.023
55	Duri	118,831	119,253	238,084	0.10	0.996
56	Kei	108,578	105,248	213,826	0.09	1.032
57	Biak-Numfor	105,843	98,572	204,415	0.09	1.074
58	Belitung	101,712	99,356	201,068	0.08	1.024
59	Alor	99,404	97,125	196,529	0.08	1.023
60	Seram	99,710	95,108	194,818	0.08	1.048
61	Rawas	96,071	96,634	192,705	0.08	0.994
62	Lio	88,616	98,539	187,155	0.08	0.899
63	Pamona	94,915	91,248	186,163	0.08	1.040
64	Sawu	90,095	87,202	177,297	0.07	1.033
65	Banggai	83,685	81,696	165,381	0.07	1.024
66	Enim	81,879	81,749	163,628	0.07	1.002
67	Lembak	81,977	81,285	163,262	0.07	1.009
68	Rambang	72,738	72,248	144,986	0.06	1.007
69	Ngalik	71,253	62,559	133,812	0.06	1.139
70	Mamasa	67,952	65,707	133,659	0.06	1.034
71	Ternate	68,225	64,885	133,110	0.06	1.051
72	Asmat	69,313	63,678	132,991	0.06	1.088

73	Selayar	63,706	67,507	131,213	0.06	0.944
74	Mbojo	64,279	63,693	127,972	0.05	1.009
75	Daya	60,763	60,526	121,289	0.05	1.004
76	Buol	60,448	59,265	119,713	0.05	1.020
77	Arab	59,679	59,187	118,866	0.05	1.008
78	Tobelo	58,736	57,210	115,946	0.05	1.027
79	Tanimbar	55,738	54,859	110,597	0.05	1.016
80	Mamuju	54,409	53,820	108,229	0.05	1.011
81	Galela	51,806	50,650	102,456	0.04	1.023
82	Yapen	51,693	47,612	99,305	0.04	1.086
83	Dauwa	53,777	45,462	99,239	0.04	1.183
84	Alas	49,003	49,220	98,223	0.04	0.996
85	Saluan	48,681	48,453	97,134	0.04	1.005
86	Talaud	47,996	46,441	94,437	0.04	1.033
87	Tomini	47,280	46,599	93,879	0.04	1.015
88	Makian	46,181	44,779	90,960	0.04	1.031
89	Saparua	44,597	45,077	89,674	0.04	0.989
90	Tidore	44,467	43,057	87,524	0.04	1.033
91	Sula	43,056	41,802	84,858	0.04	1.030
92	Bawean	39,741	43,668	83,409	0.04	0.910
93	Arfak	38,135	35,693	73,828	0.03	1.068
94	Pasir	37,639	35,711	73,350	0.03	1.054
95	Lauje	36,805	35,566	72,371	0.03	1.035
96	Mentawai	35,514	33,631	69,145	0.03	1.056
97	Simeulue	34,350	33,372	67,722	0.03	1.029
98	Aneuk Jamee	30,667	32,690	63,357	0.03	0.938
99	Moni	31,561	31,748	63,309	0.03	0.994
100	Dompu	30,752	31,065	61,817	0.03	0.990
101	Buru	29,530	27,991	57,521	0.02	1.055
102	Singkil	26,353	26,629	52,982	0.02	0.990
103	Tamiang	26,737	26,164	52,901	0.02	1.022
104	Ayfat	27,085	25,569	52,654	0.02	1.059
105	Mariri	22,860	22,690	45,550	0.02	1.007
106	Ta'a	22,382	22,197	44,579	0.02	1.008
107	Muko-Muko	22,368	21,382	43,750	0.02	1.046
108	Ketengban	22,511	19,514	42,025	0.02	1.154
109	Tialo	20,972	20,731	41,703	0.02	1.012
110	Kaur	20,662	20,201	40,863	0.02	1.023
111	Moronene	19,378	20,647	40,025	0.02	0.939

continued on next page

Table 4.38 — *cont'd*

Rank	Ethnic Group	Males	Females	Total	Distribution %	Sex Ratio
112	Marind Anim	19,246	18,312	37,558	0.02	1.051
113	Pattae	17,346	17,616	34,962	0.01	0.985
114	Geser-Gorom	17,134	16,464	33,598	0.01	1.041
115	Haruku	15,601	15,451	31,052	0.01	1.010
116	Aru	15,758	15,184	30,942	0.01	1.038
117	Sentani	15,700	14,961	30,661	0.01	1.049
118	Ngalum	15,597	13,589	29,186	0.01	1.148
119	Pekal	14,932	14,241	29,173	0.01	1.049
120	Mimika	15,010	13,635	28,645	0.01	1.101
121	Laloda	14,349	13,783	28,132	0.01	1.041
122	Kisar	14,140	13,823	27,963	0.01	1.023
123	Akik/Akit	14,199	13,570	27,769	0.01	1.046
124	Babar	13,835	13,615	27,450	0.01	1.016
125	Hupla	14,089	13,264	27,353	0.01	1.062
126	Waropen	14,029	13,044	27,073	0.01	1.076
127	Baham	12,693	11,828	24,521	0.01	1.073
128	Bali Aga	12,131	11,695	23,826	0.01	1.037
129	Tobaru	12,227	11,477	23,704	0.01	1.065
130	Banda	11,553	11,694	23,247	0.01	0.988
131	Kau	11,568	11,402	22,970	0.01	1.015
132	Damal	11,900	10,579	22,479	0.01	1.125
133	Mooi	11,334	10,589	21,923	0.01	1.070
134	Yaghay	10,803	10,318	21,121	0.01	1.047
135	Patani	9,782	9,605	19,387	0.01	1.018
136	Galumpang	9,459	8,891	18,350	0.01	1.064
137	Wandamen	8,674	7,888	16,562	0.01	1.100
138	Tehid	8,310	8,088	16,398	0.01	1.027
139	Suwawa	8,386	7,988	16,374	0.01	1.050
140	Kore	8,021	8,292	16,313	0.01	0.967
141	Irahutu	6,067	5,966	12,033	0.01	1.017
142	Kokoda	5,165	4,981	10,146	0.00	1.037
143	Inanwatan	4,960	4,725	9,685	0.00	1.050
144	Wamesa	4,936	4,612	9,548	0.00	1.070
145	Atinggola	3,107	2,983	6,090	0.00	1.042
146	Others	1,112,393	1,087,163	2,199,556	0.93	1.023
	Total	119,054,061	117,674,318	236,728,379	100.00	1.012

Source: Calculated by the authors, based on tabulations provided by the BPS.

the Kokoda, the Inanwatan and the Wamesa, all from the province of West Papua. Each of these three ethnic groups comprised only about 10,000 people. Furthermore, the list also includes 29 small ethnic groups, with each contributing to only 0.01 per cent of Indonesia's total population.

Beyond the fifteen largest ethnic groups in Indonesia, there were seven ethnic groups each with more than one million people. The Makassarese, another local ethnic group from South Sulawesi, turned out to be the largest one amongst these seven ethnic groups. The other six were the Cirebonese (a local ethnic group from West Java), the Lampung (a local ethnic group from Lampung), the Palembang (a local ethnic group from South Sumatra), the Gorontalo (a local ethnic group from Gorontalo), the Minahasa (a local ethnic group from North Sulawesi) and the Nias (a local group from North Sumatra). Thus, there were 22 ethnic groups in Indonesia each with more than a million people. The remaining 123 ethnic groups in the list were smaller than this and some were even much smaller.

In terms of male and female composition, most ethnic groups have almost equal composition, with a sex ratio of at least 0.98 and at most 1.02. The sex ratio indicates the numbers of males in relation to females. A sex ratio of 1 means that the number of males is the same as that of females. A sex ratio above 1 reveals that there are more males than females; below 1 implies that there are more females than males.

Amongst the fifteen largest ethnic groups in Indonesia, the Sundanese, Bantenese and Dayak had relatively larger numbers of males, with sex ratios of 1.03 for the Sundanese and 1.04 for each of the Bantenese and Dayak. On the other hand, the Sasak and Madurese have more females than males. The Sasak had a much lower sex ratio, at 0.92; and the Madurese, at 0.96. Further discussion on the sex ratios of these five ethnic groups can be found in Chapter 5.

Amongst the 145 ethnic groups, the Flores was an outlier. It had the highest sex ratio of 1.38, much larger than that of other ethnic groups. The number of Flores males was 38 per cent higher than that of Flores females. Perhaps it is related to the feminization of international migration, which may have resulted in a much larger number of Flores females going overseas, both legally and illegally. This phenomenon needs further studies to be better understood.

The next largest sex ratios, but still much smaller than that of the Flores, were those above 1.10, amongst the people of Dauwa (1.18), Ketengban (1.15), Ngalum (1.15), Ngalik (1.14), Dani (1.13), Damal (1.12), Wandamen

(1.10) and Mimika (1.10). All of these groups originate in the province of Papua, except for the Wandamen, who are from the province of West Papua.

On the other hand, the Bawean or Boyanese ethnic group provides a case of a community with a large excess of females. Bawean is an island located in the north of East Java Province and is part of the administrative territory of the regency of Gresik. The Bawean had the second lowest sex ratio, 0.91, after Lio (0.90), an ethnic group from Flores, East Nusa Tenggara. Interestingly, as shown in Table 4.8, the Bawean living in East Java province had a lower sex ratio of 0.89 than the overall Bawean. This phenomenon may indicate the Bawean men's inclination to migrate to other provinces and even overseas. Mantra (1998) showed the tendency of Bawean males to work overseas, particularly in Singapore and Malaysia. This tendency may have existed for a long time. The Bawean exist in Singapore as part of the Malay community. As discussed in Malte and Sakemink (2009), the Bawean were also present in Vietnam, contributing to the minority Muslim community, but many of them were stateless citizens. The Bawean migrated to Vietnam after the Second World War. As discussed by Mantra, the very low sex ratio of the Lio may also have been because of the heavy migration of its male population to work overseas.

Two other ethnic groups with an excess of females, indicated with a sex ratio below 1, were the Lamahot (0.92), an ethnic group originating in East Nusa Tenggara and the Muna (0.95), originally from Southeast Sulawesi.

UBIQUITY OF ETHNIC GROUPS

This section presents the extent to which an ethnic group in the extended list of ethnic groups discussed earlier is ubiquitous, that is, one that can be found "everywhere" across Indonesia. An ethnic group is defined to be ubiquitous if it is one of the ten largest ethnic groups in at least two provinces. From the 145 ethnic groups, there are thirty-three ubiquitous ethnic groups. In other words, the other 112 ethnic groups in the list were only importantly seen in their own home provinces.

Therefore, Table 4.39 is a matrix of 33×33, listing the thirty-three provinces based on the rank of ubiquity of each of the thirty-three ethnic groups. The ethnic groups are ordered based on the number of provinces in which they are amongst the ten largest ethnic groups. Clearly, the order of the first fifteen ethnic groups in Table 4.39 is not the same as that of the fifteen largest ethnic groups in Table 4.3.

As is clearly shown in this table, the Javanese, the largest ethnic group in Indonesia, was the most ubiquitous, with an important share of the population in almost all provinces. The Javanese made up a significant community in thirty-two out of thirty-three provinces, contributing at least 1.5 per cent of the population in each of these provinces. The province of East Nusa Tenggara was the only exception, where the Javanese were not one of the ten largest ethnic groups, although the Javanese were present in East Nusa Tenggara. More importantly, the Javanese were found as the top three largest ethnic groups in twenty-five provinces, leaving only eight provinces where the Javanese ranked between the fourth and tenth largest groups.

Furthermore, the Javanese were number one in rank in eight provinces: the three adjacent home provinces (Yogyakarta, Central Java and East Java), Jakarta, South Sumatra and Lampung, East Kalimantan and even in West Papua. The Javanese ranked number two in eleven provinces: Aceh, North Sumatra, Riau, Jambi, Bengkulu, the Riau Archipelago, West Java, Bali, Central Kalimantan, South Kalimantan and Gorontalo. They were number three in six provinces: West Sumatra, Bangka-Belitung, Banten, West Kalimantan, Central Sulawesi and Papua.

In other words, the Javanese have become an important migrant ethnic group in twenty-nine provinces. They may be the first generation to live in those areas. On the other hand, the Javanese may have been in those provinces for many generations and may have adopted local cultures, even though they still identify themselves as Javanese. They may not speak Javanese or may not speak it fluently. It is thus important to find out whether they are the first generation of migrants or lifetime migrants by assessing the Javanese places of birth. This is beyond the scope of this book, but it deserves further analysis.

This ubiquity of the Javanese may dispel the perception that the Javanese are an ethnic group who are bound to their homes, with its traditional saying of *mangan ora mangan pokoke kumpul* (to eat or not to eat, the most important thing is to be together). With the group's mobility, the Javanese today may indeed see life as *kumpul ora kumul, pokoke mangan* (together or not, the most important thing is to eat)

As the second largest ethnic group in Indonesia, the Sundanese were amongst the ten largest ethnic groups in each of twenty provinces, a smaller number than the Javanese. As the second most ubiquitous ethnic group, it was only the largest three in six provinces. The Sundanese ranked number one only in their home province of West Java. They were second

Table 4.39
The Ubiquity of the Ethnic Groups: Indonesia, 2010

Rank	Ethnic Groups		Province's Code — Rank Order of Ethnic Groups																																	
			11	12	13	14	15	16	17	18	19	21	31	32	33	34	35	36	51	52	53	61	62	63	64	71	72	73	74	75	76	81	82	91	94
1	Javanese	32	2	2	3	2	2	1	2	1	3	2	1	2	1	1	1	3	2	6		3	2	2	1	4	3	5	5	2	6	7	8	1	3
2	Sundanese	20		10	7	8	8	9	6	3	8	6	3	1	2	2	6	2	8			7	6	7	8	5	2	1						5	
3	Buginese	20				6	7			6	6	7	9	1		10			9	8		6	7	3	2	5	2	1	2	5	2				8
4	Batak	18	4		2	3	5	2	9	10	10	3	5	5	4	5	9	6				8	8	9											
5	Malay	17		4	5	1	1	2	1	5	7	1	7	8	8	3		7	4			2	4												
6	Chinese	17	5	5	8	7	10		5		4	5	4	6	3	4	4	5	7			4		8		9	9								
7	Minangkabau	13	10	6	1	4	4	5		9		4	6	7	10	7		8					10			9	7	10	8						
8	Balinese	11								8						9			1	5			10	10		6				9					
9	Madurese	10				5	6				9	10	8		6	6	2		3			5	5	5	9										
10	Banjarese	8		7																		10	3	1	3										
11	Palembang	8					9	3	6	6	5	9	10	10			10	10																	
12	Butonese	5								2														10				1			1				
13	Lampung	5												9	7		10	9															7	7	
14	Dayak	5														8						1	1	4	4			2	6		9				
15	Makassarese	4																								8		2	6		9				

No.	Ethnic group																					
									2	3	9		4		9			7	6			
16	Betawi	4																7	6	3			
17	Bajao	4																	3			9	
18	Minahasa	3																		3		3	
19	Ambonese	3	1						8			9		1									
20	Acehnese	3	8											7									
21	Nias	3	10	9																			
22	Flores	3	6			8					10												
23	Gorontalo	3											3	8				1					
24	Bantenese	3	9	4				1															
25	Mandar	3					6					8				1							
26	Kerinci	2	9	3			6																
27	Ogan	2		4	7																		
28	Arab	2				5	9																
29	Sasak	2						5	1														
30	Mongondow	2											2				8						
31	Ternate	2											10									3	
32	Biak-Numfor	2																			3		3	4
33	Yapen	2									9												9	9

Note: The province codes refer to Table 4.1.
Source: Compiled by the authors from Tables 4.5 to 4.38

in the provinces of Banten, Central Java and Yogyakarta and third in the provinces of Jakarta and Lampung. The Sundanese were mostly spread out in the western part of Indonesia.

Interestingly, although the Buginese were only the eighth largest group at the national level, they contributed a significant portion in twenty provinces, the same number as the Sundanese. The Buginese were the third most ubiquitous ethnic group. These twenty provinces are spread out from the west in the province of Jambi to the east in the province of Papua — perhaps reflecting one of their famous traits as *perantau*.[4] Like the Sundanese, the Buginese were number one only in their home province, South Sulawesi. The Buginese were the second in four provinces (East Kalimantan, Central Sulawesi, West Sulawesi and Southeast Sulawesi) and the third only in South Kalimantan.

Coming in fourth at the national level, the Batak contributed importantly in eighteen provinces. They were the fourth most ubiquitous ethnic group, being amongst the first three in three provinces on the island of Sumatra and one province on the island of Java. They were only number one in their home province of North Sumatra.

Unlike the Buginese, the Malay ranked third at the national level and were one of the ten largest ethnic groups in seventeen provinces. They were the fifth most ubiquitous ethnic group, found in seventeen provinces. These provinces are located in the western islands, namely Sumatra, Java and Kalimantan. The Malay were amongst the largest three in seven provinces and number one in four provinces (Riau, the Riau Archipelago, Jambi and Bengkulu).

The Chinese ranked fifteenth at the national level and accounted for one of the ten largest ethnic groups in nine provinces. However, they were found in seventeen provinces, the same number as that of the Malay. They ranked as the sixth most ubiquitous ethnic group, because, unlike the Malay, they were never at number one or two. They were ranked between three and five in nine provinces only.

The case of the Chinese was in stark contrast to that of the Sasak. The Sasak were one rank higher than the Chinese at the national level. However, the Sasak were only seen in two provinces, where they contributed significantly. These two include their home province, West Nusa Tenggara, where the Sasak were number one. The other province was Bali, the neighbouring province, where the Sasak were number five.

The Sasak were one of the nine least ubiquitous ethnic groups in our list, each of them found in only two provinces. The eight other ethnic groups were the Kerinci, Ogan, Arabs, Mongondow, Ternate, Biak-Numfor and Yapen. The Arabs was another ethnic group with "foreign origins" that was also ubiquitous, but they were one of the ten largest ethnic groups in only two provinces: number five in the province of Central Java and number nine in the province of East Java.

Although the Minangkabau are known for their *merantau,* or wandering tradition, they were only found in thirteen provinces, located either on the island of Sumatra itself or on the nearby island of Java. They were only the seventh most ubiquitous ethnic group and were the largest ethnic group in their home province of West Sumatra. They ranked fourth largest in the nearby provinces of Jambi, Riau and the Riau Archipelago and came fifth in the other nearby province of South Sumatra. The Minangkabau were one of the ten largest groups in all provinces on the island of Java, except for East Java.

The Dayak featured significantly in five provinces. Four of these were in their home provinces, all four provinces being in Kalimantan. Beyond the island of Kalimantan, the Dayak ranked eighth in the province of Yogyakarta.

The Palembang, Butonese, Lampung and Makassarese were not amongst the fifteen largest ethnic groups in Indonesia but were found to be ubiquitous in Indonesia. The Palembang, an ethnic group originating in the province of South Sumatra, were found in eight provinces, where they were one of the ten largest ethnic groups, although mostly amongst the five smallest ones. The Palembang were only the third largest ethnic group in their own home province, South Sumatra, after the Javanese and Malay. They were the fifth largest ethnic group in the province of Bangka-Belitung, which used to be part of the province of South Sumatra. Overall, they were the eleventh most ubiquitous ethnic group.

The Butonese, the twelfth most ubiquitous ethnic group, is an ethnic group originating in Southeast Sulawesi. They were found in five provinces, mostly in eastern Indonesia. They were number one in Southeast Sulawesi and Maluku. The Makassarese, originating in South Sulawesi, were found in four provinces. They were never ranked as number one. Their highest rank was number two in South Sulawesi, their home province.

The Lampung can be seen in five provinces but, as with the Palembang and Butonese, they were not number one in any province, even in their own home province, bordering South Sumatra. They ranked as the thirteenth most ubiquitous ethnic group, were number two in the province of Lampung and were found in four provinces on the island of Java. They ranked only number seven in Central Java, number nine in West Java and Banten and number ten in East Java.

On the other hand, the Betawi, Bantenese and Acehnese were amongst the fifteen largest ethnic groups but they numbered among the ten largest groups in fewer than five but more than two provinces. The Betawi belonged to the top ten in only four provinces but were never ranked number one; the Acehnese were the ten largest in three provinces, being the number one in their home province; the Bantenese were ranked as the tenth largest in three provinces.

It is interesting to note that the Flores people were originally from East Nusa Tenggara, yet they were not one of the ten largest ethnic groups in their home province. Instead, they were in the ten largest ethnic groups in the provinces of the Riau Archipelago, Bali and Central Kalimantan.

In short, the Javanese are the most ubiquitous ethnic group, as they are to be found in thirty-two out of the thirty-three provinces. This is in large contrast to the least ubiquitous group, the Yapen, who can only be found in two provinces and ranked only number nine in both of these provinces.

Notes

1. See discussions in Chapter 2 for the types of questionnaires.
2. See Suryadinata, Arifin and Ananta (2003).
3. See Chapter 3 under "Foreign origins" for a discussion on Timor-Leste.
4. See the discussion on the Minangkabau in the section "Almost heterogeneous provinces" in this chapter.

5

THE FIFTEEN LARGEST ETHNIC GROUPS: Age-Sex Structure and Geographical Distribution

This chapter elaborates on the various ethnic group populations, who can be seen as both consumers and producers of development. Specifically, the chapter examines the age-sex and geographical distribution of these ethnic groups. These data are especially useful for marketing and for both commercial and non-commercial purposes. In democratizing Indonesia, this knowledge is also very important for analysing electoral behaviour and understanding geopolitics.

In Chapter 4, we showed how we have classified 145 ethnic groups as belonging either to the ten largest, the fifteen largest or the twenty-five largest ethnic groups in the various provinces. However, it is beyond the scope of this chapter to discuss all of these groups in detail. Instead, we focus here on the age-sex structure (often called the population pyramid) and the geographical distribution of the fifteen largest ethnic groups in Indonesia in 2010.

LIFE-CYCLE APPROACH

Following a life-cycle approach, we disaggregate the population into different stages, each with a different impact on society and the economy. In this book, we classify a population into five age groups: infants and toddlers (0–4), children (5–14), youths (15–24), prime-working-age adults (25–59) and older persons (60 years and above).

Infants and toddlers (0–4) are highly physically and financially dependent and potential recipients of health services in their early years. They need caregivers to support them. Children (5–14) are also potential 'customers', as they are financially dependent on adults. At these ages, they cost their parents most in terms of their education. Altogether, the population aged 0–14 potentially burdens the economy with spending on health and education. At the same time, this expenditure can also be seen as investment in human capital for the nation.

Next to the dependent infants, toddlers and children are the youths (15–24). This group can be costly if the parents have higher aspirations to provide their children with tertiary education (until age 24). Therefore, youths may be added to the group of dependants (infants, toddlers and young children). In addition, youths are in transition to adulthood, ranging from entering the labour market, searching for a partner, starting a career and building a family. The youth bulge, often associated with negative things such as crime, is defined when the percentage of youths exceeds 20 per cent.

The top part of the population pyramid is the group of older persons, aged 60 years and above. They may have stopped working and may depend on others for their consumption needs, such as health care and social support. This group may also need more care if they can no longer care for themselves. On the other hand, if the older persons can become active, productive and healthy, they can be an untapped asset. They can also be the potential actors in politics as well as the custodians of cultural heritage. From this perspective, intergenerational relations should be cultivated so as to help prepare for the less active years.

The last age group segment are the prime-working-age adults, aged 25–59. In Indonesia, the working-age population covers all people of 15 years old and above, including older persons and youths. The working-age population are those who are supposed to have the ability to work and to contribute to the economy. Because youths are still often relying on their parents at this stage of their lives and persons over 60 years old may have stopped working, the group aged 25–59 can be termed the "prime-working-age population".

This group has the capacity to produce goods and services for themselves and their dependents. The burden of supporting others can be reduced if the older persons remain healthy, independent and active and if fertility is kept relatively low.[1]

Furthermore, the prime-working-age population can be divided into three groups: 25–34, 35–49 and 50–59. The young prime-working-age population (25–34) consists of people who are mostly in their early careers, are struggling to climb the ladder and are just starting to form a family, thus likely to be preoccupied with young children. Therefore, they may not have sufficient savings.

The mature prime-working-age population (35–49) covers those who may earn and save more to finance their children and invest in housing. The pre-elderly prime-working-age population (50–59) are those who are likely to be at the peak of their career and earning the highest income because of their work experience. They may save more compared to those aged 25–49. At the same time, this group may consume more if they become unhealthy.

Finally, as an ageing population has become one of three mega-demographic trends in Indonesia,[2] we have adopted the classification of this ageing population posed by Arifin and Ananta (2009) to describe the changing age structure in each ethnic group in Indonesia. This classification uses percentage of older persons to total population as the criteria. A population is considered *very young* when the percentage is below 6 per cent, *youthful* between 6 per cent and 8 per cent, *transitional* between 8 per cent and 12 per cent and *old* when above 12 per cent. Arifin and Ananta (2014) added another group, the *super-old*, for when the percentage is higher than 20 per cent.

JAVANESE

Transitional Population

Figure 5.1 shows the overall age-sex structure of the Javanese population, which forms a constrictive pyramid. The base, showing the youngest age group of 0–4, was slightly smaller than those in ages 5–9 and 10–14. This may indicate a relatively low fertility rate amongst the Javanese. Indeed, Ananta, Arifin and Bakhtiar (2005) found that the Javanese population

Figure 5.1
Population Age-Sex Structure: Javanese, 2010

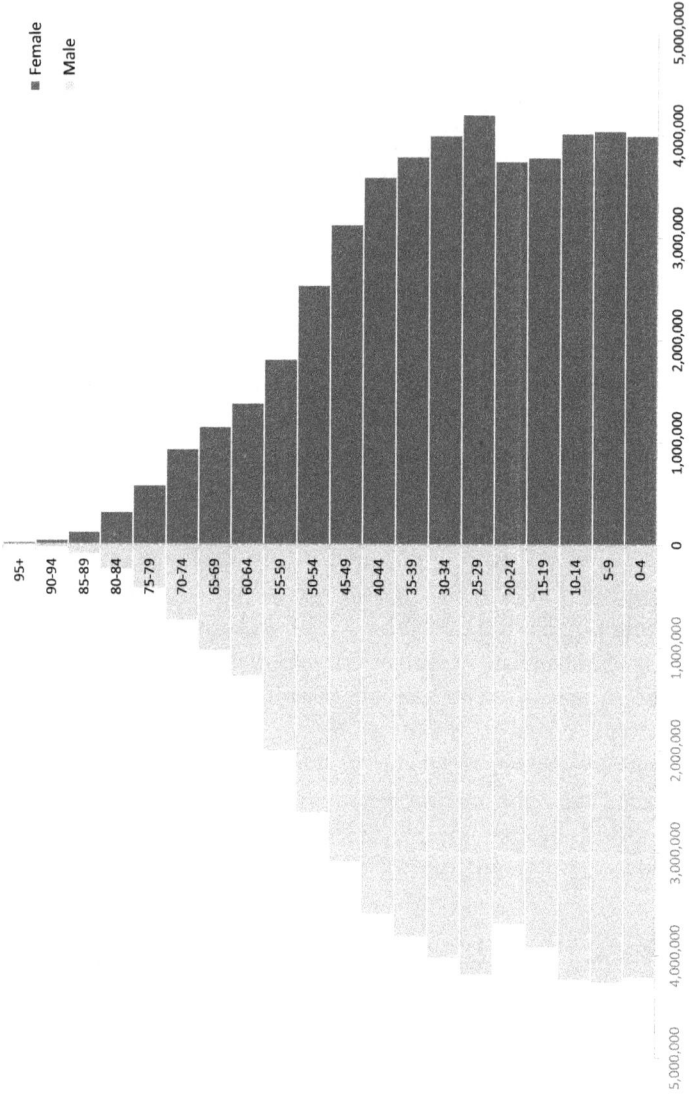

Source: Drawn from Table 5.1.

already had a low fertility rate, even below the replacement level. The TFR (total fertility rate) was 1.96 during 2000–2005. This means that if the fertility rate will remain below replacement until 2040, the absolute number of Javanese will eventually decline. Indeed, the Javanese have one of the lowest fertility rates in Indonesia.

With a population of 95 million in 2010, the Javanese formed the largest ethnic group in Indonesia, with 8.67 per cent being infants and toddlers and 17.48 per cent young children. In other words, about a quarter of the Javanese population in 2010 were below 15 years old. In absolute terms, the number of Javanese below 15 years old was very large, at 24.8 million in 2010.

Moreover, Javanese youths accounted for 15.98 per cent. As Javanese couples have one of the lowest fertility rates in Indonesia, they may also have higher aspirations for their children and are likely to commit to financing their children until tertiary education. Therefore, Javanese youth may still be dependent on their parents. Along with the younger groups, 42.13 per cent of the Javanese population may be still dependent on the prime-working-age population, although the youths are likely to have different needs from the children under 15 years old.

Nevertheless, the prime-working-age population of Javanese only accounted for almost a half (48.96 per cent) of the total Javanese population, although this was larger than the dependent population under 25 years old. This prime-working-age population may also be shouldering the burden of supporting older persons in their families.

In terms of its older persons, the Javanese are already considered a transitional population. The Javanese older persons accounted for 8.91 per cent of the total Javanese, or 8.5 million Javanese older persons. As discussed later in this chapter, the Javanese together with the Madurese, Balinese and Chinese are four ethnic groups that are at the transitional stage of an ageing population. These groups have completed their first demographic transition and already have below the replacement level of fertility.

As Indonesians are living longer, so the Javanese are also living longer and had the highest live expectancy at birth as compared to the Sundanese, Malay, Batak and Madurese. Ananta, Arifin and Bakhtiar (2005) calculated that life expectancy at birth was already 69.3 for Javanese females and 63.2 for Javanese males in 1995–2000. However, many Javanese outlived this life expectancy, as the number of Javanese aged 95 and above was relatively large in 2010 (see Table 5.1). They numbered 42,300, which was even larger than the total population of some districts in Papua, such as Intan Jaya (40,490) and Central Mamberamo (39,537).

Table 5.1 also shows the gender composition of the Javanese, comparing the number of male and female Javanese within each age group. We use sex ratio to measure an excess in the male or female population. A ratio of 1 indicates that the numbers of males and females are the same. A ratio of above 1 means an excess of males and a ratio of less than 1 shows an excess of females.

Overall, there was an excess of male over female Javanese. However, the picture was different for Javanese older persons. There were many more female than male Javanese older persons, with a sex ratio of 0.85.

Table 5.1
Number and Percentage of Javanese Population by Age and Sex: Indonesia, 2010

Age Group	Males	Females	Total	Per cent	Sex Ratio
0–4	4,226,175	3,995,830	8,222,005	8.67	1.058
5–9	4,271,738	4,042,789	8,314,527	8.77	1.057
10–14	4,245,465	4,015,973	8,261,438	8.71	1.057
15–19	3,926,898	3,784,573	7,711,471	8.13	1.038
20–24	3,700,759	3,743,423	7,444,182	7.85	0.989
25–29	4,192,427	4,203,126	8,395,553	8.85	0.997
30–34	4,036,407	3,995,091	8,031,498	8.47	1.010
35–39	3,829,628	3,789,766	7,619,394	8.03	1.011
40–44	3,604,621	3,587,786	7,192,407	7.58	1.005
45–49	3,093,376	3,124,369	6,217,745	6.56	0.990
50–54	2,623,259	2,531,860	5,155,119	5.44	1.036
55–59	2,012,345	1,812,009	3,824,354	4.03	1.111
60–64	1,287,839	1,378,312	2,666,151	2.81	0.934
65–69	1,033,854	1,152,612	2,186,466	2.31	0.897
70–74	739,634	937,571	1,677,205	1.77	0.789
75–79	433,794	580,454	1,014,248	1.07	0.747
80–84	245,194	321,682	566,876	0.60	0.762
85–89	96,330	126,551	222,881	0.23	0.761
90–94	30,105	47,073	77,178	0.08	0.640
95+	14,799	27,576	42,375	0.04	0.537
Total	47,644,647	47,198,426	94,843,073	100.00	1.009

Source: Calculated by the authors, based on tabulations provided by the BPS.

Furthermore, the sex ratio goes lower as we look at the much older persons. The sex ratio declined from 0.93 between ages 60–64, to 0.54 at ages 95 years and above, implying a high number of female older persons of advanced age. The highest sex ratio was seen at ages 55–59. With a sex ratio at 1.11, there were 111 Javanese males aged 55–59 to 100 Javanese females of the same age.

Geographical Distribution

The following discussion shows how the Javanese were spreading out all over the other provinces. Most of the Javanese (68.06 per cent or 64.55 million) lived in their own home provinces: with 33.28 per cent living in Central Java, 31.17 per cent in East Java and 3.51 per cent in Yogyakarta. Seen from the concentration level (relative number of the total population) in each province, Yogyakarta was exclusively Javanese, where the Javanese formed 96.53 per cent. Central Java was also exclusively Javanese, with the Javanese forming an even larger percentage, 97.72 per cent. These regions are in contrast to East Java, where the Javanese concentration was only 79.72 per cent, because of the presence of another, relatively large, local ethnic group — the Madurese (for a more detailed discussion, see Chapter 4).

As seen in Table 5.2, the Javanese populations living in the provinces of West Java, Jakarta and Banten were quite large (5.7 million, 3.4 million and 1.6 million, respectively). Outside the island of Java, Javanese populations over more than one million were found in Lampung, North Sumatra, South Sumatra, Riau and East Kalimantan.

The concentration of Javanese in each province was also relatively high. In addition to the three home provinces, a high concentration of the Javanese was found in Lampung, in the southern part of the island of Sumatra. Lampung used to be the most important destination of the Transmigration programme since its inception ("transmigration" was called "colonization" during the Dutch colonial period in 1905). The transmigration programme aimed to develop sparsely populated regions of Indonesia by bringing people in from the densely populated islands of Java and Bali. The large number of Javanese who participated in this programme may explain the relatively high concentration of Javanese in Lampung. Later on, the transmigration programme expanded to send people to other regions on the island of Sumatra and also to Kalimantan, Sulawesi and Papua. The programme also recruited people from Nusa Tenggara. It should be noted

Table 5.2
Number, Distribution and Concentration of Javanese by Province: Indonesia, 2010

Province	Males	Females	Total	Sex Ratio	Distribution	Concentration
Aceh	202,832	197,144	399,976	1.029	0.42	8.94
North Sumatra	2,159,926	2,158,830	4,318,756	1.001	4.55	33.40
West Sumatra	115,654	101,430	217,084	1.140	0.23	4.49
Riau	846,325	761,858	1,608,183	1.111	1.70	29.20
Jambi	469,257	423,876	893,133	1.107	0.94	29.09
South Sumatra	1,062,149	975,362	2,037,511	1.089	2.15	27.41
Bengkulu	204,382	182,893	387,275	1.117	0.41	22.64
Lampung	2,499,577	2,357,228	4,856,805	1.060	5.12	64.06
Bangka-Belitung	57,501	42,379	99,880	1.357	0.11	8.19
Riau Archipelago	213,667	196,761	410,428	1.086	0.43	24.55
Jakarta	1,742,759	1,709,409	3,452,168	1.020	3.64	36.16
West Java	2,965,309	2,744,241	5,709,550	1.081	6.02	13.28
Central Java	15,665,118	15,895,252	31,560,370	0.986	33.28	97.72
Yogyakarta	1,638,007	1,693,296	3,331,303	0.967	3.51	96.53
East Java	14,669,780	14,990,795	29,660,575	0.979	31.27	79.72

Banten	864,714	792,568	1,657,282	1.091	1.75	15.63
Bali	197,576	174,474	372,050	1.132	0.39	9.59
West Nusa Tenggara	42,037	36,784	78,821	1.143	0.08	1.76
East Nusa Tenggara	27,014	26,997	54,011	1.001	0.06	1.16
West Kalimantan	231,280	195,958	427,238	1.180	0.45	9.74
Central Kalimantan	264,750	213,643	478,393	1.239	0.50	21.67
South Kalimantan	283,883	240,393	524,276	1.181	0.55	14.51
East Kalimantan	568,815	500,790	1,069,605	1.136	1.13	30.24
North Sulawesi	38,864	32,044	70,908	1.213	0.07	3.13
Central Sulawesi	115,349	105,617	220,966	1.092	0.23	8.42
South Sulawesi	120,852	108,159	229,011	1.117	0.24	2.86
Southeast Sulawesi	82,786	76,366	159,152	1.084	0.17	7.14
Gorontalo	18,599	16,679	35,278	1.115	0.04	3.39
West Sulawesi	29,340	27,615	56,955	1.062	0.06	4.92
Maluku	41,165	38,142	79,307	1.079	0.08	5.19
North Maluku	23,302	19,400	42,702	1.201	0.05	4.12
West Papua	58,695	52,486	111,181	1.118	0.12	14.76
Papua	123,383	109,557	232,940	1.126	0.25	8.38
Indonesia	47,644,647	47,198,426	94,843,073	1.009	100.00	40.06

Source: Calculated by the authors, based on tabulations provided by the BPS.

that Lampung changed its status as a destination of transmigration into an origin of transmigration in 2007, with West Kalimantan and Central Kalimantan as the planned areas of destinations.[3]

The next highest concentration of the Javanese was in the province of Jakarta, Indonesia's capital city, on the island of Java. This may be because of spontaneous migration by the Javanese, partly due to the relatively easy transportation to Jakarta from the three home provinces. The custom of *mudik* (returning home from big cities to home towns in small cities and rural areas) amongst the Javanese, particularly during the end of Ramadhan, the Islamic fasting month, has continued. Many Javanese in Jakarta who go for *mudik* may return to Jakarta, bringing more Javanese relatives and acquaintants, thus increasing the number of Javanese in Jakarta (Sairin 2010).

A relatively high concentration of Javanese was also seen in North Sumatra (33.40 per cent), East Kalimantan (30.24 per cent), Riau (29.20 per cent), Jambi (29.09 per cent), South Sumatra (27.41 per cent) and Bengkulu (22.64 per cent). These provinces also used to be destinations for the transmigration programme.

The smallest concentration of Javanese (1.16 per cent) was in East Nusa Tenggara, followed by West Nusa Tenggara (1.76 per cent). However, the Javanese numbered 54,000 and 78,800 in these two provinces, respectively. These numbers were larger than the Javanese living in Gorontalo and North Maluku. On the other hand, the concentration of Javanese was relatively high in West Papua (14.76 per cent) and Papua (8.38 per cent). These Javanese may have come here through the transmigration programme or they may have come to West Papua and Papua on their own.

In essence, the Javanese presence can be seen in all of Indonesia's provinces. This further supports the finding that the Javanese were the most ubiquitous ethnic group (see Chapter 4) as they have been seen to be willing to migrate to capture any opportunities, anywhere.

SUNDANESE

Youthful Population

In 2010, there were 36.7 million Sundanese in Indonesia. The age structure of the population of Sundanese is presented in Figure 5.2 and Table 5.3. At a glance, the age structure of the Sundanese population may look the same as that of the Javanese. However, the Sundanese had a younger

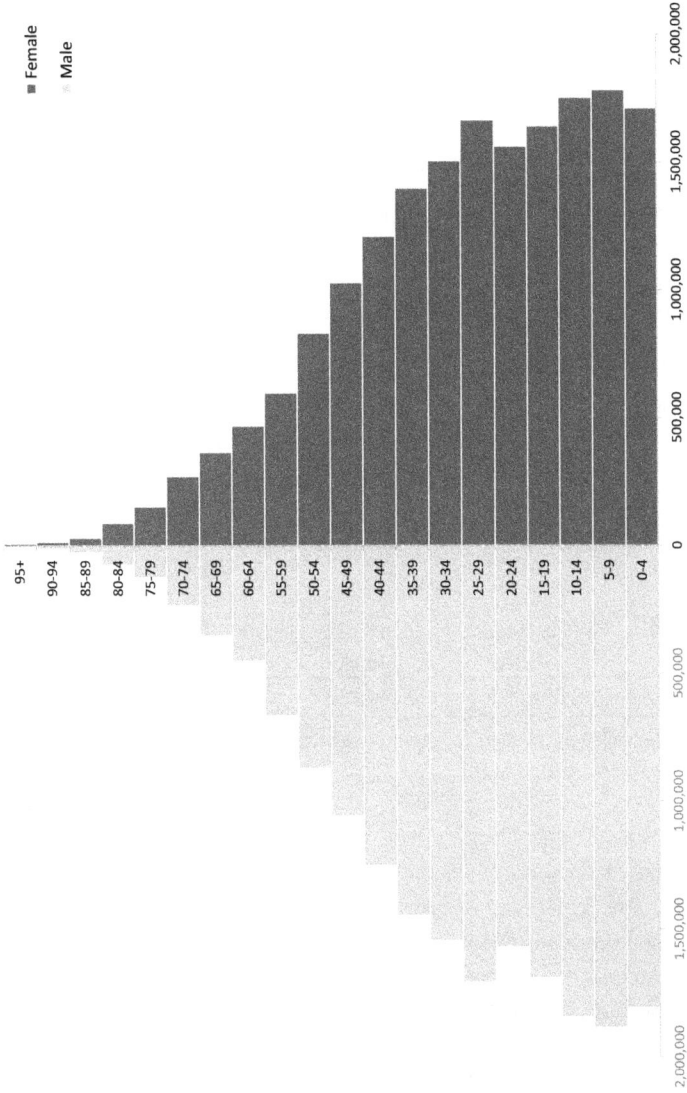

Figure 5.2
Population Age-Sex Structure: Sundanese, 2010

Source: Drawn from Table 5.3.

Table 5.3
Number and Percentage of Sundanese Population by
Age and Sex: Indonesia, 2010

Age Group	Males	Females	Total	Per cent	Sex Ratio
0–4	1,805,861	1,710,922	3,516,783	9.58	1.055
5–9	1,884,417	1,783,040	3,667,457	9.99	1.057
10–14	1,842,242	1,753,837	3,596,079	9.80	1.050
15–19	1,691,034	1,640,422	3,331,456	9.08	1.031
20–24	1,569,661	1,562,187	3,131,848	8.53	1.005
25–29	1,707,763	1,664,713	3,372,476	9.19	1.026
30–34	1,544,495	1,505,268	3,049,763	8.31	1.026
35–39	1,445,155	1,398,443	2,843,598	7.75	1.033
40–44	1,249,813	1,211,142	2,460,955	6.70	1.032
45–49	1,057,703	1,029,398	2,087,101	5.69	1.027
50–54	870,023	832,016	1,702,039	4.64	1.046
55–59	663,858	599,496	1,263,354	3.44	1.107
60–64	448,563	468,461	917,024	2.50	0.958
65–69	350,529	366,400	716,929	1.95	0.957
70–74	231,743	272,043	503,786	1.37	0.852
75–79	122,164	153,637	275,801	0.75	0.795
80–84	74,766	90,717	165,483	0.45	0.824
85–89	26,323	32,496	58,819	0.16	0.810
90–94	10,965	16,422	27,387	0.07	0.668
95+	6,179	10,627	16,806	0.05	0.581
Total	18,603,257	18,101,687	36,704,944	100.00	1.028

Source: Calculated by the authors, based on tabulations provided by the BPS.

population. The portion of infants and toddlers was 9.58 per cent, larger than that of the Javanese, indicating that Sundanese fertility was higher. Indeed, the TFR of the Sundanese was 2.55 during 2000–2005, higher than the Javanese (Ananta, Arifin and Bakhtiar 2008). It was still above the replacement level rate. Unlike the Javanese, who face the prospect of depopulation, the number of Sundanese will keep increasing if the fertility remains at the current rate.

On the other hand, the percentage of infants and toddlers was smaller than the percentages of children aged 5–9 and 10–14 (see Table 5.3). This phenomenon indicates that Sundanese fertility may have been declining before 2010.

Sundanese youths accounted for 17.61 per cent, which was higher than Javanese in the same age group. If Sundanese parents are committed to having their children pursue tertiary education, then the Sundanese dependent population (those under 25 years old) will account for 46.98 per cent, close to half the total Sundanese population, which is larger than Javanese dependants.

However, the percentage of the Sundanese prime-working-age population was only 45.72 per cent, lower than that of the Javanese. Therefore, potentially, the Sundanese faced a heavier burden than the Javanese in taking care of their young under 25 years old.

The Sundanese older persons formed a smaller percentage, 7.30 per cent, than that of the Javanese. In terms of older persons, the Sundanese were still younger than the Javanese, which may mean that the Sundanese had fewer older persons to take care of, compared to the Javanese. Overall, the burden of dependants was higher amongst the Sundanese than the Javanese.

With regard to sex composition, the Sundanese had three similarities to the Javanese population. First, the Sundanese had an excess of males over females. However, the sex ratio of the Sundanese (1.03) was higher than that of the Javanese (1.01), implying a higher excess of males amongst the Sundanese. Second, the sex ratio was below 1 for older persons, an excess of females. The third similarity was that the largest excess of males was also seen with those aged 55–59.

Geographical Distribution

The province of West Java is the home province of the Sundanese, with 84.16 per cent of all Sundanese living in this province. This province shares its border with the Javanese home province of Central Java in the east, Jakarta, a cosmopolitan and capital city of Indonesia in the north and west and Banten in the west. The province of Banten used to be part of the province of West Java. They separated in year 2000 because the people of Banten believed that Bantenese were not the same as Sundanese. A total of 6.55 per cent of all Sundanese were living in Banten. Jakarta was another province where the Sundanese reached above a population of one million. The number of Sundanese living in Central Java was much lower than for the capital city (Table 5.4).

Unlike the Javanese, no significant numbers of Sundanese could be found residing in the provinces of Gorontalo or West Sulawesi, compared to the total population of Sundanese in Indonesia. These numbers were in contrast to the significant number of Sundanese in Papua, who perhaps moved and lived there during the former transmigration programme. Some

Table 5.4
Number, Distribution and Concentration of Sundanese by Province: Indonesia, 2010

Province	Males	Females	Total	Sex Ratio	Distribution	Concentration
Aceh	5,896	4,976	10,872	1.185	0.03	0.24
North Sumatra	18,054	17,535	35,589	1.030	0.10	0.28
West Sumatra	8,865	7,075	15,940	1.253	0.04	0.33
Riau	40,653	37,323	77,976	1.089	0.21	1.42
Jambi	41,196	38,016	79,212	1.084	0.22	2.58
South Sumatra	85,384	77,512	162,896	1.102	0.44	2.19
Bengkulu	27,126	25,393	52,519	1.068	0.14	3.07
Lampung	376,338	352,377	728,715	1.068	1.99	9.61
Bangka-Belitung	10,449	8,517	18,966	1.227	0.05	1.56
Riau Archipelago	25,266	24,173	49,439	1.045	0.13	2.96
Jakarta	704,955	690,285	1,395,240	1.021	3.80	14.61
West Java	15,621,893	15,268,609	30,890,502	1.023	84.16	71.87
Central Java	226,262	225,128	451,390	1.005	1.23	1.40
Yogyakarta	13,020	10,749	23,769	1.211	0.06	0.69
East Java	25,753	21,900	47,653	1.176	0.13	0.13

Banten	1,230,751	1,171,622	2,402,373	1.050	6.55	22.66
Bali	6,508	5,202	11,710	1.251	0.03	0.30
West Nusa Tenggara	2,361	2,235	4,596	1.056	0.01	0.10
East Nusa Tenggara	1,013	975	1,988	1.039	0.01	0.04
West Kalimantan	26,903	22,627	49,530	1.189	0.13	1.13
Central Kalimantan	15,651	12,929	28,580	1.211	0.08	1.29
South Kalimantan	13,462	11,130	24,592	1.210	0.07	0.68
East Kalimantan	29,946	25,713	55,659	1.165	0.15	1.57
North Sulawesi	1,721	1,197	2,918	1.438	0.01	0.13
Central Sulawesi	8,162	7,005	15,167	1.165	0.04	0.58
South Sulawesi	5,836	5,044	10,880	1.157	0.03	0.14
Southeast Sulawesi	13,056	12,357	25,413	1.057	0.07	1.14
Gorontalo	738	562	1,300	1.313	0.00	0.13
West Sulawesi	963	837	1,800	1.151	0.00	0.16
Maluku	2,303	2,172	4,475	1.060	0.01	0.29
North Maluku	1,473	1,121	2,594	1.314	0.01	0.25
West Papua	4,027	3,167	7,194	1.272	0.02	0.95
Papua	7,273	6,224	13,497	1.169	0.04	0.49
Indonesia	18,603,257	18,101,687	36,704,944	1.028	100.00	15.51

Source: Calculated by the authors, based on tabulations provided by the BPS.

may have migrated there quite recently, but there is insufficient information on the recent migration of the Sundanese to this region.

Small Sundanese communities also existed in many other provinces, such as in the provinces of West Nusa Tenggara, East Nusa Tenggara, North Sulawesi, Maluku and North Maluku. All of these provinces are in Eastern Indonesia. In sum, the Sundanese can be found in all provinces, although the numbers in some were very small.

As shown in Table 5.4, the concentration of Sundanese in each province varies, from the lowest concentration at 0.13 per cent in Gorontalo to the highest at 71.87 per cent in West Java, their home province. Because of the migration of other ethnic groups from other provinces to West Java, this province is not an exclusively Sundanese province. A more detailed ethnic composition for West Java can be found in Chapter 4. In other provinces, the concentration of Sundanese, unlike the Javanese, was small. The next highest province was only 22.66 per cent, in the province of Banten, which borders West Java. The third highest was Jakarta (14.61 per cent), also bordering West Java. The fourth was Lampung (9.61 per cent), across the Sunda Strait on the island of Sumatra.

MALAY

Very Young Population

The Malay numbered 8.75 million in 2010. The population pyramid of Malay presented in Figure 5.3 is different from that of the Javanese and Sundanese. The Malay had an even younger population, even compared to the Sundanese. The base of the pyramid, particularly those aged 0–4, was 10.81 per cent, larger than those amongst the Javanese and Sundanese. Indeed, Ananta, Arifin and Bakhtiar (2005) estimated that the fertility rate of the Malay was relatively high, with TFR = 2.86 during 2000–2005. It was also still above the replacement level. If the fertility rate is maintained, the Malay will continue to increase in number.

Youths contributed 18.7 per cent towards the Malay population. Therefore, if Malay parents aim for their children to pursue tertiary education, the young dependent groups will form 50.88 per cent of the total Malay population, larger than the young Javanese and Sundanese. This young dependent population is larger than the prime-working-age population, which only constituted 44.28 per cent.

Figure 5.3
Population Age-Sex Structure: Malay, 2010

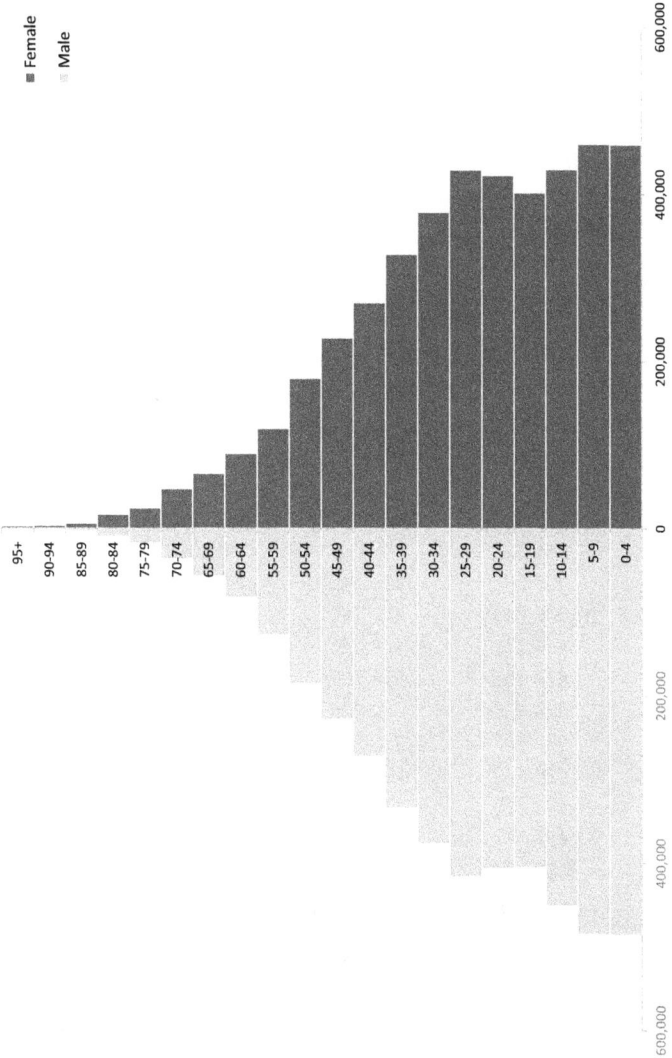

Source: Drawn from Table 5.5.

Moreover, the Malay population was still much younger than the youthful Sundanese population. Older persons only accounted for 5.34 per cent, lower than for the Javanese and Sundanese older persons. The prime-working-age population faced less burden in taking care of their older persons. Overall, the need to take care of the young and old was the highest amongst the Malay, relative to the Javanese and Sundanese.

The overall sex ratio of the Malay population was similar to the Javanese. For those below 60, the sex ratios were above 1, meaning that there were more males than females. However, Malay females aged 20–34 (Table 5.5), a marriageable age group, outnumbered their male counterparts. The sex ratio of older persons was 0.82, lower than the Javanese and Sundanese. In other words, there were very many more older females amongst the Malay than amongst the Javanese and Sundanese.

Table 5.5
Number and Percentage of Malay Population by Age and Sex: Indonesia, 2010

Age Group	Males	Females	Total	Per cent	Sex Ratio
0–4	486,710	459,786	946,496	10.81	1.059
5–9	485,389	460,651	946,040	10.81	1.054
10–14	451,031	430,067	881,098	10.07	1.049
15–19	405,591	402,145	807,736	9.23	1.009
20–24	406,503	422,740	829,243	9.47	0.962
25–29	416,346	429,451	845,797	9.66	0.969
30–34	377,108	378,882	755,990	8.64	0.995
35–39	334,626	327,978	662,604	7.57	1.020
40–44	272,677	270,054	542,731	6.20	1.010
45–49	228,142	228,311	456,453	5.21	0.999
50–54	185,490	179,679	365,169	4.17	1.032
55–59	127,787	119,496	247,283	2.82	1.069
60–64	82,534	89,524	172,058	1.97	0.922
65–69	57,558	65,747	123,305	1.41	0.875
70–74	37,075	47,574	84,649	0.97	0.779
75–79	17,576	24,649	42,225	0.48	0.713
80–84	10,200	16,767	26,967	0.31	0.608
85–89	3,690	6,202	9,892	0.11	0.595
90–94	1,482	3,250	4,732	0.05	0.456
95+	928	2,395	3,323	0.04	0.387
Total	4,388,443	4,365,348	8,753,791	100.00	1.005

Source: Calculated by the authors, based on tabulations provided by the BPS.

Geographical Distribution

Compared to the Javanese and Sundanese, the Malay were more evenly distributed across provinces, especially on the island of Sumatra, where 76.25 per cent of the Malay resided. The largest Malay population resided in the province of Riau, but they only contributed 20.94 per cent to the total Malay population. Amongst the Malay, 17.45 per cent lived in South Sumatra, 14.15 per cent in Jambi and smaller percentages in North Sumatra, Bengkulu and the Riau Archipelago. Outside the island of Sumatra, a significant Malay population (16.95 per cent or 1.5 million) lived in West Kalimantan, where they lived alongside the local Dayak groups. West Kalimantan is in the east of the island of Borneo, separated from Sumatra by the Karimata Strait. The numbers of Malay in other provinces in Kalimantan were very small. On the island of Java, the largest Malay population was found in West Java, numbering just 211,000 people (see Table 5.6).

Unlike the Javanese and Sundanese, there were no very high concentrations of Malay in any province. The highest concentration was in the province of Jambi, but that was only 40.35 per cent, followed by Riau (33.28 per cent), Bengkulu (32.12 per cent), the Riau Archipelago (30.23 per cent) and South Sumatra (20.54 per cent). In each of these provinces, the Malay were the largest ethnic group, followed by the Javanese. An exception was in South Sumatra, where the Javanese were the largest ethnic group, followed by the Malay. For information on other residents of these provinces besides the Malay, see the respective tables presented in Chapter 4.

Outside the island of Sumatra, it was only in West Kalimantan where the Malay contributed significantly (33.84 per cent) to the province's population. Yet, the Malay can be found in all provinces, with the lowest concentration at 0.01 per cent in West Sulawesi, or about 167 persons.

BATAK

Very Young Population

The Batak originated in the province of North Sumatra, bordering the province of Aceh in the north and the provinces of West Sumatra and Riau in the south. The province of Aceh is the home province for the Acehnese, West Sumatra for the Minangkabau, and Riau one of the home provinces of the Malay.

Table 5.6
Number, Distribution and Concentration of Malay by Province: Indonesia, 2010

Province	Males	Females	Total	Sex Ratio	Distribution	Concentration
Aceh	11,236	11,422	22,658	0.984	0.26	0.51
North Sumatra	383,443	389,752	773,195	0.984	8.83	5.98
West Sumatra	21,527	20,901	42,428	1.030	0.48	0.88
Riau	919,713	913,175	1,832,888	1.007	20.94	33.28
Jambi	620,048	618,497	1,238,545	1.003	14.15	40.35
South Sumatra	769,478	757,717	1,527,195	1.016	17.45	20.54
Bengkulu	275,961	273,513	549,474	1.009	6.28	32.12
Lampung	81,033	79,997	161,030	1.013	1.84	2.12
Bangka-Belitung	11,828	10,092	21,920	1.172	0.25	1.80
Riau Archipelago	255,819	249,572	505,391	1.025	5.77	30.23
Jakarta	57,218	53,907	111,125	1.061	1.27	1.16
West Java	110,349	101,071	211,420	1.092	2.42	0.49
Central Java	5,424	5,213	10,637	1.040	0.12	0.03
Yogyakarta	9,463	7,322	16,785	1.292	0.19	0.49
East Java	6,732	6,406	13,138	1.051	0.15	0.04

Banten	49,921	48,253	98,174	1.035	1.12	0.93
Bali	11,706	11,415	23,121	1.025	0.26	0.60
West Nusa Tenggara	671	872	1,543	0.769	0.02	0.03
East Nusa Tenggara	656	712	1,368	0.921	0.02	0.03
West Kalimantan	730,600	753,485	1,484,085	0.970	16.95	33.84
Central Kalimantan	44,639	42,709	87,348	1.045	1.00	3.96
South Kalimantan	2,282	1,732	4,014	1.318	0.05	0.11
East Kalimantan	3,845	3,179	7,024	1.209	0.08	0.20
North Sulawesi	271	226	497	1.199	0.01	0.02
Central Sulawesi	632	590	1,222	1.071	0.01	0.05
South Sulawesi	1,138	1,178	2,316	0.966	0.03	0.03
Southeast Sulawesi	360	437	797	0.824	0.01	0.04
Gorontalo	93	71	164	1.310	0.00	0.02
West Sulawesi	77	90	167	0.856	0.00	0.01
Maluku	698	557	1,255	1.253	0.01	0.08
North Maluku	146	139	285	1.050	0.00	0.03
West Papua	272	217	489	1.253	0.01	0.06
Papua	1,164	929	2,093	1.253	0.02	0.08
Indonesia	4,388,443	4,365,348	8,753,791	1.005	100.00	3.70

Source: Calculated by the authors, based on tabulations provided by the BPS.

In the 2010 population census, the Batak were grouped into six categories: Mandailing, Angkola, Toba, Dairi or Pakpak Dairi, Simalungun and Karo. From the linguistic point of view, there are three groups of languages. One group is Mandailing, Angkola and Toba, the second, Pakpak and Karo and the third is Simalungun.

Batak is one of the groups in Indonesia with the *merantau*[4] tradition. Later on in this section, this tradition of the Batak can be seen by their presence everywhere in Indonesia and not just in their home province.

As can be seen in Figure 5.4, the shape of the age-sex structure of the Batak is different from those of the three largest ethnic groups. The population structure still resembles a pyramid, with a large base and a rapidly declining number at older ages. The broadest base representing the large number of the population aged 0–4 and also the older age group of 5–9 indicates that the Batak have a much higher fertility rate than others. The percentage of infants and toddlers was about 11.34 per cent. In 2000–2005, as estimated by Ananta, Arifin and Bakhtiar (2005), the total fertility rate of the Batak was relatively high at 3.18, the highest amongst the five largest ethnic groups (the Javanese, Sundanese, Malay, Batak and Madurese).

As a result, the Batak population is not likely to decline in the next few decades. Quite the contrary, their number will continue to grow in future. In the next twenty years, the large portion of young population below 15 will move into their reproductive phase, where many of them will have families of their own. The Batak will most likely grow faster than the Javanese and Sundanese and even the Malay.

Youths contributed 18.05 per cent of the Batak population, while the prime-working-age population accounted for 42.98 per cent. As the Batak place much importance on education, tertiary education is a goal for many. Therefore, the Batak young dependent population are those under 25, constituting 51.61 per cent, more than half the Batak population. On the other hand, the prime-working-age population contributed only 42.99 per cent, much smaller than the percentage of the young dependent population. Thus, the Batak may be facing greater challenges in supporting their young ones, especially compared to the Javanese.

However, the percentage of older persons amongst the Batak was only 5.41, the lowest amongst the first four ethnic groups. The Batak population was also very young, making the younger persons those most in need of support by working-age people.

Figure 5.4
Population Age-Sex Structure: Batak, 2010

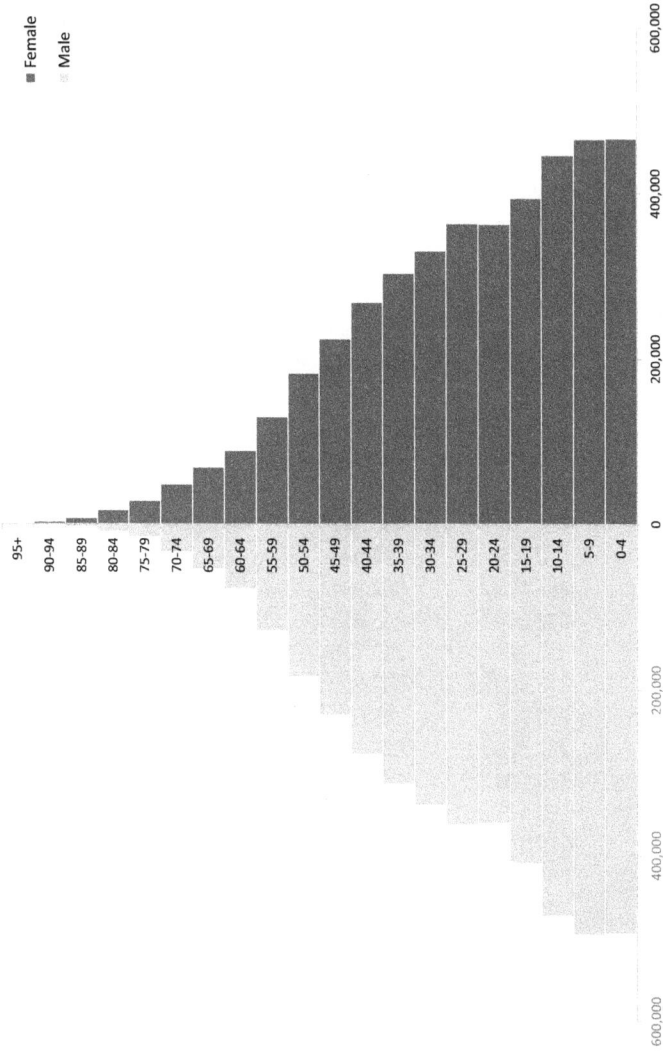

Female
Male

95+	
90-94	
85-89	
80-84	
75-79	
70-74	
65-69	
60-64	
55-59	
50-54	
45-49	
40-44	
35-39	
30-34	
25-29	
20-24	
15-19	
10-14	
5-9	
0-4	

600,000   400,000   200,000   0   200,000   400,000   600,000

Source: Drawn from Table 5.7.

With regard to sex composition, although the Batak are known to follow a patrilineal system, Table 5.7 does not show an unusual pattern of sex ratio by age group. The sex ratio of the youngest group of 0–4 was 1.06, just the same as the other ethnic groups discussed earlier, with sex ratios above 1 amongst those aged below 60, and below 1 for those aged 60 and above. However, the sex ratio for those above 60 was 0.74, the smallest amongst the four largest ethnic groups, suggesting a greater number of females amongst Batak older persons.

Table 5.8 depicts a different picture, where the Batak living in their home province even had a sex ratio below 1, meaning more females than males in North Sumatra. An excess of Batak females was also seen in the

Table 5.7
Number and Percentage of Batak Population by Age and Sex: Indonesia, 2010

Age Group	Males	Females	Total	Per cent	Sex Ratio
0–4	494,130	466,310	960,440	11.34	1.060
5–9	496,324	465,610	961,934	11.36	1.066
10–14	473,057	445,992	919,049	10.85	1.061
15–19	410,002	394,044	804,046	9.50	1.040
20–24	361,135	362,884	724,019	8.55	0.995
25–29	363,040	363,599	726,639	8.58	0.998
30–34	339,228	330,106	669,334	7.91	1.028
35–39	313,940	302,969	616,909	7.29	1.036
40–44	278,295	267,994	546,289	6.45	1.038
45–49	230,398	224,095	454,493	5.37	1.028
50–54	184,294	182,752	367,046	4.34	1.008
55–59	129,167	129,360	258,527	3.05	0.999
60–64	78,147	88,791	166,938	1.97	0.880
65–69	54,248	68,670	122,918	1.45	0.790
70–74	33,613	47,906	81,519	0.96	0.702
75–79	15,755	28,422	44,177	0.52	0.554
80–84	8,641	16,994	25,635	0.30	0.508
85–89	3,096	7,495	10,591	0.13	0.413
90–94	990	3,019	4,009	0.05	0.328
95+	574	1,883	2,457	0.03	0.305
Total	4,268,074	4,198,895	8,466,969	100.00	1.016

Source: Calculated by the authors, based on tabulations provided by the BPS.

Riau Archipelago and East Nusa Tenggara. In other provinces, there were more Batak males than females.

Geographical Distribution

The Batak living in their home province accounted for 68.33 per cent of the total Batak in the country. Some (12.54 per cent) lived in the three neighbouring provinces: Riau (8.17 per cent), West Sumatra (2.63 per cent) and Aceh (1.74 per cent). A relatively large number lived in Jakarta (3.86 per cent) and its surrounding provinces (West Java, 5.52 per cent) and Banten (1.64 per cent) on the island of Java, and also in the Riau Archipelago (2.46 per cent) (see Table 5.8).

Although the Batak originated in the province of North Sumatra, the concentration in this province was not very high, only 44.75 per cent. The second largest ethnic group in North Sumatra were the Javanese (33.40 per cent). In North Sumatra, the Batak also lived alongside the Nias group (7.05 per cent), the Malay (5.98 per cent), the Chinese (2.63 per cent) and the Minangkabau (2.58 per cent), as well as other smaller ethnic groups.

As an ethnic group with a *merantau* tradition, the concentration of Batak in their neighbouring provinces was also relatively high: Riau (12.55 per cent), West Sumatra (4.61 per cent) and Aceh (3.29 per cent). We can also include the Riau islands, to the east of Riau, not far from North Sumatra, which had 12.48 per cent. The Batak can be found in all provinces in Indonesia, although the numbers in Gorontalo and West Sulawesi were not significant compared to the total number of Batak in Indonesia.

MADURESE

Transitional Population

The Madurese ethnic group's culture is perhaps best known for its *karapan sapi*, or bull race, one of several annual traditions held throughout September and attracting visitors from Indonesia and overseas. The Madurese were the fifth largest ethnic group in 2010, originating on the small island of Madura, alongside the northeastern coast of Java. The island comprises an area approximately of 5,025 km², or 3 per cent of Java Island's area. This island is administered as part of the province of East Java, a Javanese home province.

Table 5.8
Number, Distribution and Concentration of Batak by Province: Indonesia, 2010

Province	Males	Females	Total	Sex Ratio	Distribution	Concentration
Aceh	74,367	72,928	147,295	1.020	1.74	3.29
North Sumatra	2,877,719	2,907,997	5,785,716	0.990	68.33	44.75
West Sumatra	111,140	111,409	222,549	0.998	2.63	4.61
Riau	361,796	329,603	691,399	1.098	8.17	12.55
Jambi	57,241	49,008	106,249	1.168	1.25	3.46
South Sumatra	24,958	20,751	45,709	1.203	0.54	0.61
Bengkulu	18,135	14,837	32,972	1.222	0.39	1.93
Lampung	28,007	24,304	52,311	1.152	0.62	0.69
Bangka-Belitung	5,225	4,227	9,452	1.236	0.11	0.78
Riau Archipelago	99,420	109,258	208,678	0.910	2.46	12.48
Jakarta	167,173	159,472	326,645	1.048	3.86	3.42
West Java	244,159	223,279	467,438	1.094	5.52	1.09
Central Java	13,178	11,179	24,357	1.179	0.29	0.08
Yogyakarta	5,799	4,059	9,858	1.429	0.12	0.29
East Java	28,302	28,037	56,339	1.009	0.67	0.15

Banten	72,358	66,901	139,259	1.082	1.64	1.31
Bali	3,574	2,915	6,489	1.226	0.08	0.17
West Nusa Tenggara	800	774	1,574	1.034	0.02	0.04
East Nusa Tenggara	1,605	1,625	3,230	0.988	0.04	0.07
West Kalimantan	15,289	11,197	26,486	1.365	0.31	0.60
Central Kalimantan	7,249	5,075	12,324	1.428	0.15	0.56
South Kalimantan	7,063	5,345	12,408	1.321	0.15	0.34
East Kalimantan	20,933	16,212	37,145	1.291	0.44	1.05
North Sulawesi	2,482	2,020	4,502	1.229	0.05	0.20
Central Sulawesi	1,869	1,359	3,228	1.375	0.04	0.12
South Sulawesi	2,706	2,250	4,956	1.203	0.06	0.06
Southeast Sulawesi	1,113	839	1,952	1.327	0.02	0.09
Gorontalo	228	154	382	1.481	0.00	0.04
West Sulawesi	160	107	267	1.495	0.00	0.02
Maluku	1,008	767	1,775	1.314	0.02	0.12
North Maluku	367	229	596	1.603	0.01	0.06
West Papua	3,908	3,278	7,186	1.192	0.08	0.95
Papua	8,743	7,500	16,243	1.166	0.19	0.58
Indonesia	4,268,074	4,198,895	8,466,969	1.016	100.00	3.58

Source: Calculated by the authors, based on tabulations provided by the BPS.

In 2010, the Madurese numbered 7.18 million distributed across sex and age groups as seen in Figure 5.5. This figure is significantly different from the Batak but just slightly different from the Javanese. As the small base of the population pyramid shows the number of infants and toddlers, the narrowing bar indicates a low and declining fertility. Moreover, under 15 years old, the percentage of population in an age-group becomes smaller as the age group becomes older, revealing that declining fertility seems to have been occurring for several years. Indeed, Ananta, Arifin and Bakhtiar (2005) calculated that the Madurese TFR was already low, 2.08, slightly below the replacement level, during 2000–2005. It is likely, therefore, that the percentage of Madurese will keep declining.

By 2040, if not earlier, the absolute number of Madurese will start to decline.

The population aged 0–4 accounted for 8.03 per cent. The percentage of youths, 15–24, was smaller than that of children aged 5–14, at 16.19 per cent and 18.09 per cent, respectively. If Madurese parents wish their children to pursue tertiary education, then 42.31 per cent of the Madurese were still dependent on the prime-working-age population. The percentage of the dependent young population was slightly lower than that of the Javanese, making the percentage the lowest amongst the five largest ethnic groups.

The Madurese prime-working-age population aged 25–59 accounted for 48.04 per cent. The percentage of older persons aged 60 and above was relatively high at 9.66 per cent, which was larger than its neighbouring ethnic group the Javanese. As with the Javanese, the Madurese population was already a transitional population, ready to enter an old population. Amongst the five largest ethnic groups, the Madurese had the lowest percentage of young dependent population and the highest old dependent population.

As with other ethnic groups, the sex ratio of the older Madurese was below 1, as low as the Batak, 0.74. There was a relatively large excess of females amongst older persons. Although not in as large numbers as amongst older persons, we can see an excess of females in the overall Madurese population. This sex ratio was 0.96 for the total population of Madurese, differing from the first four ethnic groups, with sex ratios above 1.

As shown in Table 5.9, the sex ratios above 1 were only seen amongst the four young groups below 20 years old and the group aged 55–59. This excess of Madurese females of these ages deserves further research.

Figure 5.5
Population Age-Sex Structure: Madurese, 2010

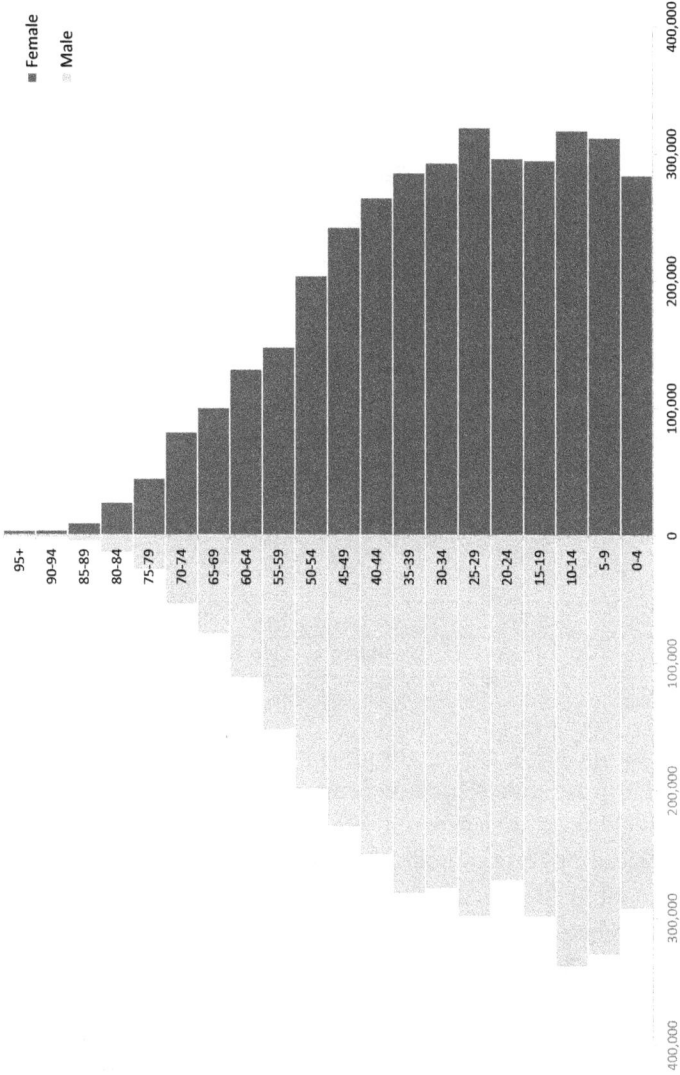

Source: Drawn from Table 5.9.

Table 5.9

Number and Percentage of Madurese Population by Age and Sex: Indonesia, 2010

Age Group	Males	Females	Total	Per cent	Sex Ratio
0–4	293,087	283,241	576,328	8.03	1.035
5–9	329,157	312,739	641,896	8.94	1.052
10–14	338,426	318,218	656,644	9.15	1.064
15–19	299,579	294,667	594,246	8.28	1.017
20–24	271,358	296,280	567,638	7.91	0.916
25–29	298,975	320,363	619,338	8.63	0.933
30–34	277,677	292,825	570,502	7.95	0.948
35–39	281,467	285,018	566,485	7.89	0.988
40–44	251,151	265,418	516,569	7.20	0.946
45–49	229,272	242,205	471,477	6.57	0.947
50–54	199,599	203,777	403,376	5.62	0.979
55–59	153,370	147,938	301,308	4.20	1.037
60–64	112,542	130,429	242,971	3.38	0.863
65–69	77,976	100,046	178,022	2.48	0.779
70–74	54,337	80,840	135,177	1.88	0.672
75–79	27,090	44,636	71,726	1.00	0.607
80–84	14,222	25,507	39,729	0.55	0.558
85–89	5,353	9,475	14,828	0.21	0.565
90–94	1,955	3,826	5,781	0.08	0.511
95+	1,768	3,547	5,315	0.07	0.498
Total	3,518,361	3,660,995	7,179,356	100.00	0.961

Source: Calculated by the authors, based on tabulations provided by the BPS.

One of the possible explanations is international migration. For a long time, Madurese males have ventured out into the world to search for better livelihoods. As shown in Smith (2006), the Madurese took part in international migration, going to Malaysia and the Middle East through government or illegal channels. In Madura, there are many agencies that recruit workers for overseas jobs in those countries. Such jobs usually include drivers, construction workers, labourers, workers on oil palm plantations or other similar heavy manual labour jobs.

On the other hand, it is also possible that some Madurese women went overseas to work as domestic helpers or servers in restaurants. This out-flow of the female population may have raised the sex ratio. Furthermore, the female migrants usually work under a two-year contract and return home at the end of the contract only to take on another overseas contract. Many of them go again and work in the same countries or different countries. Therefore, the female overseas migration may help to raise the low sex ratio. In other words, without the out-migration of female workers, the sex ratio of the Madurese may have been much lower, that is the excess of Madurese females would have been much larger.

Geographical Distribution

Not just overseas, the Madurese also move to other parts of Indonesia, particularly to the islands of Java and Kalimantan, two nearby islands. The majority of Madurese did not live on the island of Madura. In 2000, almost just one third (32.06 per cent) of Madurese in Indonesia lived on the island of Madura, although the Madurese constituted 66.82 per cent of the island's population.[5]

As indicated by Table 5.10, almost 93 per cent of the Madurese lived on the islands of Java and Madura and 90.82 per cent, or 6.5 million, lived in their home province of East Java in 2010. Yet, we do not know how many of them continued living on the island of Madura in 2010. We can therefore have a proxy by estimating the population living in the districts located on Madura Island. The population of these four districts in 2010 totalled 3.6 million. Assuming the same percentage as that of the 2000 census, about 2.5 million Madurese lived on Madura Island in 2010.

The out-migration of the Madurese to the province of East Java dates back to the thirteenth century. Their migration pattern has generally been to the eastern part of Java, located in districts such as Banyuwangi, Malang, Jember, Pasuruan, Probolinggo, Situbondo and Bondowoso as well as Surabaya (Husson 1997).

The islands of Java and Madura are separated by the narrow Strait of Madura, also known as the Suramadu. The Surabaya–Madura bridge has been in operation since 2009 to ease mobility between the two islands. The presence of this bridge may widen the propensity of the Madurese to move to the island of Java, particularly East Java. This bridge may strengthen the close connectivity of the Madurese and the eastern part of East Java. The Madurese are also known to be expert sailors.

Because of the very large population in East Java, the concentration of Madurese in East Java was only 17.53 per cent, making the Madurese the second largest ethnic group after the Javanese in the province. Apart from living alongside the majority of Javanese in this province, the Madurese

Table 5.10
Number, Distribution and Concentration of Madurese by Province: Indonesia, 2010

Province	Males	Females	Total	Sex Ratio	Distribution	Concentration
Aceh	486	380	866	1.279	0.01	0.02
North Sumatra	1,568	1,202	2,770	1.304	0.04	0.02
West Sumatra	250	174	424	1.437	0.01	0.01
Riau	2,881	2,387	5,268	1.207	0.07	0.10
Jambi	671	513	1,184	1.308	0.02	0.04
South Sumatra	3,563	2,969	6,532	1.200	0.09	0.09
Bengkulu	1,377	1,023	2,400	1.346	0.03	0.14
Lampung	3,398	2,758	6,156	1.232	0.09	0.08
Bangka-Belitung	8,302	7,127	15,429	1.165	0.21	1.27
Riau Archipelago	1,754	1,296	3,050	1.353	0.04	0.18
Jakarta	42,697	37,228	79,925	1.147	1.11	0.84
West Java	24,247	18,754	43,001	1.293	0.60	0.10
Central Java	7,263	5,657	12,920	1.284	0.18	0.04
Yogyakarta	2,986	2,303	5,289	1.297	0.07	0.15
East Java	3,171,662	3,348,741	6,520,403	0.947	90.82	17.53

Banten	5,217	4,227	9,444	1.234	0.13	0.09
Bali	15,853	14,011	29,864	1.131	0.42	0.77
West Nusa Tenggara	1,110	972	2,082	1.142	0.03	0.05
East Nusa Tenggara	865	747	1,612	1.158	0.02	0.03
West Kalimantan	139,815	135,054	274,869	1.035	3.83	6.27
Central Kalimantan	22,121	20,547	42,668	1.077	0.59	1.93
South Kalimantan	27,498	25,504	53,002	1.078	0.74	1.47
East Kalimantan	25,303	21,520	46,823	1.176	0.65	1.32
North Sulawesi	256	179	435	1.430	0.01	0.02
Central Sulawesi	1,124	922	2,046	1.219	0.03	0.08
South Sulawesi	1,446	1,190	2,636	1.215	0.04	0.03
Southeast Sulawesi	506	430	936	1.177	0.01	0.04
Gorontalo	121	104	225	1.163	0.00	0.02
West Sulawesi	176	141	317	1.248	0.00	0.03
Maluku	552	488	1,040	1.131	0.01	0.07
North Maluku	206	180	386	1.144	0.01	0.04
West Papua	690	471	1,161	1.465	0.02	0.15
Papua	2,140	1,541	3,681	1.389	0.05	0.13
Indonesia	3,518,361	3,660,995	7,179,356	0.961	100.00	3.03

Source: Calculated by the authors, based on tabulations provided by the BPS.

also lived with the Osing or Using, another local ethnic group from East Java. The Osing were the third largest ethnic group. The presence of other ethnic groups in East Java is further discussed in Chapter 4.

The Madurese also crossed the Java Sea to the island of Kalimantan. In 2010, there were 5.81 per cent of Madurese living in Kalimantan, especially in West Kalimantan, where 3.83 per cent of the total population in that province were Madurese. This is larger than the percentage of Madurese living in all other provinces on the island of Java. As seen in Table 5.10, the Madurese accounted for a significant portion of 6.27 per cent of the West Kalimantan population. In other provinces in Kalimantan, the concentration of Madurese ranged between 1.32 per cent and 1.93 per cent.

Another province with more than 1 per cent of Madurese was Bangka-Belitung, the province located just across from West Kalimantan, separated by the Karimata Strait. In other provinces, the numbers of Madurese were very small, mostly below 1 per cent of the province's population.

However, just like many other ethnic groups, the Madurese were present everywhere in Indonesia. One of the reasons why the Madurese migrated was Madura Island's rather harsh living conditions. The island is dry and has infertile soil, so it requires an enormous effort on the part of the Madurese to make a living from agriculture. Other types of economic activity outside agriculture are limited and therefore this is another reason for people to leave the island.

BETAWI

Very Young Population

The Betawi originated in Batavia (the old name for Jakarta, the capital of Indonesia). The Betawi emerged as a relatively new ethnic group created during the Dutch colonial era as a mix of several ethnic and racial groups: the Ambonese, Balinese, Buginese, Javanese, Makassarese, Malay and Sundanese, as well as other racial groups such as Arab, Chinese, Portugese and others (Tjahjono 2003). This mix produced a unique new language, types of dance, music, architecture and theatre for more than two centuries. From a historical point of view, Batavia was then regarded as an excellent example of a melting-pot phenomenon, and this mixed culture continues to be handed down proudly from one generation to the next.

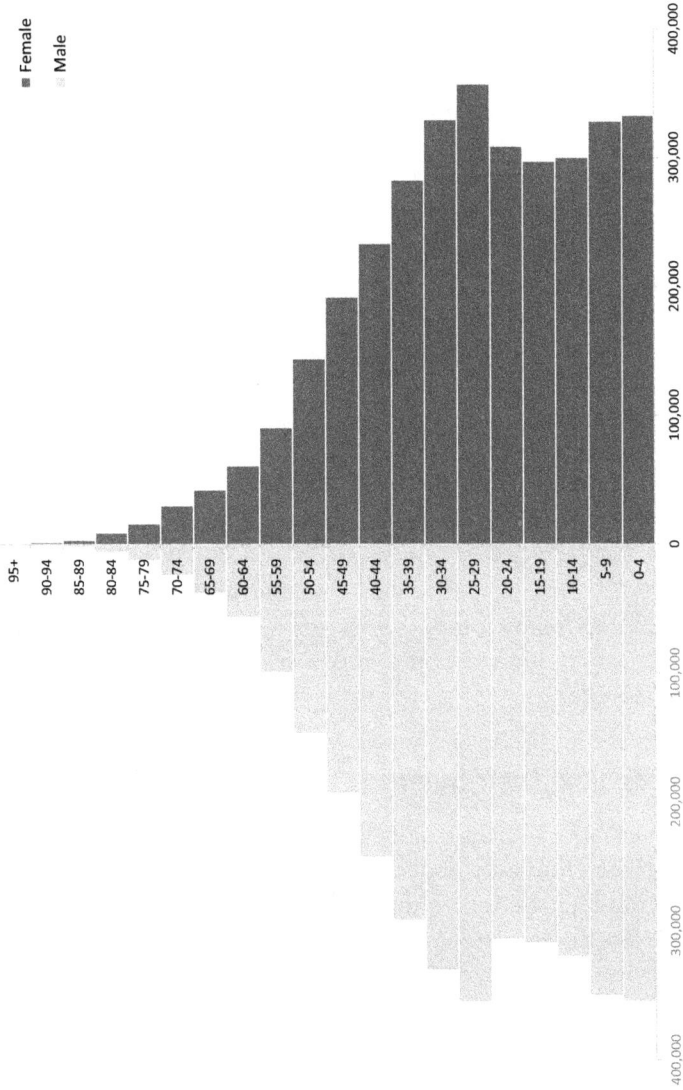

Figure 5.6
Population Age-Sex Structure: Betawi, 2010

Source: Drawn from Table 5.11.

In 2010, the Betawi numbered 6.8 million. Older persons accounted for only 4.52 per cent, making it a very young population and the youngest amongst the six largest ethnic groups. This means the Betawi were supporting fewer older persons but more younger persons.

On the other hand, the population pyramid in Figure 5.6 has a wide base, representing the youngest age group of 0–4 years. The population size in successive age groups gets smaller, indicating the existence of a high fertility rate.

As seen in Table 5.11, the Betawi aged 0–4 accounted for 10.10 per cent. The young aged 5–14 were 19.08 per cent, larger than the 0–4 group, which was larger than the youths, 17.96 per cent. Altogether, the young dependent population of Betawi formed 47.14 per cent, almost half of the total of the Betawi population in Indonesia.

The prime-working-age Betawi accounted for 48.34 per cent, slightly larger than the young dependent population, aged below 25 years old. Compared to the first five ethnic groups, the Betawi had fewer young to support financially.

The Betawi population had more males than females, with the sex ratio at 1.02, similar to the Batak. As seen in Table 5.11, the sex ratios were above 1 for those below 60 years old, but with exceptions amongst those aged 20–29. Amongst this marriageable group, females outnumbered males. As in many other ethnic groups, older persons followed the same pattern, with a sex ratio of 0.85 indicating a large number of older Betawi females.

Geographical Distribution

As seen in Table 5.12, the majority of Betawi did not live in Jakarta, but those who did made up only about 39.67 per cent of the city's total population, or 2.7 million. If we follow the conditions in 2000, many of them perhaps lived in South, East and West Jakarta (BPS 2001). About the same number lived in the two surrounding provinces of West Java (39.13 per cent) to the east and south and a smaller portion in Banten (20.06 per cent) in the west. The Betawi were found in other provinces, but their numbers were insignificant compared to those in Jakarta, West Java and Banten.

In other words, the Betawi contributed a significant portion only in these three provinces. The highest concentration of Betawi was found in Jakarta (28.29 per cent). However, in their home province of Jakarta,

Table 5.11
Number and Percentage of Betawi Population by Age and Sex: Indonesia, 2010

Age Group	Males	Females	Total	Per cent	Sex Ratio
0–4	354,905	332,823	687,728	10.10	1.066
5–9	350,305	328,309	678,614	9.97	1.067
10–14	320,079	300,399	620,478	9.11	1.066
15–19	309,533	297,339	606,872	8.91	1.041
20–24	306,875	309,078	615,953	9.05	0.993
25–29	354,971	357,641	712,612	10.47	0.993
30–34	330,554	329,722	660,276	9.70	1.003
35–39	291,925	282,989	574,914	8.44	1.032
40–44	242,476	233,756	476,232	7.00	1.037
45–49	192,756	192,158	384,914	5.65	1.003
50–54	146,679	144,439	291,118	4.28	1.016
55–59	99,852	90,935	190,787	2.80	1.098
60–64	56,963	61,205	118,168	1.74	0.931
65–69	37,911	42,760	80,671	1.18	0.887
70–74	23,934	30,408	54,342	0.80	0.787
75–79	12,290	16,359	28,649	0.42	0.751
80–84	6,176	9,471	15,647	0.23	0.652
85–89	2,235	3,440	5,675	0.08	0.650
90–94	936	1,803	2,739	0.04	0.519
95+	493	1,086	1,579	0.02	0.454
Total	3,441,848	3,366,120	6,807,968	100.00	1.022

Source: Calculated by the authors, based on tabulations provided by the BPS.

the Betawi were only the second largest ethnic group, after the Javanese (36.16 per cent). The second largest concentration of the Betawi was seen in the home province of Banten and accounted for 12.88 per cent as the fourth group. The Betawi in the province of West Java, the home province of the Sundanese, accounted for 6.20 per cent, making the third largest ethnic group.

MINANGKABAU

Youthful Population

The Minangkabau numbered 6.46 million in 2010. The age structure of the Minangkabau population, as seen in Figure 5.7, took a similar shape as

Table 5.12
Number, Distribution and Concentration of Betawi by Province: Indonesia, 2010

Province	Males	Females	Total	Sex Ratio	Distribution	Concentration
Aceh	414	540	954	0.767	0.01	0.02
North Sumatra	2,182	2,110	4,292	1.034	0.06	0.03
West Sumatra	466	546	1,012	0.853	0.01	0.02
Riau	1,405	1,339	2,744	1.049	0.04	0.05
Jambi	969	981	1,950	0.988	0.03	0.06
South Sumatra	4,799	4,539	9,338	1.057	0.14	0.13
Bengkulu	759	736	1,495	1.031	0.02	0.09
Lampung	4,931	4,690	9,621	1.051	0.14	0.13
Bangka-Belitung	1,070	1,039	2,109	1.030	0.03	0.17
Riau Archipelago	2,542	2,388	4,930	1.064	0.07	0.29
Jakarta	1,362,884	1,337,838	2,700,722	1.019	39.67	28.29
West Java	1,348,166	1,315,977	2,664,143	1.024	39.13	6.20
Central Java	4,899	4,620	9,519	1.060	0.14	0.03
Yogyakarta	1,291	1,170	2,461	1.103	0.04	0.07
East Java	4,329	4,354	8,683	0.994	0.13	0.02

Banten	691,064	674,550	1,365,614	1.024	20.06	12.88
Bali	1,080	983	2,063	1.099	0.03	0.05
West Nusa Tenggara	447	474	921	0.943	0.01	0.02
East Nusa Tenggara	521	600	1,121	0.868	0.02	0.02
West Kalimantan	935	850	1,785	1.100	0.03	0.04
Central Kalimantan	634	493	1,127	1.286	0.02	0.05
South Kalimantan	1,083	888	1,971	1.220	0.03	0.05
East Kalimantan	2,238	1,842	4,080	1.215	0.06	0.12
North Sulawesi	359	274	633	1.310	0.01	0.03
Central Sulawesi	391	327	718	1.196	0.01	0.03
South Sulawesi	673	708	1,381	0.951	0.02	0.02
Southeast Sulawesi	243	243	486	1.000	0.01	0.02
Gorontalo	113	82	195	1.378	0.00	0.02
West Sulawesi	29	32	61	0.906	0.00	0.01
Maluku	136	197	333	0.690	0.00	0.02
North Maluku	185	161	346	1.149	0.01	0.03
West Papua	195	194	389	1.005	0.01	0.05
Papua	416	355	771	1.172	0.01	0.03
Indonesia	3,441,848	3,366,120	6,807,968	1.022	100.00	2.88

Source: Calculated by the authors, based on tabulations provided by the BPS.

Figure 5.7
Population Age-Sex Structure: Minangkabau, 2010

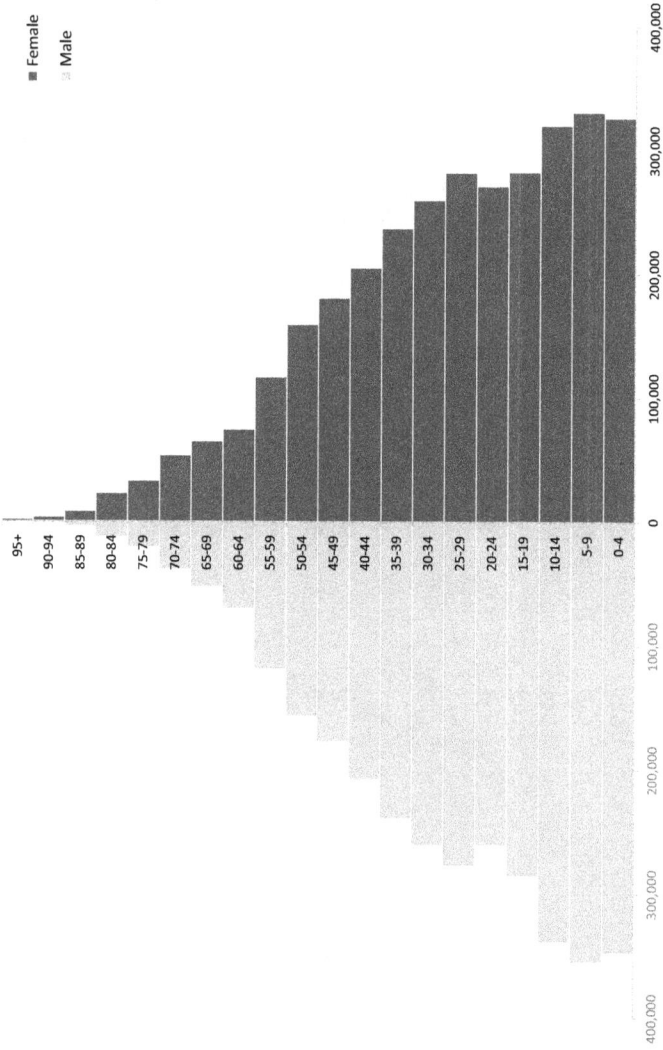

■ Female
▣ Male

Source: Drawn from Table 5.13.

the Batak, a neighbouring ethnic group from North Sumatra. Table 5.13 shows that the infants and toddlers provide a wide base for the pyramid, indicating a large number of infants born between 2005 and 2010. They accounted for 10.43 per cent, just about the same percentage as those aged 5–9 years. The young children group, 5–14, accounted for 20.82 per cent. Therefore, the population below 15 altogether made up almost one third of the Minangkabau. Youths accounted for 17.03 per cent, smaller than the young aged 5–14. The prime working-age Minangkabau population comprised 44.56 per cent. Older persons accounted for 7.17 per cent, larger than the Batak, meaning that the Minangkabau population was still a youthful population, like the Sundanese.

In contrast to other ethnic groups in Indonesia, especially the Batak, the Minangkabau have a matrilineal family system. As discussed under "Almost Homogeneous provinces" in Chapter 4, the Minangkabau are well known for being both traders and fortune seekers in the *merantau* tradition, meaning that young Minangkabau males may no longer rely on their parents. Therefore, Minangkabau parents have less need to support their male children, compared to other ethnic groups. The Minangkabau as a whole have an excess of females. There were larger numbers of females amongst those aged 20–24 and 25–29, indicated by sex ratios of 0.96 and 0.98. Some Minangkabau males at these ages may have gone for their *merantau* overseas. They may return home after 30 years old, as is indicated by the sex ratio equal to 1 at ages 30–34 and higher than 1 after ages 35–39 and 40–44 (see Table 5.13).

As with other ethnic groups, there were more female than male older persons and this excess of females become larger the older the age. Similar to the Malay and Batak, the sex ratio for the oldest ones, aged 95 years old and above, was only 0.30, implying that there were ten Minangkabau females aged 95 years old and above for every three males of the same age.

Geographical Distribution

The Minangkabau originated in the province of West Sumatra, bordering North Sumatra in the north, Riau in the east and Jambi and Bengkulu in the south. Table 5.14 shows that most of them lived in their home province, West Sumatra (65.29 per cent). The Minangkabau may have followed their *merantau* to nearby provinces — Riau (10.47 per cent), North Sumatra (5.16 per cent) and the Riau Archipelago (4.21 per cent). The Minangkabau

Table 5.13
Number and Percentage of Minangkabau Population by
Age and Sex: Indonesia, 2010

Age Group	Males	Females	Total	Per cent	Sex Ratio
0–4	347,561	326,317	673,878	10.43	1.065
5–9	355,486	330,757	686,243	10.62	1.075
10–14	339,107	319,968	659,075	10.20	1.060
15–19	285,696	282,572	568,268	8.79	1.011
20–24	261,022	271,248	532,270	8.24	0.962
25–29	277,316	282,063	559,379	8.66	0.983
30–34	260,966	259,836	520,802	8.06	1.004
35–39	239,447	237,052	476,499	7.37	1.010
40–44	208,341	204,916	413,257	6.39	1.017
45–49	177,372	180,569	357,941	5.54	0.982
50–54	156,885	159,369	316,254	4.89	0.984
55–59	119,068	116,625	235,693	3.65	1.021
60–64	70,083	74,483	144,566	2.24	0.941
65–69	52,574	65,013	117,587	1.82	0.809
70–74	38,462	53,636	92,098	1.43	0.717
75–79	20,441	33,117	53,558	0.83	0.617
80–84	12,780	23,034	35,814	0.55	0.555
85–89	3,796	8,282	12,078	0.19	0.458
90–94	1,366	3,614	4,980	0.08	0.378
95+	577	1,896	2,473	0.04	0.304
Total	3,228,346	3,234,367	6,462,713	100.00	0.998

Source: Calculated by the authors, based on tabulations provided by the BPS.

living on the island of Sumatra numbered 5.80 million, forming 89.73 per cent of the total Minangkabau population in Indonesia. The majority of those living outside Sumatra were on the island of Java, numbering about 629,000, or 9.73 per cent.

The highest sex ratios of the Minangkabau living outside West Sumatra were seen in South Kalimantan (1.39), followed by Yogyakarta (1.32) and Bangka-Belitung (1.32) — revealing an excess of Minangkabau males in those provinces. West Sumatra, the home province of the Minangkabau, was the only province where the sex ratio of Minangkabau was below 1, revealing a greater number of Minangkabau females in the province. Interestingly, the sex ratios, although greater than 1, in other provinces in Sumatra, were not high, still below 1.10. In other words, the larger number

Table 5.14
Number, Distribution and Concentration of Minangkabau by Province: Indonesia, 2010

Province	Males	Females	Total	Sex Ratio	Distribution	Concentration
Aceh	16,962	16,150	33,112	1.050	0.51	0.74
North Sumatra	169,914	163,327	333,241	1.040	5.16	2.58
West Sumatra	2,078,142	2,141,587	4,219,729	0.970	65.29	87.33
Riau	344,600	332,348	676,948	1.037	10.47	12.29
Jambi	82,642	81,118	163,760	1.019	2.53	5.33
South Sumatra	33,216	31,187	64,403	1.065	1.00	0.87
Bengkulu	36,416	35,056	71,472	1.039	1.11	4.18
Lampung	35,932	33,720	69,652	1.066	1.08	0.92
Bangka-Belitung	2,411	1,821	4,232	1.324	0.07	0.35
Riau Archipelago	81,254	81,198	162,452	1.001	2.51	9.72
Jakarta	140,883	131,135	272,018	1.074	4.21	2.85
West Java	126,167	115,002	241,169	1.097	3.73	0.56
Central Java	4,776	3,819	8,595	1.251	0.13	0.03
Yogyakarta	2,927	2,225	5,152	1.316	0.08	0.15
East Java	3,500	3,104	6,604	1.128	0.10	0.02
Banten	49,788	46,057	95,845	1.081	1.48	0.90
Bali	1,175	904	2,079	1.300	0.03	0.05
West Nusa Tenggara	825	712	1,537	1.159	0.02	0.03
East Nusa Tenggara	1,472	1,216	2,688	1.211	0.04	0.06

continued on next page

Table 5.14 — cont'd

Province	Males	Females	Total	Sex Ratio	Distribution	Concentration
West Kalimantan	4,365	3,718	8,083	1.174	0.13	0.18
Central Kalimantan	533	416	949	1.281	0.01	0.04
South Kalimantan	998	720	1,718	1.386	0.03	0.05
East Kalimantan	3,565	3,105	6,670	1.148	0.10	0.19
North Sulawesi	400	291	691	1.375	0.01	0.03
Central Sulawesi	957	825	1,782	1.160	0.03	0.07
South Sulawesi	935	810	1,745	1.154	0.03	0.02
Southeast Sulawesi	346	310	656	1.116	0.01	0.03
Gorontalo	82	64	146	1.281	0.00	0.01
West Sulawesi	72	58	130	1.241	0.00	0.01
Maluku	756	629	1,385	1.202	0.02	0.09
North Maluku	762	583	1,345	1.307	0.02	0.13
West Papua	314	251	565	1.251	0.01	0.07
Papua	1,259	901	2,160	1.397	0.03	0.08
Indonesia	3,228,346	3,234,367	6,462,713	0.998	100.00	2.73

Source: Calculated by the authors, based on tabulations provided by the BPS.

of Minangkabau males in the Sumatran provinces was not that great, except in Bangka-Belitung. In contrast, the sex ratios of the Minangkabau outside Sumatra were very large, greater than 1.10. The sex ratio reached 1.397 in Papua, meaning that there were 1,397 Minangkabau males for every 1,000 Minangkabau females living in Papua. Perhaps the migration out of West Sumatra to areas outside Sumatra was more dominated by Minangkabau males. The female Minangkabau may be more likely to migrate to nearby provinces on the island of Sumatra.

The Minangkabau living in their home province of West Sumatra accounted for 87.33 per cent. This was followed by the surrounding provinces: Riau (12.29 per cent), the Riau Archipelago (9.72 per cent) and Jambi (5.33 per cent). Outside Sumatra, the Minangkabau accounted for a significant portion (2.84 per cent, or 272,000) in Jakarta. The Minangkabau living in West Java were smaller in number than in Jakarta (241,000), making up only 0.56 per cent of the West Java population.

Nevertheless, Table 5.14 shows that the Minangkabau can be seen even in far-away provinces such as Papua. The Minangkabau living in Papua numbered 2,160, larger than the numbers of Minangkabau living in South Sulawesi or South Kalimantan.

BUGINESE

Youthful Population

The Buginese, also known as the Uginese (Ugi), are famed seafarers. In 2010, they numbered 6.4 million. As seen in Figure 5.8, the shape of their population pyramid resembled that of the Minangkabau. The youngest were fewer than those aged 5–9. Together with those aged 10–14, those aged 5–14 made up 20.58 per cent. They were fewer than the youths (17.48 per cent). The older persons comprised 7.37 per cent, meaning that the Buginese population was still youthful. The prime-working-age group accounted for 44.36 per cent.

Like the Minangkabau, the number of Buginese males is almost the same as the number of Buginese females. As seen in Table 5.15, the sex ratios were below 1 for the population at 20–35 years old. The male population may have migrated, followed the *merantau*, gone abroad and returned at age 35.

There was also an excess of females amongst the older persons. This excess of females is attributed to a higher mortality rate amongst male

Figure 5.8
Population Age-Sex Structure: Buginese, 2010

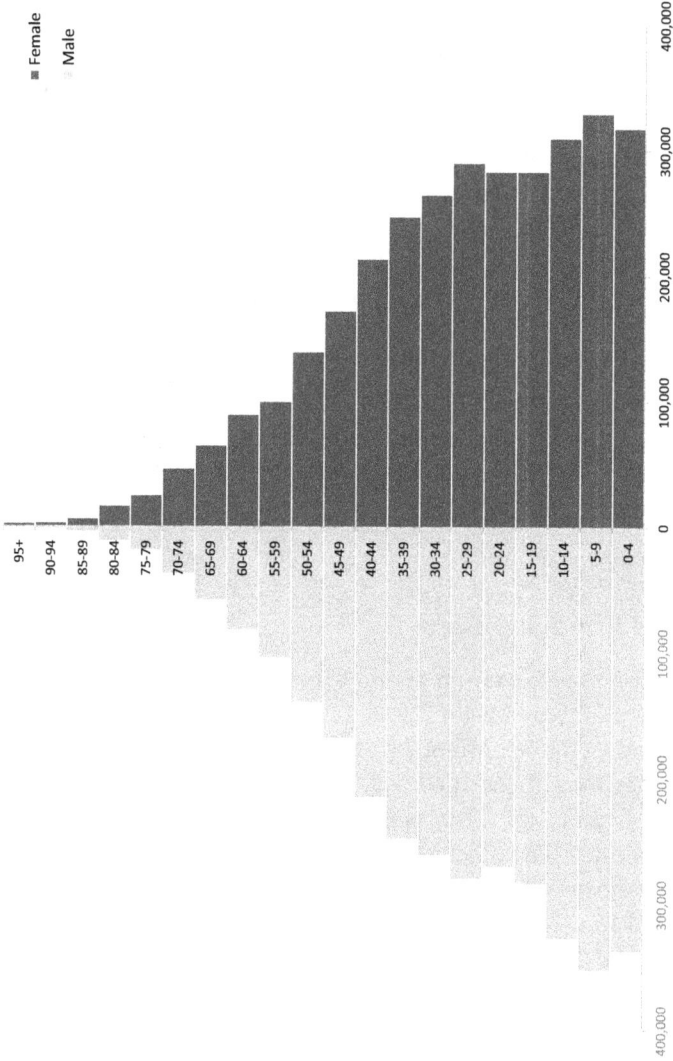

Source: Drawn from Table 5.15.

Table 5.15
Number and Percentage of Buginese Population by Age and Sex: Indonesia, 2010

Age Group	Males	Females	Total	Per cent	Sex Ratio
0–4	337,723	317,950	655,673	10.22	1.062
5–9	352,694	329,671	682,365	10.64	1.070
10–14	327,529	309,890	637,419	9.94	1.057
15–19	284,132	283,515	567,647	8.85	1.002
20–24	270,335	283,459	553,794	8.63	0.954
25–29	279,760	290,449	570,209	8.89	0.963
30–34	261,109	265,245	526,354	8.20	0.984
35–39	248,412	247,582	495,994	7.73	1.003
40–44	215,192	213,535	428,727	6.68	1.008
45–49	168,308	172,169	340,477	5.31	0.978
50–54	140,059	139,789	279,848	4.36	1.002
55–59	104,354	99,998	204,352	3.19	1.044
60–64	82,145	89,563	171,708	2.68	0.917
65–69	58,683	65,060	123,743	1.93	0.902
70–74	37,347	46,719	84,066	1.31	0.799
75–79	18,571	25,546	44,117	0.69	0.727
80–84	11,250	17,016	28,266	0.44	0.661
85–89	4,224	6,707	10,931	0.17	0.630
90–94	1,850	3,319	5,169	0.08	0.557
95+	1,488	2,756	4,244	0.07	0.540
Total	3,205,165	3,209,938	6,415,103	100.00	0.999

Source: Calculated by the authors, based on tabulations provided by the BPS.

older persons. The sex ratio for the population aged 95 years old and above amongst the Buginese was 0.54, meaning that for every two female older persons aged 95 years old there was only one male of the same age. However, the Buginese sex ratio for the oldest ones (0.54) was not as low as that in the Minangkabau (0.30). That means the excess of females amongst the Buginese oldest population was not as large as that of the Minangkabau oldest population.

Geographical Distribution

The Buginese originated in the province of South Sulawesi and have three sub-ethnic groups: the Bugis Pagatan or Pagatan; the Amatoa, Ammatowa

Table 5.16
Number, Distribution and Concentration of Buginese by Province: Indonesia, 2010

Province	Males	Females	Total	Sex Ratio	Distribution	Concentration
Aceh	548	451	999	1.215	0.02	0.02
North Sumatra	2,655	2,304	4,959	1.152	0.08	0.04
West Sumatra	402	267	669	1.506	0.01	0.01
Riau	54,941	52,256	107,197	1.051	1.67	1.95
Jambi	48,380	47,766	96,146	1.013	1.50	3.13
South Sumatra	22,637	20,465	43,102	1.106	0.67	0.58
Bengkulu	2,008	1,686	3,694	1.191	0.06	0.22
Lampung	11,509	9,573	21,082	1.202	0.33	0.28
Bangka-Belitung	18,101	15,491	33,592	1.168	0.52	2.75
Riau Archipelago	20,223	16,922	37,145	1.195	0.58	2.22
Jakarta	36,698	31,668	68,366	1.159	1.07	0.72
West Java	19,468	15,314	34,782	1.271	0.54	0.08
Central Java	2,322	2,136	4,458	1.087	0.07	0.01
Yogyakarta	1,927	1,434	3,361	1.344	0.05	0.10
East Java	11,035	9,898	20,933	1.115	0.33	0.06
Banten	8,257	6,912	15,169	1.195	0.24	0.14

Bali	4,806	4,486	9,292	1.071	0.14	0.24
West Nusa Tenggara	10,051	9,967	20,018	1.008	0.31	0.45
East Nusa Tenggara	11,402	11,117	22,519	1.026	0.35	0.48
West Kalimantan	71,664	65,618	137,282	1.092	2.14	3.13
Central Kalimantan	9,301	7,803	17,104	1.192	0.27	0.77
South Kalimantan	53,338	48,389	101,727	1.102	1.59	2.81
East Kalimantan	391,713	344,106	735,819	1.138	11.47	20.81
North Sulawesi	12,103	9,936	22,039	1.218	0.34	0.97
Central Sulawesi	212,729	197,012	409,741	1.080	6.39	15.62
South Sulawesi	1,736,718	1,881,965	3,618,683	0.923	56.41	45.12
Southeast Sulawesi	255,460	240,972	496,432	1.060	7.74	22.28
Gorontalo	5,078	3,757	8,835	1.352	0.14	0.85
West Sulawesi	74,082	70,472	144,554	1.051	2.25	12.49
Maluku	13,430	12,089	25,519	1.111	0.40	1.67
North Maluku	11,227	9,580	20,807	1.172	0.32	2.01
West Papua	21,770	18,317	40,087	1.189	0.62	5.32
Papua	49,182	39,809	88,991	1.235	1.39	3.20
Indonesia	3,205,165	3,209,938	6,415,103	0.999	100.00	2.71

Source: Calculated by the authors, based on tabulations provided by the BPS.

or Orang Kajang; and the Tolotang. The Buginese are another *perantau* ethnic group. It is not surprising, therefore, that the Buginese living in their own province were not the predominant group. Only about 56.41 per cent (3.6 million) of the total population of the Buginese lived in South Sulawesi. A significant percentage lived in the surrounding provinces: Southeast Sulawesi (7.74 per cent) to the east and Central Sulawesi (6.39 per cent) to the north. However, a larger number of Buginese were also found in East Kalimantan (11.47 per cent or 736,000). The province of East Kalimatan lies to the west of the province of South Sulawesi, separated by the Makassar Strait. This large percentage was probably contributed by the Bugis Pagatan or Pagatan. We found 4.0 per cent of the Buginese living in three other Kalimantan provinces, 2.3 per cent living on the island of Java, especially in Jakarta. The number of Buginese living on the island of Sumatra, especially in the provinces of Jambi and Riau, was larger than their number in Java.

In their home province, the Buginese formed 45.12 per cent of the South Sulawesi population. The second and fourth largest concentrations were in the bordering provinces, Southeast Sulawesi (22.28 per cent) and Central Sulawesi (15.62 per cent). East Kalimantan had the third largest concentration (20.81 per cent). As can be seen in Table 5.16, the concentration of Buginese in many provinces was significant and, as discussed in Chapter 4, the Buginese were amongst the ten largest ethnic groups in twenty provinces.

BANTENESE

Very Young Population

As the ninth largest ethnic group in Indonesia, the Bantenese numbered 4.64 million. The shape of age structure of the population of Bantenese indicated a declining fertility rate, as seen in Figure 5.9. The base of the pyramid showing the number of infants and toddlers was smaller than in the older groups. The Bantenese aged 0–4 accounted for 10.03 per cent, as compared to 10.74 per cent for those aged 5–9. The young aged 5–14 years accounted for 22.23 per cent, more than double the infants and toddlers. Youths comprised 19.42 per cent. Therefore, the young dependent population, under 25 years old, formed 52.39 per cent of the total Bantenese population. On the other hand, the prime-working-age population, who are supposed to take care of the young dependent population, made up only

Figure 5.9
Population Age-Sex Structure: Bantenese, 2010

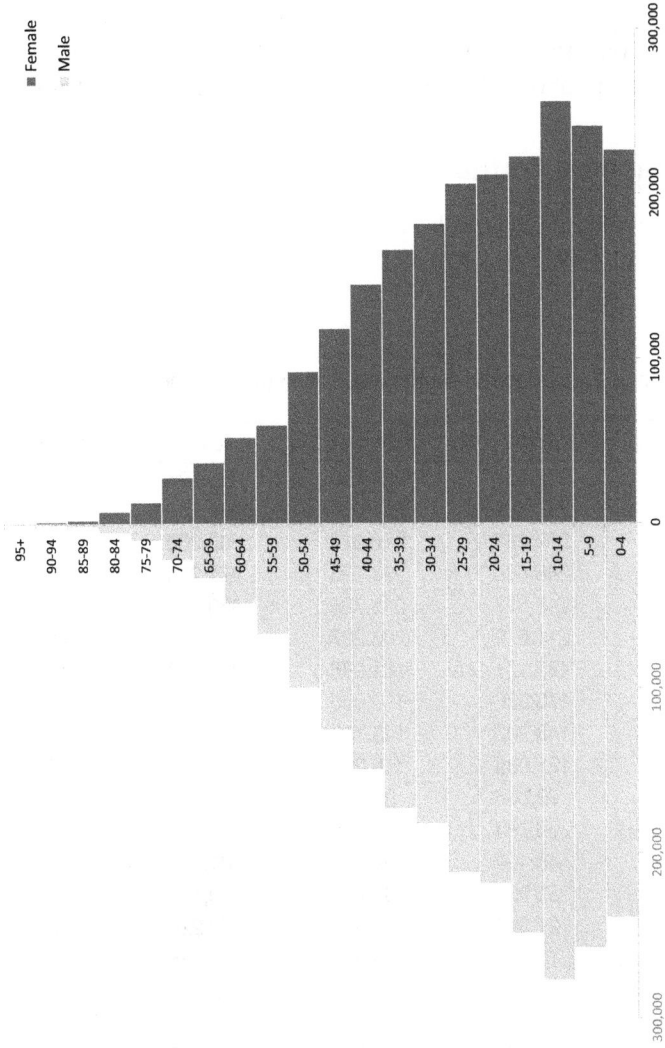

Source: drawn from Table 5.17.

42.59 per cent. In addition, older persons aged 60 and above accounted for 5.72 per cent, making a very young Bantenese population.

The overall sex ratio of Bantenese was 1.04, meaning that there were more Bantenese males than females. As seen in more detail in Table 5.17, a sex ratio of above 1 was seen in all age groups below 60, with the highest seen amongst those aged 15–19 and 55–59. Yet, the ratios were below 1 for all age groups above 60. The sex ratio for those aged 60 and above was 0.85.

Geographical Distribution

The Bantenese have no sub-ethnic groups. They originated in the province of Banten, formerly part of the province of West Java. As discussed

Table 5.17
Number and Percentage of Bantenese Population by Age and Sex: Indonesia, 2010

Age Group	Males	Females	Total	Per cent	Sex Ratio
0–4	239,287	226,509	465,796	10.03	1.056
5–9	257,625	241,064	498,689	10.74	1.069
10–14	277,237	256,013	533,250	11.49	1.083
15–19	248,689	222,526	471,215	10.15	1.118
20–24	218,517	211,796	430,313	9.27	1.032
25–29	211,679	206,227	417,906	9.00	1.026
30–34	182,171	181,988	364,159	7.84	1.001
35–39	173,036	166,086	339,122	7.30	1.042
40–44	148,903	145,192	294,095	6.33	1.026
45–49	125,085	118,358	243,443	5.24	1.057
50–54	99,666	92,273	191,939	4.13	1.080
55–59	66,793	59,955	126,748	2.73	1.114
60–64	48,460	52,567	101,027	2.18	0.922
65–69	32,954	37,201	70,155	1.51	0.886
70–74	21,914	28,306	50,220	1.08	0.774
75–79	10,038	13,397	23,435	0.50	0.749
80–84	5,489	7,694	13,183	0.28	0.713
85–89	1,713	2,361	4,074	0.09	0.726
90–94	808	1,342	2,150	0.05	0.602
95+	553	917	1,470	0.03	0.603
Total	2,370,617	2,271,772	4,642,389	100.00	1.044

Source: Calculated by the authors, based on tabulations provided by the BPS.

earlier, in 2000 the province of West Java split into the current West Java and Banten provinces. Thus, the province borders Jakarta and West Java to the east. Almost all Bantenese (92.83 per cent of 4.64 million) lived in their home province. The number of Bantenese living in the capital city was very small, only 28,300. A greater number of Bantenese lived in the province of West Java (60,100). However, the number of Bantenese living in the province of Lampung (172,400) was even larger than the numbers in West Java and Jakarta. Lampung is located in the southern part of the island of Sumatra, separated by the Sunda Straits, to the north of Banten. In addition to Lampung, relatively large numbers of Bantenese were also found in South Sumatra (17,100) and North Sumatra (46,600).

However, in percentage terms, the contribution of the Bantenese in those three Sumatran provinces was low. The share was only 2.27 per cent in Lampung and less than 0.5 per cent in each of North Sumatra and South Sumatra. Even in their home province, their contribution was low, at only 40.65 per cent. See Table 5.18.

BANJARESE

Very Young Population

The Banjarese, as the tenth largest ethnic group, totalled 4.13 million. As seen in Figure 5.10, the Banjarese age-sex structure indicated both a declining fertility and mortality, although the fertility rate was not low. The base of the age-sex structure, which indicates the number of births occurring between 2005 and 2010, was still relatively large, with the youngest population accounting for almost 10 per cent. However, this youngest population was already smaller than its next older population, 5–9 years old, hinting at a decline in fertility rate. Furthermore, the children aged 5–14 were almost double the number of the youngest group. The youths, aged 15–24, who are likely to be schooling at the senior high school and university level, accounted for 18.21 per cent.

On the other hand, the prime-working-age Banjarese accounted for 46.39 per cent, slightly lower than the population under 25 years old. It is therefore likely to be a big challenge for the Banjarese to finance their children until tertiary education.

The older Banjarese, aged 60 and above, accounted for 5.65 per cent, still relatively low. With their very young population, the Banjarese working-age population does not need to support too many older persons.

Table 5.18
Number, Distribution and Concentration of Bantenese by Province: Indonesia, 2010

Province	Males	Females	Total	Sex Ratio	Distribution	Concentration
Aceh	885	756	1,641	1.171	0.04	0.04
North Sumatra	24,168	22,453	46,621	1.076	1.00	0.36
West Sumatra	152	130	282	1.169	0.01	0.01
Riau	770	574	1,344	1.341	0.03	0.02
Jambi	371	341	712	1.088	0.02	0.02
South Sumatra	9,169	7,926	17,095	1.157	0.37	0.23
Bengkulu	79	58	137	1.362	0.00	0.01
Lampung	90,541	81,830	172,371	1.106	3.71	2.27
Bangka-Belitung	363	279	642	1.301	0.01	0.05
Riau Archipelago	233	190	423	1.226	0.01	0.03
Jakarta	14,315	13,959	28,274	1.026	0.61	0.30
West Java	30,601	29,475	60,076	1.038	1.29	0.14
Central Java	201	199	400	1.010	0.01	0.00
Yogyakarta	75	56	131	1.339	0.00	0.00
East Java	233	233	466	1.000	0.01	0.00

Banten	2,197,303	2,112,355	4,309,658	1.040	92.83	40.65
Bali	30	35	65	0.857	0.00	0.00
West Nusa Tenggara	16	38	54	0.421	0.00	0.00
East Nusa Tenggara	10	11	21	0.909	0.00	0.00
West Kalimantan	339	308	647	1.101	0.01	0.01
Central Kalimantan	52	36	88	1.444	0.00	0.00
South Kalimantan	93	65	158	1.431	0.00	0.00
East Kalimantan	250	173	423	1.445	0.01	0.01
North Sulawesi	32	24	56	1.333	0.00	0.00
Central Sulawesi	8	7	15	1.143	0.00	0.00
South Sulawesi	33	37	70	0.892	0.00	0.00
Southeast Sulawesi	13	6	19	2.167	0.00	0.00
Gorontalo	6	5	11	1.200	0.00	0.00
West Sulawesi	2	2	4	1.000	0.00	0.00
Maluku	58	53	111	1.094	0.00	0.01
North Maluku	22	22	44	1.000	0.00	0.00
West Papua	54	43	97	1.256	0.00	0.01
Papua	140	93	233	1.505	0.01	0.01
Indonesia	2,370,617	2,271,772	4,642,389	1.044	100.00	1.96

Source: Calculated by the authors, based on tabulations provided by the BPS.

Figure 5.10
Population Age-Sex Structure: Banjarese, 2010

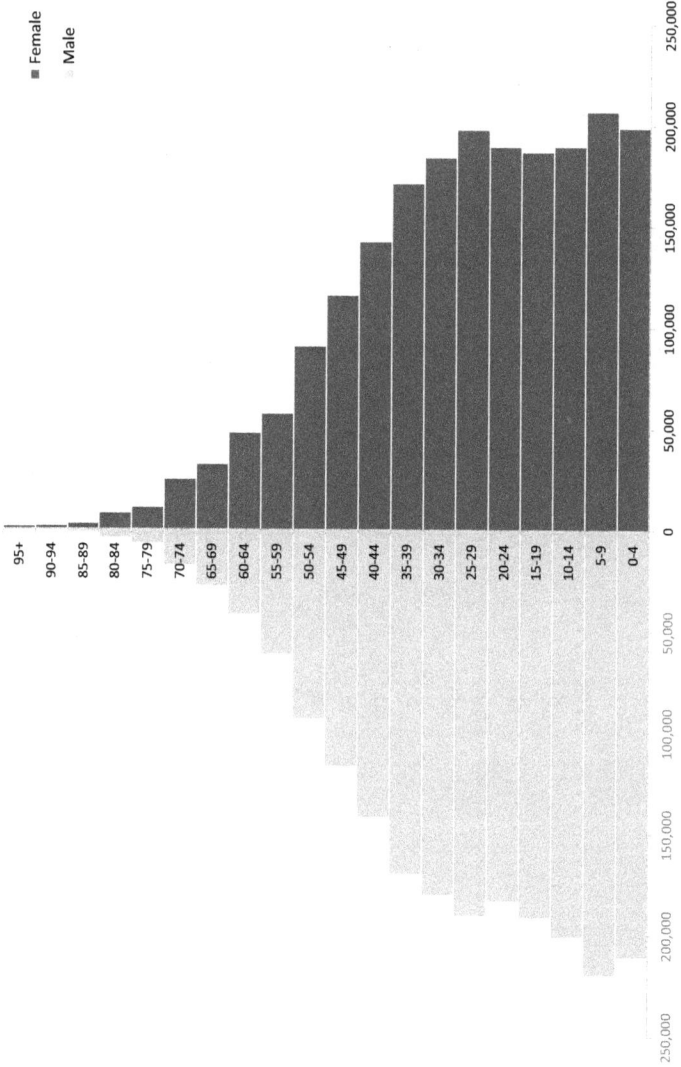

Source: drawn from Table 5.19.

Overall, the sex ratio of the Banjarese was the same as the Buginese, with a balanced sex composition between males and females. As can be seen in Table 5.19, there was an excess of males for those younger than 20 years old and those between 45 and 59 years old. The sex ratio of those aged 60 and above was 0.77, much smaller than that of the Bantenese and the Buginese. The excess of females amongst older persons becomes larger the older the age group.

Geographical Distribution

As with the Minangkabau, the Banjarese are known as both traders and *merantau*, originating in the province of South Kalimantan, which

Table 5.19
Number and Percentage of Banjarese Population by Age and Sex: Indonesia, 2010

Age Group	Males	Females	Total	Per cent	Sex Ratio
0–4	211,123	198,775	409,898	9.93	1.062
5–9	219,933	206,852	426,785	10.34	1.063
10–14	201,259	189,646	390,905	9.47	1.061
15–19	191,816	187,042	378,858	9.18	1.026
20–24	183,309	189,518	372,827	9.03	0.967
25–29	190,633	197,921	388,554	9.41	0.963
30–34	180,279	184,214	364,493	8.83	0.979
35–39	169,930	171,300	341,230	8.27	0.992
40–44	141,957	142,334	284,291	6.89	0.997
45–49	116,844	115,917	232,761	5.64	1.008
50–54	93,401	90,796	184,197	4.46	1.029
55–59	61,643	57,494	119,137	2.89	1.072
60–64	41,876	48,064	89,940	2.18	0.871
65–69	27,907	32,497	60,404	1.46	0.859
70–74	17,648	25,185	42,833	1.04	0.701
75–79	7,051	11,292	18,343	0.44	0.624
80–84	4,314	8,242	12,556	0.30	0.523
85–89	1,535	2,893	4,428	0.11	0.531
90v94	771	1,818	2,589	0.06	0.424
95+	540	1,555	2,095	0.05	0.347
Total	2,063,769	2,063,355	4,127,124	100.00	1.000

Source: Calculated by the authors, based on tabulations provided by the BPS.

Table 5.20
Number, Distribution and Concentration of Banjarese by Province: Indonesia, 2010

Province	Males	Females	Total	Sex Ratio	Distribution	Concentration
Aceh	1,396	1,338	2,734	1.043	0.07	0.06
North Sumatra	63,997	61,710	125,707	1.037	3.05	0.97
West Sumatra	192	163	355	1.178	0.01	0.01
Riau	115,488	111,751	227,239	1.033	5.51	4.13
Jambi	51,543	50,694	102,237	1.017	2.48	3.33
South Sumatra	730	712	1,442	1.025	0.03	0.02
Bengkulu	104	76	180	1.368	0.00	0.01
Lampung	210	201	411	1.045	0.01	0.01
Bangka-Belitung	134	115	249	1.165	0.01	0.02
Riau Archipelago	6,279	5,532	11,811	1.135	0.29	0.71
Jakarta	4,257	4,315	8,572	0.987	0.21	0.09
West Java	4,931	4,452	9,383	1.108	0.23	0.02
Central Java	1,111	1,225	2,336	0.907	0.06	0.01
Yogyakarta	1,371	1,174	2,545	1.168	0.06	0.07
East Java	6,234	6,171	12,405	1.010	0.30	0.03
Banten	1,290	1,282	2,572	1.006	0.06	0.02

Bali	183	166	349	1.102	0.01	0.01
West Nusa Tenggara	508	575	1,083	0.883	0.03	0.02
East Nusa Tenggara	91	109	200	0.835	0.00	0.00
West Kalimantan	7,735	6,695	14,430	1.155	0.35	0.33
Central Kalimantan	236,248	228,012	464,260	1.036	11.25	21.03
South Kalimantan	1,332,563	1,354,064	2,686,627	0.984	65.10	74.34
East Kalimantan	222,489	217,964	440,453	1.021	10.67	12.45
North Sulawesi	287	307	594	0.935	0.01	0.03
Central Sulawesi	1,800	1,652	3,452	1.090	0.08	0.13
South Sulawesi	1,773	2,064	3,837	0.859	0.09	0.05
Southeast Sulawesi	261	238	499	1.097	0.01	0.02
Gorontalo	66	68	134	0.971	0.00	0.01
West Sulawesi	83	138	221	0.601	0.01	0.02
Maluku	111	102	213	1.088	0.01	0.01
North Maluku	46	56	102	0.821	0.00	0.01
West Papua	85	80	165	1.063	0.00	0.02
Papua	173	154	327	1.123	0.01	0.01
Indonesia	2,063,769	2,063,355	4,127,124	1.000	100.00	1.74

Source: Calculated by the authors, based on tabulations provided by the BPS.

borders Central Kalimantan to the west, East Kalimantan to the north, the Makassar Strait to the east and the Java Sea to the south. The Banjarese are active in running trading and seafaring ventures, and thus they are not only scattered in the archipelago of Indonesia, but also live in some Malaysian states such as Johor, Selangor, Perak, Pulau Penang and Pahang.

The Banjarese living in their home province numbered 2.69 million, or 65.10 per cent of the total Banjarese. Many of them migrated to neighbouring provinces such as East Kalimantan (440,000) and Central Kalimantan (464,000). Table 5.20 shows that 11.46 per cent of the Banjarese lived in provinces on the island of Sumatra such as in Riau (227,000), North Sumatra (126,000) and Jambi (102,000). There were not many Banjarese in other provinces.

The Banjarese formed 74.34 per cent of the South Kalimantan population, 21.03 per cent in Central Kalimantan and 12.45 per cent in East Kalimantan. In Central Kalimantan, the Banjarese were the third largest ethnic group, after the Dayak and Javanese. In East Kalimantan, the Banjarese were also the third largest group, after the Javanese and Buginese. The concentrations of Banjarese in two Sumatran provinces (Riau and Jambi) were also significant. They were the fifth largest ethnic group in Riau, forming 4.13 per cent and the sixth in Jambi, constituting 3.33 per cent.

It would be interesting to know why the Banjarese migrated to live in Riau and Jambi. These two provinces have wide areas of long uninhabited, unexploited swamp forests, which produce extreme heat and humidity, making them highly unfavourable for living (Abe 1997). However, the Banjarese have long been experts in reclaiming these swampy lands and turning them into agricultural farms, comprising rice fields, coconut, coffee and banana plantations. The Buginese are also known to be experts in transforming these swampy forests, arriving there later in the 1960s (Collier et al. 1984).

BALINESE

Transitional Population

The Balinese originated from the island of Bali, including a few smaller islands such as Nusa Penida and Nusa Dua. The Lombok Strait separates

Bali to the east from the island of Lombok, the home of the Sasak. The Bali Strait separates Bali to the west from the island of Java, next to the province of East Java, home to the Javanese and Madurese. The Balinese comprised only 3.9 million people. Figure 5.11 indicates that the Balinese population has had a low fertility rate for several decades. As a proxy for the Balinese, the total fertility rate for the province of Bali has been low since the late 1980s and reached below the replacement level in the early 1990s. The base, the population aged 0–4, accounted for 8.59 per cent, fewer than those aged 5–9. The children aged 5–14 comprised 18.04 per cent. Balinese youths made up 14.41 per cent, the smallest percentage of youths amongst other ethnic groups. The prime-working-age population accounted for 48.66 per cent. The older persons aged 60 and above comprised 10.30 per cent, the second largest after the Chinese. The Balinese population is a transitional population and is almost about to enter an old population phase. The Balinese prime-working-age population should ready itself to support the rising percentage of older persons.

The sex ratio of the Balinese was 1.01. As seen in Table 5.21, the sex ratios were above 1 amongst those aged below 20, 35–49 and 55–59, meaning that there was an excess of males in those age groups. The other groups had ratios below 1. The sex ratio of older persons aged 60 and above was 0.89, showing an excess of female older persons.

The sex ratio was always above 1 for the Balinese living outside the island of Bali, with 1.03 as the lowest in West Nusa Tenggara. An outlier was seen amongst the Balinese in Maluku, with a very high sex ratio, at 1.64, hinting at a very large excess of Balinese males over Balinese females in Maluku.

Geographical Distribution

A very large percentage (84.54 per cent) of the Balinese live in their home province of Bali. The second largest number (although only 3.03 per cent) was in West Nusa Tenggara, a Balinese neighbouring province. The Balinese were also found living in Central Sulawesi (2.95 per cent) and in Lampung (2.67 per cent). Smaller numbers of Balinese lived in other provinces (Table 5.22).

The highest concentration of Balinese was also in Bali (85.50 per cent), followed by Central Sulawesi (4.41 per cent), Southeast Sulawesi (2.22 per cent), Lampung (1.38 per cent) and West Sulawesi (1.26 per cent). In

Figure 5.11
Population Age-Sex Structure: Balinese, 2010

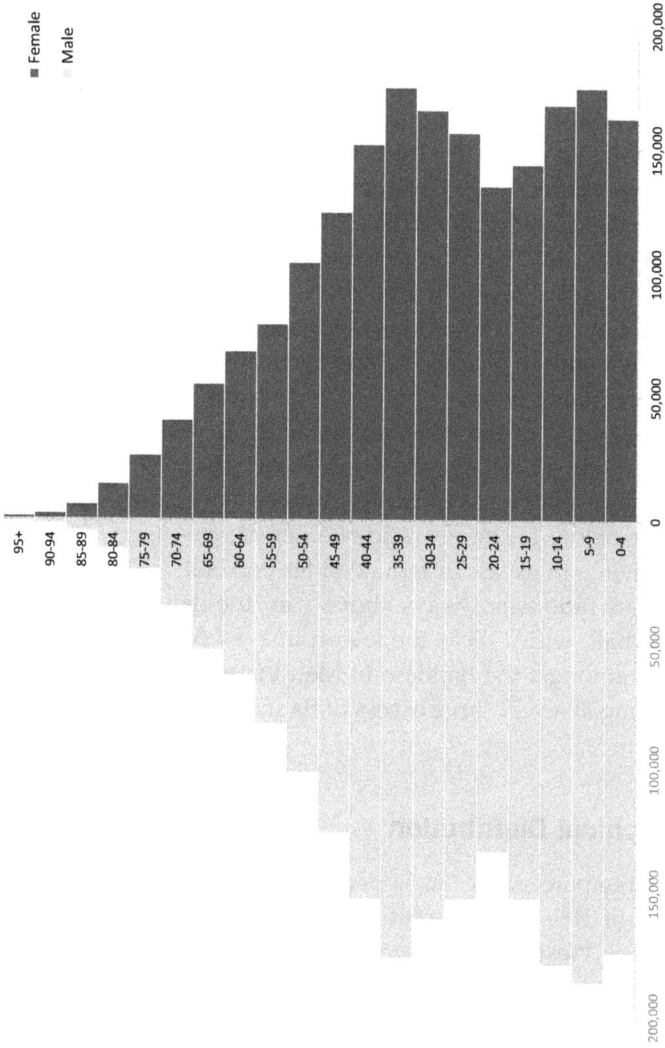

Source: Drawn from Table 5.21.

Table 5.21
Number and Percentage of Balinese Population by Age and Sex: Indonesia, 2010

Age Group	Males	Females	Total	Per cent	Sex Ratio
0–4	174,712	162,524	337,236	8.59	1.075
5–9	186,397	174,637	361,034	9.20	1.067
10–14	179,301	167,834	347,135	8.84	1.068
15–19	153,056	143,796	296,852	7.56	1.064
20–24	133,729	135,031	268,760	6.85	0.990
25–29	152,920	156,515	309,435	7.88	0.977
30–34	161,079	165,495	326,574	8.32	0.973
35–39	176,644	174,627	351,271	8.95	1.012
40–44	153,131	151,617	304,748	7.76	1.010
45–49	126,209	124,153	250,362	6.38	1.017
50–54	102,054	103,847	205,901	5.25	0.983
55–59	82,390	79,076	161,466	4.11	1.042
60–64	62,840	68,054	130,894	3.33	0.923
65–69	52,855	54,833	107,688	2.74	0.964
70–74	35,122	40,242	75,364	1.92	0.873
75–79	20,375	26,007	46,382	1.18	0.783
80–84	12,012	14,520	26,532	0.68	0.827
85–89	4,764	6,042	10,806	0.28	0.788
90–94	1,764	2,466	4,230	0.11	0.715
95+	945	1,293	2,238	0.06	0.731
Total	1,972,299	1,952,609	3,924,908	100.00	1.010

Source: Calculated by the authors, based on tabulations provided by the BPS.

other provinces, the Balinese contributed less than one per cent of the respective populations.

ACEHNESE

Youthful Population

The Acehnese are one of the many local ethnic groups from the province of Aceh, situated on the northern tip of the island of Sumatra, bordering North Sumatra to the south. The Acehnese numbered 3.40 million in 2010. As seen in Figure 5.12, the Acehnese seem to have a relatively high fertility rate, seen from the wide base of the pyramid. The population aged 0–4 accounted for the largest group, 10.85 per cent. The young aged 5–14 made

Table 5.22
Number, Distribution and Concentration of Balinese by Province: Indonesia, 2010

Province	Males	Females	Total	Sex Ratio	Distribution	Concentration
Aceh	80	62	142	1.290	0.00	0.00
North Sumatra	605	541	1,146	1.118	0.03	0.01
West Sumatra	102	90	192	1.133	0.00	0.00
Riau	585	439	1,024	1.333	0.03	0.02
Jambi	267	189	456	1.413	0.01	0.01
South Sumatra	20,007	18,451	38,458	1.084	0.98	0.52
Bengkulu	2,207	2,108	4,315	1.047	0.11	0.25
Lampung	54,358	50,248	104,606	1.082	2.67	1.38
Bangka-Belitung	600	507	1,107	1.183	0.03	0.09
Riau Archipelago	740	571	1,311	1.296	0.03	0.08
Jakarta	8,167	6,827	14,994	1.196	0.38	0.16
West Java	11,358	9,174	20,532	1.238	0.52	0.05
Central Java	1,971	1,458	3,429	1.352	0.09	0.01
Yogyakarta	1,898	1,555	3,453	1.221	0.09	0.10
East Java	10,616	8,872	19,488	1.197	0.50	0.05

Banten	4,293	3,589	7,882	1.196	0.20	0.07
Bali	1,655,358	1,662,707	3,318,065	0.996	84.54	85.50
West Nusa Tenggara	60,236	58,591	118,827	1.028	3.03	2.65
East Nusa Tenggara	3,360	2,647	6,007	1.269	0.15	0.13
West Kalimantan	1,063	808	1,871	1.316	0.05	0.04
Central Kalimantan	3,971	3,377	7,348	1.176	0.19	0.33
South Kalimantan	6,300	5,666	11,966	1.112	0.30	0.33
East Kalimantan	4,660	3,954	8,614	1.179	0.22	0.24
North Sulawesi	7,400	6,910	14,310	1.071	0.36	0.63
Central Sulawesi	60,073	55,687	115,760	1.079	2.95	4.41
South Sulawesi	14,067	13,218	27,285	1.064	0.70	0.34
Southeast Sulawesi	25,739	23,650	49,389	1.088	1.26	2.22
Gorontalo	1,918	1,774	3,692	1.081	0.09	0.36
West Sulawesi	7,533	7,054	14,587	1.068	0.37	1.26
Maluku	1,002	610	1,612	1.643	0.04	0.11
North Maluku	136	94	230	1.447	0.01	0.02
West Papua	510	374	884	1.364	0.02	0.12
Papua	1,119	807	1,926	1.387	0.05	0.07
Indonesia	1,972,299	1,952,609	3,924,908	1.010	100.00	1.66

Source: Calculated by the authors, based on tabulations provided by the BPS.

Figure 5.12
Population Age-Sex Structure: Acehnese, 2010

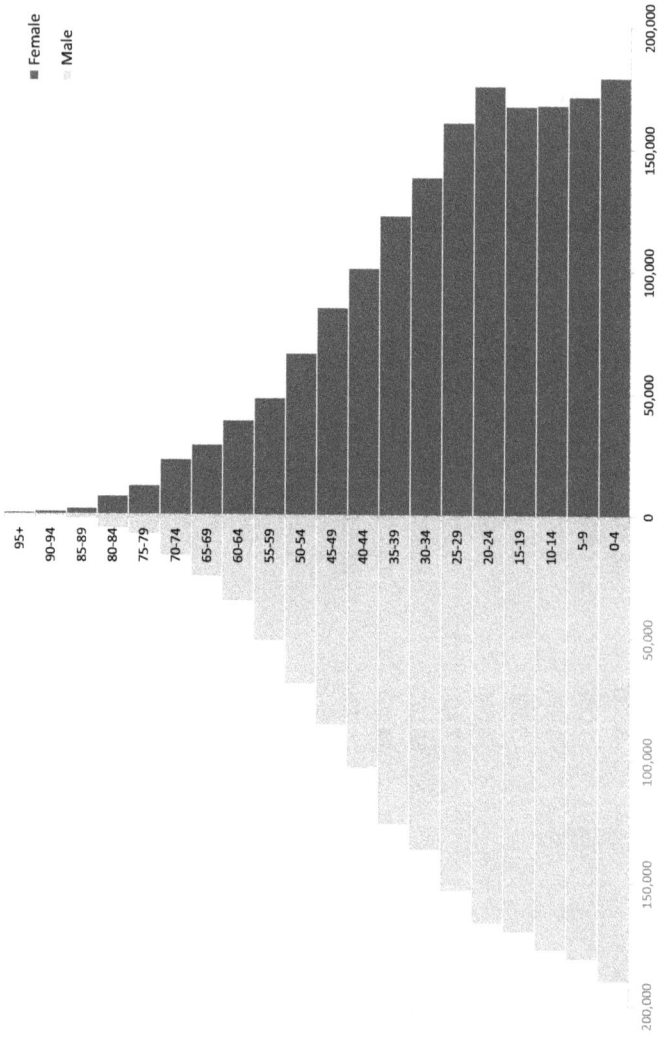

Source: Drawn from Table 5.23.

up 20.51 per cent. Thus, the population below 15 comprised almost one third of the total Acehnese.

Youths comprised 19.98 per cent. If the Acehnese aim for their children to pursue tertiary education, the prime-working-age population will be supporting the population under 25 years old, accounting for 51.34 per cent. On the other hand, the prime-working-age population constituted only 42.53 per cent.

The Acehnese population is still youthful, with older persons aged 60 contributing 6.13 per cent of the total Acehnese population. Therefore, currently, the Acehnese working adults are supporting more younger than older dependants.

Table 5.23 shows that, overall, the Acehnese had a balanced sex composition. The males outnumbered the females aged below 20 and

Table 5.23

Number and Percentage of Acehnese Population by Age and Sex: Indonesia, 2010

Age Group	Males	Females	Total	Per cent	Sex Ratio
0–4	190,189	179,275	369,464	10.85	1.061
5–9	181,139	171,601	352,740	10.36	1.056
10–14	177,435	168,038	345,473	10.15	1.056
15–19	170,093	167,466	337,559	9.92	1.016
20–24	166,751	175,823	342,574	10.06	0.948
25–29	153,179	160,770	313,949	9.22	0.953
30–34	136,521	138,456	274,977	8.08	0.986
35–39	126,290	122,699	248,989	7.31	1.029
40–44	103,377	101,158	204,535	6.01	1.022
45–49	85,635	85,030	170,665	5.01	1.007
50–54	68,979	66,289	135,268	3.97	1.041
55–59	51,312	48,064	99,376	2.92	1.068
60–64	35,011	38,868	73,879	2.17	0.901
65–69	25,151	28,888	54,039	1.59	0.871
70–74	16,905	22,929	39,834	1.17	0.737
75–79	7,825	12,119	19,944	0.59	0.646
80–84	5,544	7,727	13,271	0.39	0.717
85–89	1,815	2,528	4,343	0.13	0.718
90–94	697	1,357	2,054	0.06	0.514
95+	290	886	1,176	0.03	0.327
Total	1,704,138	1,699,971	3,404,109	100.00	1.002

Source: Calculated by the authors, based on tabulations provided by the BPS.

Table 5.24
Number, Distribution and Concentration of Acehnese by Province: Indonesia, 2010

Province	Males	Females	Total	Sex Ratio	Distribution	Concentration
Aceh	1,574,245	1,586,483	3,160,728	0.992	92.85	70.65
North Sumatra	64,127	60,399	124,526	1.062	3.66	0.96
West Sumatra	1,223	940	2,163	1.301	0.06	0.04
Riau	6,416	5,494	11,910	1.168	0.35	0.22
Jambi	1,522	1,234	2,756	1.233	0.08	0.09
South Sumatra	1,579	1,353	2,932	1.167	0.09	0.04
Bengkulu	841	503	1,344	1.672	0.04	0.08
Lampung	1,399	1,121	2,520	1.248	0.07	0.03
Bangka-Belitung	340	180	520	1.889	0.02	0.04
Riau Archipelago	6,515	4,937	11,452	1.320	0.34	0.68
Jakarta	15,302	12,533	27,835	1.221	0.82	0.29
West Java	17,113	13,670	30,783	1.252	0.90	0.07
Central Java	1,096	895	1,991	1.225	0.06	0.01
Yogyakarta	802	588	1,390	1.364	0.04	0.04
East Java	1,602	1,444	3,046	1.109	0.09	0.01
Banten	6,222	4,962	11,184	1.254	0.33	0.11

Bali	216	180	396	1.200	0.01	0.01
West Nusa Tenggara	133	137	270	0.971	0.01	0.01
East Nusa Tenggara	131	134	265	0.978	0.01	0.01
West Kalimantan	463	359	822	1.290	0.02	0.02
Central Kalimantan	131	136	267	0.963	0.01	0.01
South Kalimantan	283	230	513	1.230	0.02	0.01
East Kalimantan	963	765	1,728	1.259	0.05	0.05
North Sulawesi	128	113	241	1.133	0.01	0.01
Central Sulawesi	232	172	404	1.349	0.01	0.02
South Sulawesi	384	366	750	1.049	0.02	0.01
Southeast Sulawesi	81	118	199	0.686	0.01	0.01
Gorontalo	36	28	64	1.286	0.00	0.01
West Sulawesi	24	16	40	1.500	0.00	0.00
Maluku	149	110	259	1.355	0.01	0.02
North Maluku	93	92	185	1.011	0.01	0.02
West Papua	116	106	222	1.094	0.01	0.03
Papua	231	173	404	1.335	0.01	0.01
Indonesia	1,704,138	1,699,971	3,404,109	1.002	100.00	1.44

Source: Calculated by the authors, based on tabulations provided by the BPS.

35–59. Older persons aged 60 and above had a sex ratio of 0.81, indicating that there were more female than male Acehnese older persons.

However, as is shown in Table 5.24, a different picture emerges when we see where the Acehnese were living. Amongst the Acehnese who lived in Aceh, the sex ratio was below 1, indicating more Acehnese females. An excess of Acehnese females was also seen amongst the Acehnese living in East Nusa Tenggara, West Nusa Tenggara, Central Kalimantan and Southeast Sulawesi. The sex ratio in Southeast Sulawesi was very low, at 0.69, implying a very large number of Acehnese females living in Southeast Sulawesi. It should be noted, however, that the number of Acehnese living in each of these four provinces was very small, less than 300 people in each.

Geographical Distribution

Table 5.24 shows that almost all of the Acehnese (92.85 per cent) lived in their own province of Aceh. The next largest number of Acehnese (3.66 per cent) was seen in the neighbouring province of North Sumatra. Those Acehnese migrating to the island of Java (2.24 per cent) were fewer than those migrating to North Sumatra.

The highest concentration (70.65 per cent) was also in Aceh. The concentration in each of other provinces was very small, below 1 per cent.

DAYAK

Very Young Population

The Dayak are perhaps the most complex ethnic group in Indonesia. They originated from the island of Kalimantan. Some also originated from the state of Sarawak, Malaysia, on the same island of Borneo. The island of Borneo consists of four Indonesian provinces (West Kalimantan, South Kalimantan, Central Kalimantan and East Kalimantan),[6] two Malaysian states (Sabah and Sarawak) and one country (Brunei). However, we limit the discussion here to the Dayak originating in Indonesian Borneo, excluding those from other parts of Borneo. As shown in Appendix 1, in Indonesia, the Dayak include 375 coded categories.

The Dayak totalled 3.22 million in Indonesia in 2010. As can be seen in Figure 5.13, the age-sex structure of the Dayak resembled that of the Banjarese. The youngest population accounted for 10.31 per cent, which

Figure 5.13
Population Age-Sex Structure: Dayak, 2010

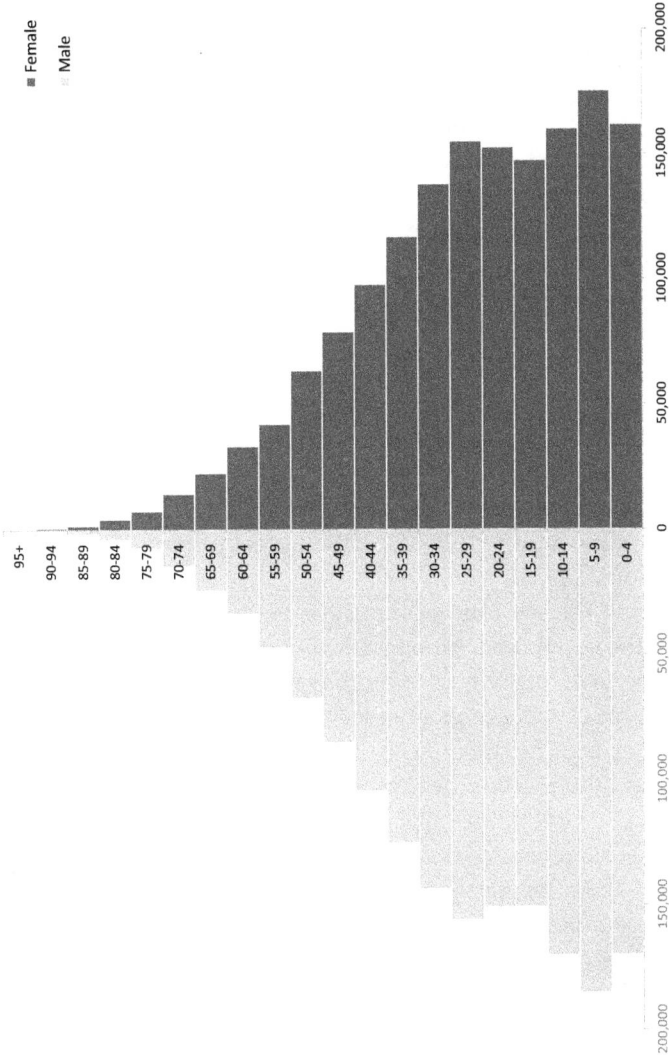

Source: Drawn from Table 5.25.

was smaller than those aged 5–9 (11.20 per cent), indicating a declining fertility. The children, aged 5–14, made up 21.46 per cent. Youths accounted a slimmer 18.70 per cent.

The prime-working-age population comprised 44.18 per cent. If the Dayak children pursue tertiary education, the young dependent population will be those under 25 years old, comprising 50.47 per cent of the total Dayak population. The percentage of the young dependent population was much higher than the percentage of prime-working-age adults, implying heavy economic challenges for young Dayak who wish to pursue tertiary education.

On the other hand, the percentage of older persons amongst the Dayak was still relatively low, at 5.36 per cent, meaning fewer elderly for the prime-working-age population to support. The Dayak population is still very young.

Differing from other ethnic groups, as seen in Table 5.25, the sex ratios above 1 were seen amongst those aged below 75 years, except those aged 20–24. In other ethnic groups, except for the Chinese, the sex ratios below 1 started at age 60 years old. The excess of females only occurs at 75 years old and above amongst the Dayak, rather than at 60 years old in other ethnic groups, although the Chinese excess of older females starts from 45 years old.

Overall, the sex ratio of the Dayak was 1.04, indicating an excess of males in the population. Amongst the Dayak who lived in West Kalimantan, the excess, with a sex ratio at 1.05, was larger than the overall sex ratio. High sex ratios were seen amongst the Dayak who lived on the island of Sumatra, except for those seen in North Sumatra. The largest excess of males was 1.39 amongst the Dayak who lived in Bangka-Belitung, followed by 1.36 in nearby Jambi.

On the other hand, an excess of females was only seen in nine provinces, with East Nusa Tenggara as the lowest at 0.83 and West Nusa Tenggara at 0.84. The smallest excess of females were found amongst the Dayak who lived in East Java, with a sex ratio at 0.96. An excess of Dayak females was also found in South Kalimantan.

Geographical Distribution

Most of the Dayak live in West Kalimantan (47.58 per cent), Central Kalimantan (31.97 per cent), East Kalimantan (10.92 per cent) and South

Table 5.25
Number and Percentage of Dayak Population by Age and Sex: Indonesia, 2010

Age Group	Males	Females	Total	Per cent	Sex Ratio
0–4	170,016	161,824	331,840	10.31	1.051
5–9	185,058	175,382	360,440	11.20	1.055
10–14	170,162	160,179	330,341	10.26	1.062
15–19	150,800	147,555	298,355	9.27	1.022
20–24	150,936	152,780	303,716	9.43	0.988
25–29	155,998	155,101	311,099	9.66	1.006
30–34	143,567	138,136	281,703	8.75	1.039
35–39	125,371	116,941	242,312	7.53	1.072
40–44	104,504	98,023	202,527	6.29	1.066
45–49	85,029	79,100	164,129	5.10	1.075
50–54	67,440	63,567	131,007	4.07	1.061
55–59	47,241	42,260	89,501	2.78	1.118
60–64	33,637	33,377	67,014	2.08	1.008
65–69	24,396	22,726	47,122	1.46	1.073
70–74	14,614	14,533	29,147	0.91	1.006
75–79	7,426	7,477	14,903	0.46	0.993
80–84	3,942	4,288	8,230	0.26	0.919
85–89	1,673	1,774	3,447	0.11	0.943
90–94	645	900	1,545	0.05	0.717
95+	569	679	1,248	0.04	0.838
Total	1,643,024	1,576,602	3,219,626	100.00	1.042

Source: Calculated by the authors, based on tabulations provided by the BPS.

Kalimantan (2.51 per cent). They can also be found on the island of Java, especially in Jakarta (1.41 per cent) and West Java (1.40 per cent). The percentages in the remaining provinces were very small (less than 1 per cent). In other words, the Dayak lived mostly on the island of Kalimantan (Table 5.26).

The largest number of the Dayak was in the province of West Kalimantan, but the highest concentration of Dayak was in Central Kalimantan (46.62 per cent). The Dayak in West Kalimantan accounted for 34.93 per cent of the population. The Dayak had the third highest concentration in East Kalimantan (9.94 per cent) and South Kalimantan (2.23 per cent). The concentrations were very small (less than 1 per cent) in the remaining provinces in Indonesia.

Table 5.26
Number, Distribution and Concentration of Dayak by Province: Indonesia, 2010

Province	Males	Females	Total	Sex Ratio	Distribution	Concentration
Aceh	631	593	1,224	1.064	0.04	0.03
North Sumatra	1,784	1,926	3,710	0.926	0.12	0.03
West Sumatra	468	370	838	1.265	0.03	0.02
Riau	1,877	1,587	3,464	1.183	0.11	0.06
Jambi	202	148	350	1.365	0.01	0.01
South Sumatra	6,145	5,184	11,329	1.185	0.35	0.15
Bengkulu	1,378	1,145	2,523	1.203	0.08	0.15
Lampung	1,969	1,762	3,731	1.117	0.12	0.05
Bangka-Belitung	1,126	811	1,937	1.388	0.06	0.16
Riau Archipelago	1,559	1,521	3,080	1.025	0.10	0.18
Jakarta	23,374	22,011	45,385	1.062	1.41	0.48
West Java	23,938	21,295	45,233	1.124	1.40	0.11
Central Java	2,431	2,697	5,128	0.901	0.16	0.02
Yogyakarta	2,520	2,097	4,617	1.202	0.14	0.13
East Java	7,227	7,514	14,741	0.962	0.46	0.04

Banten	10,619	9,409	20,028	1.129	0.62	0.19
Bali	948	1,016	1,964	0.933	0.06	0.05
West Nusa Tenggara	570	679	1,249	0.839	0.04	0.03
East Nusa Tenggara	1,352	1,628	2,980	0.830	0.09	0.06
West Kalimantan	785,755	746,234	1,531,989	1.053	47.58	34.93
Central Kalimantan	522,618	506,564	1,029,182	1.032	31.97	46.62
South Kalimantan	39,849	40,859	80,708	0.975	2.51	2.23
East Kalimantan	178,624	172,813	351,437	1.034	10.92	9.94
North Sulawesi	2,589	2,485	5,074	1.042	0.16	0.22
Central Sulawesi	833	855	1,688	0.974	0.05	0.06
South Sulawesi	13,967	15,287	29,254	0.914	0.91	0.36
Southeast Sulawesi	1,826	1,733	3,559	1.054	0.11	0.16
Gorontalo	526	494	1,020	1.065	0.03	0.10
West Sulawesi	821	819	1,640	1.002	0.05	0.14
Maluku	775	775	1,550	1.000	0.05	0.10
North Maluku	975	929	1,904	1.050	0.06	0.18
West Papua	1,111	980	2,091	1.134	0.06	0.28
Papua	2,637	2,382	5,019	1.107	0.16	0.18
Indonesia	1,643,024	1,576,602	3,219,626	1.042	100.00	1.36

Source: Calculated by the authors, based on tabulations provided by the BPS.

SASAK

Youthful Population

The Sasak originated from the island of Lombok, the westernmost island of the archipelagic province of West Nusa Tenggara, lying between the island of Bali to the west, separated by the Lombok Strait, and Sumbawa to the east, separated by the Alas Strait. The provincial capital of Mataram is located on Lombok.

In 2010, the Sasak population in Indonesia totalled 3.18 million. As can be seen in Figure 5.14, the Sasak had a relatively high fertility rate shown by the wide base of the population pyramid, representing the number of infants born between 2005 and 2010. The base group aged 0–4, accounted for 10.61 per cent, the largest size amongst the five-year age groups. The young population aged 5–14 was twice as large (20.30 per cent) as the youngest group. Youths made up 18.37 per cent. The prime-working-age population comprised 43.66 per cent. The older Sasak aged 60 and above accounted for 7.06 per cent, a relatively high percentage, although still within the stage of a youthful population.

Historically, amongst other provinces, the province of West Nusa Tenggara has always had the highest infant mortality rate, at 189 per 1,000 live births, while the overall figure for Indonesia was 109 per 1,000 live births in the middle of the 1970s. The rate declined to 48 in the middle of the 2000s, still higher than the national rate of 26 per 1,000 live births.

With regard to sex composition, the number of Sasak females was larger than that of males, with a sex ratio of 0.92. The excess of Sasak females was seen amongst the young groups, aged between 15 years old and 55 years old. This may indicate a male-dominated migration tendency of the Sasak to work in other countries such as Malaysia. It is also possible that male mortality was higher than female mortality amongst the prime-working-age population, especially during the early ages of the working-age population.

The possibility of there being a male-dominated pattern of migration was also seen inside Indonesia. As mentioned earlier, the sex ratio for the Sasak as a whole implies an excess of females. On the other hand, an excess of males can be found for all Sasak living in other provinces outside West Nusa Tenggara, and this excess of males was very high. Amongst the Sasak living in West Sumatra, there were more than four Sasak males for every one Sasak female. The next highest ratios were in Bangka-Belitung

Figure 5.14
Population Age-Sex Structure: Sasak, 2010

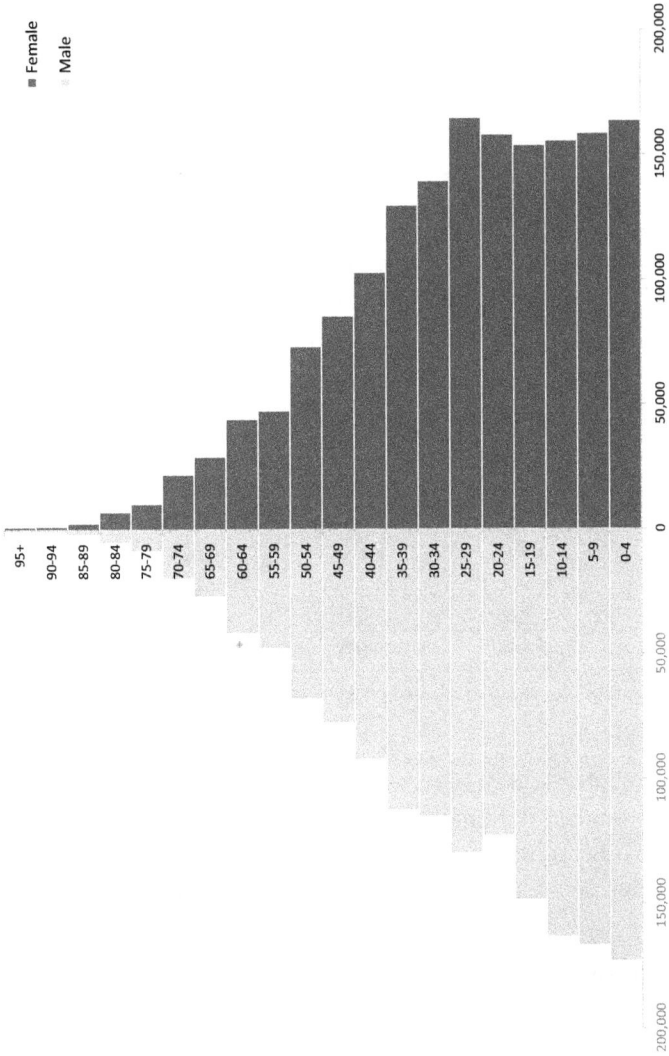

Source: Drawn from Table 5.27.

Table 5.27
Number and Percentage of Sasak Population by Age and Sex: Indonesia, 2010

Age Group	Males	Females	Total	Per cent	Sex Ratio
0–4	173,022	163,731	336,753	10.61	1.057
5–9	166,869	158,690	325,559	10.25	1.052
10–14	163,435	155,657	319,092	10.05	1.050
15–19	148,438	153,902	302,340	9.52	0.964
20–24	122,968	158,089	281,057	8.85	0.778
25–29	129,664	164,804	294,468	9.27	0.787
30–34	115,025	139,633	254,658	8.02	0.824
35–39	112,463	129,855	242,318	7.63	0.866
40–44	92,184	102,879	195,063	6.14	0.896
45–49	77,526	85,592	163,118	5.14	0.906
50–54	67,758	73,400	141,158	4.45	0.923
55–59	47,688	47,641	95,329	3.00	1.001
60–64	41,526	44,178	85,704	2.70	0.940
65–69	26,786	29,236	56,022	1.76	0.916
70–74	19,658	22,186	41,844	1.32	0.886
75–79	8,550	10,362	18,912	0.60	0.825
80–84	5,362	7,211	12,573	0.40	0.744
85–89	1,981	2,647	4,628	0.15	0.748
90–94	905	1,401	2,306	0.07	0.646
95+	828	1,276	2,104	0.07	0.649
Total	1,522,636	1,652,370	3,175,006	100.00	0.921

Source: Calculated by the authors, based on tabulations provided by the BPS.

and Jambi, also in Sumatra, where there were at least three Sasak males for every one Sasak female.

As in other ethnic groups, there was also an excess of females amongst Sasak older persons, and this becomes larger with the higher the age.

Geographical Distribution

As seen in Table 5.28, the Sasak live in many provinces in Indonesia. Yet, almost all of the Sasak, 95.55 per cent or 3 million, lived in their own home province of West Nusa Tenggara. The percentage of Sasak living in each of the other provinces was very small, less than 1 per cent of the total Sasak population. However, in absolute terms, there

Table 5.28
Number, Distribution and Concentration of Sasak by Province: Indonesia, 2010

Province	Males	Females	Total	Sex Ratio	Distribution	Concentration
Aceh	83	46	129	1.804	0.00	0.00
North Sumatra	330	197	527	1.675	0.02	0.00
West Sumatra	113	27	140	4.185	0.00	0.00
Riau	1,564	641	2,205	2.440	0.07	0.04
Jambi	378	125	503	3.024	0.02	0.02
South Sumatra	258	168	426	1.536	0.01	0.01
Bengkulu	33	19	52	1.737	0.00	0.00
Lampung	111	74	185	1.500	0.01	0.00
Bangka-Belitung	1,370	434	1,804	3.157	0.06	0.15
Riau Archipelago	2,180	1,129	3,309	1.931	0.10	0.20
Jakarta	1,486	1,181	2,667	1.258	0.08	0.03
West Java	2,224	1,590	3,814	1.399	0.12	0.01
Central Java	683	514	1,197	1.329	0.04	0.00
Yogyakarta	1,386	900	2,286	1.540	0.07	0.07
East Java	2,384	1,960	4,344	1.216	0.14	0.01
Banten	592	406	998	1.458	0.03	0.01
Bali	12,533	10,139	22,672	1.236	0.71	0.58
West Nusa Tenggara	1,443,226	1,590,436	3,033,662	0.907	95.55	67.58
East Nusa Tenggara	1,254	835	2,089	1.502	0.07	0.04
West Kalimantan	1,734	1,130	2,864	1.535	0.09	0.07

continued on next page

Table 5.28 — cont'd

Province	Males	Females	Total	Sex Ratio	Distribution	Concentration
Central Kalimantan	2,857	1,947	4,804	1.467	0.15	0.22
South Kalimantan	6,615	5,280	11,895	1.253	0.37	0.33
East Kalimantan	12,781	9,586	22,367	1.333	0.70	0.63
North Sulawesi	95	51	146	1.863	0.00	0.01
Central Sulawesi	10,719	9,739	20,458	1.101	0.64	0.78
South Sulawesi	5,963	5,373	11,336	1.110	0.36	0.14
Southeast Sulawesi	3,627	3,307	6,934	1.097	0.22	0.31
Gorontalo	789	694	1,483	1.137	0.05	0.14
West Sulawesi	3,200	2,911	6,111	1.099	0.19	0.53
Maluku	200	136	336	1.471	0.01	0.02
North Maluku	113	76	189	1.487	0.01	0.02
West Papua	412	304	716	1.355	0.02	0.10
Papua	1,343	1,015	2,358	1.323	0.07	0.08
Indonesia	1,522,636	1,652,370	3,175,006	0.921	100.00	1.34

Source: Calculated by the authors, based on tabulations provided by the BPS.

were some provinces with relatively large numbers of Sasak. About 22,700 Sasak live in neighbouring Bali, about 22,400 Sasak in East Kalimantan and 11,900 in South Kalimantan. About 20,500 Sasak live in Central Sulawesi and 11,300 in South Sulawesi. The number of Sasak migrating to eastern neighbouring provinces was very small, only about 2,000 people.

CHINESE

Moving to Old Population

The term Chinese here refers to Indonesian citizens of Chinese descent. Unlike other ethnic groups, there is no home province for the Chinese. The Chinese may be the fifth or sixth generation living in Indonesia, and some even longer. Some may just be third generation and some others may be second generation Indonesian-born citizens. Some others may be the first generation, coming from the People's Republic of China (PRC) or Taiwan. Those who have been in Indonesia for more than one generation have in particular adapted to local cultures.

Therefore, the Chinese Indonesians are very heterogeneous. Their ethnic identity is determined by their places of residence. For example, the Chinese living alongside the Javanese community may have adopted Javanese culture. In addition to Bahasa Indonesia, they may also speak Javanese fluently and enjoy Javanese food very much. They may like drinking "very sweet" tea as most Javanese do. Similarly, the Chinese living alongside the Sundanese community may speak Sundanese and eat Sundanese food. Just like the Sundanese, they may not like "sweet" tea. Similarly with the Balinese. On the island of Sumatra, however, the Chinese groups are different. They usually speak Chinese, in addition to Bahasa Indonesia. Similarly, the Chinese in West Kalimantan speak Chinese. More discussion on the languages of the Chinese can be found in Chapter 7.

The Chinese are one of the ethnic groups with "foreign origins". As shown in Appendix 1, the 2010 population census recorded many groups of Indonesian citizens with foreign origins such as those from Timor-Leste, the Arab states, the United States, India, Malaysia, Pakistan and Singapore. The Arab can only be found in the provinces of Central Java and East Java, where they were the fifth and ninth largest ethnic group, respectively, although only constituting a very tiny percentage, 0.04 per cent and 0.08 per cent, of the respective populations. The Arab may also be found in other provinces, but they were not one of the ten largest ethnic groups in the province. The group of those with Timor-Leste origins was the sixth largest group in the province of East Nusa Tenggara. Timor-Leste borders the province of East Nusa Tenggara and used to be a province of the Republic of Indonesia.

The total number of Chinese in Indonesia was 2.83 million in 2010. The population pyramid of the Chinese, depicted in Figure 5.15, has a narrowing base indicating a very low fertility rate. The population aged 0–4 accounted for 7.13 per cent. A rapid decline in population amongst those aged below 25 indicates that the fertility rate has been low during the past several decades. The young aged 5–14 made up 15.77 per cent and the youth accounted for a slightly higher percentage, 15.99 per cent. The young dependent population, under 25 years, formed only 38.89 per cent of the total Chinese population. This was the lowest percentage of young dependent populations amongst all ethnic groups. On the other hand, the prime-working-age Chinese made up almost a half (49.76 per cent) of the population, much larger than the percentage of the young dependent population. The Chinese prime-working-age population thus had fewer young people to support financially.

On the other hand, the population aged 60 and above accounted for 11.35 per cent, which made the Chinese the oldest population amongst the fifteen largest ethnic groups. It is still a transitional population, but close to 12 per cent, the threshold to enter the old population phase. Amongst all ethnic groups, the Chinese have the oldest age-structure in their population, the closest stage to an old population. The Balinese have the second highest percentage of older persons, followed by the Madurese and the Javanese.

The overall sex ratio of the Chinese was the same as the Balinese, 1.01. The excess of Chinese males over females was seen amongst those aged below 45 (Table 5.29). As in other ethnic groups, the sex ratio of older persons aged 60 and above was below 1 (0.87). As depicted in Table 5.30, the sex ratio of the Chinese was different in many provinces. In many provinces, Chinese males outnumbered females with sex ratios even higher than the overall ratio. The highest ratio was in Papua with 1.25, indicating that there were 25 per cent more Chinese males than females. Except for Banten, the Chinese population in all other provinces on the island of Java had more females than males. Three other provinces (North Sumatra,

Figure 5.15
Population Age-Sex Structure: Chinese, 2010

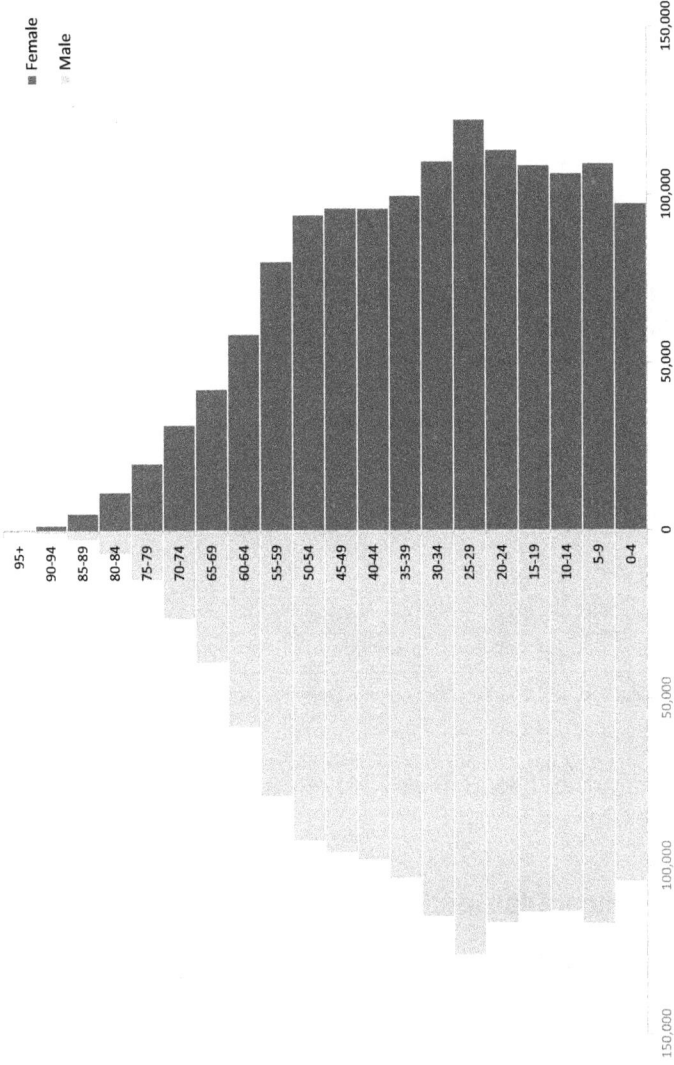

Source: Drawn from Table 5.29.

Table 5.29
Number and Percentage of Chinese Population by Age and Sex: Indonesia, 2010

Age Group	Males	Females	Total	Per cent	Sex Ratio
0–4	104,536	97,521	202,057	7.13	1.072
5–9	117,111	109,469	226,580	8.00	1.070
10–14	113,497	106,505	220,002	7.77	1.066
15–19	113,693	108,810	222,503	7.86	1.045
20–24	116,824	113,464	230,288	8.13	1.030
25–29	126,453	122,467	248,920	8.79	1.033
30–34	114,909	110,066	224,975	7.94	1.044
35–39	103,658	99,912	203,570	7.19	1.037
40–44	97,954	96,087	194,041	6.85	1.019
45–49	95,833	96,158	191,991	6.78	0.997
50–54	92,435	94,142	186,577	6.59	0.982
55–59	79,170	80,264	159,434	5.63	0.986
60–64	58,525	58,692	117,217	4.14	0.997
65–69	39,431	42,256	81,687	2.88	0.933
70–74	26,125	31,709	57,834	2.04	0.824
75–79	14,518	20,234	34,752	1.23	0.718
80–84	6,853	11,757	18,610	0.66	0.583
85–89	2,710	5,360	8,070	0.28	0.506
90–94	785	1,827	2,612	0.09	0.430
95+	216	574	790	0.03	0.376
Total	1,425,236	1,407,274	2,832,510	100.00	1.01

Source: Calculated by the authors, based on tabulations provided by the BPS.

West Sumatra and South Sulawesi) saw a sex ratio below 1, indicating an excess of Chinese females.

Geographical Distribution

Amongst provinces, there was no province dominantly inhabited by the Chinese. The largest number of Chinese lived in Jakarta, the capital of Indonesia, but this was only 22.33 per cent. This means that a significant number of the Chinese lived in many other provinces. If we include Jakarta's two neighbours, West Java (9 per cent) and Banten (6.49 per cent), then 37.82 per cent of the Chinese lived in the adjacent provinces of Jakarta, West Java, Banten. Because the number of Chinese in these three other

Table 5.30
Number, Distribution and Concentration of Chinese by Province: Indonesia, 2010

Province	Males	Females	Total	Sex Ratio	Distribution	Concentration
Aceh	4,936	4,684	9,620	1.054	0.34	0.22
North Sumatra	169,842	170,478	340,320	0.996	12.01	2.63
West Sumatra	5,340	5,459	10,799	0.978	0.38	0.22
Riau	52,742	49,122	101,864	1.074	3.60	1.85
Jambi	19,160	18,086	37,246	1.059	1.31	1.21
South Sumatra	36,854	35,721	72,575	1.032	2.56	0.98
Bengkulu	1,521	1,369	2,890	1.111	0.10	0.17
Lampung	20,492	19,487	39,979	1.052	1.41	0.53
Bangka-Belitung	50,897	48,727	99,624	1.045	3.52	8.17
Riau Archipelago	66,890	61,814	128,704	1.082	4.54	7.70
Jakarta	311,848	320,524	632,372	0.973	22.33	6.62
West Java	127,063	127,857	254,920	0.994	9.00	0.59
Central Java	67,932	71,946	139,878	0.944	4.94	0.43
Yogyakarta	5,716	5,829	11,545	0.981	0.41	0.33
East Java	118,947	125,446	244,393	0.948	8.63	0.66
Banten	92,262	91,427	183,689	1.009	6.49	1.73
Bali	7,668	7,302	14,970	1.050	0.53	0.39
West Nusa Tenggara	3,785	3,603	7,388	1.051	0.26	0.16
East Nusa Tenggara	4,085	3,954	8,039	1.033	0.28	0.17
West Kalimantan	188,662	169,789	358,451	1.111	12.65	8.17

continued on next page

Table 5.28 – *cont'd*

Province	Males	Females	Total	Sex Ratio	Distribution	Concentration
Central Kalimantan	2,864	2,266	5,130	1.264	0.18	0.23
South Kalimantan	6,688	6,312	13,000	1.060	0.46	0.36
East Kalimantan	17,194	15,563	32,757	1.105	1.16	0.93
North Sulawesi	4,383	4,149	8,532	1.056	0.30	0.38
Central Sulawesi	6,577	5,943	12,520	1.107	0.44	0.48
South Sulawesi	21,550	22,296	43,846	0.967	1.55	0.55
Southeast Sulawesi	1,518	1,372	2,890	1.106	0.10	0.13
Gorontalo	634	585	1,219	1.084	0.04	0.12
West Sulawesi	360	300	660	1.200	0.02	0.06
Maluku	2,393	2,163	4,556	1.106	0.16	0.30
North Maluku	1,232	1,072	2,304	1.149	0.08	0.22
West Papua	1,312	1,113	2,425	1.179	0.09	0.32
Papua	1,889	1,516	3,405	1.246	0.12	0.12
Indonesia	1,425,236	1,407,274	2,832,510	1.013	100.00	1.20

Source: Calculated by the authors, based on tabulations provided by the BPS.

provinces in Java were also relatively large, the Chinese living on the island of Java accounted for just about half of the total Chinese (51.80 per cent) in Indonesia.

After Jakarta, the largest number of Chinese live in West Kalimantan, followed by North Sumatra. The Chinese living on the island of Sumatra comprised almost 30 per cent, with the largest number living in North Sumatra (340,000), followed by those in the Riau Archipelago (129,000) and Riau (102,000).

In terms of concentrations in each province, the Chinese had a unique pattern. The highest concentration was in the province of Bangka-Belitung (8.17 per cent) and West Kalimantan (8.17 per cent), followed by the Riau Archipelago (7.70 per cent) and Jakarta (6.62 per cent). Although the Chinese could be found in each of the remaining provinces in Indonesia, the concentrations were mostly under 1 per cent, except in North Sumatra (2.63 per cent), Riau (1.85 per cent) and Jambi (1.21 per cent).

In Bangka-Belitung, the Chinese were the fourth largest ethnic group. Ahok (Basuki Tjahaja Purnama), the current governor of Jakarta, was one of the Bangka-Belitung Chinese. In this province, the Chinese live with the Bangka as the largest ethnic group, followed by the Belitung and Javanese. The Chinese was also the fourth largest ethnic group in the province of West Kalimantan, sharing a population size with the Dayak as the largest ethnic group, followed by the Malay and the Javanese. In Jakarta, the Chinese were number four, after the Javanese, the Betawi and the Sundanese. Similarly, the Chinese were number four in Yogyakarta and East Java and even number three in Central Java, but their contributions were very small — less than 1 per cent in each of the three Javanese provinces. As discussed in Chapter 4, the Chinese were amongst the largest ten ethnic groups in seventeen provinces.

Notes

1. It is still a debatable point how low fertility should go. Should it be that the TFR equals 1.7, below the replacement level, or should the fertility be at the replacement level, with the TFR at about 2.1, or should the TFR be a little higher than the replacement level, with the TFR around 2.4? Definitely, it should not be higher than 3.
2 See Arifin and Ananta (2013) for a detailed discussion on three mega demographic trends in Indonesia.
3. Muslihat, Eni. "Lampung Makin Padat, Tiap Tahun Kirim Transmigrasi",

KBR68H, PortalKBR.com, 3 December 2013, downloaded from http://www.portalkbr.com/nusantara/acehdansumatera/3045129_4264.html on 15 December 2013.

4. See a discussion on *merantau* in sub-section "Almost Homogenous Provinces" in Chapter 4.

5. The percentage is calculated from two sources. The total number of Madurese in Indonesia is cited from Suryadinata, Arifin and Ananta (2003), totalling 6,771,727 in 2000. The number of Madurese living on the island of Madura in 2000 is calculated from the BPS (2001) figures by adding the number of Madurese in the four districts on the island of Madura: Bangkalan, Pamekasan, Sampang and Sumenep. Based on the calculation, the population in these four districts totalled 3,249,488 and the Madurese living there numbered 2,171,271.

6. The province of East Kalimantan split into North Kalimantan and East Kalimantan in 2013. The discussion in this book follows the definition of 2010.

6

CHANGE IN SIZE AND COMPOSITION OF ETHNIC GROUPS: Indonesia, 2000–2010

As Indonesia collected information on ethnicity for the first time since the colonial era in the 2000 population census, the discussion on the dynamics of Indonesia's ethnic groups is focused on the period of 2000–2010. However, this chapter also provides a brief discussion relating to the period 1930–2000, as the colonial population census in 1930 collected information on ethnicity. Special caution should be exercised when interpreting the statistics from 1930, especially when comparing with those in 2000 and 2010, as the concepts and coverage of the statistics as well as classification of ethnic groups can be different. Because of space and time limitations, we have concentrated on the dynamics of the fifteen largest ethnic groups in Indonesia according to the 2010 population censuses.

To understand the changes in population numbers, we first need to examine changes in the three basic demographic components: fertility, mortality and migration. The fertility rate has a positive impact on the size of a population by adding to the number of people. On the other hand, the mortality rate has a negative impact by reducing the number of people. Migration can increase or reduce the number of people depending on the flows of out-migration and in-migration. The fertility rate affects the age structure through the youngest population aged 0–4 years old. Mortality and migration can have an impact on all age groups. In addition to these three demographic components, we have checked for any possible differences on the coverage of samples and classifications of ethnic groups over time.

In the next section, we discuss the classifications of ethnic groups in 2000 and compare them with those in 2010. We then compare the coverage of the 2000 and 2010 population censuses, especially the underestimation in the 2000 population census. With this background, this chapter discusses the change of the composition of ethnic groups in Indonesia.

ETHNIC CLASSIFICATION IN 2000

The ethnic groups in 2000, presented in the book, *Indonesia's Population: Ethnicity and Religion in a Changing Political Landscape* (Suryadinata, Arifin and Ananta 2003), was based on publications by BPS. BPS published the results of the 2000 population census in a series of thirty-one volumes, one volume for each of the thirty provinces and one volume for Indonesia as a whole.

Amongst many other things, this series contains statistics on ethnicity in Indonesia as a whole and within each province. The statistics on ethnicity covered the eight largest ethnic groups in Indonesia as a whole and within each province. The publication for Indonesia as a whole provided data for the eight largest ethnic groups in Indonesia: the Javanese, Sundanese, Madurese, Minangkabau, Betawi, Buginese, Bantenese and Banjarese. This publication missed out the Malay and Batak. As shown in Table 6.1, the corrected order should be the Javanese, Sundanese, Malay, Batak, Madurese, Minangkabau, Betawi, Buginese, Bantenese and Banjarese.

Each ethnic group in 2000 was classified in a very simple way, merely based on its main category, without taking into account any sub-ethnic groups or aliases. The data for each ethnic group was published as it was coded. Yet, there were exceptions for a few cases discussed later here.

The 2000 classification used in this book mainly follows the same classification presented in Suryadinata, Arifin and Ananta (2003), which was based on BPS publications. Nevertheless, we use the revised version wherever the data is available. In contrast, the 2010 classification utilizes

Table 6.1
Change in Ethnic Composition as Ordered by the 2010 Rank: Indonesia, 2000–2010

Rank	Ethnic Group	1930**** Number (000)	1930**** Percentage	2000 Number (000)	2000 Percentage	2010 Number (000)	2010 Percentage
1	Javanese	27,809	47.02	83,866*	41.71	94,843	40.06
2	Sundanese	8,595	14.53	30,978*	15.41	36,705	15.51
3	Malay	954	1.61	8,950*	4.45	8,754	3.70
4	Batak	1,208	2.04	6,891*	3.43	8,467	3.58
5	Madurese	4,306	7.28	6,772*	3.37	7,179	3.03
6	Betawi	981	1.66	5,042	2.51	6,808	2.88
7	Minangkabau	1,989	3.36	5,475	2.72	6,463	2.73
8	Buginese	1,533	2.59	5,010	2.49	6,415	2.71
9	Bantenese	n.a	n.a	4,113	2.05	4,642	1.96
10	Banjarese	899	1.52	3,496	1.74	4,127	1.74
11	Balinese	1,112	1.88	3,028^	1.51	3,925	1.66
12	Acehnese	831	1.41	872	0.43^^^	3,404	1.44
13	Dayak	651	1.10	n.a	n.a	3,220	1.36
14	Sasak	659	1.12	2,611^^	1.3	3,175	1.34
15	Chinese	1,233	2.03***	1,739	0.86**	2,833	1.20
	Others	6,378	10.78	32,249	16.02	35,769	15.11

Note: * The 2000 data for these five ethnic groups refer to the revised version, presented in Ananta, Arifin and Bakhtiar (2005). However, the revised version produced different numbers for only three ethnic groups: the Javanese, Malay and Batak. Therefore, we have followed the data of Suryadinata, Arifin and Ananta (2003) for the numbers of Sundanese and Madurese. The data for the remaining ethnic groups as well those for the 1930 census refer to Suryadinata, Arifin and Ananta (2003). The 2010 figures are the authors' calculations, based on tabulations provided by the BPS (Statistics, Indonesia).

** Underestimated figure. The re-estimated figure (Suryadinata, Arifin and Ananta 2003) was about 1.5 per cent.

*** Regardless of their citizenships, the Chinese totalled 1,233,000 in 1930 and therefore the percentage of the Chinese was calculated using the total population as the denominator, while others used the indigenous population as its denominator.

**** The 1930 data included Palembang as the thirteenth largest ethnic group, contributing 1.30 per cent; but did not have the Bantenese, as they were classified under the Sundanese.

^ The Balinese may have been underestimated, as this figure was estimated from five provinces only.

^^ The Sasak may have been underestimated, as this figure was estimated from two provinces only.

^^^ The Achenese may have been underestimated due to security reasons during data collection.

the New Classification, created from the coded raw data set of the 2010 population census, which has taken the complexity of the data on ethnicity into account.

Therefore, this difference should be taken into account when comparing the 2000 and 2010 classifications. For example, in 2000, the Javanese were classified simply from one coded category, "Jawa". On the other hand, as seen in Appendix 1, the New Classification includes four additional codes as sub-ethnic groups of the Javanese.

The Sundanese only consisted of one coded category, "Sunda", in the 2000 classification. However, the 2010 New Classification data also includes Naga, a sub-ethnic group of the Sundanese with a different code.

Four ethnic groups (Madurese, Betawi, Minangkabau and Bantenese) had the same classification for both 2000 and 2010. They have neither sub-ethnic groups nor aliases. However, three ethnic groups had a somewhat complex change of classifications. They are the Malay, Batak and Chinese.

The Malay in the 2000 classification covered thirteen sub-ethnic groups residing in fourteen provinces. Seven of these are the same as those in the 2010 New Classification. They are Melayu, Melayu Riau, Melayu Jambi, Melayu Bengkulu, Melayu Semendo, Melayu Pasemah and Melayu Pontianak. The remaining six sub-ethnic groups of Malay were recorded in 2000, but not in the 2010 census. They were the Melayu Musi Sekayu, Melayu Bangka, Melayu Belitung, Melayu Enim, Melayu Palembang and Melayu Pegagan. As shown in Appendix 1 and discussed in Chapter 3, the New Classification found Musi to be a separate ethnic group, different from the Malay; and the Musi Sekayu is a sub-ethnic group of the Musi. Furthermore, the Bangka, Belitung, Enim, Palembang and Pegagan are separate ethnic groups, not part of the Malay group.

As the 2000 publication may miss some Malay who lived outside the fourteen provinces, Ananta, Arifin and Bakhtiar (2005) revised the statistics for the Malay, using the raw data set of the 2000 population census, to include all Malay living in Indonesia. The revised version of the Malay is compared with the corresponding figure in 2010, which includes many more categories under the Malay, as described in Chapter 3 and listed in Appendix 1.

In the 2000 classification, the Batak, also known as the Batak Tapanuli, included four out of six sub-ethnic groups of Batak. They were the Angkola, Mandailing (also recorded as the Angkola Mandailing in the census), the

Karo and Toba. The Simalungun and Dairi/Pakpak were not included. Later, Ananta, Arifin and Bakhtiar (2005) revised the estimate of the Batak by including all six sub-ethnic groups derived from the complete raw 2000 data set. The revised version of the Batak is used here to examine the change between 2000 and 2010.

The classification of the Chinese was more complicated. In 2000, as discussed in Suryadinata, Arifin and Ananta (2003, p. 76), the Chinese were defined as consisting of Indonesian citizens self-identified as Chinese. Apart from these, there were non-Indonesian Chinese, the citizens of the People's Republic of China and Taiwan. They were included in the estimation of the Chinese Indonesians. Suryadinata, Arifin and Ananta assumed that these foreign Chinese were poor Chinese who could not afford to become Indonesians. They might have been born in Indonesia, grown up there and now work in Indonesia, speaking Bahasa Indonesia fluently.

In 2006, the Government of Indonesia issued Law No. 12/2006 relating to the citizenship of Indonesia. One of the points of this law mentioned that Indonesian citizens included anybody born in Indonesia regardless of the citizenship of their parents. Therefore, with this law, the Indonesian born stateless Chinese, as assumed above, were automatically Indonesian citizens after 2006. They may still not have the official documents to prove that they are Indonesian citizens, but by law they are already Indonesian citizens.

In the 2010 population census, the categories for people with PRC and Taiwan origins were put under Indonesian citizens, not foreigners. Therefore, there is no different category in the 2000 and 2010 classifications for the Chinese. However, regardless of the above classification, the Chinese in 2000 remained underestimated, as is discussed later in this chapter.

Nevertheless, the simple classification of ethnic groups in 2000 has been significantly helpful in bridging and filling the gap in information on ethnicity. It has enriched and improved understanding of ethnicity in Indonesia.

UNDERESTIMATION IN 2000

This section focuses on the underestimation of the estimates of the population of three ethnic groups in the 2000 population census: the Acehnese, Dayak and Chinese. The reason for this underestimation is different for each of these three ethnic groups. Because of the underestimation of these ethnic groups in the 2000 population census, it is not possible to present and examine their dynamics in the same ways as we do for the other ethnic groups during 2000–2010.

In addition to these three ethnic groups, we also have underestimations for the Balinese and Sasak, because of the limited coverage in the BPS publications. As the BPS publication for Indonesia as a whole did not include the Balinese and Banjarese, Suryadinata, Arifin and Ananta (2003) tried to get the statistics for the Balinese and Banjarese from the publications for each of the thirty provinces. Unfortunately, each publication only covered the eight largest ethnic groups in a province. As a result, the Balinese and Banjarese may not be amongst the eight largest ethnic groups in some provinces.

Therefore, because we do not know the age-sex structure of the underestimated ethnic groups, we cannot examine the changes in the age-sex structure of those five ethnic groups during 2000–2010.

Acehnese: Political and Security Reasons

The Acehnese were not included in the fifteen largest ethnic groups in 2000 because there was no accurate information on the population in the province of Aceh. The political and security situation in this province during the 2000 population census was not conducive for conducting interviews and accurately gathering the data. The province of Aceh was in decades of long internal conflict over demands for its independence. The GAM (Gerakan Aceh Merdeka, Free Aceh Movement) emerged in the 1970s, primarily driven by Acehnese nationalism. A larger conflict occurred in 1989, which turned Aceh into a DOM (*Daerah Operasi Militer*, Military Operations Zone). The GAM insurgency was defeated in 1992, but the troops remained there. The collapse of the New Order regime in 1998 permitted the anti-military and anti-Jakarta sentiment in Aceh to grow high. To restore confidence in the central government, the government lifted the DOM status in Aceh in 1998. However, the democratizing reforms gave space for the GAM to re-establish and launch a series of violent conflicts against the government. The military and police were sent there again in increasing numbers. The conflict continued until the province was struck by the strong earthquake followed by the deadliest tsunami in the world on 26 December 2004.

Amidst this political turmoil and high security conditions, there was significant under-coverage of the population in Aceh, as the interviewers could not enter and enumerate the population in the conflict areas. The enumerators in the 2000 population census were only able to enumerate in several areas which were relatively safe. They only managed to cover less than 50 per cent of the Aceh population, leaving about 2.2 million unrecorded, almost one per cent of Indonesia's total population.

The serious lack of data centred on the regencies of North and East Aceh, as well as in the regency of Bireuen. The most serious omission was indicated by the absence of data in the regency of Pidie, which disappeared altogether from the list of districts in the BPS publication. Yet, these regencies do have Acehnese as the majority ethnic group. Thus, the serious under-coverage in these regencies resulted in a large underestimation of Acehnese in 2000. This underestimation produced only about 872,000 persons identifying themselves as Acehnese in 2000. There should have been a much larger number, as they accounted for 3.4 million, contributing 1.44 per cent of the Indonesian population in 2010.

Dayak: A Matter of Classification

The "no show" of the Dayak of Kalimantan in the 2000 census is also because of an underestimation, but for different reasons. It was not because of difficulties found in field enumeration and interviews, but rather a matter of classification. In the 2010 census, the Dayak were classified into hundreds of categories which could be sub-ethnic and sub-sub-ethnic groups as well as aliases. However, in the publication of the 2000 census, a large number of sub-ethnic groups were not combined into a single ethnic group of the Dayak. Instead, categories of the Dayak were treated as distinct ethnic groups. As a result, there were only small numbers of categories appearing as Dayak in the 2000 publication and classification. For example, the 2000 classification mentioned that there were only four sub-ethnic groups of the Dayak (the Sambas, Kendayan, Darat and Pesaguan) in West Kalimantan. The publication only listed the eight largest ethnic categories in the province. Apparently, many Dayak categories were not captured in the eight largest categories.

Similarly, in Central Kalimantan, the publication only mentioned the Ngaju, Dayak Sampit, Bakumpai, Katingan and Maanyan. The list in

South Kalimantan recorded only the Bukat and Bakumpai, while in East Kalimantan there was just one category, the Dayak Kenyah.

There was no other information on the Dayak in other provinces presented in the series of publications in 2000. This made the statistics of the Dayak highly underestimated.

Thus, with the New Classification, the Dayak were "fully" estimated in 2010 and combined into one ethnic group to enable comparison with other ethnic groups. "Fully" means that it is still possible that there are still more Dayak sub-ethnic groups which have not been identified in the New Classification.

Chinese: Political Change

Not long after the New Order regime came to power, the government implemented a series of assimilationist regulations by banning the three pillars of Chinese identity: clan association, ethnic media and Chinese-language schools. The regulation also prohibited circulating newspapers and other kinds of Chinese-language mass media for the public. Chinese language materials were not allowed to enter the country. The public use and display of Chinese characters were strictly forbidden. Chinese New Year celebrations could not be carried out in public. Confucianism was no longer recognized as an official religion in Indonesia. The Chinese Indonesians were strongly encouraged to change their names to "Indonesian" names.[1] After this policy took place, it was no longer easy to identify the Chinese through their names. In short, any expression of Chinese culture and religion was not permitted to be displayed in public. These assimilationist regulations lasted from 1966 until 1999.[2]

The 2000 census was conducted just about two years after the collapse of the New Order regime in 1998, coloured with "anti-Chinese" riots in several cities. The trauma of being ethnic Chinese might still be felt. Thus, the statistics on the size of the Chinese population in 2000 may be still underestimated.

Suryadinata, Arifin and Ananta (2003) argued that some respondents in 2000 did not want to identify themselves as Chinese because of the political situation. Therefore, the 2000 census recorded that the Chinese formed only 0.82 per cent of the total population of Indonesia. This estimate was derived from only eleven provinces where the Chinese were one of the eight largest ethnic groups. It was possible that the

Chinese could live in other provinces, but they were not amongst the eight largest ethnic groups. Because of the possibility of missing some Chinese, Suryadinata, Arifin and Ananta then re-estimated the percentage to be between 1.5 per cent and 2 per cent. With the finding in Ananta, Arifin and Bakhtiar (2005), it is likely that the figure for 2000 is closer to 1.5 per cent than 2 per cent. The Chinese could have been at least in twelfth position in 2000.

UNCHANGING TREND: SKEWED DISTRIBUTION

Table 6.1 shows an unequal distribution amongst ethnic groups during the eighty-year period of 1930–2010 with a very large percentage of the Javanese. The Javanese have always been the largest and most dominant ethnic group in Indonesia, comprising more than 40 per cent of the total number of citizens in that period. The difference with the second largest ethnic group, the Sundanese, was very large. The Sundanese only contributed about 15 per cent, a difference of about 25 percentage points between the two groups in 2010. Yet this difference has been declining from about 32 percentage points in 1930.

Furthermore, the difference between the second and third largest groups has been widening, from 7.25 percentage points (between the Sundanese and Madurese) in 1930 to 10.96 percentage points in 2000 (between the Sundanese and Malay) and 11.81 percentage points (between the Sundanese and Malay) in 2010. On the other hand, the difference between the third and fourth narrowed from 3.92 percentage points (between the Madurese and Minangkabau) in 1930 to only 0.12 percentage points (between the Malay and Batak) in 2010. The differences amongst the smaller ethnic groups were also very small.

With regard to the islands of origin, five of the fifteen largest ethnic groups originated from the island of Java. They were the Javanese, Sundanese, Madurese, Betawi and Bantenese. These five Java-origin ethnic groups have always dominated all ethnic groups between 1930 and 2010, although the contribution declined from 70.49 per cent in 1930 to 63.44 per cent in 2010. On the other hand, the contribution from the four largest ethnic groups originating in Sumatra (Malay, Batak, Minangkabau and Acehnese) was much smaller, but there was an increasing trend between 1930 and 2010, from 8.42 per cent to 11.45 per cent. Therefore, in terms of the Java–Sumatra difference, the gap in the contribution of the ethnic groups has narrowed. Moreover, the percentage of population living on Java Island in 2010 was smaller than the percentage of the five largest Java-origin ethnic groups, 57.48 per cent vs. 63.44 per cent. This may indicate that the five largest Java-origin ethnic groups have been migrating to islands outside Java.

The nine ethnic groups from Java and Sumatra continued to dominate the ethnic composition. They contributed about three quarters to the total Indonesian population between 1930 and 2000, although the percentage has slightly declined from 78.91 per cent in 1930 to 74.89 per cent in 2010.

STABLE RANKING OF ELEVEN ETHNIC GROUPS IN 2000–2010

The order of the eleven largest ethnic groups hardly changed at all between the 2000 and 2010 censuses, although the number and percentage contributions have changed. The Javanese, Sundanese, Malay, Batak and Madurese have always been the first five largest groups. The Betawi and Minangkabau swapped their positions. The Minangkabau were sixth in 2000 but the seventh in 2010. On the other hand, the Betawi were the seventh in 2000 and rose to the sixth in 2010. The next four ethnic groups did not change their positions. Buginese always came in eighth place, followed by the Bantenese, Banjarese and Balinese.

All of the eleven groups can also be seen as the eleven largest ethnic groups in 1930. An exception was the absence of the Bantenese in 1930, who were categorized under Sundanese in the 1930 census. The ranking is, however, somewhat different from that in 1930. For example, the Madurese were the third largest in 1930, rather than the fifth; the Malay, the ninth, rather than the third; and the Balinese, the seventh, rather than the eleventh.

DECLINING PERCENTAGES: JAVANESE, MALAY, MADURESE, BANTENESE AND CHINESE

Javanese

As the first largest ethnic group, the percentage of Javanese declined from 41.71 per cent in 2000 to 40.01 per cent in 2010, although the number still grew.[3] This decline occurred even though some small ethnic groups were added to the Javanese in 2010 under the New Classification. This decline is very likely because the Javanese has one of the lowest fertility rates in Indonesia. Another possible reason is that there has been a large outflow of international migration amongst the Javanese, particularly those who worked as overseas workers. Indeed, the decline in the percentage of the Javanese in the period 2000–2010 is actually a continuation of the decline between 1930 and 2000.

As shown in Figure 6.1, the decline in the percentage of the Javanese may be attributed to the decline in the percentages amongst the younger age groups, those under 35 years old. The percentage of infants and toddlers, aged 0–4, declined from 9.1 per cent in 2000 (Table 6.2) to 8.7 per cent in 2010. A declining percentage was also seen amongst the young, aged 5–14. Furthermore, the Javanese did not have a youth bulge in 2000 and the percentage of youths declined rapidly from 19.8 per cent in 2000 to 16 per cent in 2010.

Table 6.2
The Javanese Population by Age and Sex: 2000

Age Group	Males	Females	Total	Per cent	Sex Ratio
0–4	3,882.5	3,722.7	7,605.2	9.07	1.04
5–9	3,971.0	3,771.4	7,742.4	9.23	1.05
10–14	4,053.5	3,854.0	7,907.5	9.43	1.05
15–19	4,369.7	4,254.6	8,624.3	10.28	1.03
20–24	3,895.1	4,076.2	7,971.3	9.50	0.96
25–29	3,830.5	3,931.1	7,761.6	9.25	0.97
30–34	3,549.6	3,567.1	7,116.7	8.49	1.00
35–39	3,251.1	3,285.4	6,536.5	7.79	0.99
40–44	2,816.8	2,661.7	5,478.5	6.53	1.06
45–49	2,253.0	2,021.6	4,274.6	5.10	1.11
50–54	1,634.1	1,591.1	3,225.2	3.85	1.03
55–59	1,333.4	1,330.3	2,663.7	3.18	1.00
60–64	1,194.0	1,328.6	2,522.6	3.01	0.90
65–69	819.8	977.6	1,797.4	2.14	0.84
70–74	666.6	740.9	1,407.5	1.68	0.90
75+	551.7	679.0	1,230.7	1.47	0.81
Total	42,072.4	41,793.3	83,865.7	100.00	1.01

Notes: This is the revised version, slightly different from the one presented in Suryadinata, Arifin and Ananta (2003).

Figure 6.1
Trend in Population Shares by Specific Age Group: Javanese, 2000 and 2010

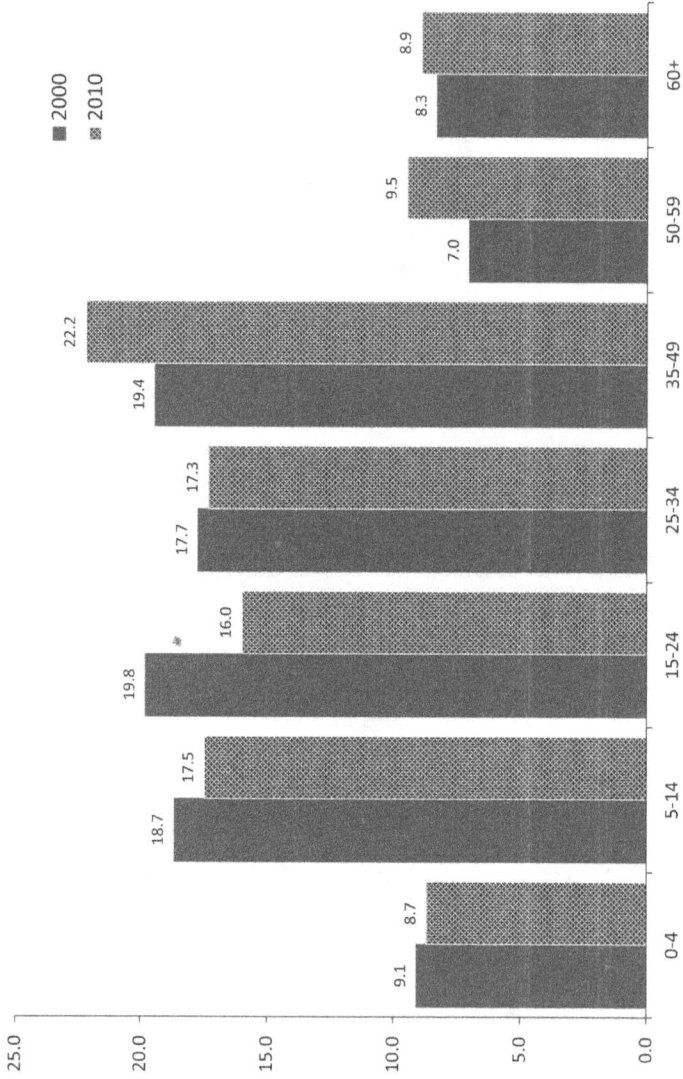

Source: The statistics for 2000 are based on Table 6.2; and for 2010, on Table 5.1.

The Javanese were relatively advanced in their age-structure transition in 2010. With the classification of the age-structure transition discussed in Chapter 5, the Javanese population has become a transitional population, almost an old population. The percentage of older persons rose between 2000 and 2010, but not much, from 8.30 per cent to 8.91 per cent. An interesting phenomenon is that the percentages of older persons aged 60–64, 65–69 and 70–74 declined between 2000 and 2010, although the percentage of older persons aged 75+ rose, from 1.47 per cent in 2000 to 2.02 per cent in 2010. Further studies should be done to explain this phenomenon.

Furthermore, the percentage of Javanese young prime-working-age adults (25–34) declined slightly.[4] However, a percentage of the mature prime-working-age population (35–49) rose from 19.4 per cent in 2000 to 22.2 per cent in 2010, making the largest contribution to the Javanese population. At the same time, the percentage of pre-elderly (50–59) increased faster than the elderly aged 60 and above in the same period.

Overall, if these trends continue, the percentage of Javanese will continue to decline, because of the continuous decline of the percentages of the younger age groups. The prime-working-age population will have to support an increasingly larger number of older persons.

Malay

Malay is a complex ethnic group, constantly shifting, making difficult comparison over time. The percentage of the Malay declined from 4.45 per cent in 2000 to 3.70 per cent in 2010, although it remained the third largest ethnic group. The Malay even declined in its absolute number, with about 200,000 fewer population in 2010. It should also be noted that the 4.45 per cent for Malay in 2000 is cited from Ananta, Arifin and Bakhtiar (2005), a revision from the 3.45 per cent as estimated in Suryadinata, Arifin and Ananta (2003). With the revision, the total number of Malay rose from 6.95 million to 8.95 million. The revised version of the Malay population by age and sex in 2000 is presented in Table 6.3.

Figure 6.2 suggests a different age structure of Malay between 2000 and 2010. The percentage of each of the age-groups below 25 declined during 2000 and 2010, but each of the age-groups above 25 rose. The percentage of infants and toddlers declined slightly from 11.1 per cent to 10.8 per cent, indicating a decline in fertility rate. A larger decline was seen amongst those aged 5–14 years old. The youth bulge[5] disappeared

Table 6.3
The Malay Population by Age and Sex: 2000

Age Group	Males	Females	Total	Per cent	Sex Ratio
0–4	503.0	494.5	997.5	11.14	1.02
5–9	510.0	491.6	1,001.6	11.19	1.04
10–14	543.4	527.1	1,070.5	11.96	1.03
15–19	516.9	527.6	1,044.5	11.67	0.98
20–24	444.8	490.7	935.5	10.45	0.91
25–29	411.0	427.1	838.1	9.36	0.96
30–34	343.2	338.4	681.6	7.62	1.01
35–39	313.0	312.8	625.8	6.99	1.00
40–44	266.8	240.6	507.4	5.67	1.11
45–49	197.8	174.0	371.8	4.15	1.14
50–54	136.7	125.9	262.6	2.93	1.09
55–59	97.4	92.1	189.5	2.12	1.06
60–64	85.8	86.7	172.5	1.93	0.99
65–69	49.2	54.8	104.0	1.16	0.90
70–74	38.7	42.4	81.1	0.91	0.91
75+	28.8	37.5	66.3	0.74	0.77
Total	4,486.5	4,463.8	8,950.3	100.00	1.01

Notes: This is the revised version, covering all thirty provinces and estimated from the raw data of the 2000 population census. The Malay in 2000, as presented in Suryadinata, Arifin and Ananta (2003) totalled 6.94 million, derived from fourteen provinces only.

as the youth declined significantly from 22.1 per cent in 2000 to 18.7 per cent in 2010. Overall, the decline amongst the population below 25 may indicate a future slower growth of the Malay population.

The percentage of the mature working-age population has risen from 16.8 per cent to 19 per cent, the pre-elderly from 5.1 per cent to 7 per cent, and older persons from 4.7 per cent to 5.3 per cent. Therefore, the Malay population is moving towards a youthful population, leaving the very young population phase.

This decline (in both absolute and percentage) of the Malay can be attributed to the different classifications of Malay in 2000 and 2010. As mentioned earlier, the New Classification uncovered the Bangka, Palembang, Enim, Belitung and Pegagan ethnic groups as being separate, not being grouped with the Malay as in the 2000 census. These groups may initially be Malay but, as discussed in Melalatoa (1995) and Hidayah

Figure 6.2
Trend in Population Shares by Specific Age Group: Malay, 2000–2010

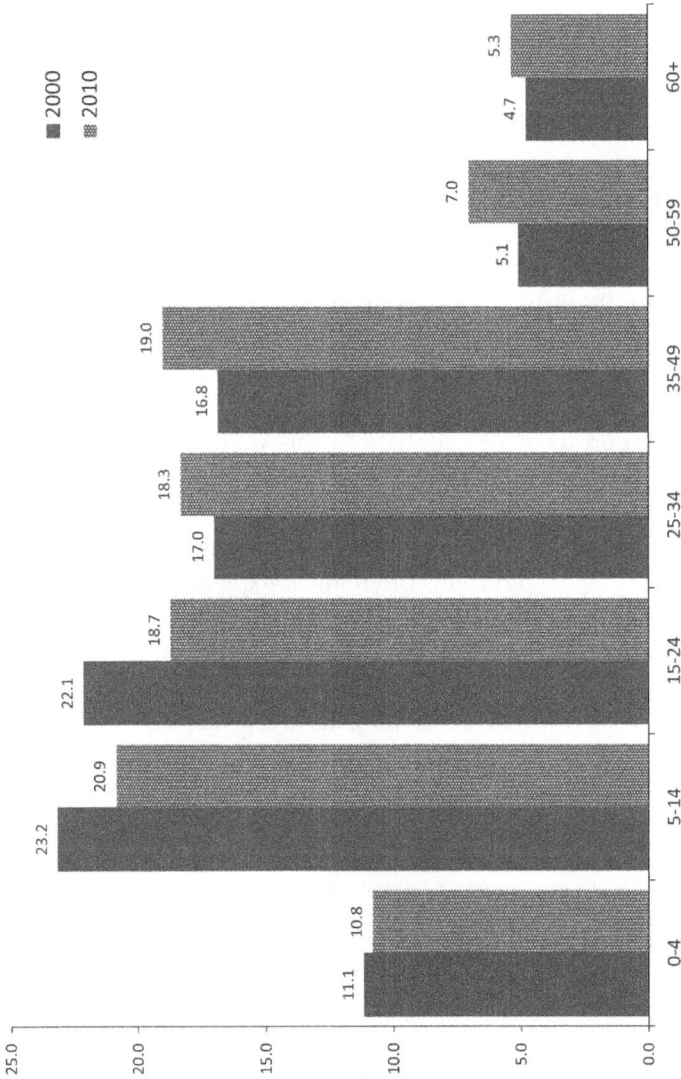

Source: Statistics for 2000 are based on Table 6.3, and 2010 on Table 5.5.

(1996), they may have identified themselves as the Palembang (*Wong* Palembang), Bangka (*Orang* Bangka), Belitung (*Urang* Belitong), Enim or Pegagan because of their growing identities. Pegagan is a sub-ethnic of the Ogan ethnic group. All of these groups also originate from the island of Sumatra.

In other words, the removal of these groups from the Malay main grouping in the New Classification may explain the decline of the Malay in 2010. However, the New Classification also uncovered some ethnic groups that were not in the 2000 census: the Melayu Banyu Asin, Melayu Deli, Langkat/Melayu Langkat, Asahan, Melayu Asahan, Melayu Lahat, Serawai, Dayak Melayu Pontianak and the Dayak Melayu Sambas. In short, a deeper study should be conducted into what extent the New Classification has resulted in the decline of both the number and percentage of the Malay.

It is also possible that there have been important demographic changes amongst the Malay. Is it possible that Malay fertility declined very fast between 2000 and 2010? Is it possible that the Malay had a large flow of out-migration to other countries in this period? We have excluded the possibility of a rising mortality rate amongst the Malay because there has been no major event which could have had such a result. Deeper studies analysing both the 2000 and 2010 censuses could help to explain whether the fertility and migration differentials explain the decline in both the number and percentage of the Malay.

Moreover, we may also study whether it is possible that some Malay who have been living outside the island of Sumatra no longer identify themselves as Malay; instead, they may now identify themselves with the local ethnic groups in the provinces where they presently live. Is it possible that there were many marriages with other ethnic groups, resulting in new ethnic identities?

It is interesting to note that the percentage of the Malay was very low in 1930, only 1.61 per cent, then rising during 1930–2000. It is not clear whether the increase was because of a different definition, high fertility or more awareness amongst groups of being of a Malay identity. Without further deep studies, these questions cannot be answered.

Madurese

As mentioned earlier, there is no change in the classification of the Madurese. It is likely that the declining percentage of the Madurese, from

Figure 6.3
Trend in Population Shares by Specific Age Group: Madurese, 2000 and 2010

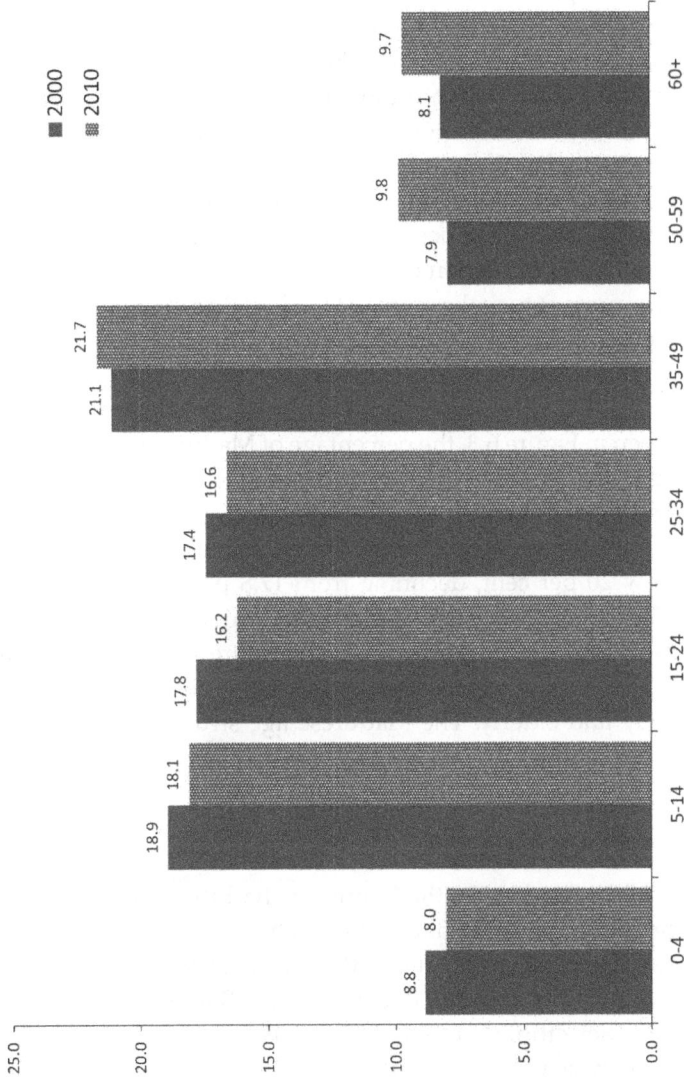

■ 2000
▓ 2010

Age	2000	2010
0-4	8.8	8.0
5-14	18.9	18.1
15-24	17.8	16.2
25-34	17.4	16.6
35-49	21.1	21.7
50-59	7.9	9.8
60+	8.1	9.7

Source: The statistics for 2000 are based on Suryadinata, Arifin and Ananta (2003), and for 2010 on Table 5.9.

3.37 per cent in 2000 to 3.03 per cent in 2010, is because of the group's relatively low fertility and/or its relatively large flow of out-migration to other countries. It is also perhaps because of a rising mortality amongst the Madurese, particularly those who lived in Kalimantan. The interethnic violence in Sampit, Central Kalimantan, in 2000–2001 may have caused a rising number of deaths amongst the Madurese. The Norwegian Refugee Council (2010) noted that the number of deaths was claimed to be between 500 and 1,300. A more important explanation was perhaps the change of self-perception after the long conflict against the Madurese in Kalimantan. Sukandar (2007) argued that being the losers in the conflict, the Madurese in Kalimantan may have been reluctant to reveal their identity, including during the 2010 population census.

It is important to make more detailed studies of the factors that caused the declining percentage of the Madurese. It is highly interesting because the contribution of the Madurese was relatively very high in 1930, at 7.28 per cent.

As seen in Figure 6.3, the percentage of Madurese infants and toddlers declined in the period 2000–2010, indicating a decline in the fertility rate. The percentage of children aged 5–14 declined as fast as the youngest ones, a decline of 0.8 percentage points. The contribution of youths aged 15–24 was below 20 per cent, declining from 17.8 per cent in 2000 to 16.2 per cent in 2010. The percentage of the young prime-working-age population aged 25–34 also declined. However, the figure shows that the Madurese aged above 35 years increased, with the higher increase seen amongst the pre-elderly and elderly. The Madurese age structure is moving towards an old population.

Bantenese

Similar to the Madurese, the Bantenese had the same classification for both the 2000 and 2010 data. The slight decline in percentage of the Bantenese, from 2.05 per cent in 2000 to 1.96 per cent in 2010, may indicate a relatively faster fertility decline in the Bantenese population than amongst other ethnic groups. Figure 6.4 indicates that the percentages of the Bantenese population below 25 years old decreased significantly. Compared with Figure 6.1 for the Javanese and Figure 6.5 for the Sundanese, the decline in percentage points of infants and toddlers (0–4) and children (5–14) amongst the Bantenese was relatively larger than

Figure 6.4
Trend in Population Shares by Specific Age Group: Bantenese, 2000 and 2010

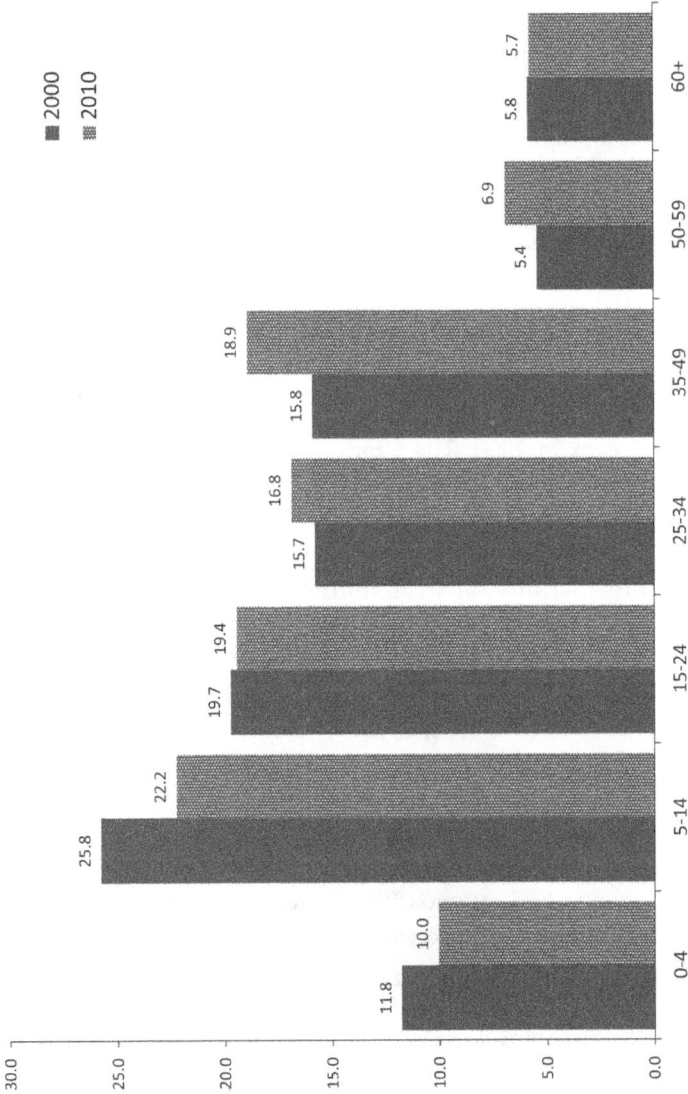

■ 2000
▨ 2010

	0-4	5-14	15-24	25-34	35-49	50-59	60+
2000	11.8	25.8	19.7	15.7	15.8	5.4	5.8
2010	10.0	22.2	19.4	16.8	18.9	6.9	5.7

Source: The statistics for 2000 are based on Suryadinata, Arifin and Ananta (2003), and 2010 on Table 5.17.

amongst the Javanese and Sundanese. Therefore, the Bantenese may have experienced a faster fertility decline relative to these two ethnic groups.[6]

Nevertheless, Bantenese youths remained at 19.7 per cent and their percentage is much larger than that of the young working-age population, which increased from 15.7 per cent in 2000 to 16.8 per cent in 2010. Currently, the population of Bantenese, who were still considered a very young population, may be moving towards a youthful population. The number of older age groups have been increasing, although the percentage of Bantenese older persons declined by 0.1 percentage point. The mature working-age population increased significantly from 15.8 per cent to 18.9 per cent. The pre-elderly increased from 5.4 per cent to 6.9 per cent.

Chinese

The percentage of the Chinese declined from 2.03 per cent in 1930 to close to 1.5 per cent in 2000. The Chinese may be the twelfth largest ethnic group in 2000, declining from sixth place in 1930. Heavy international out-migration ("going back home" to China) in the 1950s and early 1960s may have contributed to the decline during this period. The second reason was their low fertility rate. The third reason is that some of them did not choose to become Indonesian citizens.

On the other hand, during the period 2000–2010, there were significant political changes that enabled the Chinese Indonesians to feel more comfortable with belonging to the Chinese ethnic group in Indonesia. In 2000, President Abdurrahman Wahid allowed the expression of Chinese culture and religion in public. Chinese New Year, called *Imlek* in Indonesia, could then be celebrated publicly. In 2002, President Megawati Sukarnoputri announced that Chinese New Year was a national holiday. In 2006, President Susilo Bambang Yudhoyono officially recognized Confucianism as one of the official religions in Indonesia.

Another "revolution" in government policy occurred in 2006. The Chinese, although they are Indonesian citizens, were often treated as non-indigenous (non Indonesia *asli*). However, Law Number 12/2006 on citizenship redefines "Indonesia asli", to include all people born as Indonesian citizens and never becoming citizens of other countries of their own will. Therefore, all Chinese born as Indonesian citizens who do not hold citizenship in other countries willingly are automatically defined as Indonesia *asli.*

By the constitution, a local-born Chinese Indonesian can now become the President of the Republic of Indonesia. Currently, there is an increasing number of Chinese contributing to a variety of jobs outside business. Some are in politics, especially because of regional autonomy.

As the political situation in 2010 was very much more open relative to 2000, there was only a very small possibility that the Chinese in the 2010 population census were still reluctant to identify themselves as Chinese, if they wanted to. If they did not want to identify themselves as Chinese, that was more likely because they did not feel they were Chinese, rather than because of the political situation. They may have freely felt that they were more comfortable in identifying themselves with local ethnic groups, such as the Javanese or Sundanese, or being just "Indonesian" rather than Chinese. Although racially they might be Chinese, the census recorded whatever they answered to the race question. However, the census did not have an option of answering "Indonesian" as an ethnic group. Therefore, future censuses/surveys should consider including an option of "Indonesian" to answer the question on ethnicity.

With this political background, the recorded 1.20 per cent, as the percentage of the Chinese in the 2010 population, does not require any adjustment. The estimate of 1.20 per cent is also consistent with an earlier estimate for 2005 (Ananta, Arifin and Bakhtiar 2008), using the 2005 Intercensal Population Survey data, giving the percentage of 1.20 per cent.

The decline in percentage and position of the Chinese during 2000–2010 is likely because the Chinese had one of the lowest fertility rates in Indonesia. It is also possible that there was a heavy out-migration amongst the Chinese from Indonesia during that period. They may have gone to study, work or live in other countries. Moreover, there may have been a trend that some Chinese more comfortably identified themselves with local ethnic groups. The decline in the ranking of the Chinese, from the twelfth to the fifteenth place from 2000 to 2010, may also be attributable to the "full" estimation of the Acehnese and the Dayak in the 2010 census.

RISING PERCENTAGES: SUNDANESE, BATAK, BETAWI, BUGINESE, BALINESE AND DAYAK

Sundanese

Unlike the Javanese, the percentage of Sundanese slightly increased from 15.41 per cent in 2000 to 15.51 per cent in 2010. This pattern was also seen

Figure 6.5
Trend in Population Shares by Specific Age Group: Sundanese, 2000 and 2010

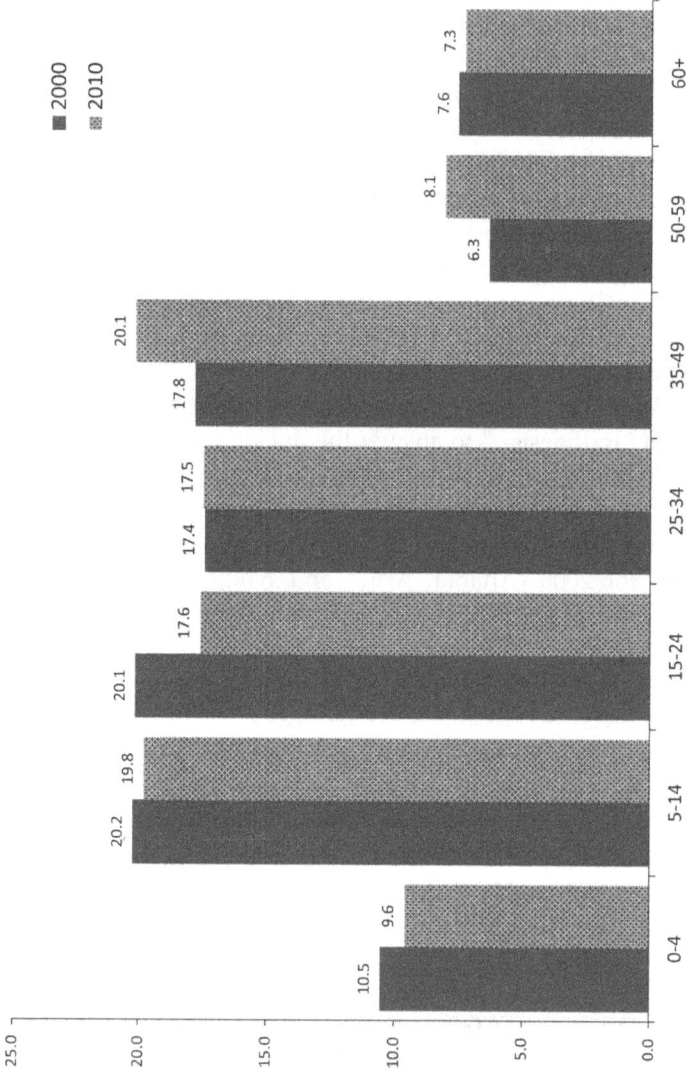

- 2000
- 2010

Age Group	2000	2010
0-4	10.5	9.6
5-14	20.2	19.8
15-24	20.1	17.6
25-34	17.4	17.5
35-49	17.8	20.1
50-59	6.3	8.1
60+	7.6	7.3

Source: The statistics for 2000 are based on Suryadinata, Arifin and Ananta (2003), and for 2010 on Table 5.3.

in 1930, when the Sundanese contributed 14.53 per cent, and rose slightly between 1930 and 2000.

As mentioned in Chapter 5, Sundanese fertility was still above the replacement level. Figure 6.5 also indicates the relatively high fertility rate of the Sundanese and its slow decline. The percentage of infants and toddlers declined slightly from 10.5 per cent in 2000 to 9.6 per cent in 2010. In addition, the number of Sundanese children aged 5–14 old remained large in the past decade, about one fifth of the total Sundanese population. The youth bulge disappeared from 2000 to 2010; the percentage of youths declined significantly from 20.1 per cent in 2000 to 17.6 per cent in 2010. The percentages of all other older groups increased during this period, except for the elderly.

Batak

The contribution of the Batak rose from 3.43 per cent to 3.58 per cent. The rise in the Batak percentage was also seen between 1930 and 2000. The increase in the last decade may be because of a relatively higher fertility amongst the Batak and/or a larger coverage of the Batak in the New Classification. In the New Classification, the Batak also included the Batak Pakpak Dairi, Dairi and Batak Simalungun. The estimate of 3.43 per cent of the Batak in 2000 was cited from Ananta, Arifin and Bakhtiar (2005), a revision from 3.02 per cent as an estimate in Suryadinata, Arifin and Ananta (2003). The revision brought the total number of the Batak from 6.08 million to 6.89 million. Table 6.4 provides the revised Batak age-sex structure of the population in 2000.

Figure 6.6 suggests the relatively high fertility of the Batak recorded in the two censuses. The percentage of Batak infants and toddlers declined very slowly, only from 11.8 per cent in 2000 to 11.3 per cent in 2010. Batak children aged 5–14 made up the largest portion, although this declined in both years. A significant decline in percentage was seen amongst the Batak youths, with the disappearance of the youth bulge from 2000 to 2010.

The Batak age-structure shows a very young population. The proportion of older persons has risen from 5.0 per cent in 2000 to 5.4 per cent in 2010. At the same time, the percentage of the pre-elderly rose to 7.4 per cent from 5.5 per cent. Thus, the percentage of Batak older persons may pass 6 per cent, so entering the youthful population, in 2020.

Overall, the Batak prime-working-age population has been shifting its financial burden, reducing the support for younger persons below 25

Figure 6.6
Trend in Population Shares by Specific Age Group: Batak, 2000 and 2010

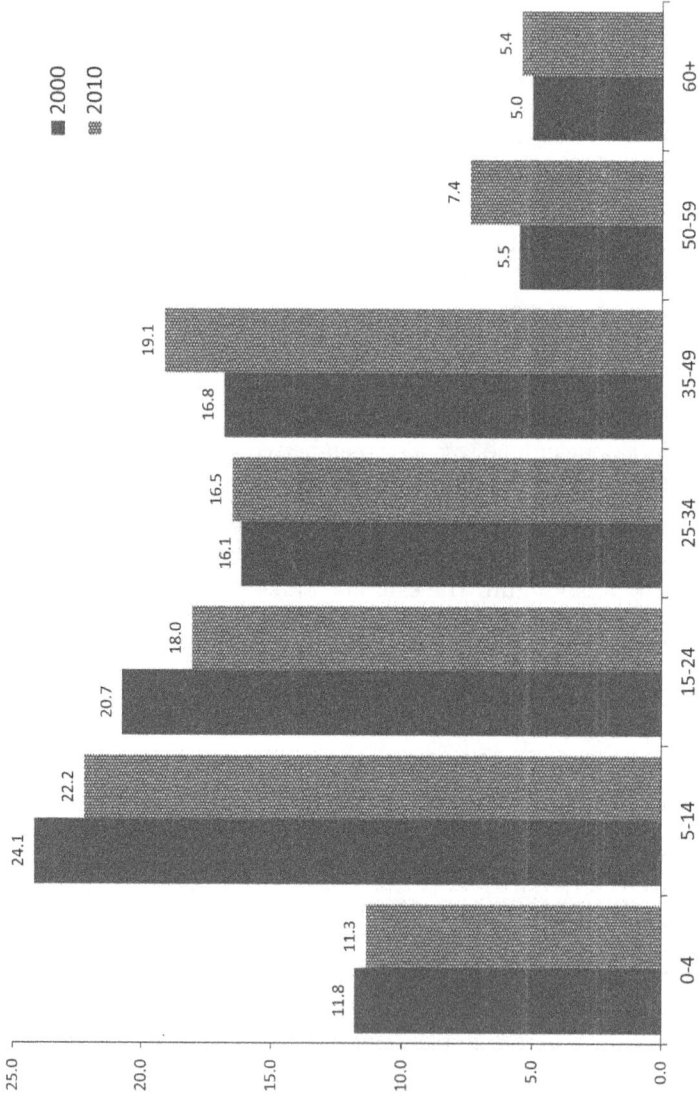

■ 2000
▓ 2010

Age Group	2000	2010
0-4	11.8	11.3
5-14	24.1	22.2
15-24	20.7	18.0
25-34	16.1	16.5
35-49	16.8	19.1
50-59	5.5	7.4
60+	5.0	5.4

Source: The statistics for 2000 are based on Table 6.4, and for 2010 on Table 5.7.

Table 6.4
The Batak Population by Age and Sex: 2000

Age Group	Males	Females	Total	Per cent	Sex Ratio
0–4	413.3	398.3	811.6	11.78	1.04
5–9	420.6	398.2	818.8	11.88	1.06
10–14	432.8	411.3	844.1	12.25	1.05
15–19	396.5	394.6	791.1	11.48	1.00
20–24	305.1	330.5	635.6	9.22	0.92
25–29	286.9	298.6	585.5	8.50	0.96
30–34	264.5	261.1	525.6	7.63	1.01
35–39	236.6	230.1	466.7	6.77	1.03
40–44	203.9	190.1	394.0	5.72	1.07
45–49	154.3	141.8	296.1	4.30	1.09
50–54	109.1	105.2	214.3	3.11	1.04
55–59	81.5	82.1	163.6	2.37	0.99
60–64	66.4	69.6	136.0	1.97	0.95
65–69	39.2	47.1	86.3	1.25	0.83
70–74	29.1	34.9	64.0	0.93	0.83
75+	23.6	34.3	57.9	0.84	0.69
Total	3,463.4	3,427.8	6,891.2	100.00	1.01

Notes: This is a revised version, taking into account all six sub-ethnic groups of the Batak living in thirty provinces. This is estimated from the raw data set of the 2000 population census.

years old and increasing the support of older persons aged 60 years old and above.

Betawi

The Betawi had no sub-ethnic group and are considered to be the "native people" (*bumi putera*) of Jakarta, the capital city. Their contribution to the total Indonesian population increased from 2.51 per cent in 2000 to 2.88 per cent in 2010, or from 5.0 million to 6.8 million.

As can be seen in Figure 6.7, the population of Betawi still had its youth bulge in 2000, with a population aged 15–24 accounting for a significant portion of 22.3 per cent of the Betawi population. However, the youth bulge disappeared between 2000 and 2010; the percentage of youths declined to 18.0 per cent in 2010. This large group were likely to have been starting families, creating a population momentum, with a large

Figure 6.7
Trend in Population Shares by Specific Age Group: Betawi, 2000 and 2010

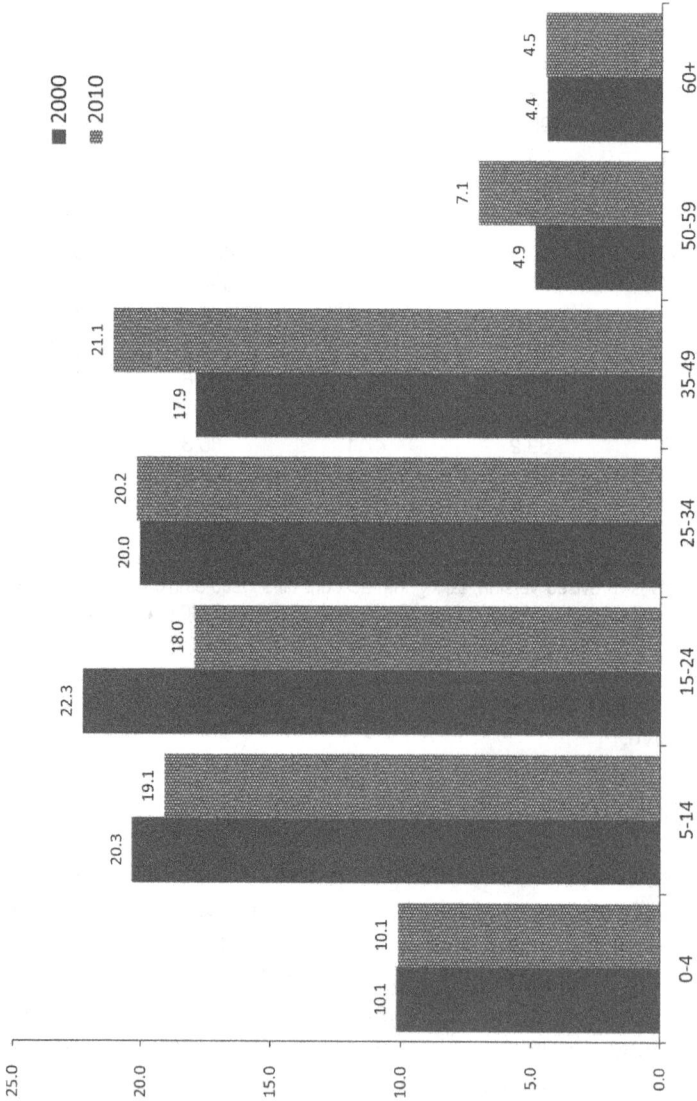

Legend: ■ 2000 ▦ 2010

Age Group	2000	2010
0-4	10.1	10.1
5-14	20.3	19.1
15-24	22.3	18.0
25-34	20.0	20.2
35-49	17.9	21.1
50-59	4.9	7.1
60+	4.4	4.5

Source: The statistics for 2000 are based on Suryadinata, Arifin and Ananta (2003), and for 2010 on Table 5.11.

increase in the number of births because of a large increase in the number of women, starting from 2000–2010.

During this period, the percentage of infants and toddlers remained stable at about 10 per cent of the total Betawi population. In addition, the children aged 5–14 still accounted for a high percentage with a slight decline in this period.

Another possibility of the growth of the Betawi population was the increased awareness of Betawi identity, resulting in a rising percentage of those who proudly identified themselves as Betawi. The trend of a rising percentage was also seen between 1930 and 2000.

Buginese

The Buginese also experienced an increase in their percentage, from 2.49 per cent in 2000 to 2.71 per cent in 2010. This increase could partly be because in 2010, the New Classification included more categories for the Buginese, as well as higher fertility rates (see Appendix 1).

However, the pattern between 1930 and 2000 was different. The contribution of the Buginese declined a little from 2.59 per cent in 1930 to 2.49 per cent in 2000. Further studies should be carried out to explain this decline and rise in percentage for the Buginese.

Figure 6.8 suggests a relatively stable proportion of the infants and toddlers at about 10 per cent. The children were also stable at around 21 per cent, but the youths declined from 20.1 per cent to 17.5 per cent. The young working-age population remained stable at about 17 per cent. The mature working-age population increased significantly. At the same time, the percentages of the pre-elderly and older persons rose significantly, although the Buginese population remained at the stage of a youthful population.

Balinese

The percentage of the Balinese rose from 1.51 per cent in 2000 to 1.66 per cent in 2010, although the Balinese also had one of the lowest fertility rates in Indonesia; indeed, it was already below the replacement level. One possibility for the increase in the percentage was that, as mentioned earlier in this chapter, the number of Balinese in 2000 was underestimated because of the coverage of the BPS publication. It was calculated from only

Figure 6.8
Trend in Population Shares by Specific Age Group: Buginese, 2000 and 2010

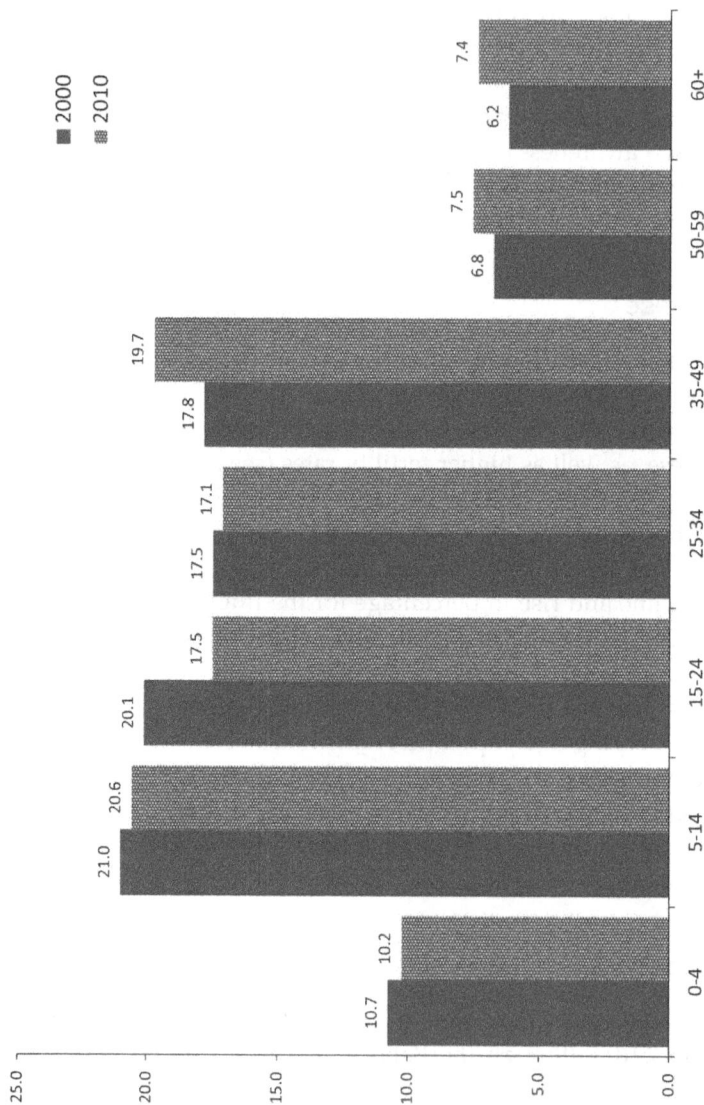

■ 2000
▒ 2010

	0-4	5-14	15-24	25-34	35-49	50-59	60+
2000	10.7	21.0	20.1	17.5	17.8	6.8	6.2
2010	10.2	20.6	17.5	17.1	19.7	7.5	7.4

Source: The statistics for 2000 are based on Suryadinata, Arifin and Ananta (2003), and for 2010 on Table 5.15.

five provinces (Bali, Central Sulawesi, West Nusa Tenggara, Southeast Sulawesi and Yogyakarta) where the Balinese were one of the eight largest ethnic groups. The Balinese may be living in other provinces where they are not one of the eight largest ethnic groups.

Another possibility could be because of a different classification. In 2010 the Balinese also consisted of the Bali Majapahit, which group was not included in the 2000 classification. However, the number of Bali Majapahit may not be sufficiently large to increase the percentage of the Balinese. Another possibility is an increase in Balinese fertility between 2000 and 2010. A rise in fertility when fertility is already below the replacement level is not unusual, as fertility usually fluctuates at this stage. The last possibility is that Balinese mortality has declined much faster than in other ethnic groups.

Like the Buginese, the percentage of Balinese also declined between 1930 and 2000, from 1.88 in 1930 to 1.51 per cent in 2000. The very low fertility amongst the Balinese may explain this declining trend between 1930 and 2000, as the province of Bali was one of the earlier provinces to start the family planning programme in Indonesia. More detailed studies should be done on the decline and rise of the percentage of the Balinese.

Dayak

As elaborated earlier in this chapter, the number of Dayak was underestimated in 2000. We have the data for the 1930 census but it is not clear whether there was an underestimation. Is the increase in the percentage of the Dayak from 1.10 per cent in 1930 to 1.36 per cent in 2010 an actual one? This question deserves further research. In terms of absolute number, it would have been a significant increase from 0.65 million to 3.2 million within eighty years.

CONSTANT PERCENTAGES: MINANGKABAU, BANJARESE, ACEHNESE AND SASAK

Minangkabau

The Minangkabau have no sub-ethnic group, comprising about the same percentage of about 2.72 per cent in both 2000 and 2010. As presented in

Figure 6.9, the change in the age structure of the Minangkabau in 2000 and 2010 does not seem to be significant, except for the youths, the mature working-age population and the pre-elderly working-age population. The percentage of youths declined significantly but the percentages of the mature and pre-elderly working-age population rose considerably. The youth bulge disappeared, as the percentage declined from 20.4 per cent in 2000 to 17.0 per cent in 2010.

Banjarese

The percentage of Banjarese in the total Indonesian population remained at 1.74 per cent in both 2000 and 2010. As seen in Figure 6.10, the percentage of infants and toddlers declined by just 0.4 percentage points from 10.3 per cent to 9.9 per cent. The Banjarese children aged 5–14 declined in relative number from 21.4 per cent to 19.8 per cent. A more significant decline was seen amongst the youth, declining from 20.9 per cent in 2000 to 18.2 per cent 2010.

On the other hand, the percentage of the population aged 35 years old and above has risen. The contribution of the older persons increased to 5.7 per cent but still lay in the stage of a very young population. However, the percentage of the pre-elderly working-age population rose a great deal, from 5.7 per cent in 2000 to 7.3 per cent in 2010. The percentage of older persons will pass 6 per cent, entering the youthful population stage in 2020.

As with many other ethnic groups, the Banjarese prime-working-age population is also transitioning, from the heavy support of younger persons below 25 years old to more support for older persons 60 years old and above.

Sasak

The percentage of Sasak was relatively constant at 1.30 per cent in 2000 and 1.34 per cent in 2010. As mentioned earlier in this chapter, the statistics for the Sasak in 2000 may have been underestimated because of the coverage of the BPS publication. The statistics for the Sasak were only provided for their home province of West Nusa Tenggara and the neighbouring province of Bali. The Sasak may live in other provinces but they were not one of the eight largest ethnic groups in the provinces

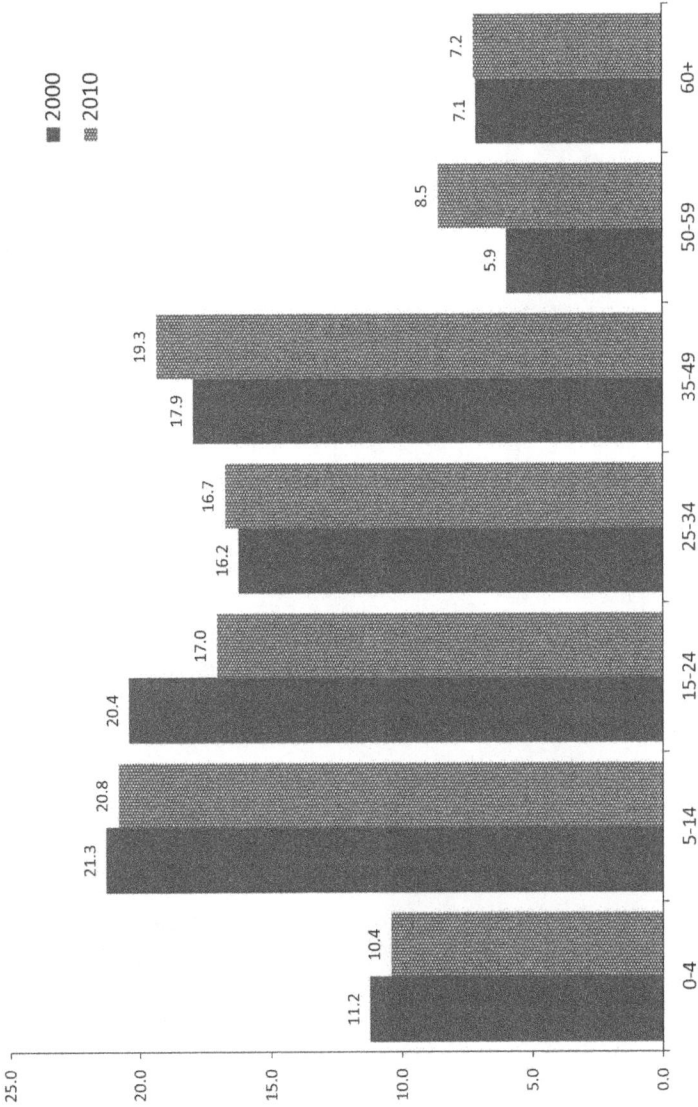

Figure 6.9
Trend in Population Shares by Specific Age Group: Minangkabau, 2000 and 2010

■ 2000
▨ 2010

Age	0-4	5-14	15-24	25-34	35-49	50-59	60+
2000	11.2	21.3	20.4	16.2	17.9	5.9	7.1
2010	10.4	20.8	17.0	16.7	19.3	8.5	7.2

Source: The statistics for 2000 are based on Suryadinata, Arifin and Ananta (2003), and for 2010 on Table 5.13.

Figure 6.10
Trend in Population Shares by Specific Age Group: Banjarese, 2000 and 2010

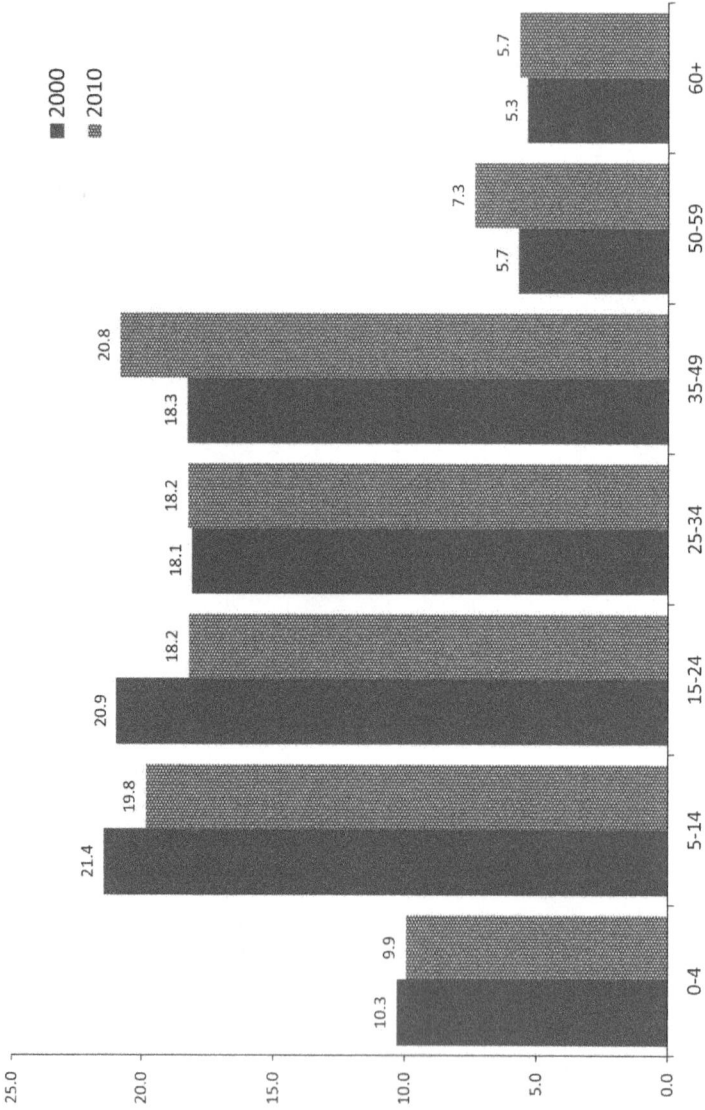

■ 2000
▨ 2010

	0-4	5-14	15-24	25-34	35-49	50-59	60+
2000	10.3	21.4	20.9	18.1	18.3	5.7	5.3
2010	9.9	19.8	18.2	18.2	20.8	7.3	5.7

Source: The statistics for 2000 are based on Suryadinata, Arifin and Ananta (2003), and for 2010 on Table 5.19.

and therefore their possible numbers elsewhere were not revealed by the statistics at that time.

The percentage rose from 1.12 per cent in 1930, partly because of a higher fertility amongst the Sasak. Because of the underestimation of both the Acehnese and the Dayak in the 2000 census, the Sasak, originating in West Nusa Tenggara, stood in the twelfth position in 2000. Their ranking declined to fourteenth place in 2010, because of the much better coverage of the Acehnese and the improved classification of the Dayak, although the percentage contribution of the Sasak remained the same between 2000 and 2010, contributing about 1.30 per cent.

Acehnese

We do not know exactly what happened to the Acehnese between 2000 and 2010 because, as explained earlier in this chapter, the number of Acehnese was underestimated in 2000. Yet the data in 1930 indicates that the Acehnese contributed 1.41 per cent at that time. Therefore, we estimate that the percentage of the Acehnese may have been almost constant for the whole period of 1930–2010. The Acehnese may have contributed about 1.42 per cent in 2000, rather than only 0.43 per cent, as was recorded in the 2000 population census.

Notes

1. It was not clear what was meant by "Indonesian" names. The Chinese then resorted to using any name but Chinese ones. They might use Javanese names, names from other local languages, Sanskrit or even Western names, particularly from the Bible.
2. For the history and discussion on the Chinese Indonesians during the New Order Era, refer to Mackie (1976) and Suryadinata (2005).
3. The data for the Javanese were cited from Ananta, Arifin and Bakhtiar (2005), a revision of that by Suryadinata, Arifin and Ananta (2003). Although the total number of Javanese did not change significantly, we present the revised age-structure in Table 6.2.
4. See the discussion in Chapter 5 for the definition of the working-age population in Indonesia and its grouping used in this book.
5. A youth bulge is defined when the percentage of youths (15–24 years old) is larger than 20 per cent, indicating problems that may be associated with such a large number.

6. We do not have the fertility rate for the Bantenese. However, we do have the data for the province of Banten. The province's fertility declined from 2.72 in 1996–99 to 2.35 in 2006–9 (BPS 2011b). As is shown in Chapter 4, the Bantenese contributed 40.65 per cent of the population in the province of Banten in 2010. Therefore, there is a possibility that the Bantenese fertility was also declining.

7

RELIGION AND LANGUAGE:
Two Important Ethnic Markers

Earlier chapters have shown the richness of Indonesia in terms of its ethnic groups: the ethnic composition at the national level, the variation of the ethnic composition at the provincial level and the dynamics of ethnic composition across time. As religion and language are closely intertwined with ethnicity and the data are available from the 2010 population census, this chapter examines the religions and languages of each of the fifteen largest ethnic groups in Indonesia. This is the first detailed statistical information on the religion and language of ethnic groups ever published for the whole of Indonesia and its fifteen largest ethnic groups. However, this chapter does not assume that there is any meaningful relationship between religion and the usual language spoken at home.

This chapter begins by examining the religious composition of Indonesia, including politically inherited problems concerning statistics on religion. Although Indonesia is well known as a Muslim majority country, this chapter examines and shows the spatial distribution of religious followers, that there is a considerable variation of religious compositions across provinces and within each province. Furthermore, this chapter studies the religions of each of the fifteen largest ethnic groups, the first quantitative measurement of religions amongst ethnic groups in Indonesia.

It shows the composition of religious followers in each of the ethnic groups. This section provides an interesting answer to whether or not, for example, there is a significant percentage of Sundanese recording themselves as embracing Protestantism. Do the Chinese embrace only Buddhism or Christianity? What percentage of the Chinese Indonesians are Muslims?

This chapter also studies the composition of groups of language speakers in Indonesia, which may be different from that of ethnic groups. It also analyses what languages each of the fifteen largest ethnic groups speak daily at home. It is the first quantitative analysis on the language of ethnic groups in Indonesia. For example, it calculates the percentage of Javanese, the largest ethnic group in Indonesia, who speak their own language, who speak Bahasa Indonesia, the national language and/or who speak some other languages. Another example is the language proficiency of the Chinese Indonesians. How many Chinese speak Bahasa Indonesia, how many of them speak their own language (Chinese) and/or how many speak some other local languages, such as Javanese?

It should be noted that, in earlier censuses such as the 1980 and 1990 population censuses, information on language was gathered and treated as a proxy for an ethnic group. The 2000 population census collected information on ethnicity, but not on language. The 2010 population census improved on this by collecting information on both ethnicity and language. Language is seen as one of the important markers of ethnicity, rather than a proxy of ethnicity. The two, language and ethnicity, although these may overlap, are not necessarily measuring the same concept as assumed in the 1980 and 1990 censuses.

As mentioned in Chapter 2, there were two questions related to language: the ability to speak the national language (Bahasa Indonesia) and the language spoken daily at home. Before discussing the languages spoken daily at home, this chapter examines the ability to speak Bahasa Indonesia as the national language to unite the multi-ethnic Indonesians. Bahasa Indonesia is a compulsory subject at school, taught from primary school and the language of instruction in all schools in Indonesia.

RELIGIOUS FOLLOWERS

Limited Freedom of Religion

The Indonesian state is based on the official philosophical foundation of Pancasila, a Sanskrit word. *Panca* means five and *sila* means principle. In other words, combined this means the Five Principles, consisting of divinity, humanism, nationalism, consensual decision making and social justice. Pancasila was declared by Sukarno, who later became the first president of Indonesia, on 1 June 1945, as the philosophic basis on which to build Indonesia as a new independent nation. Pancasila is a pluralistic ideology that embraces people of different ethnic groups, religions and regions residing alongside one another in a country that itself is huge, diverse and geographically complex.

The first principle is divinity, the belief in God, and this is often interpreted as meaning that every Indonesian citizen must have a religion, whatever the religion is. However, in 1965, the government curtailed Indonesians' freedom to choose their religions. In the explanation of Presidential Decree No. 1/PNPS 1965, the government mentioned only six "official" religions, namely Islam, Protestantism, Catholicism, Hinduism, Buddhism and Confucianism. The explanation that accompanied this decree also stated that other religions such as Judaism, Zoroastrianism, Shintoism and Taoism were not forbidden in Indonesia. However, it should be noted that all religions mentioned in the decree are world religions. Actually, in Indonesia there are many traditional beliefs, such as Kebatinan amongst the Javanese, Subud, originally from the Javanese, Sunda Wiwitan amongst the Baduy in the province of Banten, the Madrais or Cigugur religion in the regency of Kuningan of the province of West Java, Kaharingan of Dayak on the island of Kalimantan, Aluk To Dolo of the Toraja on the island of Sulawesi and Wetu Telu amongst the Sasak on the island of Lombok.

In addition, the religion is stated on the identity card (KTP-Kartu Tanda Penduduk) and, therefore, Indonesians have to choose one of these six official religions to appear on their card.[1] A citizen with a non-official religion (for example Wetu Telu) must choose to be recorded as a Muslim, Catholic, Protestant, Buddhist, Hindu or Confucian.

There are also a number of Indonesian Jews in the country, largely in North Sulawesi and East Java, and they must choose to be recorded as either Muslim, Protestant, Catholic, Hindu, Buddhist or Confucian. Furthermore, Sikhs may identify themselves as Hindus. Atheism is not allowed legally. On the other hand, anecdotal observation shows that some people may not follow any religious practice, although they are officially recorded as embracing one of the six official religions.

When Soeharto, the second president, came to power in 1967, he continued his predecessor's policy on religion. However, in 1979 his cabinet decided not to recognize Confucianism as an official religion, because Confucianism is closely linked to the ethnic Chinese. Since then, only five official religions were recognized. The Confucians then identified themselves either as Christians or Buddhists (Ong 2008).

The fall of the New Order regime and the arrival of the Reform era brought about significant changes. Under the fourth president, Abdurrahman Wahid (affectionately known as Gus Dur), the government abolished all discriminatory laws in order to improve relations between different ethnic groups and religions. For instance, the ban on public displays of Chinese culture was abolished in 2000. In February 2000, the president and his cabinet members attended the celebration of the Chinese New Year organized by Matakin (Majelis Tinggi Agama Khonghucu Indonesia, the Supreme Council for the Confucian Religion in Indonesia). Later, the minister of home affairs on 31 March 2000 abolished the 1978 circular that recognized only five religions. Therefore, Confucianism was once again recognized as one of the religions in the country. It was in January 2006 that President Susilo Bambang Yudhoyono declared that Confucianism was one of the official religions in Indonesia.

Another example of change during the Reform era was Kaharingan, a local religion of the Dayak in Kalimantan. It is not one of the official religions. Therefore, in their identification cards and for other administrative purposes, the people of Kaharingan had to mention one of the official religions, instead of Kaharingan. In 1980, the Ministry of Religion recognized Kaharingan as a variety of Hinduism. Earlier, beliefs and practices associated with Kaharingan were deemed custom (*adat*). However, because of the decentralization since 1999, which provides sub-national governments more power to make their own policies, the people of Kaharingan have been successful in obtaining official recognition from the Government of South Kalimantan. Now, they can proudly show "Kaharingan" as their religion on their identification cards. However, Kaharingan is still not an official religion at the national level.

Within this legal framework of religion in Indonesia, we go on to discuss the statistics on religions gathered in the series of the decennial censuses. The following section focuses on the religious composition in Indonesia based on the 2010 population census.

Composition of Religious Followers in Indonesia

Although officially the people of Indonesia must have a religion and choose one of the official religions, the question on religion in the population census has been more democratic. The question is based on what respondents wanted to say about their own religions. It is a semi-open ended questionnaire. "Apakah agama yang Bapak/Ibu anut?" (What is your religion?). The 2010 census provides seven options to answer the question — six official religions and "Others". The answer may not be the same as that recorded in the respondent's KTP (identity card).

The option of "Others" means that if a respondent did not feel comfortable with any of the six official religions or that the respondent did not have any religion, the respondent could choose "Others" and mentioned the belief/religion if they wished to do so. However, the census does not report in detail what the "Others" were.

In 2010, although very rarely, there were some respondents who did not mention one of the six official religions. Only 0.13 per cent of Indonesian citizens answered "Others" for the question of religion. Compared with data in 1971 and 2000, as shown in Table 7.1, we find that the percentage of "Others" has declined over time. This may mean that they may have been absorbed into one of the six official religions. Further studies should be done on this tiny group, especially during the democratizing era, when people are becoming more aware of their rights.

Confucianism was recorded as one of the answers to the religion question in the 1961 and 1971 population censuses. The results for responses to the religion question were not published for the census of 1961 but they were for the one of 1971. The following three censuses (1980, 1990 and 2000) did not record Confucianism, but listed it under the category of

Table 7.1
Population by Religious Followers: Indonesia, 1971, 2000 and 2010

Religious Followers	1971	2000	2010
Muslims	87.51	88.22	87.51
Christians	7.39	8.92	9.90
Hindus	1.94	1.81	1.69
Buddhists	0.92	0.84	0.72
Confucians	0.82	n/a	0.05
Others	1.42	0.20	0.13
Total	100.0	100.0	100.0

Notes: n/a = not available
The population total includes foreigners, with insignificant numbers.
Source: The 1971 figure was calculated from the Biro Pusat Statistik (1975).
The 2000 figure was calculated from the BPS (2001).
The 2010 figure was calculated from www.bps.go.id, accessed on 25 November 2013. The percentage was calculated by omitting "not asked", that is, those people who were not asked the question on religion constituting 0.32 per cent of Indonesia's total population. These were covered under L2 and C2* diplomat (757,118 individuals).

"Others". Therefore, the numbers could not be distinguished. Although at the beginning of 2000, the government no longer banned Confucianism, the 2000 population census was too late to include this in the questionnaire. It was still recorded under "Others". The 2010 population census made a change to include Confucianism as one option to the question on religion.

Within these constraints of "official records", the religious composition of the population might best be regarded as a rough record of religious followers. About 80 per cent of the Indonesian population were recorded as Muslims in 2010. The second largest group was Protestants (about 7 per cent). If we include Catholics (about 3 per cent), nearly 10 per cent of Indonesia's population were categorized as Christians. Hindus, followed by Buddhists, Confucians and Others made up the remainder.

Table 7.1 shows that Christians are the only religious followers whose percentage continuously rose between 1971 and 2010. The percentage of Muslims rose between 1971 and 2000, but declined during 2000–2010. The percentages of Hindus, Buddhists and "Others" declined in both periods of 1971–2000 and 2000–2010. The percentage of Confucians dropped significantly between 1971 and 2010, from 0.82 per cent in 1971 to only 0.05 per cent in 2010.

The increase in the percentage of the Christians is partly because of their higher fertility rate. In addition to this, the increased percentage of the Christians can also be due to the abolition of "Confucianism" during the New Order era. Some of the Chinese who were earlier recorded as Confucians may have chosen to be recorded as Christians. The declining percentage of the Buddhists may reflect their low fertility rate compared to that of followers of other religions. The declining percentage of Buddhists may also indicate that some Chinese converted from Buddhism to Christianity. Furthermore, the decline in "Others" may hint at a shift to Christianity. Further studies should be done on this subject. The declining percentage of the Hindus may also indicate the continuously very low (the nation's lowest) fertility of the Hindus, mostly living on the island of Bali.

Religious Composition by Province

Although Muslims are predominant in the population as a whole, the religious composition can be different within some provinces. We can categorize the provinces based on the percentage of religious followers into two groups. With 50 per cent as a cut-off point, there are Muslim-majority and non-Muslim-majority provinces. As seen in Figure 7.1 and

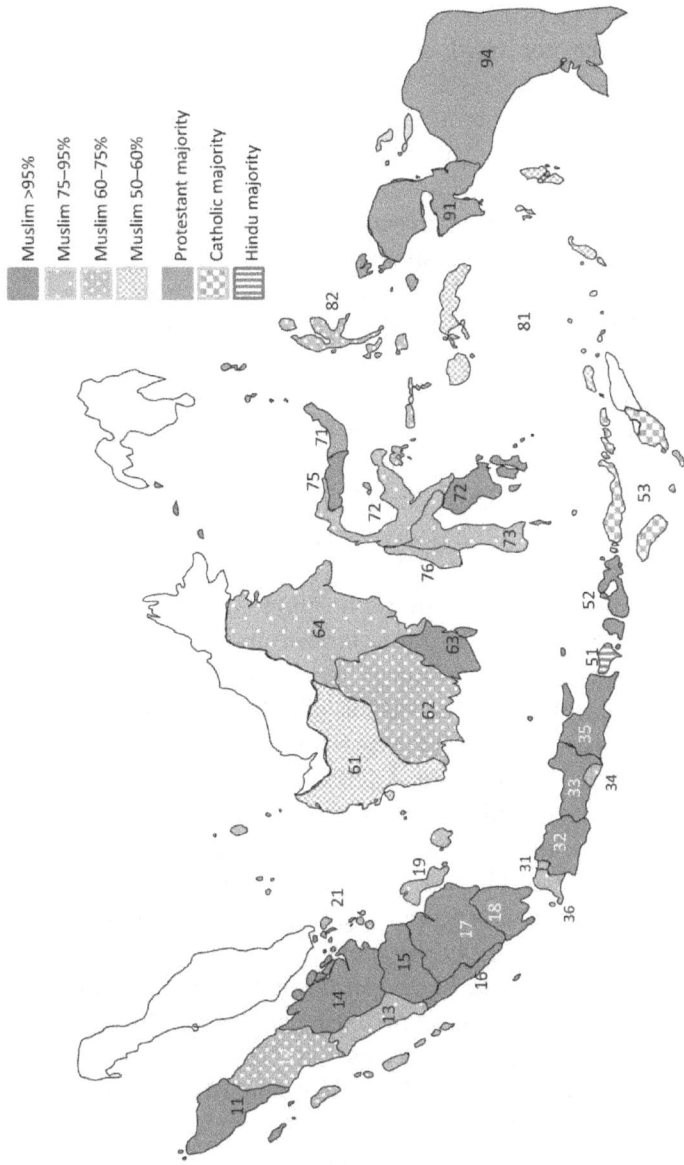

Figure 7.1
Muslim and Non-Muslim-Majority Provinces: Indonesia, 2010

Muslim >95%
Muslim 75–95%
Muslim 60–75%
Muslim 50–60%
Protestant majority
Catholic majority
Hindu majority

Source: Drawn based on Table 7.3.

Table 7.3, there were twenty-eight Muslim-majority provinces and five non-Muslim-majority provinces.

The province of East Nusa Tenggara was a province with a Catholic majority (54.25 per cent). In this province, Protestants contributed a significant percentage (34.82 per cent of the province's population); and thus Christians (Protestants and Catholics) accounted for 89.07 per cent of the population in this province. Catholics living in the province of East Nusa Tenggara accounted for 36.76 per cent of all Catholics in Indonesia and this was the largest percentage of Catholics amongst all provinces (Table 7.4). In addition, Muslims in East Nusa Tenggara were the largest minority, relative to Hindus, Buddhists and Confucians.

West Papua, Papua and North Sulawesi were Protestant majority provinces, accounting for 54.10 per cent, 66.03 per cent and 63.79 per cent, respectively. Although Protestants were the majority, those living in West Papua only formed 2.48 per cent of total Protestants in Indonesia. In West Papua, Muslims constituted the second largest group of religious followers (38.65 per cent). Catholics were the third largest, at 7.06 per cent. Hindus and Buddhists were very small minorities. Confucians were not found in West Papua.

Protestants living in Papua contributed a relatively large percentage (11.24 per cent) of the total Protestants in Indonesia. In Papua, Catholics were the second largest group of religious followers, at 17.81 per cent. The percentage of Muslims was just slightly below that of the Catholics, at 16.02 per cent. As in West Papua, Hindus and Buddhists were also very small minorities in Papua. No Confucians were recorded in Papua.

The province of Bali was a province with a Hindu majority, contributing 83.67 per cent of the province's population. Hindus in Bali accounted for 81.06 per cent of all Hindus in Indonesia. Other significant percentages of Hindus were seen in Lampung (2.83 per cent), East Java (2.80 per cent) and Central Sulawesi (2.49 per cent).

There was no Buddhist or Confucian majority province. The highest concentration of Buddhists was 6.64 per cent in the Riau Archipelago and the highest one for Confucians was 3.26 per cent in Bangka-Belitung.

North Sulawesi, another Protestant majority province, split into two with the Gorontalo gaining their own Muslim majority province in 2000. In the current North Sulawesi, Catholics accounted for 4.41 per cent and thus the percentage of Christians made up 68.20 per cent. Muslims there made up a relatively large number, with 13.40 per cent, but this was in

Table 7.2
Number of Population in Each Province According to Religion: Indonesia, 2010

Province	Muslims	Protestants	Catholics	Hindus	Buddhists	Confucians	Others	Total
Aceh	4,413,026	50,265	3,302	129	7,012	34	269	4,474,037
North Sumatra	8,579,544	3,509,553	515,988	14,549	303,369	977	5,079	12,929,059
West Sumatra	4,721,836	69,221	40,395	206	3,397	64	488	4,835,607
Riau	4,872,788	484,708	44,128	1,041	114,273	3,752	1,991	5,522,681
Jambi	2,950,148	82,297	13,233	549	29,965	1,446	301	3,077,939
South Sumatra	7,218,691	72,074	42,260	39,165	59,166	647	151	7,432,154
Bengkulu	1,669,062	28,700	6,352	3,719	2,009	39	129	1,710,010
Lampung	7,264,646	115,157	68,971	113,498	24,081	586	652	7,587,591
Bangka-Belitung	1,088,772	22,047	14,734	1,026	51,870	39,767	320	1,218,536
Riau Archipelago	1,330,883	187,004	37,976	1,132	110,980	3,354	124	1,671,453
Jakarta	8,195,794	715,485	299,559	17,113	312,937	5,081	1,102	9,547,071
West Java	41,761,041	775,859	249,298	18,271	91,708	14,322	5,330	42,915,829
Central Java	31,327,897	571,531	317,445	17,155	52,686	2,945	5,591	32,295,250
Yogyakarta	3,178,770	93,826	164,722	5,159	3,409	146	465	3,446,497
East Java	36,112,355	636,028	232,811	112,017	59,921	5,724	1,814	37,160,670
Banten	10,065,178	267,653	115,393	8,050	130,526	3,101	11,610	10,601,511
Bali	519,866	62,222	30,618	3,246,922	20,613	385	94	3,880,720

continued on next page

Table 7.2 – cont'd

Province	Muslims	Protestants	Catholics	Hindus	Buddhists	Confucians	Others	Total
West Nusa Tenggara	4,341,122	13,686	8,835	118,069	14,585	135	33	4,496,465
East Nusa Tenggara	423,880	1,626,998	2,535,019	5,205	316	86	81,126	4,672,630
West Kalimantan	2,603,260	500,119	1,008,293	2,705	237,697	29,720	2,891	4,384,685
Central Kalimantan	1,643,667	353,222	58,200	11,143	2,133	375	138,407	2,207,147
South Kalimantan	3,505,794	47,940	15,972	16,051	11,661	236	16,432	3,614,086
East Kalimantan	3,033,521	336,909	138,446	7,603	16,318	1,070	800	3,534,667
North Sulawesi	701,649	1,443,840	99,879	13,130	3,031	506	1,354	2,263,389
Central Sulawesi	2,047,882	447,345	21,626	99,579	3,905	138	2,575	2,623,050
South Sulawesi	7,200,682	612,391	124,088	58,360	19,667	348	4,717	8,020,253
Southeast Sulawesi	2,126,094	41,074	12,836	45,441	975	38	8	2,226,466
Gorontalo	1,017,370	16,530	759	3,612	926	11	17	1,039,225
West Sulawesi	957,726	164,657	11,867	16,042	320	35	6,535	1,157,182
Maluku	776,096	634,740	103,586	5,669	245	114	6,278	1,526,728
North Maluku	771,100	258,451	5,378	200	85	212	122	1,035,548
West Papua	292,004	408,741	53,374	858	513	25	0	755,515
Papua	450,043	1,854,723	500,278	2,414	1,371	74	174	2,809,077
Total	207,162,187	16,504,996	6,895,621	4,005,782	1,691,670	115,493	296,979	236,672,728

Notes: This table does not include foreigners.
Source: Calculated from tabulations provided by the BPS.

Table 7.3
Religious Composition across Provinces: Indonesia, 2010

Province	Muslims	Protestants	Catholics	Hindus	Buddhists	Confucians	Others	Total
Aceh	98.64	1.12	0.07	0.00	0.16	0.00	0.01	100.00
Gorontalo	97.90	1.59	0.07	0.35	0.09	0.00	0.00	100.00
West Sumatra	97.65	1.43	0.84	0.00	0.07	0.00	0.01	100.00
Bengkulu	97.61	1.68	0.37	0.22	0.12	0.00	0.01	100.00
West Java	97.31	1.81	0.58	0.04	0.21	0.03	0.01	100.00
East Java	97.18	1.71	0.63	0.30	0.16	0.02	0.00	100.00
South Sumatra	97.13	0.97	0.57	0.53	0.80	0.01	0.00	100.00
Central Java	97.00	1.77	0.98	0.05	0.16	0.01	0.02	100.00
South Kalimantan	97.00	1.33	0.44	0.44	0.32	0.01	0.45	100.00
West Nusa Tenggara	96.55	0.30	0.20	2.63	0.32	0.00	0.00	100.00
Jambi	95.85	2.67	0.43	0.02	0.97	0.05	0.01	100.00
Lampung	95.74	1.52	0.91	1.50	0.32	0.01	0.01	100.00
Southeast Sulawesi	95.49	1.84	0.58	2.04	0.04	0.00	0.00	100.00
Banten	94.94	2.52	1.09	0.08	1.23	0.03	0.11	100.00
Yogyakarta	92.23	2.72	4.78	0.15	0.10	0.00	0.01	100.00
South Sulawesi	89.78	7.64	1.55	0.73	0.25	0.00	0.06	100.00
Bangka-Belitung	89.35	1.81	1.21	0.08	4.26	3.26	0.03	100.00

continued on next page

Table 7.3 — cont'd

Province	Muslims	Protestants	Catholics	Hindus	Buddhists	Confucians	Others	Total
Riau	88.23	8.78	0.80	0.02	2.07	0.07	0.04	100.00
Jakarta	85.85	7.49	3.14	0.18	3.28	0.05	0.01	100.00
East Kalimantan	85.82	9.53	3.92	0.22	0.46	0.03	0.02	100.00
West Sulawesi	82.76	14.23	1.03	1.39	0.03	0.00	0.56	100.00
Riau Archipelago	79.62	11.19	2.27	0.07	6.64	0.20	0.01	100.00
Central Sulawesi	78.07	17.05	0.82	3.80	0.15	0.01	0.10	100.00
Central Kalimantan	74.47	16.00	2.64	0.50	0.10	0.02	6.27	100.00
North Maluku	74.46	24.96	0.52	0.02	0.01	0.02	0.01	100.00
North Sumatra	66.36	27.14	3.99	0.11	2.35	0.01	0.04	100.00
West Kalimantan	59.37	11.41	23.00	0.06	5.42	0.68	0.07	100.00
Maluku	50.83	41.58	6.78	0.37	0.02	0.01	0.41	100.00
West Papua	38.65	54.10	7.06	0.11	0.07	0.00	0.00	100.00
North Sulawesi	31.00	63.79	4.41	0.58	0.13	0.02	0.06	100.00
Papua	16.02	66.03	17.81	0.09	0.05	0.00	0.01	100.00
Bali	13.40	1.60	0.79	83.67	0.53	0.01	0.00	100.00
East Nusa Tenggara	9.07	34.82	54.25	0.11	0.01	0.00	1.74	100.00
Total	87.53	6.97	2.91	1.69	0.71	0.05	0.13	100.00

Source: Calculated from Table 7.2.

stark contrast with its neighbouring province of Gorontalo as an exclusively Muslim province.

Maluku is another example of one province (Maluku) breaking into two (Maluku and North Maluku), in 2001, resulting in different compositions of religious followers. In the current province of Maluku, Muslims made up 50.83 per cent. Christians in Maluku altogether accounted for 48.36 per cent. On the other hand, in North Maluku Muslims made up almost three quarters of the population. However, in this archipelagic region, it is possible that there were some Muslim-majority islands as well as Christian-majority islands.

West Kalimantan can be considered as a significant multi-religious province, as all religions exist, each with a relatively significant representation. Muslims as the majority (59.37 per cent) live alongside Christians, who form one third (Protestants 11.41 per cent and Catholics 23.0 per cent) of the population. Buddhists there account for 5.42 per cent and this constitutes the second largest concentration of Buddhists amongst provinces (Table 7.3). Confucians account for 0.68 per cent, also the second largest concentration of Confucians amongst provinces. The significant multi-religiosity in West Kalimantan may reflect its past harmony amongst the main ethnic groups resulting in the birth of a cultural product known as Tidayu. Tidayu stands for *Tionghoa* (Chinese Indonesian), Dayak and *Melayu* (Malay). Tidayu is used for dance and batik in Singkawang, a district in West Kalimantan.

North Sumatra, Central Kalimantan and North Maluku are provinces where Muslims comprised between 60 and 75 per cent. However, several points are important to understand these three provinces. Although North Sumatra is a Muslim majority province, the number of Protestants living in this province, as seen in Table 7.4, made up the largest percentage in Indonesia, forming 21.26 per cent of all Protestants in Indonesia, or 3.5 million. This number accounted for 27.14 per cent of the North Sumatra population. In addition, Buddhists were also relatively significant (2.35 per cent) due to the presence of Chinese in Medan, the region's capital. Sikhism exists there as seen in the presence of Gurdwara, the Sikh temple. Yet, Sikhism was identified under Hinduism, which accounted for 0.11 per cent in North Sumatra.

In Central Kalimantan, the Muslim majority lived alongside Christians as well as "Others". The "Others" in this provinces accounted for 6.27 per cent, the largest percentage amongst provinces. As discussed earlier,

Table 7.4
Geographic Distribution of Religious Followers: Indonesia, 2010

Province	Muslims	Protestants	Catholics	Hindus	Buddhists	Confucians	Others
Aceh	2.13	0.30	0.05	0.00	0.41	0.03	0.09
North Sumatra	4.14	21.26	7.48	0.36	17.93	0.85	1.71
West Sumatra	2.28	0.42	0.59	0.01	0.20	0.06	0.16
Riau	2.35	2.94	0.64	0.03	6.76	3.25	0.67
Jambi	1.42	0.50	0.19	0.01	1.77	1.25	0.10
South Sumatra	3.48	0.44	0.61	0.98	3.50	0.56	0.05
Bengkulu	0.81	0.17	0.09	0.09	0.12	0.03	0.04
Lampung	3.51	0.70	1.00	2.83	1.42	0.51	0.22
Bangka-Belitung	0.53	0.13	0.21	0.03	3.07	34.43	0.11
Riau Archipelago	0.64	1.13	0.55	0.03	6.56	2.90	0.04
Jakarta	3.96	4.33	4.34	0.43	18.50	4.40	0.37
West Java	20.16	4.70	3.62	0.46	5.42	12.40	1.79
Central Java	15.12	3.46	4.60	0.43	3.11	2.55	1.88
Yogyakarta	1.53	0.57	2.39	0.13	0.20	0.13	0.16
East Java	17.43	3.85	3.38	2.80	3.54	4.96	0.61
Banten	4.86	1.62	1.67	0.20	7.72	2.69	3.91
Bali	0.25	0.38	0.44	81.06	1.22	0.33	0.03
West Nusa Tenggara	2.10	0.08	0.13	2.95	0.86	0.12	0.01
East Nusa Tenggara	0.20	9.86	36.76	0.13	0.02	0.07	27.32
West Kalimantan	1.26	3.03	14.62	0.07	14.05	25.73	0.97
Central Kalimantan	0.79	2.14	0.84	0.28	0.13	0.32	46.60
South Kalimantan	1.69	0.29	0.23	0.40	0.69	0.20	5.53
East Kalimantan	1.46	2.04	2.01	0.19	0.96	0.93	0.27
North Sulawesi	0.34	8.75	1.45	0.33	0.18	0.44	0.46
Central Sulawesi	0.99	2.71	0.31	2.49	0.23	0.12	0.87
South Sulawesi	3.48	3.71	1.80	1.46	1.16	0.30	1.59
Southeast Sulawesi	1.03	0.25	0.19	1.13	0.06	0.03	0.00
Gorontalo	0.49	0.10	0.01	0.09	0.05	0.01	0.01
West Sulawesi	0.46	1.00	0.17	0.40	0.02	0.03	2.20
Maluku	0.37	3.85	1.50	0.14	0.01	0.10	2.11
North Maluku	0.37	1.57	0.08	0.00	0.01	0.18	0.04
West Papua	0.14	2.48	0.77	0.02	0.03	0.02	0.00
Papua	0.22	11.24	7.26	0.06	0.08	0.06	0.06
Total	100.00	100.00	100.00	100.00	100.00	100.00	100.00

this can be explained by the presence of Kaharingan as Kaharingan is not officially recognized by the central government.

Amongst other Muslim majority provinces, Muslims generally co-reside with Christians, being either Protestants or Catholics. Yet there were some provinces in 2010 where Muslims co-reside more either with Hindus, Buddhists or Confucians. In West Nusa Tenggara where Muslims accounted for 96.55 per cent, Hindus formed 2.63 per cent, as the third largest concentration of Hindus after those in Bali and Central Sulawesi. Hindus here are most likely to be the Hindu Balinese from the neighbouring island of Bali. Furthermore, Hindus made a relatively significant contribution in some other provinces: Lampung (1.50 per cent), Southeast Sulawesi (2.04 per cent), West Sulawesi (1.39 per cent) and Central Sulawesi (3.80 per cent). The ancient Prambanan temple is a landmark of Hinduism, standing in the border area between Central Java and Yogyakarta, where Hindus are no longer significant in these provinces.

In Bangka-Belitung, where Muslims accounted for 89.35 per cent, Buddhists and Confucians had more significant percentages than Christians. Buddhists made up 4.26 per cent and Confucians made up 3.26 per cent. The concentration of Confucians in this province was the largest in Indonesia. Buddhists were also quite significant in the following provinces: Jakarta, West Sumatra and the Riau Archipelago. The well-known landmark of Buddhism, the ancient Borobudur temple, is located in Central Java, although only 0.05 per cent of Buddhists lived in Central Java, or about 17,000 Buddhists, a comparable number with those in West Sulawesi (16,000), as seen in Table 7.2.

Amongst the Muslim majority, as seen in Table 7.3 and Figure 7.1, we find thirteen provinces which were almost exclusively Muslim, forming at least 95 per cent of the province's population. Aceh had the highest percentage (98.64 per cent) and Southeast Sulawesi had the lowest percentage (95.49 per cent) of this group.

RELIGIOUS COMPOSITION OF THE LARGEST ETHNIC GROUPS

Before we discuss the religions of each of the largest ethnic groups, it should be noted that the data on ethnicity is limited to Indonesian citizens. As a result, the discussion of religion as associated with ethnicity is also limited to Indonesian citizens only, who were enumerated under the C1 and C2 General and C2* Apartment types of questionnaire.

Figure 7.2 and Tables 7.5–7.6 reveal that the Javanese were almost exclusively Muslim, as 97.17 per cent of them were Muslims, or 92.1 million. A small minority embraced Protestantism (1.59 per cent) and Catholicism (0.97 per cent). Those Javanese embracing Hinduism or Buddhism were a much smaller minority (with 0.10 per cent each). Furthermore, despite a very tiny number (0.01 per cent), some Javanese did not associate themselves with any of the six official religions. As seen in Table 7.5, although the percentages of non-Muslim Javanese were small, the size of the Javanese population is very large. Thus, Protestant Javanese totalled 1.5 million. Almost 10,000 Javanese were not recorded as adhering to any of the six official religions.

The Sundanese were almost exclusively Muslim, forming 99.41 per cent of the total Sundanese population. In other words, the Muslim Sundanese numbered 36.5 million in 2010, leaving 0.2 million non-Muslim Sundanese. The Muslim Malay accounted for 98.77 per cent and a small minority, almost 1 per cent, were Christian Malay (Protestants, 0.71 per cent, and Catholics, 0.26 per cent).

As shown in Table 7.6, the Batak, the fourth largest ethnic group in Indonesia, were a Christian majority ethnic group, mostly Protestant. Yet, not all Batak were Christians. Indeed, the Batak are more pluralistic with regard to religion, compared to the three largest ethnic groups. The majority (49.56 per cent) of the Batak were Protestants. Including Catholics (6.07 per cent), the contribution of Christians was 55.63 per cent, more than half the population of the Batak. The second largest group of religious followers amongst the Batak were Muslims (44.17), almost equalling the Christians. The remaining ones were very small minorities; Buddhist (0.11 per cent), "Others" (0.07 per cent) and a tiny minority were Hindus (0.02 per cent). Although very small, the presence of "Others" indicates the existence of some local religions or no religion amongst the Batak, and they numbered about 6,000, twice as many as the "Others" for the Sundanese.

The Madurese were exclusively Muslims, as the Muslim Madurese made up 99.88 per cent. The Muslim Betawi accounted for 97.15 per cent amongst the Betawi. Protestants formed 1.62 per cent and Catholics 0.61 per cent. The Betawi had another minority, Buddhists (0.58 per cent), but their number was larger than that of the Buddhist Malay and Buddhist Sundanese (Table 7.5). Interestingly, although a very tiny group (0.03 per

Figure 7.2
Religious Composition of the Fifteen Largest Ethnic Groups: Indonesia, 2010

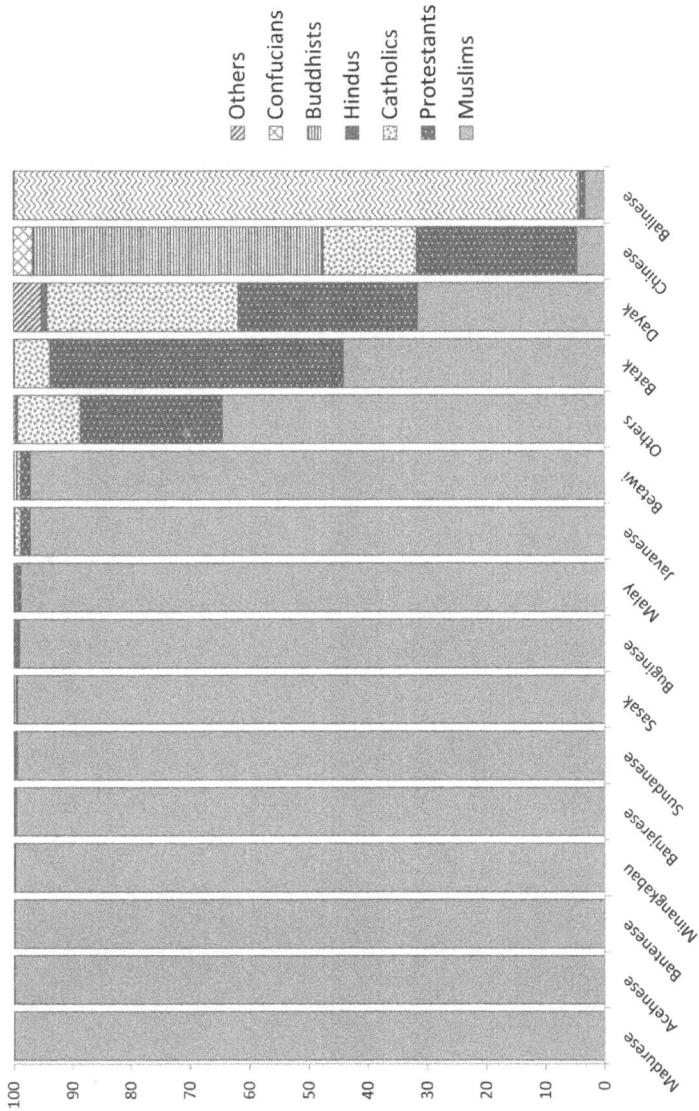

Source: Drawn from Table 7.6.

Table 7.5
Religions of the Fifteen Largest Ethnic Groups: Indonesia, 2010

Province	Muslims	Protestants	Catholics	Hindus	Buddhists	Confucians	Others	Total
Javanese	92,107,046	1,506,208	921,913	150,855	90,465	2,857	9,599	94,788,943
Sundanese	36,450,022	129,085	52,317	1,851	24,528	4,854	3,235	36,665,892
Malay	8,643,370	62,571	22,913	1,031	19,848	1,243	242	8,751,218
Batak	3,738,660	4,194,282	513,376	1,476	9,190	315	6,305	8,463,604
Madurese	7,157,518	5,576	2,119	368	435	32	43	7,166,091
Betawi	6,607,019	109,966	41,463	1,161	39,278	1,805	252	6,800,944
Minangkabau	6,441,071	11,665	5,157	179	1,255	49	44	6,459,420
Buginese	6,348,200	29,771	5,745	26,102	957	47	2,395	6,413,217
Bantenese	4,634,374	3,593	1,217	101	2,680	70	242	4,642,277
Banjarese	4,108,104	12,313	3,462	994	1,396	62	410	4,126,741
Balinese	127,274	36,046	13,339	3,736,993	10,378	142	473	3,924,645
Acehnese	3,398,818	3,289	745	70	1,028	7	4	3,403,961
Dayak	1,016,697	971,644	1,046,226	12,140	17,502	568	154,219	3,218,996
Sasak	3,153,671	3,693	1,847	4,555	10,682	7	439	3,174,894
Chinese	131,682	765,536	446,156	3,552	1,388,829	94,005	1,114	2,830,874
Others	23,057,923	8,621,275	3,815,048	63,909	73,027	9,422	117,848	35,758,452
Total	207,121,449	16,466,513	6,893,043	4,005,337	1,691,478	115,485	296,864	236,590,169

Notes: The total population was smaller than the earlier tables. This was due to the selection process to meet the needs of the analysis, which covered citizens only. These were aged five years old and above. The information on religion was enumerated under the C1 and C2 General and C2* Apartment types of questionnaire.
Source: Calculated from tabulations provided by the BPS.

Table 7.6
Religious Composition of the Fifteen Largest Ethnic Groups, Indonesia: 2010

Ethnic Group	Religion							
	Muslims	Protestants	Catholics	Hindus	Buddhists	Confucians	Others	Total
Javanese	97.17	1.59	0.97	0.16	0.10	0.00	0.01	100.00
Sundanese	99.41	0.35	0.14	0.01	0.07	0.01	0.01	100.00
Malay	98.77	0.71	0.26	0.01	0.23	0.01	0.00	100.00
Batak	44.17	49.56	6.07	0.02	0.11	0.00	0.07	100.00
Madurese	99.88	0.08	0.03	0.01	0.01	0.00	0.00	100.00
Betawi	97.15	1.62	0.61	0.02	0.58	0.03	0.00	100.00
Minangkabau	99.72	0.18	0.08	0.00	0.02	0.00	0.00	100.00
Buginese	98.99	0.46	0.09	0.41	0.01	0.00	0.04	100.00
Bantenese	99.83	0.08	0.03	0.00	0.06	0.00	0.01	100.00
Banjarese	99.55	0.30	0.08	0.02	0.03	0.00	0.01	100.00
Balinese	3.24	0.92	0.34	95.22	0.26	0.00	0.01	100.00
Acehnese	99.85	0.10	0.02	0.00	0.03	0.00	0.00	100.00
Dayak	31.58	30.18	32.50	0.38	0.54	0.02	4.79	100.00
Sasak	99.33	0.12	0.06	0.14	0.34	0.00	0.01	100.00
Chinese	4.65	27.04	15.76	0.13	49.06	3.32	0.04	100.00
Others	64.48	24.11	10.67	0.18	0.20	0.03	0.33	100.00
Total	87.54	6.96	2.91	1.69	0.71	0.05	0.13	100.00

Source: Calculated from Table 7.5.

cent), there were some Confucian Betawi, more than the Confucian Malay (Table 7.5).

The Muslim Minangkabau made up 99.72 per cent. Yet, there was a small Christian minority (0.26 per cent) and a very tiny Buddhist minority (0.02 per cent) amongst the Minangkabau. The number of Christian Minangkabau was larger than the Christian Madurese.

Muslims made up 98.99 per cent of the Buginese population. Christians, a very small minority (0.55 per cent), were seen amongst the Buginese. Interestingly, there were some respondents who mentioned "Others", not one of the official religions, although the number was very small (0.04 per cent). It is not clear what their religious inclinations were.

The Balinese, who mostly lived in the province of Bali and were the eleventh largest ethnic group, were almost exclusively Hindus, with 95.2 per cent (3.7 million). Muslim Balinese accounted for 3.2 per cent, or 127,000 people. The Muslim Balinese are not necessarily the same as Muslims living in the province of Bali, such as local ethnic groups of Nyama Selam and Loloan, as well as some migrant ethnic groups. The Muslim Balinese may also be the Balinese living and becoming Muslims on the island of Lombok, where the Muslim Sasak are the majority group.

The province of Aceh, known as Indonesia's Veranda of Mecca (Serambi Mekah Indonesia), was exclusively Muslim, 99.85 per cent. Nevertheless, there were some Christian Acehnese (0.12 per cent) and a few Buddhist Acehnese (0.03 per cent).

The Dayak can be considered the most multi-religious ethnic group, with a Christian majority, constituting 62.7 per cent of all Dayak in Indonesia. Christians consisted of Protestants (30.2 per cent) and Catholics (32.5 per cent). The percentage of Muslim Dayak was also relatively high, 31.6 per cent. As discussed earlier, Kaharingan has been recognized as an official religion in South Kalimantan, but is not officially recognized by the Government of Indonesia. Therefore, in the 2010 population census there was still no option for "Kaharingan" as an answer for the question on religion. Indeed, the proportion of "Others" for the question of religion was 4.79 per cent amongst the Dayak, the highest amongst all of the fifteen largest ethnic groups in Indonesia. Future surveys/censuses may ask the respondents to detail the answer of "Others". This answer could be a local religion, another world religion or no religion at all. For some ethnic groups, the percentage of "Others" can be relatively large. In addition, although small, the percentages of Hindu and Buddhist

Dayak were relative large compared to the same religions in other ethnic groups.

The Sasak were exclusively Muslims, making up 99.33 per cent. The Muslim Sasak can be divided into two groups, the Wetu Telu and the Wetu Lima. The difference between the two is that the Wetu Telu adherents practise a religious syncretism combining Islam and Hinduism. They are just like the Abangan Muslim syncretists amongst the Javanese (Budiwanti 2000). Meanwhile, the Wetu Lima adherents follow the Islamic fundamentals as taught by the prophet Muhammad. The Bayan Sasak are the stronghold of the Wetu Telu. Amongst the non-Muslim Sasak, the number of Buddhists was larger than that of Christians (Table 7.5). There was also a Hindu minority of 4,555 people.

The Chinese were very pluralistic in terms of their religions. There were no dominant religious followers. The largest number was that of the followers of Buddhism, but they only accounted for half (49.06 per cent) of the 2.8 million Chinese. Furthermore, this group of Buddhists may actually include people who follow other religions such as Taoism and Confucianism. Although Confucianism has become an official religion, some Confucians might not have known that this option was already available. The percentage of Confucians was relatively small, only 3.32 per cent, even lower than the Muslim Chinese (4.65 per cent). The Protestant Chinese were the second largest group (27.04 per cent), followed by the Catholics (15.76 per cent). Nevertheless, only a very small percentage (0.13 per cent) of the Chinese followed Hinduism. Compared to other ethnic groups, the percentage of Chinese who did not choose one of the six official religions, those who answered "Others", was relatively large, at 0.04 per cent.

It is interesting to see the change in religious composition of the Chinese. Based on the 2000 population census, Ananta, Arifin and Bakhtiar (2008) estimated the religious composition of the Chinese. Comparing their results, we found that the percentage of the Buddhist Chinese declined from 53.82 per cent in 2000 to less than half (49.06 per cent) in 2010. The "Others" accounted for 3.91 per cent in 2000 (when Confucianism was not an option), declining dramatically to 0.04 per cent in 2010 (when Confucianism was an option). The Hindu Chinese and Muslim Chinese declined by 1.64 and 0.76 percentage points, respectively, within the observed period. In 2000, the Hindu Chinese accounted for 1.77 per cent, and the Muslim Chinese, 5.41 per cent. On the other hand, the Christian Chinese increased significantly by 7.71 percentage points, from 35.09 per cent in 2000.

LANGUAGE SPEAKERS

According to the United Nations (2008), there are three types of data on language. The first is the mother tongue, usually spoken at home in early childhood. The second is the usual language spoken at home, regardless of age. The third is the ability to speak a given language. The Indonesian 2010 population census collected two types of information on language. First was the ability to speak Bahasa Indonesia, the official and national language of Indonesia. The second was the language spoken daily at home. The census did not collect information on the mother tongue.

In the 2010 population census, the question on language was only asked to the population aged five and above, which numbered 214.0 million, smaller than 236.7 million for the whole population.

Bahasa Indonesia: A Unifying Language

Indonesia is not only a multi-ethnic but also a multilingual country. The 2010 population census recorded more than 1,400 languages spoken daily at home, larger than that of ethnic categories. It is therefore interesting to learn what language each of the ethnic groups spoke daily at home. Of particular interest was to compare the percentage of those who spoke their own languages, Bahasa Indonesia and "other languages". As with the discussion on ethnicity, the discussion here is limited to the fifteen largest ethnic groups in Indonesia.

The existence of the huge number of different languages poses a challenge for communication and unity of Indonesia, yet Indonesia has been quite successful in developing a national language policy with the use of Bahasa Indonesia (Paauw 2009). This success partly lies in a historical perspective in the early period of nation building. The Sumpah Pemuda (Youth Oath), "Satu Nusa, Satu Bangsa, Satu Bahasa" (One Land, One Nation, One Language) was declared on 28 October 1928. This oath was used to unify people living in a single homeland, Indonesia, as a single nation, Indonesia, and speaking the same language, Bahasa Indonesia (the Indonesian national language).

Bahasa Indonesia has its roots in Malay dialects spoken in the coastal areas of the Strait of Malacca and the Riau Islands. It also functioned as a lingua franca for trade throughout the archipelago long before Indonesia was born. Bahasa Indonesia has a dual function in Indonesian society: it is the language of national identity and the language of education, literacy, modernization and social mobility.

Bahasa Indonesia is very similar to Malay. People who speak Malay can understand Bahasa Indonesia and vice versa. Jakarta's local ethnic group the Betawi speak Betawi, a language that is similar to Bahasa Indonesia or Malay. Some call the Betawi language a dialect of Bahasa Indonesia or Malay. Because of its location in the capital city, we can also hear people from outside Jakarta who speak Betawi.

Bahasa Indonesia has existed and developed within the context of a large number of local languages. Bahasa Indonesia has unified people over time from different ethnic groups. Indeed, in 2010, most (92.08 per cent) of the Indonesian population aged five years old and above had the ability to speak Bahasa Indonesia. Table 7.7 shows that in all provinces Indonesians were mostly able to speak Bahasa Indonesia, ranging from 74.11 per cent in Papua to 98.91 per cent in Jakarta. The ability to speak Bahasa Indonesia here includes simple Bahasa Indonesia. Respondents were said to be able to speak Bahasa Indonesia if they could answer question number 211 in the population census "Apakah [Nama] mampu berbahasa Indonesia?" ("Is [Name] able to use Bahasa Indonesia?") The answer was dichotomous with a yes/no answer. To assess a respondent's ability in Bahasa Indonesia, the question must not be translated into a local language, although the interview was conducted in a local language. It must be read out as it is written in Bahasa Indonesia. If the person asked somebody else to answer the question, then this person was registered as not being able to speak Bahasa Indonesia. If the person could understand the question, then the person was assumed to be able to speak Bahasa Indonesia (BPS 2009, p. 117).

Nevertheless, the ability to speak Bahasa Indonesia does not necessarily mean that the respondents used Bahasa Indonesia as the language spoken daily at home. Thus, citizens of Indonesia are expected to be at least bi-lingual, speaking Bahasa Indonesia and a local language. Migration to a place with a different language than the persons' native language may affect the persons' language spoken daily at home. This is seen as part of an adaptation strategy to a new place of residence.

Therefore, the census also collected information on languages spoken daily at home in question number 210: "Apakah bahasa sehari-hari yang digunakan [Nama] di rumah? ([What is [Name]'s language spoken daily at home?")

Table 7.7
Ability to Speak Bahasa Indonesia: Indonesia, 2010

Province	Number	Per cent
Aceh	3,661,134	91.51
North Sumatra	11,028,331	95.64
Sumatera Barat	3,851,683	88.67
West Sumatra	4,737,149	96.83
Jambi	2,582,635	93.22
South Sumatra	6,158,908	92.15
Bengkulu	1,442,653	93.70
Lampung	6,679,423	97.23
Bangka-Belitung	1,028,655	93.90
Riau Archipelago	1,455,766	98.49
Jakarta	8,682,223	98.91
West Java	36,549,385	93.89
Central Java	26,923,107	90.74
Yogyakarta	2,937,776	91.79
East Java	29,925,211	86.61
Banten	9,123,281	95.21
Bali	3,218,380	90.50
West Nusa Tenggara	3,301,688	82.03
East Nusa Tenggara	3,598,626	88.02
West Kalimantan	3,648,262	92.51
Central Kalimantan	1,839,479	92.94
South Kalimantan	3,000,834	91.76
East Kalimantan	3,112,017	98.42
North Sulawesi	2,015,561	97.44
Central Sulawesi	2,295,804	97.88
South Sulawesi	6,650,411	91.81
Southeast Sulawesi	1,896,685	96.57
Gorontalo	911,041	97.60
West Sulawesi	950,142	93.10
Maluku	1,318,416	97.95
North Maluku	885,257	97.21
West Papua	653,859	98.07
Papua	1,867,461	74.11
Indonesia	197,931,243	92.08

Note: The question was collected from those aged five years old and above.
Source: Calculated from tabulations provided by the BPS.

This question is of an open-ended type. The language spoken daily at home is the language used at home to communicate with all members of the household. This is not necessarily inherited; it can be developed through social interaction.

At home someone can speak a language different from his/her own ethnic origin. For instance, a Sundanese person married to a Javanese lives in a Javanese community for years. She may develop proficiency in Javanese and then speak it daily at home. As explained in the census manual (BPS 2009, p. 116), in her case, the enumerator recorded her as speaking Javanese daily at home, although she is of Sundanese origin and can still speak Sundanese.

In a case that a person speaks both Bahasa Indonesia and an ethnic language daily at home, the census recorded the ethnic language as the language spoken daily at home. If a person used more than one ethnic language, then the census recorded the language spoken more often. In addition, if the person spoke a foreign language, the country of that language was recorded.

Language Spoken Daily at Home

We have outlined the twenty largest groups of the "languages spoken daily at home" (hereafter referred to as "language"). To create the classification of groups of language speakers, we used three sources: the code book of the 2010 population census, literature such as Melalatoa (1995), Hidayah (1996) and www.ethnologue.com, as well as tabulations prepared by the BPS (Statistics, Indonesia). We also used local expertise and Internet searches. Further studies should definitely be made to improve this classification.

We chose twenty groups to make sure that all languages associated with the fifteen largest ethnic groups were included in the list. See Table 7.8, which describes the twenty largest groups of language speakers in Indonesia in 2010. It is ordered by the number of speakers and it is differentiated by the sex of the speakers. Javanese is the largest group of language speakers and Chinese is the smallest one.

The twenty groups of language speakers already accounted for 93.68 per cent of the Indonesian population aged five years old and above. Although very important, the discussion of many small groups of language speakers is beyond the scope of this book. However, these smaller languages certainly deserve to be studied further.

Table 7.8
20 Languages Ordered by Number of Speakers: Indonesia, 2010

Rank	Language	Males	Females	Total	Sex Ratio
1	Javanese	34,085,092	34,129,676	68,214,768	0.999
2	Bahasa Indonesia	21,512,862	21,175,733	42,688,595	1.016
3	Sundanese	15,783,384	15,224,065	31,007,449	1.037
4	Malay	7,370,438	7,249,162	14,619,600	1.017
5	Madurese	3,777,660	4,003,427	7,781,087	0.944
6	Minangkabau	2,094,188	2,143,597	4,237,785	0.977
7	Banjarese	1,833,102	1,820,098	3,653,200	1.007
8	Buginese	1,712,939	1,799,165	3,512,104	0.952
9	Balinese	1,685,906	1,686,270	3,372,176	1.000
10	Batak	1,653,355	1,677,522	3,330,877	0.986
11	Cirebonese	1,591,804	1,497,903	3,089,707	1.063
12	Acehnese	1,359,370	1,381,497	2,740,867	0.984
13	Lombok/Sasak	1,274,565	1,416,559	2,691,124	0.900
14	Betawi	1,146,860	1,106,538	2,253,398	1.036
15	Dayak	977,549	901,047	1,878,596	1.085
16	Makassarese	906,088	961,619	1,867,707	0.942
17	Bantenese	733,589	695,636	1,429,225	1.055
18	Nias	368,826	379,482	748,308	0.972
19	Bangka	364,871	347,771	712,642	1.049
20	Chinese	325,423	319,798	645,221	1.018
	Others	6,821,160	6,717,446	13,538,606	1.015
	Total	107,379,031	106,634,011	214,013,042	1.007

Notes: This table describes the languages spoken daily at home by Indonesians aged five years and above.
Source: Calculated from tabulations provided by the BPS.

However, as discussed later in this chapter, there are several reasons which may make the number of speakers of a given language different from that of the population of the associated ethnic groups. One of them is the sample of analysis. The information for ethnicity was collected for the whole population, including those under five years old. On the other hand, the information on language was only asked for citizens aged five years old and above. Therefore, for a comparison between ethnic groups and groups of language speakers, as seen in Table 7.9, we have to limit this discussion to the population aged five years old and above.

Table 7.9
Rankings of Ethnic Group versus Group of Language Speakers:
Indonesia's Population, aged 5 years old and above, 2010

	Ethnic Group			Group of Language Speakers	
No	Name	Percentage	No	Name	Percentage
1	Javanese	40.47	1	Javanese	31.87
2	Sundanese	15.50	2	Bahasa Indonesia	19.95
3	Malay	3.65	3	Sundanese	14.49
4	Batak	3.51	4	Malay	6.83
5	Madurese	3.09	5	Madurese	3.64
6	Betawi	2.86	6	Minangkabau	1.98
7	Minangkabau	2.70	7	Banjarese	1.71
8	Buginese	2.69	8	Buginese	1.64
9	Bantenese	1.95	9	Balinese	1.58
10	Banjarese	1.74	10	Batak	1.56
11	Balinese	1.68	11	Cirebonese	1.44
12	Acehnese	1.42	12	Acehnese	1.28
13	Dayak	1.35	13	Lombok	1.26
14	Sasak	1.33	14	Betawi	1.05
15	Chinese	1.22	15	Dayak	0.88
			16	Makasarese	0.87
			17	Bantenese	0.67
			18	Nias	0.35
			19	Bangka	0.33
			20	Chinese	0.30
	Others	14.86		Others	6.32
	Total	100.00		Total	100.00

Notes: The percentage of ethnic composition was slightly different from Table 4.3, because the ethnic composition in this table refers to the population aged five years old and above, as the data for language is recorded for this segment of the population.
Source: Calculated from tabulations provided by the BPS.

As mentioned earlier, the list of groups of language speakers includes all languages associated with the fifteen largest ethnic groups in Indonesia. However, there are five groups of language speakers that are not associated with any of the fifteen largest ethnic groups in Indonesia. The first is Bahasa Indonesia (Indonesian), which has no associated ethnic groups. The other four are the languages of Cirebonese, Makassarese, Nias and Bangka.

The Bahasa Indonesia–speaking group is significant, standing as the second largest group in Indonesia. They numbered 42.7 million, contributing

19.95 per cent. In other words, on average one in five Indonesians spoke Bahasa Indonesia daily at home in 2010. In other words, although some are able to speak Bahasa Indonesia, they may not use it daily at home.

Cirebonese is the language of the Cirebonese, originally living in Cirebon, on the border between the Sundanese province of West Java and the Javanese province of Central Java. The Cirebonese are considered a separate ethnic group because they are neither Javanese nor Sundanese. They also have their own language, a mix of the Javanese and Sundanese languages. The existence of Cirebonese as one of the fifteen largest groups of language speakers may indicate that many non-Cirebonese ethnic groups may speak Cirebonese. The group of Cirebonese speakers was the eleventh largest group in Indonesia.

Makassarese is the language of the Makassarese, originating in South Sulawesi. The ethnic groups of the Makassarese and Buginese may have many similarities, but they are two different ethnic groups, with two different languages. The number of Makassarese speakers was larger than those speaking Bantenese, making the Makassarese the sixteenth largest group of language speakers.

The Nias language belongs to the ethnic group of Nias, originating from the island of Nias and the nearby mainland in the province of North Sumatra. Bangka is the language of the Bangka ethnic group. As a language, Bangka is close to the Malay language. The ethnic group of Bangka also originated from the island of Bangka, in the province of Bangka-Belitung, Sumatra. The numbers of each of the Nias and Bangka speakers was larger than that of Chinese speakers. The group of Nias speakers were the eighteenth largest ethnic group and the Bangka speakers were the nineteenth.

The list of the twenty largest groups of language speakers also includes Lombok, which is not seen in the list of the fifteen largest ethnic groups. Nevertheless, Lombok was originally spoken by the Sasak ethnic group from the island of Lombok, West Nusa Tenggara, who were one of the fifteen largest ethnic groups in Indonesia. It is also often called the Sasak language.

Finally, as seen in Table 7.8, there were seventeen languages each spoken by more than one million Indonesians. Three other languages, including Chinese, were each spoken by fewer than one million Indonesians.

With regard to sex composition, more male Indonesians spoke Bahasa Indonesia than females. The same pattern is seen amongst the Indonesians who spoke the following languages: Sundanese, Malay, Banjarese,

Cirebonese, Betawi, Dayak, Bantenese, Bangka and Chinese. On the other hand, other languages had more female speakers. For example, there were more female Indonesians who spoke Javanese than males. The speakers of Lombok had the lowest sex ratio, 0.90, implying that there were only ninety male speakers of Lombok for every one hundred female speakers. The Balinese speakers had an almost equal number of male and female Balinese speakers.

LANGUAGE SPOKEN BY ETHNIC GROUP

Own Language and Bahasa Indonesia

Table 7.10 and Figure 7.3 show the languages spoken by each of the fifteen largest ethnic groups, focusing on one's own languages, Bahasa Indonesia and "Others". For example, Table 7.10 indicates that 77.36 per cent of Javanese spoke their own language, Javanese. Only 16.33 per cent of Javanese spoke Bahasa Indonesia. The remaining 6.32 per cent spoke other languages, mostly other local languages in Indonesia.

There was a large variation in terms of speaking their own languages. The highest percentage was seen amongst the Sasak (93.94 per cent), followed by the Balinese (92.69 per cent) and Madurese (91.12 per cent). The smallest percentage of speaking one's own language was seen amongst the Chinese (24.07 per cent) and the Betawi (25.41 per cent). For the Buginese it was 59.14 per cent and the Batak 43.11 per cent.

Almost all ethnic groups did not speak other languages. Less than 10 per cent of each ethnic group spoke other languages. An exception was only seen in three ethnic groups, the Bantenese (54.54 per cent), Dayak (24.28 per cent) and Chinese (15.44 per cent).

With regard to speaking Bahasa Indonesia, Table 7.10 shows that the Betawi mainly spoke Bahasa Indonesia. The majority of the Betawi (72.57 per cent) spoke Bahasa Indonesia. Therefore, although the Betawi were the sixth largest ethnic group, the group of Betawi speakers only came fourteenth.

Meanwhile, the majority (60.49 per cent) of the Chinese also spoke Bahasa Indonesia. The Chinese were the fifteenth largest ethnic group, but the Chinese speakers only came twentieth. It should be noted that in this book Bahasa Indonesia Peranakan, a mix of Bahasa Indonesia with Malay, Chinese and local languages, spoken by some Chinese, is not classified

Table 7.10
Percentage Distribution of Groups of Language Speakers
by Ethnic Group: Indonesia, 2010

Rank	Ethnic Group	Bahasa Indonesia	Own language	Others	Total
1	Javanese	16.33	77.36	6.32	100.00
2	Sundanese	13.31	83.70	2.99	100.00
3	Malay	18.95	76.23	4.82	100.00
4	Batak	52.56	43.11	4.33	100.00
5	Madurese	3.30	91.12	5.58	100.00
6	Betawi	72.57	25.41	2.02	100.00
7	Minangkabau	23.87	71.19	4.94	100.00
8	Buginese	32.15	59.14	8.71	100.00
9	Bantenese	10.32	33.13	56.54	100.00
10	Banjarese	10.85	86.13	3.02	100.00
11	Balinese	6.29	92.69	1.02	100.00
12	Acehnese	14.67	84.17	1.16	100.00
13	Dayak	14.11	61.62	24.28	100.00
14	Sasak	4.45	93.94	1.62	100.00
15	Chinese	60.49	24.07	15.44	100.00
	Others	22.66	31.59	45.75	100.00
	Total	19.95	67.58	12.47	100.00

Note: The data is limited to the population aged five years old and above.
Source: Calculated from tabulations provided by the BPS.

as Bahasa Indonesia. The percentage of the Chinese who spoke Bahasa Indonesia would have been higher if we had classified Bahasa Indonesia Peranakan as Bahasa Indonesia. However, we decided to treat Bahasa Indonesia Peranakan as a separate language, as Betawi and Malay are classified as languages different from Bahasa Indonesia.

Batak was the fourth largest ethnic group but the Batak language was only the tenth largest language, spoken by only 43.11 per cent of the Batak population. A larger percentage (52.56 per cent) of the Batak spoke Bahasa Indonesia.

The following sub-sections elaborate the languages spoken by the fifteen largest ethnic groups in Indonesia. Tables 7.10–7.25 present the ten largest groups of language speakers in each of the fifteen largest ethnic groups in Indonesia. It should be noted, however, that the examination of groups of language speakers within each ethnic group is limited to the

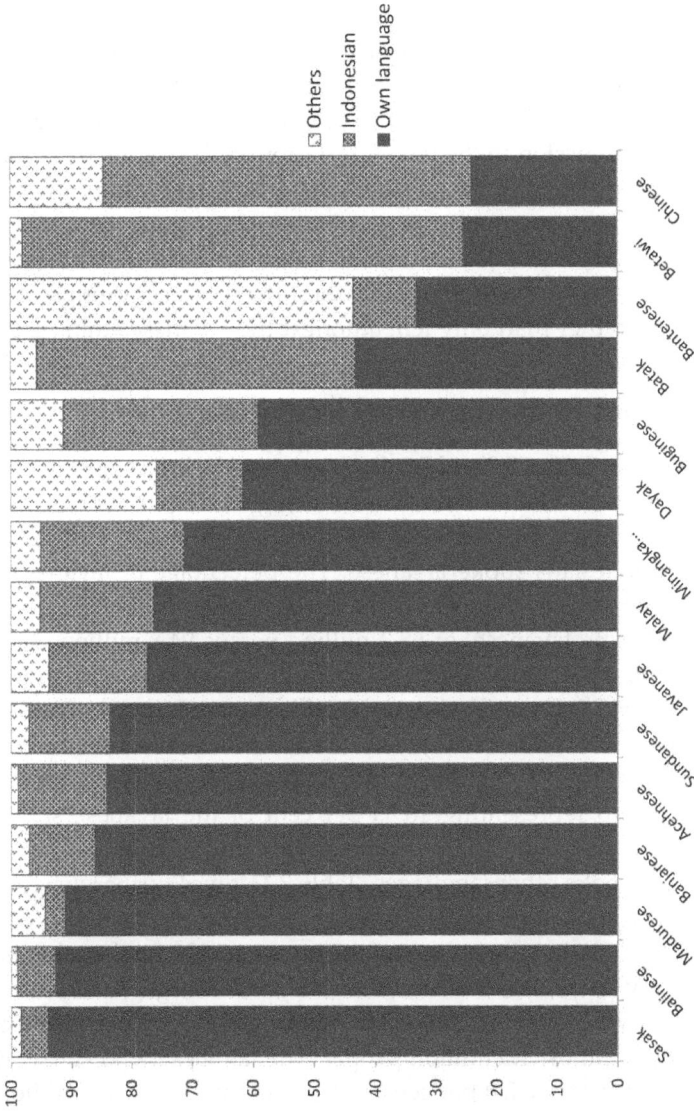

Figure 7.3
Language Spoken Daily at Home by Ethnic Group: Indonesia, 2010

Source: Drawn from Table 7.10.

twenty largest language groups in Indonesia as a whole, as discussed earlier. Yet, the twenty largest groups of language speakers at the national level may not necessarily be the same as the twenty largest groups of language speakers of each ethnic group. A large percentage of "Others" may indicate the presence of other groups of language speakers, which should have been included in the ten largest groups of language speakers within that ethnic group. Fortunately, there are not many such cases, especially as we limit the discussion to the ten largest groups. Therefore, this case will not affect the accuracy of the analysis on the language composition.

There is an exception in presenting the composition of groups of language speakers. Because of the dominant feature of the Javanese as an ethnic group, we have presented the fifteen largest groups of language speakers, rather than only ten, amongst the Javanese ethnic group.

Languages of the Javanese: Mostly Javanese

As shown in Tables 7.8 and 7.9, Javanese was the largest group of language speakers, with 68.2 million, contributing 31.87 per cent of Indonesia's population aged five years old and above. This means that almost one in three Indonesians spoke Javanese. The percentage of Javanese speakers was much smaller than 40.47, the percentage of Indonesians identifying themselves as Javanese, or 68.2 million versus 94.8 million, respectively. This implies that not all Javanese spoke their own language. Indeed, out of 68.2 million Javanese speakers, 67.0 million were Javanese. In other words, there were 1.2 million non-Javanese who spoke Javanese. As is shown in Table 7.10, only 77.35 per cent of the Javanese spoke Javanese.

A group representing 16.33 per cent of the Javanese spoke Bahasa Indonesia. As the Javanese people were found everywhere in Indonesia, they also spoke other languages. Table 7.11 gives further insight on other languages spoken by the Javanese.

Although the percentages of the Javanese who spoke other languages were very small, in absolute terms they were large. As an example, the Javanese who spoke Cirebonese accounted for 1.7 per cent only, but numbered almost 1.5 million people. The Javanese who spoke Madurese accounted for only 2.0 per cent, but this amounted to 1.7 million people. It should be mentioned that both the Cirebonese and Madurese languages are closely related to the Javanese language.

The fifth largest (1.03 per cent) language spoken by the Javanese was Malay. Malay and Bahasa Indonesia are relatively similar. Therefore, from

Table 7.11
Languages Spoken Daily at Home by the Javanese: Indonesia, 2010

Rank	Language	Males	Females	Total	Per cent	Sex Ratio
1	Javanese	33,467,283	33,521,309	66,988,592	77.35	0.998
2	Bahasa Indonesia	7,147,907	6,990,991	14,138,898	16.33	1.022
3	Madurese	844,355	889,869	1,734,224	2.00	0.949
4	Cirebonese	759,006	712,377	1,471,383	1.70	1.065
5	Malay	469,523	423,704	893,227	1.03	1.108
6	Sundanese	363,846	322,023	685,869	0.79	1.130
7	Betawi	108,140	100,892	209,032	0.24	1.072
8	Banjarese	81,566	67,050	148,616	0.17	1.216
9	Bangka	17,396	13,155	30,551	0.04	1.322
10	Minangkabau	16,160	12,952	29,112	0.03	1.248
11	Batak	11,107	12,582	23,689	0.03	0.883
12	Acehnese	9,505	9,764	19,269	0.02	0.973
13	Balinese	6,564	10,638	17,202	0.02	0.617
14	Bantenese	9,178	7,418	16,596	0.02	1.237
15	Dayak	7,951	5,870	13,821	0.02	1.355
	Others	93,514	90,946	184,460	0.21	1.028
	Total	43,423,823	43,203,952	86,604,541	100.00	1.005

Source: Calculated from tabulations provided by the BPS.

the five largest languages spoken by the Javanese, there were only two groups of language speakers. First, the largest one included the Javanese and its "close" languages (Madurese and Cirebonese). The second consists of Bahasa Indonesia and its "close" language of Malay. Altogether, these five largest languages were spoken by 98.41 per cent of the Javanese in Indonesia.

It is interesting to note that only 0.79 per cent of the Javanese spoke Sundanese, the language of the second largest ethnic group in Indonesia. They may be Javanese who lived in Sundanese communities or there may have been some inter-marriages between these two groups.

With the transmigration programme, many Javanese lived outside Java, including Sumatra and Kalimantan. The fact that 0.17 per cent of the Javanese spoke Banjarese may indicate that they were Javanese descendants living in Banjarese communities in South Kalimantan. They may be the so-called "Pujakekal" (Putra Jawa Kelahiran Kalimantan — Javanese born in Kalimantan). Indeed, the Javanese were the second largest ethnic group in the province of South Kalimantan, forming 14.51 per cent. In addition, 0.02 per cent of the Javanese spoke Dayak, the languages spoken by a large ethnic group from the island of Kalimantan. Some Javanese also spoke the languages in Sumatra, such as Bangka, Minangkabau, Batak and Acehnese. Altogether, 0.12 per cent of the Javanese spoke one of these languages. They may be the so-called "PUJAKESUMA" (Putra Jawa Kelahiran Sumatra, Javanese born in Sumatra).

Languages of the Sundanese: Mostly Sundanese

There were 31.0 million Sundanese speakers aged five years and above, the third largest language in Indonesia. The number of Sundanese speakers was smaller than the number of Sundanese aged five years old and above (33.2 million). Although the absolute difference was relatively large (2.2 million), the percentages were very close (15.50 per cent versus 14.49 per cent), indicating that not many other ethnic groups spoke Sundanese. Furthermore, not all Sundanese spoke their own language, Sundanese. About 83.70 per cent of the Sundanese spoke Sundanese daily at home. See Table 7.12.

The second language spoken by the Sundanese was Bahasa Indonesia (13.31 per cent). The number of Sundanese who spoke Betawi (1.16 per cent) was greater than the number who spoke Javanese (0.68 per cent). A small percentage (0.42 per cent) spoke Malay. Therefore, the Sundanese spoke only two languages, their own Sundanese and Bahasa Indonesia, Betawi or Malay. These four groups of language speakers already accounted for 98.59 per cent of the Sundanese. The fifth largest group (0.42 per cent) spoke Cirebonese, or about 170,000 Sundanese.

Languages of the Malay: Mostly Malay

The number of Malay speakers ranked fourth after Javanese, Bahasa Indonesia and Sundanese speakers. Unlike the Javanese and Madurese, as compared in Tables 7.8 and 7.13, Malay speakers (14.6 million) were almost double the number of the Malay aged five years old and above (7.8 million). Furthermore, as depicted in Table 7.13, the Malay who spoke Malay totalled only about 6 million. In other words, many non-Malay such as Javanese, Sundanese and Batak spoke Malay.

The Malay who spoke their own language made up 76.23 per cent and those speaking Bahasa Indonesia accounted for 18.95 per cent. These two

Table 7.12
Languages Spoken Daily at Home by the Sundanese: Indonesia, 2010

Rank	Language	Males	Females	Total	Per cent	Sex Ratio
1	Sundanese	14,114,099	13,661,068	27,775,167	83.70	1.033
2	Bahasa Indonesia	2,174,258	2,240,779	4,415,037	13.31	0.970
3	Betawi	193,520	189,814	383,334	1.16	1.020
4	Javanese	116,426	109,787	226,213	0.68	1.060
5	Cirebonese	88,274	81,885	170,159	0.51	1.078
6	Malay	71,217	68,328	139,545	0.42	1.042
7	Bantenese	10,220	8,906	19,126	0.06	1.148
8	Banjarese	4,276	3,630	7,906	0.02	1.178
9	Bangka	2,665	2,285	4,950	0.01	1.166
10	Minangkabau	1,927	1,798	3,725	0.01	1.072
	Others	18,508	18,544	37,052	0.11	0.998
	Total	16,795,390	16,386,824	33,182,214	100.00	1.025

Source: Calculated from tabulations provided by the BPS.

Table 7.13
Languages Spoken Daily at Home by the Malay: Indonesia, 2010

Rank	Language	Males	Females	Total	Per cent	Sex Ratio
1	Malay	2,976,196	2,973,865	5,950,061	76.23	1.001
2	Bahasa Indonesia	737,325	741,695	1,479,020	18.95	0.994
3	Javanese	17,106	19,923	37,029	0.47	0.859
4	Minangkabau	15,070	13,934	29,004	0.37	1.082
5	Dayak	14,240	13,985	28,225	0.36	1.018
6	Betawi	8,931	8,453	17,384	0.22	1.057
7	Sundanese	8,409	7,298	15,707	0.20	1.152
8	Banjarese	7,079	6,718	13,797	0.18	1.054
9	Bangka	7,056	6,046	13,102	0.17	1.167
10	Batak	5,396	6,270	11,666	0.15	0.861
	Others	104,143	106,461	210,604	2.70	0.978
	Total	3,900,951	3,904,648	7,805,599	100.00	0.999

Source: Calculated from tabulations provided by the BPS.

languages formed 95.18 per cent. Practically, only one language, "Malay-Bahasa Indonesia", was spoken by the Malay. All other languages were only spoken by much smaller numbers of Malay.

As seen in Table 7.13, the Malay who spoke Javanese numbered 37,029 persons, larger than 29,004, the number of Malay who spoke Minangkabau. More than 10,000 Malay spoke each of the following languages: Dayak and Banjarese on the island of Kalimantan, Sundanese and Betawi on the island of Java, Bangka and Batak on the island of Sumatra. Apart from all these languages, it would be interesting to investigate the very small percentage (0.02 per cent, or 1,900 Malay, not presented in Table 7.13) who spoke Chinese. Were these Malay who spoke Chinese married to Chinese persons?

Languages of the Batak: Majority Bahasa Indonesia

The Batak speakers numbered 3.3 million and those who spoke Batak numbered 3.2 million. In other words, Batak speakers were mostly the Batak themselves. This does not mean that the Batak ethnic group mostly spoke their own language in everyday life at home. Table 7.14 indicates that the Batak who spoke Bahasa Indonesia were the majority, as compared to the Batak speaking their own language (52.56 per cent versus 43.11 per cent). Therefore, the Batak-speaking group ranked as the tenth largest group, although as an ethnic group the Batak were the fourth largest.

A significant number of the Batak spoke Malay (2.23 per cent). The next most common language spoken by the Batak was Javanese, with 49,504 speakers, which was larger than the number of Javanese who spoke Batak. This was probably because some Batak had migrated to Javanese provinces. As indicated in Table 5.8, there were 90,554 Batak who lived in the Javanese provinces of Yogyakarta, Central Java or East Java.

On the other hand, as seen in Table 7.14, the Batak who spoke Sundanese numbered only 14,391 people, a very much smaller group than the 467,438 Batak living in the Sundanese province of West Java. Similarly, the number of Batak who spoke Betawi was just 15,949, very much smaller than the Batak who lived in Jakarta (326,645). Does this mean that the Batak living in the Javanese provinces assimilated better with the local communities? Or, were the Batak more likely to speak Bahasa Indonesia in Jakarta and West Java? There were also the Batak who spoke neighbouring languages such as Minangkabau and Acehnese as well as those who spoke Javanese.

Interestingly, although very small, we found that 0.02 per cent or almost 1,500 Batak spoke Chinese (this data is not presented in Table 7.14). These may be the Batak who lived in the city of Medan, the capital

Table 7.14
Languages Spoken Daily at Home by the Batak: Indonesia, 2010

Rank	Language	Males	Females	Total	Per cent	Sex Ratio
1	Bahasa Indonesia	1,997,708	1,946,691	3,944,399	52.56	1.026
2	Batak	1,604,974	1,630,016	3,234,990	43.11	0.985
3	Malay	88,764	78,404	167,168	2.23	1.132
4	Javanese	25,011	24,493	49,504	0.66	1.021
5	Minangkabau	11,176	10,561	21,737	0.29	1.058
6	Acehnese	9,110	9,327	18,437	0.25	0.977
7	Betawi	8,495	7,454	15,949	0.21	1.140
8	Sundanese	8,238	6,153	14,391	0.19	1.339
9	Banjarese	2,381	1,752	4,133	0.06	1.359
10	Madurese	1,612	2,030	3,642	0.05	0.794
	Others	15,521	14,742	30,263	0.40	1.053
	Total	3,772,990	3,731,623	7,504,613	100.00	1.011

Source: Calculated from tabulations provided by the BPS.

of the province of North Sumatra, marrying Chinese or living alongside the Chinese community. As presented in Table 5.30, the Chinese living in North Sumatra accounted for about 12 per cent of all Chinese Indonesians.

Languages of the Madurese: Overwhelming Madurese

Madurese speakers were the fifth largest group, forming 3.64 per cent of all Indonesians aged five years old and above. The Madurese were also the fifth largest ethnic group, though constituting 3.09 per cent of Indonesian citizens aged five years and above. The number of Madurese speakers was larger than the number of the Madurese, indicating that some non-Madurese spoke Madurese. As mentioned earlier, some Javanese spoke Madurese.

Madurese was spoken by 7.8 million Indonesians. The number of Madurese who spoke Madurese was only 6 million. There were 1.8 million non-Madurese who spoke Madurese, mostly the Javanese (1.7 million). It is therefore important to examine whether they were the East Javanese living in the Madurese community and assimilated into this community through marriage. However, this is beyond the scope of this study. Furthermore, not all Madurese spoke their own language, although a large majority (91.02 per cent) of 6.6 million Madurese aged five years old and above spoke Madurese.

As seen in Table 7.15, the number of Madurese who spoke Javanese was much smaller in absolute terms, yet in relative terms, 4.22 per cent spoke Javanese. The Madurese who spoke Bahasa Indonesia only made up 3.30 per cent and those who spoke Malay only made up 0.56 per cent. It is interesting to note that 53,002 Madurese lived in South Kalimantan and there were 22,504 Madurese who spoke Banjarese. Their number was larger than the number of Madurese who spoke Dayak, who numbered less than 1,000 people (this data is not presented in Table 7.15).

Languages of the Betawi: Mostly Bahasa Indonesia

Differing from all ethnic groups mentioned so far, only a quarter of the 6.1 million Betawi spoke their own language (Betawi). Yet, almost three quarters of them spoke Bahasa Indonesia. This may partly be because the Betawi language is sometimes perceived as a dialect of Bahasa Indonesia, especially when spoken in the capital city of Jakarta, but which has been widely known around Indonesia. Some Betawi may have identified

Table 7.15
Languages Spoken Daily at Home by the Madurese: Indonesia, 2010

Rank	Language	Males	Females	Total	Per cent	Sex Ratio
1	Madurese	2,918,814	3,097,562	6,016,376	91.12	0.942
2	Javanese	145,095	133,738	278,833	4.22	1.085
3	Bahasa Indonesia	114,482	103,717	218,199	3.30	1.104
4	Malay	19,539	17,643	37,182	0.56	1.107
5	Banjarese	11,695	10,809	22,504	0.34	1.082
6	Bangka	1,721	1,421	3,142	0.05	1.211
7	Batak	1,417	1,491	2,908	0.04	0.950
8	Sundanese	1,592	1,129	2,721	0.04	1.410
9	Betawi	1,102	854	1,956	0.03	1.290
10	Balinese	620	585	1,205	0.02	1.060
	Others	9,166	8,770	17,936	0.27	1.045
	Total	3,225,243	3,377,719	6,602,962	100.00	0.955

Source: Calculated from tabulations provided by the BPS.

their language as Bahasa Indonesia, rather than Betawi. Altogether, most Betawi (97.98 per cent) spoke either Bahasa Indonesia or Betawi. Only small numbers of Betawi spoke languages other than Bahasa Indonesia and Betawi.

As presented in earlier Table 5.12, about 2.7 million Betawi lived in West Java, the home province of the Sundanese language. Yet, as seen in Table 7.16, only about 50,000 Betawi spoke Sundanese. Because of the larger Sundanese population, there was a much larger number of Sundanese who spoke Betawi than Betawi who spoke Sundanese (see Table 7.12). Malay and Javanese were two other languages spoken by the Betawi.

Languages of the Minangkabau: Mostly Minangkabau

As seen in Table 7.17, the majority of the Minangkabau spoke either Minangkabau (71.19 per cent) or Bahasa Indonesia (23.87 per cent) to communicate daily with members of their household. There were 3.61 per cent of the Minangkabau who spoke Malay and 0.19 per cent who spoke Betawi. As mentioned earlier, the Malay and Betawi languages are similar to Bahasa Indonesia. In other words, 27.67 per cent spoke Bahasa Indonesia,

Table 7.16
Languages Spoken Daily at Home by the Betawi: Indonesia, 2010

Rank	Language	Males	Females	Total	Per cent	Sex Ratio
1	Bahasa Indonesia	2,232,191	2,205,926	4,438,117	72.57	1.012
2	Betawi	789,706	764,512	1,554,218	25.41	1.033
3	Sundanese	26,284	23,658	49,942	0.82	1.111
4	Malay	11,195	10,947	22,142	0.36	1.023
5	Javanese	7,399	7,846	15,245	0.25	0.943
6	Dawan	7,534	7,313	14,847	0.24	1.030
7	Bantenese	1,371	1,171	2,542	0.04	1.171
8	Cirebonese	710	609	1,319	0.02	1.166
9	Banjarese	427	422	849	0.01	1.012
10	Bangka	372	338	710	0.01	1.101
	Others	7,746	7,984	15,730	0.26	0.970
	Total	3,084,935	3,030,726	6,115,661	100.00	1.018

Source: Calculated from tabulations provided by the BPS.

Table 7.17
Languages Spoken Daily at Home by the Minangkabau: Indonesia, 2010

Rank	Language	Males	Females	Total	Per cent	Sex Ratio
1	Minángkabau	2,032,497	2,088,320	4,120,817	71.19	0.973
2	Bahasa Indonesia	701,187	680,201	1,381,388	23.87	1.031
3	Malay	106,027	102,817	208,844	3.61	1.031
4	Batak	9,939	9,141	19,080	0.33	1.087
5	Betawi	5,819	5,279	11,098	0.19	1.102
6	Javanese	5,375	5,132	10,507	0.18	1.047
7	Sundanese	5,341	3,819	9,160	0.16	1.399
8	Acehnese	1,127	1,094	2,221	0.04	1.030
9	Bangka	977	801	1,778	0.03	1.220
10	Banjarese	646	488	1,134	0.02	1.324
	Others	11,503	10,552	22,055	0.38	1.090
	Total	2,880,438	2,907,644	5,788,082	100.00	0.991

Source: Calculated from tabulations provided by the BPS.

Malay or Betawi. Altogether, almost all of the Minangkabau (98.86 per cent) spoke their own language or Bahasa Indonesia/Malay/Betawi. The percentages of other languages were very small. The only relatively large one was the Batak language, although this number was also very small, only 0.33 per cent. In other words, as *perantau*,[2] the Minangkabau tended to speak their own language or Bahasa Indonesia/Malay/Betawi.

Languages of the Buginese: Majority Buginese

There were 3.5 million Buginese speakers and 3.4 million Buginese who spoke Buginese. Therefore, there were only about 100,000 non-Buginese who spoke Buginese. In other words, the Buginese speakers were mostly the Buginese.

The number of Buginese speakers was much smaller than the 5.8 million Buginese aged five years and above. In other words, not all Buginese spoke Buginese, with only about 59.14 per cent of the Buginese speaking their own language, also called Ugi. Some (1.89 per cent) of the Buginese spoke Makassarese, the fourth largest language spoken by the Buginese. As mentioned earlier, Buginese is closely related to Makassarese, both as ethnic groups and languages.

Apart from this, 32.15 per cent of the Buginese spoke Bahasa Indonesia and 3.61 per cent spoke Malay. In other words, most of the Buginese (96.79 per cent) spoke either Buginese/Makasarese or Bahasa Indonesia/Malay.

Other than Buginese and Bahasa Indonesia/Malay, the languages spoken by the Buginese were small in number (Table 7.18). The largest one was Banjarese (0.79 per cent), perhaps spoken by some Bugis Pagatan living in South Kalimantan.

Languages of the Bantenese: Majority Sundanese

The Bantenese ethnic group was unique. Only about one third (33.13 per cent) of the Bantenese aged five years old and above spoke their own language, but more than half (54.28 per cent) spoke Sundanese. Therefore, Bantenese speakers ranked as only the seventeenth largest, although the Bantenese were the ninth largest ethnic group in Indonesia.

The Bantenese identity was quite new in 2010 as the Bantenese used previously to be seen as a sub-ethnic group of the Sundanese. The province of Banten was created from the province of West Java (the home province of the Sundanese) in 2000.

Table 7.18
Languages Spoken Daily at Home by the Buginese: Indonesia, 2010

Rank	Language	Males	Females	Total	Per cent	Sex Ratio
1	Buginese	1,660,633	1,745,269	3,405,902	59.14	0.952
2	Bahasa Indonesia	946,117	905,313	1,851,430	32.15	1.045
3	Malay	110,548	97,532	208,080	3.61	1.133
4	Makassarese	52,174	56,483	108,657	1.89	0.924
5	Banjarese	24,469	20,929	45,398	0.79	1.169
6	Javanese	6,419	5,418	11,837	0.21	1.185
7	Bangka	3,540	2,589	6,129	0.11	1.367
8	Mandar	2,233	1,935	4,168	0.07	1.154
9	Sundanese	1,819	1,269	3,088	0.05	1.433
10	Madurese	1,259	1,260	2,519	0.04	0.999
	Others	58,036	53,779	111,815	1.94	1.079
	Total	2,867,247	2,891,776	5,759,023	100.00	0.992

Source: Calculated from tabulations provided by the BPS.

Furthermore, 10.32 per cent of the Bantenese spoke Bahasa Indonesia. The Bantenese also spoke Malay (0.31 per cent) and Betawi (0.23 per cent), two languages closely related to Bahasa Indonesia.

Languages of the Banjarese: Mostly Banjarese

The number of Banjarese speakers ranked the seventh amongst other groups of language speakers, with 3.7 million users. The Banjarese who spoke their own language numbered 3.2 million and only a small number of non-Banjarese spoke Banjarese. As an ethnic group, the Banjarese, also known as *perantau*,[3] were amongst the ten largest ethnic groups in eight provinces. It seems that wherever the Banjarese lived, most of them spoke Banjarese at home, with 86.13 per cent of them speaking their own language. Those speaking Bahasa Indonesia accounted for 10.83 per cent and a much smaller percentage (1.78 per cent) spoke Malay. Altogether, these three languages were spoken by 98.76 per cent of the Banjarese.

Apart from the Banjarese and Bahasa Indonesia/Malay, the numbers of languages spoken by the Banjarese were very small. Amongst these, Javanese and Dayak were spoken daily at home by the Banjarese (Table 7.20).

Table 7.19
Languages Spoken Daily at Home by the Bantenese: Indonesia, 2010

Rank	Language	Males	Females	Total	Per cent	Sex Ratio
1	Sundanese	1,158,423	1,108,742	2,267,165	54.28	1.045
2	Bantenese	709,074	674,635	1,383,709	33.13	1.051
3	Bahasa Indonesia	214,896	216,299	431,195	10.32	0.994
4	Javanese	25,380	23,293	48,673	1.17	1.090
5	Malay	6,870	6,097	12,967	0.31	1.127
6	Betawi	4,832	4,732	9,564	0.23	1.021
7	Cirebonese	1,987	2,033	4,020	0.10	0.977
8	Lampung	1,152	1,114	2,266	0.05	1.034
9	Bangka	122	101	223	0.01	1.208
10	Batak	64	74	138	0.00	0.865
	Others	8,484	8,044	16,528	0.40	1.055
	Total	2,131,284	2,045,164	4,176,448	100.00	1.042

Source: Calculated from tabulations provided by the BPS.

Table 7.20
Languages Spoken Daily at Home by the Banjarese: Indonesia, 2010

Rank	Language	Males	Females	Total	Per cent	Sex Ratio
1	Banjarese	1,597,389	1,604,167	3,201,556	86.13	0.996
2	Bahasa Indonesia	199,587	203,878	403,465	10.85	0.979
3	Malay	33,284	32,996	66,280	1.78	1.009
4	Javanese	7,958	9,561	17,519	0.47	0.832
5	Dayak	2,460	2,238	4,698	0.13	1.099
6	Buginese	761	1,161	1,922	0.05	0.655
7	Sundanese	396	347	743	0.02	1.141
8	Madurese	281	322	603	0.02	0.873
9	Betawi	237	192	429	0.01	1.234
10	Mandar	130	147	277	0.01	0.884
	Others	10,106	9,507	19,613	0.53	1.063
	Total	1,852,589	1,864,516	3,717,105	100.00	0.994

Source: Calculated from tabulations provided by the BPS.

Languages of the Balinese: Overwhelming Balinese

A large majority (92.69 per cent) of the Balinese spoke Balinese, followed by Bahasa Indonesia (6.29 per cent). In other words, almost all (98.98 per cent) of the Balinese spoke either their own language or Bahasa Indonesia. Therefore, the numbers of Balinese who spoke other languages were very small.

Few Balinese conversed with members of their households in neighbouring languages such as Javanese (0.43 per cent) and Lombok or Sasak (0.07 per cent). Some of them also spoke Malay (0.26 per cent). As seen in Table 7.21, there were almost 16,000 Balinese who spoke Javanese. This was smaller than the number of Javanese who spoke Balinese (about 17,000). There was a larger number of Sasak who spoke Balinese than Balinese who spoke Sasak.

Languages of the Acehnese: Mostly Acehnese

With around 2.7 million Acehnese speakers, this group of language speakers ranked twelfth in Indonesia. Amongst them, about 2.6 million were the Acehnese (Table 7.22). In other words, only a few non-Acehnese spoke Acehnese.

Table 7.21
Languages Spoken Daily at Home by the Balinese: Indonesia, 2010

Rank	Language	Males	Females	Total	Per cent	Sex Ratio
1	Balinese	1,664,766	1,660,481	3,325,247	92.69	1.003
2	Bahasa Indonesia	113,858	111,830	225,688	6.29	1.018
3	Javanese	8,010	7,508	15,518	0.43	1.067
4	Malay	5,007	4,412	9,419	0.26	1.135
5	Lombok	1,250	1,408	2,658	0.07	0.888
6	Banjarese	623	488	1,111	0.03	1.277
7	Sundanese	486	419	905	0.03	1.160
8	Madurese	290	367	657	0.02	0.790
9	Betawi	328	261	589	0.02	1.257
10	Dayak	106	70	176	0.00	1.514
	Others	2,744	2,721	5,465	0.15	1.008
	Total	1,797,468	1,789,965	3,587,433	100.00	1.004

Source: Calculated from tabulations provided by the BPS.

This language was spoken by a large majority (84.17 per cent) of the Acehnese. In addition to their own language, the Acehnese spoke Bahasa Indonesia (14.67 per cent). Furthermore, very few Acehnese (0.33 per cent) spoke Malay. In other words, almost all (99.17 per cent) Acehnese spoke either Acehnese or Bahasa Indonesia/Malay.

Very few Acehnese (about 2,000 or 0.08 per cent) spoke Batak, the language of the neighbouring province of North Sumatra. Interestingly, although also very few, there were about 3,000 Acehnese who spoke Javanese. As is revealed in Table 5.24, there were around 6,000 Acehnese living in Javanese provinces, either in Yogyakarta, Central Java or East Java. Almost half of them may have spoken Javanese.

Languages of the Dayak: Majority Dayak

As with their ethnic classification, the Dayak language consists of many sub-groups, as can be seen in Appendix 2. However, it is beyond the scope of this book to discuss each sub-language.

Amongst the Dayak, the majority (61.62 per cent) conversed in their own language in everyday life at home. Dayak speakers numbered about

Table 7.22
Languages Spoken Daily at Home by the Acehnese: Indonesia, 2010

Rank	Language	Males	Females	Total	Per cent	Sex Ratio
1	Acehnese	1,267,353	1,286,586	2,553,939	84.17	0.985
2	Bahasa Indonesia	227,727	217,572	445,299	14.67	1.047
3	Malay	5,645	4,471	10,116	0.33	1.263
4	Javanese	1,715	1,602	3,317	0.11	1.071
5	Batak	1,280	1,108	2,388	0.08	1.155
6	Sundanese	948	624	1,572	0.05	1.519
7	Betawi	917	637	1,554	0.05	1.440
8	Minangkabau	856	683	1,539	0.05	1.253
9	Nias	297	286	583	0.02	1.038
10	Chinese	167	183	350	0.01	0.913
	Others	6,940	6,842	13,782	0.45	1.014
	Total	1,513,845	1,520,594	3,034,439	100.00	0.996

Source: Calculated from tabulations provided by the BPS.

1.9 million, 1.8 million of whom were Dayak themselves. Thus, only about 100,000 non-Dayak spoke Dayak. The non-Dayak could be the Malay or Banjarese who interacted with the Dayak in the various provinces of Kalimantan. Indeed, there were 28,000 Malay who spoke Dayak (Table 7.13) and almost 5,000 Banjarese (Table 7.20) who spoke Dayak.

The non-Dayak could also be the Javanese. As is seen in Table 7.11, there were almost 14,000 Javanese who spoke Dayak. They were not necessarily Javanese by blood but may have become Javanese through social and political interaction.

The second largest language spoken was Bahasa Indonesia (14.11 per cent). Some Dayak spoke Malay (6.01 per cent) and Banjarese (5.80 per cent), probably because they lived nearby Malay and Banjarese communities. Altogether, the four groups of language speakers formed 87.54 per cent.

As indicated in Table 7.23, the remaining 12.46 per cent consisted of many small groups of language speakers. Amongst these, the largest one was Makassarese speakers, although they only made up 0.63 per cent. Others included those who spoke Javanese (0.40 per cent), Batak (0.11 per cent) and Betawi (0.11 per cent).

Table 7.23
Language Spoken Daily at Home by the Dayak: Indonesia, 2010

Rank	Language	Males	Females	Total	Per cent	Sex Ratio
1	Dayak	924,169	854,656	1,778,825	61.62	1.081
2	Bahasa Indonesia	197,579	209,739	407,318	14.11	0.942
3	Malay	86,253	87,342	173,595	6.01	0.988
4	Banjarese	82,069	85,282	167,351	5.80	0.962
5	Makassarese	8,721	9,398	18,119	0.63	0.928
6	Javanese	5,088	6,341	11,429	0.40	0.802
7	Batak	1,669	1,530	3,199	0.11	1.091
8	Buginese	1,526	1,585	3,111	0.11	0.963
9	Betawi	1,380	1,226	2,606	0.09	1.126
10	Sundanese	1,391	1,195	2,586	0.09	1.164
	Others	162,760	156,076	318,836	11.04	1.043
	Total	1,472,605	1,414,370	2,886,975	100.00	1.041

Source: Calculated from tabulations provided by the BPS.

Languages of the Sasak: Overwhelming Lombok

Lombok is the language of the Sasak. The number of Lombok speakers formed the thirteenth largest group of language speakers in Indonesia, while Sasak was the fourteenth largest ethnic group in Indonesia. The Sasak made up 1.33 per cent of all Indonesians aged five years old and above and the Lombok speakers contributed 1.26 per cent. The number of Sasak speakers was just slightly smaller than the number of Sasak people, 2.69 million and 2.84 million, respectively. Furthermore, the Sasak who spoke their own language (2.67 million) were fewer in number than the Sasak speakers (2.69 million). There were only about 20,000 non-Sasak people who spoke Lombok.

In other words, Lombok was mostly spoken by the Sasak, accounting for 93.94 per cent. Only 4.45 per cent of the Sasak spoke Bahasa Indonesia. Apart from these languages, as seen in Table 7.24, all other languages spoken by the Sasak were migrants' languages such as Balinese, Javanese, Malay, Banjarese, Sundanese, Buginese, Madurese and Betawi. Yet, the "Others" accounted for 1.14 per cent, or 32,200 individuals. It is possible that amongst "Others" there were a few local languages spoken

Table 7.24
Languages Spoken Daily at Home by the Sasak: Indonesia, 2010

Rank	Language	Males	Females	Total	Per cent	Sex Ratio
1	Lombok	1,262,180	1,403,933	2,666,113	93.94	0.899
2	Bahasa Indonesia	64,873	61,292	126,165	4.45	1.058
3	Balinese	2,705	2,918	5,623	0.20	0.927
4	Javanese	1,888	1,459	3,347	0.12	1.294
5	Malay	1,423	635	2,058	0.07	2.241
6	Banjarese	974	584	1,558	0.05	1.668
7	Sundanese	226	193	419	0.01	1.171
8	Buginese	168	164	332	0.01	1.024
9	Madurese	93	73	166	0.01	1.274
10	Betawi	88	73	161	0.01	1.205
	Others	14,988	17,309	32,297	1.14	0.866
	Total	1,349,606	1,488,633	2,838,239	100.00	0.907

Source: Calculated from tabulations provided by the BPS.

by at least 6,000 individuals, who might represent the third or fourth group of language speakers amongst the Sasak.

Languages of the Chinese: Majority Bahasa Indonesia

Amongst the population aged five years old and above, there were about 2.6 million Chinese in Indonesia, but there were only around 645,000 Chinese speakers, the twentieth largest group of language speakers. This was because not all Chinese spoke Chinese languages, only almost one quarter (24.07 per cent).

For more than three decades Chinese culture, including the Chinese language and products bearing Chinese characters, was banned. Many Chinese who had been living in Indonesia for generations had perhaps lost their command of Chinese. As a result, as shown in Table 7.25, the majority (60.49 per cent) of the Chinese used Bahasa Indonesia as the medium of communication at home. Some Chinese may speak Bahasa Indonesia Peranakan, referring to Bahasa Indonesia or Malay mixed with local languages and Chinese. The Chinese who spoke Malay accounted for 4.18 per cent. The Chinese had used Malay, as it was the language

Table 7.25
Languages Spoken Daily at Home by the Chinese: Indonesia, 2010

Rank	Language	Males	Females	Total	Per cent	Sex Ratio
1	Bahasa Indonesia	786,429	790,476	1,576,905	60.49	0.995
2	Chinese	317,527	309,828	627,355	24.07	1.025
3	Malay	56,612	52,292	108,904	4.18	1.083
4	Javanese	31,432	32,565	63,997	2.46	0.965
5	Bangka	27,474	26,838	54,312	2.08	1.024
6	Sundanese	12,521	12,422	24,943	0.96	1.008
7	Betawi	7,806	7,593	15,399	0.59	1.028
8	Banjarese	4,620	4,400	9,020	0.35	1.050
9	Dayak	4,488	3,022	7,510	0.29	1.485
10	Balinese	1,499	1,467	2,966	0.11	1.022
	Others	59,023	56,367	115,390	4.43	1.047
	Total	1,309,431	1,297,270	2,606,701	100.00	1.009

Source: Calculated from tabulations provided by the BPS.

of trade thoughout the archipelago over the centuries. In other words, a very large majority (88.74 per cent) of the Chinese spoke either Bahasa Indonesia/Malay or Chinese.

A significant 2.46 per cent (almost 64,000) of Chinese spoke Javanese, perhaps because of the presence of the significant absolute number of Chinese living in the three home provinces of the Javanese. Amongst the population aged five years old and above, there were about 396,000 Chinese living in these Javanese provinces.

The number of Chinese who spoke Bangka was also significant (2.06 per cent, about 54,000). The Chinese were the fourth largest ethnic group in the province of Bangka-Belitung. There were almost 100,000 Chinese living in the province of Bangka-Belitung and some of them have adapted to using the Bangka language.

As is shown in Table 7.25, some other languages were spoken by the Chinese, although the contribution of each was small: Sundanese (almost 25,000), Betawi (about 15,000), Banjarese (about 9,000) and a few others.

The fact that "Others" in Table 7.25 was still relatively large (4.43 per cent) may indicate the presence of many groups of languages spoken by the Chinese, although the numbers of each may have been very small.

In other words, some of the Chinese, who were spread all over Indonesia, may have adapted to use the languages spoken most in the area in which they resided.

Notes

1. In 2013 there was a national debate on whether to continue mentioning religion in the KTP.
2. See the sub-section, "Almost Heterogeneous Provinces", in Chapter 4.
3. *Perantau* is a person who *merantau*.

REFERENCES

Abe, Ken-ichi. "Cari Rezeki, Numpang, Siap: The Reclamation Process of Peat Swamp Forest in Riau". *Southeast Asian Studies* 34, no. 4 (1997): 622–32.

Akinwale, Omobolaji. "Change in Ethnic Group: England and Wales, 1991–2001". MSc dissertation, Department of Sociology, City University, United Kingdom, 2005 <http://www.ccsr.ac.uk/research/documents/Akinwaledissertation.pdf> (accessed 21 June 2013).

Alkatiri, Zeffry. "The Words of Magic Used during the Soeharto's Indonesian New Order Military Regime Era 1980–1997. *Asian Journal of Social Sciences & Humanities* 2, no. 1 (2013): 82–91.

Ananta, Aris. "Changing Ethnic Composition and Potential Violent Conflict in Riau Archipelago, Indonesia: An Early Warning Signal". *Population Review* 45, no. 1 (2006).

———. "The Population and Conflict". In *Aceh: A New Dawn*, edited by Aris Ananta and Lee Poh Onn. Singapore: Institute of Southeast Asian Studies, 2007.

Ananta, Aris, Evi Nurvidya Arifin, and Leo Suryadinata. *Electoral Behaviour in Indonesia: A Statistical Perspective*. Singapore: Institute of Southeast Asian Studies, 2004.

Ananta, Aris, Evi Nurvidya Arifin, and Bakhtiar. "Ethnicity and Ageing in Indonesia, 2000–2050". *Asian Population Studies* 1, no. 2 (2005).

———. "Chinese Indonesians in Indonesia and the Province of Riau Archipelago: A Demographic Analysis". In *Ethnic Chinese in Contemporary Indonesia*, edited by Leo Suryadinata. Singapore: Institute of Southeast Asian Studies, 2008.

Arifin, Evi Nurvidya and Aris Ananta. "Three Mega Demographic Trends in Indonesia". *Social Development Issue*, 2013.

Badan Perencanaan Pembangunan Nasional (Bappenas), Badan Pusat Statistik (BPS) and United Nations Population Fund (UNFPA). *Indonesia Population Projection 2010–2035*. Jakarta: Badan Pusat Statistik, 2013.

Badan Pusat Statistik. *Population of Indonesia: 1971 Population Census*, Series D. Jakarta: Badan Pusat Statistik, 1975.

———. *Population of Indonesia: Results of the 2000 Population Census*, Series 2.2. Jakarta: Badan Pusat Statistik, 2001*a*.

————. *Population of East Java: Results of the 2000 Population Census*, Series L.2.2.14. Jakarta: Badan Pusat Statistik, 2001b.

————. *Population of West Kalimantan: Results of the 2000 Population Census*, Series L.2.2.18. Jakarta: Badan Pusat Statistik, 2001c.

————. *Population of Central Kalimantan: Results of the 2000 Population Census*, Series L.2.2.19. Jakarta: Badan Pusat Statistik, 2001d.

————. *Population of South Kalimantan: Results of the 2000 Population Census*, Series L.2.2.20. Jakarta: Badan Pusat Statistik, 2001e.

————. *Population of East Kalimantan: Results of the 2000 Population Census*, Series L.2.2.21. Jakarta: Badan Pusat Statistik, 2001f.

————. *Pedoman Teknis BPS Provinsi dan BPS Kabupaten/Kota Sensus Penduduk 2010. Buku 1.* Jakarta: Badan Pusat Statistik, 2009a.

————. *Sensus Penduduk 2010. Pedoman Pencacah. Buku 6.* Jakarta: Badan Pusat Statistik, 2009b.

————. *Pedoman Kode Provinsi, Kabupaten/Kota, Negara, Suku Bangsa, Kewarganegaraan,Bahasa dan Lapangan Usaha pada Sensus Penduduk 2010. Buku 7.* Jakarta: Badan Pusat Statistik, 2009c.

————. *Kewarganegaraan, Suku Bangsa, Agama dan Bahasa Sehari-hari Penduduk Indonesia* [Citizenships, ethnicity, religion and language spoken daily of Indonesia population]. Jakarta: Badan Pusat Statistik, 2011a <http://sp2010. bps.go.id/files/ebook/kewarganegaraan%20penduduk%20indonesia/index. html>.

————. Fertilitas Penduduk Indonesia: Hasil Sensus Penduduk 2010 [Indonesia's fertility: The results of the 2010 Population Census]. Jakarta: Badan Pusat Statistik, 2011b.

Bamba, John, ed. *Mozaik Dayak: Keberagaman Subsuku dan Bahasa Dayak di Kalimantan Barat.* Pontianak, Kalimanan Barat: Institut Dayakologi, 2008.

Baumann, Timothy. "Defining Ethnicity". *SAA Archaeological Record*, 12–14 September 2004.

Budidarsono, Suseno, Bambang Arifatmi, Hubert de Foresta, and Thomas P. Tomich. "Damar Agroforest Establishment and Sources of Livelihood: A Profitability Assessment of Damar Agroforest System in Krui, Lampung, Sumatra, Indonesia". *Southeast Asia Policy Research Working Paper*, no. 17, 2000.

Budiwanti, Erni. *Islam Sasak: Wetu Telu versus Waktu Lima.* Yogyakarta: LKIS, 2000.

Bulmer, M. "The Ethnic Group Question in the 1991 Census of Population". In *Ethnicity in the 1991 Census: Volume One: Demographic Characteristics of the Ethnic Minority Populations*, edited by David Coleman and John Salt. London: HMSO, 1996.

Coleman, David. "Immigration and Ethnicity in Low Fertility Countries: A Third

Demographic Transition". *Population and Development Review* 32, no. 3 (2006): 401–46.

Collier, W., B. Rachman, Supardi, B. Ali, Rachmadi and A.M. Jurindar. "Cropping System and Marginal Land Development in the Coastal Wetlands of Indonesia". In *Workshop on Research Priorities in the Tidal Swamp Rice*. Philippines: International Rice Research Institute, 1984.

Cunningham, Clark E. "Soba: An Atoni Village of West Timor". In *Villages in Indonesia*, edited by Koentjaraningrat. Singapore: Equinox, 2007.

Eberstadt, Nicholas and Apoorva Shah. "Fertility Decline in the Muslim World, c.1975–c.2005: A Veritable Sea-change, Still Curiously Unnoticed". In *Population Dynamics in Muslim Countries: Asembling the Jigsaw,* edited by Hans Groth and Alfonso Sousa-Poza. Springer, 2012.

Espenshade, Thomas J., Juan Carlos Guzman, and Charles F. Westoff. "The Surprising Global Variation in Replacement Fertility". *Population Research and Policy Review* 22 (2003): 575–83.

Gomang, Syarifuddin R. "Muslim and Christian Alliances: "Familial Relationships" between Inland and Coastal Peoples of the Belagar Community in Eastern Indonesia". *Bijdragen tot de Taal-, Land- en Volkenkunde (BKI)* 162, no. 4 (2006): 468–89.

Haug, Michaela. "Making Local Government More Responsive to the Poor: Developing Indicators and Tools to Support Sustainable Livelihood under Decentralization. Poverty and Decentralisation in Kutai Barat: The Impacts of Regional Autonomy on Dayak Benuaq Wellbeing". *Research Report*. Bogor, Indonesia: CIFOR, 2007.

Hauser, Philip and Otis Dudley Duncan. "Overview and Conclusion". In *The Study of Population*, edited by Hauser and Duncan. Chicago: University of Chicago Press, 1959.

Hidayah, Zulyani. *Ensiklopedi Suku Bangsa di Indonesia*. Jakarta: LP3ES, 1996.

Hugo, Graeme. "Indonesia's Population: Ethnicity and Religion in a Changing Political Landscape (review)". *Population Review* 42, nos. 1–2 (2003): 45–46.

Hull, Terry H. "First Results from the 2000 Population Census". *Bulletin of Indonesian Economic Studies* 37, no. 1 (2001): 103–11.

Husson, Laurence. "Eight Centuries of Madurese Migration to East Java". *Asian and Pacific Migration Journal* 6, no. 1 (1997): 77–102.

Ichwandi, Iin and Takeo Shinohara. "Indigenous Practices for Use of Land Managing Tropical Natural Resources: A Case Study on Baduy Community in Banten, Indonesia". *TROPICS* 16, no. 2 (2007): 87–102.

Khong Dien. *Population and Ethno-Demography in Vietnam*. Bangkok: Silkworm, 2002.

King, Victor T. *The Sociology of Southeast Asia: Transformation in a Developing Region*. Copenhagen: NIAS Press, 2008.

Koentjaraningrat, J.R. Mansoben, and Y. Biakai. "Kebinekaan Kesenian Irian Jaya: Khususnya Dalam Kebudyaan Asmat". In *Irian Jaya. Membangun Masyarakat Majemuk*, edited by Koentjaraningat. Jakarta: Penerbit Djambatan, 1994.

Lai, Ah Eng. "Introduction: Beyond Rituals and Riots". In *Beyond Rituals and Riots: Ethnic Pluralism and Social Cohesion in Singapore*, edited by Lai Ah Eng. Singapore: Eastern Universities Press, 2004.

Lesthaeghe, R. "The Second Demographic Transition in Western Countries: An Interpretation". IPO-Working Paper, 1991–92.

Lontaan, J.U. *Sejarah Hukum Adat dan Istiadat Kalimantan Barat*. Pemerintah Daerah Tingkat I Kalimantan Barat. Jakarta: Bumi Restu, 1975.

Mackie, J.A.C. *The Chinese in Indonesia*. Hawaii: University of Hawai'i Press in association with Australian Institute of International Affairs, 1976.

Mantra, Ida Bagoes. "Indonesia Labour Mobility to Malaysia. A Case Study: East Flores, West Lombok and the Islands of Bawean". In *Labour Migration in Indonesia. Policies and Practices*, edited by Sukamdi, Abdul Haris, and Patrick Brownlee. Yogyakarta: Population Studies Centre, Gadjah Mada University, 1998.

Mckenney, Nampeo R. and Claudette E. Bennett. "Issues Regarding Data on Race and Ethnicity: The Census Bureau Experience". *Public Health Report* 109, no. 1 (1994): 16–25.

Melalatoa, M. Junus. *Ensiklopedi Suku Bangsa di Indonesia. Jilid A–K*. Jakarta: Departemen Pendidikan dan Kebudayaan RI, 1995a.

———. *Ensiklopedi Suku Bangsa di Indonesia. Jilid L–Z*. Jakarta: Departemen Pendidikan dan Kebudayaan RI, 1995b.

Morning, Ann. "Ethnic Classification in Global Perspective: A Cross-National Survey of the 2000 Census Round". *Popul Res Policy Rev* 27 (2008): 239–72.

Naim, Mochtar. *Merantau: Pola Migrasi Suku Minangkabau* [Merantau: Pattern of migration of Minangkabau ethnic group]. Yogyakarta: Gadjah Mada University Press, 1984.

Nooy-Palm C.H.M. "Introduction to the Sa'dan Toraja People and Their Country". *Archipel* 10 (1975): 53–91.

Norwegian Refugee Council. "Indonesia/Kalimantan: New Ethnic-related Displacement while Earlier IDPs Struggle to Make Return Sustainable". Oslo: NRC, 2010.

Notestein, F.W. "Population — The Long View". In *Food for the World*, edited by T.W. Schultz. Chicago: Chicago University Press, 1945.

Ong, Susy. "Ethnic Chinese Religions: Some Recent Developments". In *Ethnic Chinese in Contemporary Indonesia*, edited by Leo Suryadinata. Singapore: Institute of Southeast Asian Studies, 2008.

Ratcliffe, Peter. "Ethnic Group". *Sociopedia.isa*. 2010.

Riwut, Tjilik. *Kalimantan Memanggil*. Indonesia: Endang, 1958.

————. *Kalimantan Membangun Alam dan Kebudayaan* [Kalimantan develops nature and culture]. Yogyakarta: NR, 1993.

Riwut, Tjilik and Sanaman Mantikei. *Menyelami Kekayaan Leluhur.* Yogyakarta: Pusakalima, 2003.

Sairin, Sjafri. *Perubahan Sosial Masyarakat Indonesia. Perspektif Antropologi.* Yogyakarta: Pustaka Pelajar, 2002.

————. "Mudik Lebaran: Ritual Tahunan Masyarakat Indonesia". In *Riak Riak Pembangunan. Perspektif Antropologi.* Yogyakarta: Media Wacana, 2010.

Sandra, Jaida n'ha. "From 'You, Toradja' to 'We Toraya': Ethnicity in the Making". *Explorations in Southeast Asian Studies: A Journal of the Southeast Asian Studies Student Association* 2, no. 1 (1998) <http://www.hawaii.edu/cseas/pubs/explore/v2n1-sandra.html>.

Shryock, Henry S. and Jacob S. Siegel. *The Methods and Materials of Demography.* New York: Academic Press, 1976 (condensed edition by Edward G. Stockwell).

Singapore Deparment of Statistics. *Census of Population 2010: Administrative Report.* Singapore: Singapore Department of Statistics, 2011.

Skeldon, Ronald. *Population Mobility in Developing Countries.* London: Belhaven, 1990.

Skinner, G. William. "The Chinese Minority". In *Indonesia*, edited by Ruth McVey. New Haven: Yale University Southeast Asian Studies, 1963.

Smith, Glenn. "Evolving Forms of Migration and Settlement in Indonesia". In *Ethnicity/Ethnicité: Mixed Views/Regards Entrecroisés*, edited by Glenn Smith and Hélène Bouvier. Jakarta: Pusat Dokumentasi dan Informasi Ilmiah LIPI; LASEMA, 2006.

Stahl, Charles W. and Raginal T. Appleyard. "International Manpower Flows in Asia: An Overview". *Asian and Pacific Migration Journal* 1, nos. 3–4 (1992): 407–94.

Stokhof, Malte and Oscar Salemink. "State Classification and Its Discontents: The Struggle over Bawean Ethnic Identity in Vietnam". *Journal of Vietnamese Studies* 4, no. 2 (2009): 154–95.

Sukandar, Rudi. "Negotiating Post-Conflict Communication: A Case of Ethnic Conflict in Indoensia". PhD dissertation, Scripps College of Communication, Ohio University <http://www.internal-displacement.org/8025708F004CE9 0B/%28httpDocuments%29/0D1F6C3186CB7529C12577BD00426956/$file/ Negotiating+post-conflict+communication+-+a+case+of+ethnic+conflict+in +Indonesia+2007.pdf> (accessed 13 December 2013).

Suryadinata, Leo. *Pribumi Indonesians, the Chinese Minority and China: A Study of Perceptions and Policies.* Singapore: Marshall Cavendish Academic, 2005.

Suryadinata, Leo, Evi Nurvidya Arifin, and Aris Ananta. *Indonesia's Population: Ethnicity and Religion in a Changing Political Landscape.* Singapore: Institute of Southeast Asian Studies, 2003.

Thung, Ju-Lan, Yekti Manuati, and Peter Mulok Kedit. *The (Re)Construction of the "Pan Dayak" Identity in Kalimantan and Sarawak: A Study on Minority's Identity, Ethnicity and Nationality.* Jakarta: Pusat Penelitian Kemasyarakatan dan Kebudyaan, LIPI, 2004.

Tjahjono, Gunawan. "Reviving the Betawi Tradition: The Case of Setu Babakan, Indonesia". *TDSR* 15, no. 1 (2003): 59–71.

United Nations. *Principles and Recommendation for Population and Housing Census: Revision 2. Statistical Papers Series M No. 67/Rev.2.* New York: Department of Economic and Social Affairs, Statistics Division, United Nations, 2008 <http://unstats.un.org/unsd/demographic/standmeth/principles/Series_M67Rev2en.pdf> (accessed 25 March 2014).

Van de Kaa. "The Idea of a Second Demographic Transition in Industrialized Countries". Paper presented at the Sixth Welfare Policy Seminar of the National Institute of Population and Social Security, Tokyo, Japan, 29 January 2002.

Van Klinken, Gerry. "Ethnicity in Indonesia". In *Ethnicity in Asia*, edited by Colin Mackerras. RoutledgeCurzon, 2003.

Zelinsky, Wilbur. "The Hypothesis of the Mobility Transition". *Geographical Review* 61 (April 1971).

APPENDIX 1

NEW CLASSIFICATION OF ETHNIC GROUPS CATEGORIZED ACCORDING TO THE MAIN ISLAND REGIONS IN INDONESIA

Sumatra

No.	Ethnic Group	Sub-ethnic	Sub-sub-ethnic	Alias	Code
1	Acehnese	—	—	—	0001 2
	Acehnese	—	—	Achin	0001 2
	Acehnese	—	—	Akhir	0001 2
	Acehnese	—	—	Asji	0001 2
	Acehnese	—	—	A-Tse	0001 2
	Acehnese	—	—	Ureung Aceh	0001 2
	Acehnese	—	—	Lambai/ Lamuri	0105 0
2	Akit	—	—	Akik	0033 2
3	Alas	—	—	—	0002 4
4	Anak Dalam	—	—	Anak Rimbo	0041 6
	Anak Dalam	—	—	Kubu	0044 5
	Anak Dalam	—	—	Lubu	0022 6
	Anak Dalam	—	—	Ulu	0075 3
5	Aneuk Jamee	—	—	—	0003 6
6	Bangka	—	—	—	0098 4
7	Batak	—	—	Batak Tapanuli	0019 5
	Batak	Batak Angkola	—	—	0014 2
	Batak	Batak Karo	—	—	0015 4
	Batak	Batak Mandailing	—	—	0016 6
	Batak	Dairi	—	—	0021 4

No.	Ethnic Group	Sub-ethnic	Sub-sub-ethnic	Alias	Code
	Batak	Dairi	—	Batak Pakpak Dairi	0017 1
	Batak	Batak Simalungun	—	—	0018 3
	Batak	Batak Toba	—	—	0020 2
8	Batin	—	—	—	0042 1
9	Belitung	—	—	—	0099 6
10	Bonai	—	—	—	0034 4
11	Daya	—	—	—	0047 4
12	Enggano	—	—	—	0077 0
13	Enim	—	—	—	0048 6
14	Gayo	—	—	—	0004 1
	Gayo	Gayo Lut	—	—	0005 3
	Gayo	Gayo Luwes	—	—	0006 5
	Gayo	Gayo Serbe Jadi	—	—	0007 0
15	Gumbak Cadek	Gumbak Cadek	—	Muslim Gunung Ko	0103 3
	Gumbak Cadek	Gumbak Cadek	—	Orang Cumbok	no code
16	Hutan	—	—	—	0035 6
17	Kaur	—	—	—	0078 2
18	Kayu Agung	—	—	—	0050 5
19	Kerinci	—	—	—	0030 3
20	Kluet	—	—	—	0008 2
21	Kuala	—	—	—	0036 1
22	Komering	—	—	—	0053 4
23	Lampung	—	—	—	0088 3
	Lampung	Seibatin	—	—	0096 0
	Lampung	Seibatin	—	Peminggir	no code
	Lampung	Seibatin	Peminggir Semangka	—	0093 1
	Lampung	Seibatin	Skala Brak	—	0093 1
	Lampung	Seibatin	Skala Brak (Bunga Mayang)	—	0084 2
	Lampung	Seibatin	Skala Brak (Abung)	—	0084 2

No.	Ethnic Group	Sub-ethnic	Sub-sub-ethnic	Alias	Code
	Lampung	Seibatin	Teluk	—	0093 1
	Lampung	Seibatin	Melintang Rajabasa-Peminggir MR	—	0091 4
	Lampung	Seibatin	Krui	—	0087 1
	Lampung	Seibatin	Belalau	—	0085 4
	Lampung	Pepaduan	—	—	0094 3
	Lampung	Pepaduan	Siwo Megou	Sembilan Marga	0084 2
	Lampung	Pepaduan	Buay Lima	—	0086 6
	Lampung	Pepaduan	Megau Pak Tulang Bawang	—	0089 5
	Lampung	Pepaduan	Pubian	Pubian Telu Suku	0095 5
	Lampung	Pepaduan	Pubian	Pubiyan	0095 5
24	Lembak	—	—	—	0079 4
25	Lingga	—	—	—	0106 2
26	Malay	—	—	—	0107 4
	Malay	Melayu Asahan	—	—	0023 1
	Malay	Melayu Asahan	—	Asahan	0013 0
	Malay	Melayu Langkat	—	Langkat	0054 6
	Malay	Melayu Langkat	—	Melayu Deli	0024 3
	Malay	Melayu Riau	—	—	0037 3
	Malay	Melayu Banyu Asin	—	—	0058 0
	Malay	Melayu Lahat	—	—	0059 2
	Malay	Melayu Lahat	Kikim	—	0051 0
	Malay	Melayu Lahat	Lematang	—	0055 1
	Malay	Melayu Lahat	Lintang	—	0056 3
	Malay	Melayu Lahat	Pasemah	—	0066 4
	Malay	Melayu Lahat	Pasemah (Gumai)	—	0049 1
	Malay	Melayu Lahat	Pasemah (Kisam)	—	0052 2

No.	Ethnic Group	Sub-ethnic	Sub-sub-ethnic	Alias	Code
	Malay	Melayu Lahat	Pasemah (Serawai)	—	0083 0
	Malay	Melayu Lahat	Pasemah (Melayu Semendo)	—	0090 2
	Malay	Melayu Lahat	Pasemah (Melayu Semendo)	Semendo	0073 6
	Malay	Melayu Lahat	Pasemah (Semidang)	—	no code
	Malay	Dayak Melayu Pontianak	—	—	0345 5
	Malay	Dayak Melayu Sambas	—	—	0346 0
	Malay	Jambi	—	—	0043 3
	Malay	Bengkulu	—	—	0076 5
27	Mantang	—	—	—	0101 6
28	Mentawai	—	—	—	0031 5
	Mentawai	Pagai	—	—	0108 6
	Mentawai	Siberut	—	—	0027 2
29	Meranjat	—	—	—	0060 6
30	Minangkabau	—	—	—	0032 0
31	Muko-Muko	—	—	—	0080 1
32	Musi	Musi Banyuasin	—	—	0061 1
	Musi	Musi Sekayu	—	Sekayu	0062 3
33	Nias	—	—	—	0025 5
34	Ogan	—	—	—	0063 5
	Ogan	Pegagan	—	—	0068 1
35	Palembang	—	—	—	0065 2
36	Pedamaran	—	—	—	0067 6
37	Pekal	—	—	—	0081 3
	Pekal	—	—	Anak Sungai	no code
	Pekal	—	—	Orang Katau	no code
	Pekal	—	—	Orang Seblat	no code
	Pekal	—	—	Mekea	no code
	Pekal	—	—	Orang Ipuh	no code

No.	Ethnic Group	Sub-ethnic	Sub-sub-ethnic	Alias	Code
38	Penghulu	—	—	—	0045 0
39	Pesisir	—	—	—	0026 0
40	Pindah	—	—	—	0046 2
41	Rambang	—	—	—	0069 3
42	Ranau	—	—	—	0070 0
43	Rawa	—	—	—	0038 5
44	Rawas	—	—	—	0071 2
45	Rejang	—	—	—	0082 5
	Rejang	—	—	Keme	0104 5
	Rejang	—	—	Lebong	no code
	Rejang	Saling	—	—	0072 4
46	Sawang	—	—	—	0109 1
47	Sekak	—	—	—	0057 5
	Sekak	—	—	Ameng Sewang	0097 2
	Sekak	—	—	Sakai	0039 0
	Sekak	—	—	Lom	0057 5
	Sekak	—	—	Mapur	0057 5
	Sekak	—	—	Belom	0102 1
	Sekak	—	—	Anak Laut/ Laut	0100 4
	Sekak	—	—	Orang Sampan	0064 0
48	Siladang	—	—	—	0028 4
49	Simeulue	—	—	—	0010 1
	Simeulue	Sigulai	—	—	0009 4
50	Singkil	—	—	—	0011 3
51	Suban	—	—	—	0110 5
52	Talang Mamak*	—	—	—	0040 4
53	Tamiang	—	—	—	0012 5
54	Teloko	—	—	—	0074 1
55	Ulu Muara Sipongi	—	—	—	0029 6
56	Others in Sumatra	—	—	—	2000 4

Note: The names in parentheses refer to the sub-sub-sub-ethnic groups.

*Talang Mamak is a different name of Orang Dalam, which does not have a code yet in the census.

Java and Bali

No.	Ethnic Group	Sub-ethnic	Sub-sub-ethnic	Alias	Code
1	Badui		—	Baduy	0122 3
2	Balinese		—	Bali/Bali Hindu	0124 0
	Balinese		—	Bali Majapahit	0125 2
3	Bali Aga	—	—	—	0126 4
	Bali Aga	—	—	Baliaga	0197 6
	Bali Aga	—	—	Trunyan	0208 3
4	Bantenese		—	—	0123 5
5	Bawean		—	Boyan	0116 3
6	Betawi	—	—	—	0111 0
7	Cirebonese	—	—	—	0112 2
8	Javanese	—	—	—	0114 6
	Javanese	Samin	—	—	0115 1
	Javanese	Tengger	—	—	0120 6
	Javanese	Nagaring	—	—	0118 0
	Javanese	Nagarigung	—	—	0092 6
9	Loloan	—	—	—	0174 5
10	Madurese		—	—	0121 1
11	Nyama Selam	—	—	—	0186 3
12	Osing		—	Using	0119 2
13	Sundanese	—	—	—	0113 4
	Sundanese	Naga	—	—	0117 5
14	Others in Java		—	—	3000 6
15	Others in Bali & Nusa Tenggara	—	—	—	5000 3

Nusa Tenggara

No.	Ethnic Group	Sub-ethnic	Sub-sub-ethnic	Alias	Code
1	Adabe	—	—	—	0132 4
2	Alor	—	—	—	0133 6
	Alor	Abui	—	—	0131 2
	Alor	Belagar	—	—	0133 6
	Alor	Kelong	—	—	0133 6
	Alor	Manete	—	—	0133 6

No.	Ethnic Group	Sub-ethnic	Sub-sub-ethnic	Alias	Code
	Alor	Mauta	—	—	0133 6
	Alor	Seboda	—	—	0133 6
	Alor	Wersin	—	—	0133 6
	Alor	Belagar	—	Blagar	0141 3
	Alor	Deing	—	—	0145 4
	Alor	Kabola	—	—	0156 0
	Alor	Kemang	—	—	0161 5
	Alor	Kui	—	—	0167 3
	Alor	Lemma	—	—	0172 1
	Alor	Kramang	—	—	0165 6
	Alor	Kawei	—	—	0158 4
	Alor	Ndebang	—	—	no code
	Alor	Malua	—	—	no code
	Alor	Wuwuli	—	—	no code
3	Atoni*	—	—	Atanfui	0134 1
	Atoni	—	—	Atani	0134 1
	Atoni	—	—	Atoni Meto	0134 1
	Atoni	—	—	Dawan	0134 1
	Atoni	—	—	Gunung-Orang Gunung	0151 4
	Atoni	—	—	Orang Gunung	0578 1
	Atoni	—	—	Dawam	0561 0
	Atoni	—	—	Rawan	0561 0
4	Babui	—	—		0135 3
5	Bakifan	—	—	—	0137 0
6	Barawahing	—	—	—	0138 2
7	Barue	—	—	—	0139 4
8	Bima	—	—	—	0127 6
9	Boti	—	—	—	0142 5
10	Bunak	—	—	Marae	0143 0
11	Dadua	—	—	—	0144 2
12	Dompu	—	—	—	0128 1
13	Dongo	—	—	—	0146 6
14	Ende	—	—	—	0147 1
15	Fataluku	—	—	—	0148 3
	Fataluku	—	—	Dagada	0834 1
16	Faun	—	—	—	0149 5

No.	Ethnic Group	Sub-ethnic	Sub-sub-ethnic	Alias	Code
17	Flores	—	—		0150 2
18	Galoli	—	—	—	0199 3
19	Gaura		—		0562 2
20	Hahak	—	—	—	0152 6
21	Helong	—	—	—	0154 3
22	Henifeto	—	—	—	0155 5
23	Kairul	—	—	—	0202 5
24	Karera	—	—	—	0157 2
25	Kedang	—	—	—	0159 6
26	Kemak	—	—	—	0160 3
	Kemak	Marobo	—	—	0653 0
27	Kolana	—	—	—	0163 2
28	Kore	—	—	—	0164 4
29	Krowe Muhang	—	—	—	0166 1
	Krowe Muhang	—	—	Muhang	0182 2
30	Kupang	—	—	—	0168 5
31	Labala	—	—	—	0169 0
32	Lakalei	—	—	—	0203 0
33	Lamahot	—	—	Lamholot	0170 4
	Lamahot	—	—	Lamkolot	0170 4
	Lamahot	—	—	Larantuka	0171 6
	Lamahot	—	—	Solor	0193 5
	Lamahot	—	—	Solot	0193 5
	Lamahot	—	—	Ata Kiwan	0552 1
	Lamahot	—	—	Holo	no code
34	Lio	—	—	—	0173 3
35	Lomblem	—	—	—	0175 0
36	Maimaa	—	—	—	0176 2
37	Makua	—	—	—	0205 4
38	Manggarai	—	—	—	0177 4
39	Mbojo	—	—	—	0179 1
40	Mela	—	—	—	0180 5
41	Modo	—	—	—	0181 0
42	Ngada	Ngada	—	Nage	0184 6
	Ngada	—	—	Bajawa	0136 5
	Ngada	Nagekeo	—	—	0185 1

No.	Ethnic Group	Sub-ethnic	Sub-sub-ethnic	Alias	Code
	Ngada	Keo	—	—	0162 0
	Ngada	Maung	—	—	0178 6
	Ngada	Riung	—	—	0190 6
	Ngada	Rangga	—	—	0581 2
43	Noenleni	—	—	—	0574 0
44	Palue	—	—	—	0187 5
45	Pantar	—	—	—	0188 0
46	Remucles	—	—	—	0582 4
47	Rote	—	—	Roti	0191 1
48	Samoro	—	—	—	0207 1
49	Sasak	—	—	—	0129 3
	Sasak	Bayan	—	—	0198 1
50	Sawu	—	—	Hawu	0153 1
	Sawu			Sabu	0153 1
	Sawu	—	—	Rai Hawu	0580 0
	Sawu	—	—	Savu	0580 0
	Sawu	—	—	—	0580 0
51	Sikka	—	—	—	0192 3
52	Sumbawa	—	—	Semawa	0130 0
53	Sumbanese	—	—	Humba	0563 4
	Sumbanese	—	—	Tau Humba	0563 4
54	Toi Anas	—	—	—	0195 2
	Toi Anas	—	—	Anas/Toi	0550 4
55	To Uluuwai	—	—	—	0194 0

Notes: * Atoni has many aliases. Thus the Atoni can be called Atanfui, Atani, Atoni, Atoni, Meto, Dawan, Rawan, Orang Gunung. The Lamahot have many aliases and can be called Lamahot, Lamholot, Lamkolot, Solor, Solot, Larantuka, Ata Kiwan or Holo.

Kalimantan

No.	Ethnic Group	Sub-ethnic	Alias	Code
1	Banjarese	—	—	0520 1
	Banjarese	Banjar Kuala	—	0499 1
	Banjarese	Batang Banyu	—	0499 1
	Banjarese	Pahuluan	—	0499 1

No.	Ethnic Group	Sub-ethnic	Alias	Code
2	Dayak	Abai/Tidung/Tingalan/ Tudung	—	0514 1
	Dayak	Dayak Abai	—	0209 5
	Dayak	Abal	—	0497 4
	Dayak	Ahe	—	0515 3
	Dayak	Badeng	—	0517 0
	Dayak	Baka	—	0554 5
	Dayak	Bakung Metulang	—	0519 4
	Dayak	Balangan	—	0498 6
	Dayak	Banjau	—	0521 3
	Dayak	Bantai	—	0555 0
	Dayak	Bantian	—	0556 2
	Dayak	Bara Dia	—	0472 6
	Dayak	Barangas	—	0500 6
	Dayak	Barangas	Berangas	0501 1
	Dayak	Bawo	—	0557 4
	Dayak	Beketan	—	0523 0
	Dayak	Beraki	—	0558 6
	Dayak	Berau/Merau	—	0525 4
	Dayak	Bulungan/Murut	—	0527 1
	Dayak	Bungan	—	0559 1
	Dayak	Busang	—	0528 3
	Dayak	Dayak Air Durian/Dayak Air Upas/Dayak Batu Payung/Dayak Belaban/ Dayak Kendawangan/ Dayak Membulu'/Dayak Menggaling/Dayak Pelanjau/ Dayak Sekakai/Dayak Sempadian	—	0210 2
	Dayak	Dayak Air Tabun/Dayak Banjur/Dayak Demam/Dayak Begelang/Dayak Embarak// Dayak Ketungau-sesae'/Dayak Kumpang/Dayak Mandau/ Dayak Merakai/Dayak Sebaru'/Dayak Sekalau/Dayak Sekapat/Dayak Senangan/ Dayak Senangkan/Dayak Senangkatn	—	0211 4

No.	Ethnic Group	Sub-ethnic	Alias	Code
	Dayak	Dayak Ketungau/Dayak Ketungau Air Tabun/Dayak Ketungau Banjur/Dayak Ketungau Begelang/Dayak Ketungau Demam/Dayak Ketungau Embarak/Dayak Ketungau Kumpang/Dayak Ketungau Mandau/Dayak Ketungau Merakai/Dayak Ketungau Sebaru'/Dayak Ketungau Sekalau/Dayak Ketungau	—	0312 3
	Dayak	Dayak Alau'/Dayak Lau'	—	0212 6
	Dayak	Dayak Angan	—	0213 1
	Dayak	Dayak Angkabakng/Dayak Banokng/Dayak Banyuke/Dayak Banyuke-Angkabang/Dayak Banyuke-Banokng/Dayak Banyuke-Moro Batukng/Dayak Banyuke-Sakanis/Dayak Banyuke-Satolo/Dayak Banyuke-Satona/Dayak Banyuke-Songga Batukng/Dayak Moro Batukng/Dayak Sakanis	—	0214 3
	Dayak	Dayak Apalin	—	0215 5
	Dayak	Dayak Apalin	Apalin/Palin	0551 6
	Dayak	Dayak Apoyan	—	0216 0
	Dayak	Dayak Babak	—	0217 2
	Dayak	Dayak Badat	—	0218 4
	Dayak	Dayak Bahau	—	0219 6
	Dayak	Dayak Bahau	Bahau	0518 2
	Dayak	Dayak Bakati' Kanayatn Satango/Dayak Bakati' Kuma/Dayak Bakati' Lape/Dayak Bakati' Lumar/Dayak Bakati' Palayo/Dayak Bakati' Payutn/Dayak Bakati' Rara/Dayak Bakati' Riok/Dayak Bakati' Sara/Dayak Bakati' Sebiha'/Dayak Bakati' Subah/Dayak Bakati'	—	0220 3

No.	Ethnic Group	Sub-ethnic	Alias	Code
	Dayak	Dayak Balantiatn	—	0221 5
	Dayak	Dayak Balau/Dayak Daya/ Dayak Hivan/Dayak Iban/ Dayak Neban	—	0222 0
	Dayak	Dayak Bangau	—	0223 2
	Dayak	Dayak Banyadu'	—	0224 4
	Dayak	Dayak Banyur/Dayak Kualatn/Dayak Sajan/Dayak Semanakng/Dayak Simpakng	—	0225 6
	Dayak	Dayak Barai	—	0226 1
	Dayak	Dayak Bassap	—	0227 3
	Dayak	Dayak Bassap	Basap	0522 5
	Dayak	Dayak Batu Entawa'	—	0228 5
	Dayak	Dayak Batu Tajam/Dayak Kekura'/Dayak Kengkubang/ Dayak Marau/Dayak Pesaguan/Dayak Pesaguan Hulu/Dayak Pesaguan Kanan/ Dayak Sepauhan	—	0229 0
	Dayak	Dayak Bauk	—	0230 4
	Dayak	Dayak Baya	—	0231 6
	Dayak	Dayak Bawo/Mangkatip/ Taboyan	—	0496 2
	Dayak	Dayak Beah/Dayak Begeleng/ Dayak Beginci	—	0232 1
	Dayak	Dayak Behe/Dayak Benane	—	0233 3
	Dayak	Dayak Benatu/Dayak Jalai/ Dayak Penyarang/Dayak Perigi/Dayak Pringkunyit/ Dayak Riam/Dayak Sumanjawat/Dayak Tanjung/ Dayak Tembiruhan	—	0234 5
	Dayak	Dayak Benawas	—	0235 0
	Dayak	Dayak Bentian	—	0236 2
	Dayak	Ayus/Bentian/Karau/Lemper/ Leo Arak	—	0516 5
	Dayak	Dayak Benuaq	—	0237 4
	Dayak	Dayak Benuaq	Benuak	0524 2
	Dayak	Dayak BI Somu	—	0238 6

No.	Ethnic Group	Sub-ethnic	Alias	Code
	Dayak	Dayak Biatah/Dayak Bidayuh	—	0239 1
	Dayak	Dayak Bihak	—	0240 5
	Dayak	Dayak Brusu	—	0241 0
	Dayak	Dayak Brusu	Berusu	0526 6
	Dayak	Dayak Bubung	—	0242 2
	Dayak	Dayak Bugau	—	0243 4
	Dayak	Dayak Bukat/Dayak Buket/ Dayak Bukit/Dayak Bukut/ Dayak Ukit	—	0244 6
	Dayak	Bukat/Buket/Bukut/Ukit	—	0503 5
	Dayak	Dayak Bukit Talaga	—	0245 1
	Dayak	Dayak Buratmato	—	0246 3
	Dayak	Dayak Butok	—	0247 5
	Dayak	Dayak Cempedak	—	0248 0
	Dayak	Dayak Da'/Dayak Kayan	—	0249 2
	Dayak	Dayak Kayanath	—	0295 6
	Dayak	Dayak Dait	—	0250 6
	Dayak	Dayak Dalam	—	0251 1
	Dayak	Dayak Dalang/Dayak Kaluas/ Dayak Kayu Bunga	—	0252 3
	Dayak	Dayak Darai	—	0253 5
	Dayak	Dayak Darat	—	0254 0
	Dayak	Dayak Daro'	—	0255 2
	Dayak	Dayak Darok	—	0256 4
	Dayak	Dayak Dayah Sa'ban	—	0257 6
	Dayak	Dayak Desa	—	0258 1
	Dayak	Dayak Dsa	—	0261 2
	Dayak	Dayak Dosan/Dayak Dusun	—	0259 3
	Dayak	Dusun Deyah	—	0504 0
	Dayak	Dayak Dosatn	—	0260 0
	Dayak	Dayak Ella	—	0262 4
	Dayak	Dayak Embaloh/Dayak Maloh/Dayak Mbaloh/Dayak Taman Ba	—	0263 6
	Dayak	Dayak Umaloh	—	0462 5
	Dayak	Dayak Empayuh	—	0264 1
	Dayak	Dayak En Silat	—	0265 3
	Dayak	Dayak En Silat	Dayak Ensilat	0269 4

No.	Ethnic Group	Sub-ethnic	Alias	Code
	Dayak	Dayak Engkarong	—	0266 5
	Dayak	Dayak Engkode	—	0267 0
	Dayak	Dayak Ensanang	—	0268 2
	Dayak	Dayak Entabang/Dayak Entebang	—	0270 1
	Dayak	Dayak Entuka	—	0271 3
	Dayak	Dayak Entungau	—	0272 5
	Dayak	Dayak Gali/Dayak Galik	—	0273 0
	Dayak	Dayak Gerai	—	0274 2
	Dayak	Dayak Gerunggang	—	0275 4
	Dayak	Dayak Golik	—	0276 6
	Dayak	Dayak Goneh	—	0277 1
	Dayak	Dayak Gun	—	0278 3
	Dayak	Dayak Hibun	—	0279 5
	Dayak	Dayak Hovogan	—	0280 2
	Dayak	Dayak Inggar Silat	—	0281 4
	Dayak	Dayak Jagoi	—	0282 6
	Dayak	Dayak Jangkang/Dayak Jangkang Benua/Dayak Jangkang Engkarong/Dayak Jangkang Jungur Tanjung/Dayak Jangkang Kopa	—	0284 3
	Dayak	Dayak Jawan	—	0285 5
	Dayak	Dayak Jawatn	—	0286 0
	Dayak	Dayak Jelai	—	0287 2
	Dayak	Dayak Joka'	—	0288 4
	Dayak	Dayak Kalis	—	0289 6
	Dayak	Dayak Kanayan	—	0290 3
	Dayak	Dayak Kanayatn/Dayak Kanayatn Capala/Dayak Kanayatn-Ambawang-Mampawah/Dayak Kanayatn-Banana'-Mampawah-Barabas/Dayak Kanayatn-Banana'-Mampawah-Pulo Padak/Dayak Kanayatn-Banana'-Mampawah-Sabawis/Dayak Kanayatn-Banana'-Mampawal-Salutukng/Dayak Kanaya	—	0291 5

No.	Ethnic Group	Sub-ethnic	Alias	Code
	Dayak	Dayak Kancikng	—	0292 0
	Dayak	Kencing	—	0566 3
	Dayak	Dayak Kantu'/Dayak Kantuk	—	0293 2
	Dayak	Dayak Kayaan	—	0294 4
	Dayak	Dayak Kayong	—	0296 1
	Dayak	Dayak Kayung	—	0297 3
	Dayak	Dayak Kebahan	—	0298 5
	Dayak	Dayak Kebuai/Dayak Pangkalan Suka/Dayak Suka Maju/Dayak Tayap	—	0299 0
	Dayak	Dayak Kede	—	0300 5
	Dayak	Dayak Kelabit	—	0301 0
	Dayak	Dayak Kelata	—	0302 2
	Dayak	Dayak Keluas	—	0303 4
	Dayak	Dayak Keneles	—	0304 6
	Dayak	Dayak Keninjal	—	0305 1
	Dayak	Dayak Kenyah	—	0306 3
	Dayak	Kenyah Lo Bakung	—	0746 2
	Dayak	Kajang/Kejin/Kenyah	—	0549 0
	Dayak	Dayak Kenyilu	—	0307 5
	Dayak	Dayak Kepuas	—	0308 0
	Dayak	Dayak Kerabat	—	0309 2
	Dayak	Dayak Keramai/Dayak Keramay	—	0310 6
	Dayak	Dayak Ketior/Dayak Ketiur	—	0311 1
	Dayak	Dayak Klematan	—	0313 5
	Dayak	Klemantan	—	0567 5
	Dayak	Dayak Kodatn	—	0314 0
	Dayak	Dayak Koman	—	0315 2
	Dayak	Dayak Konyeh	—	0316 4
	Dayak	Dayak Kopak	—	0317 6
	Dayak	Dayak Kowotn	—	0318 1
	Dayak	Dayak Koyon	—	0319 3
	Dayak	Dayak Kriau	—	0320 0
	Dayak	Dayak Kriau	Karehan/Kriau	0564 6
	Dayak	Dayak Krio	—	0322 4
	Dayak	Dayak Krinu	—	0321 2
	Dayak	Dayak Kubitn	—	0323 6

No.	Ethnic Group	Sub-ethnic	Alias	Code
	Dayak	Dayak Labu	—	0324 1
	Dayak	Dayak Laman Tuha/Dayak Lamantawa	—	0325 3
	Dayak	Dayak Lara	—	0326 5
	Dayak	Dayak Laur	—	0327 0
	Dayak	Dayak Laut	—	0328 2
	Dayak	Dayak Lawangan	—	0329 4
	Dayak	Dayak Lawangan	Lawangan	0478 4
	Dayak	Dayak Laya	—	0330 1
	Dayak	Dayak Lebang	—	0331 3
	Dayak	Dayak Lebong	—	0332 5
	Dayak	Dayak Lemandau	—	0333 0
	Dayak	Dayak Liboy	—	0334 2
	Dayak	Dayak Limbai	—	0335 4
	Dayak	Dayak Linoh	—	0336 6
	Dayak	Dayak Lomur	—	0337 1
	Dayak	Dayak Mahap	—	0338 3
	Dayak	Dayak Mali	—	0339 5
	Dayak	Dayak Manyan	—	0340 2
	Dayak	Maanyan	—	0507 6
	Dayak	Maanyan Benua Lima/ Maanyan Paju Lima	—	0480 3
	Dayak	Maanyan Dayu	—	0481 5
	Dayak	Maanyan Paju Epat	—	0482 0
	Dayak	Maanyan Paju Sepuluh	—	0483 2
	Dayak	Maanyan Paku	—	0484 4
	Dayak	Dayak Mayan	—	0341 4
	Dayak	Dayak Mayau	—	0342 6
	Dayak	Dayak Melahoi	—	0343 1
	Dayak	Dayak Melanau	—	0344 3
	Dayak	Dayak Mentebah	—	0347 2
	Dayak	Dayak Mentebak	—	0348 4
	Dayak	Dayak Menterap Kabut	—	0349 6
	Dayak	Dayak Menterap Sekado	—	0350 3
	Dayak	Dayak Mentuka'	—	0351 5
	Dayak	Dayak Menyangka	—	0352 0
	Dayak	Dayak Menyanya	—	0353 2

No.	Ethnic Group	Sub-ethnic	Alias	Code
	Dayak	Dayak Menyuke	—	0354 4
	Dayak	Dayak Menyuke	Manyuke	1144 4
	Dayak	Dayak Merau	—	0355 6
	Dayak	Dayak Mobui	—	0356 1
	Dayak	Dayak Modang	—	0357 3
	Dayak	Medang	—	0485 6
	Dayak	Medan/Modang	—	0572 3
	Dayak	Dayak Mualang	—	0358 5
	Dayak	Dayak Muara	—	0359 0
	Dayak	Dayak Mudu'	—	0360 4
	Dayak	Dayak Muduh	—	0361 6
	Dayak	Dayak Muluk	—	0362 1
	Dayak	Dayak Nahaya'	—	0363 3
	Dayak	Dayak Nanga	—	0364 5
	Dayak	Dayak Ngabang	—	0365 0
	Dayak	Dayak Ngalampan	—	0366 2
	Dayak	Ngalampa	—	0487 3
	Dayak	Dayak Ngamukit	—	0367 4
	Dayak	Dayak Nganayat	—	0368 6
	Dayak	Dayak Nganayat	Nganayath	0573 5
	Dayak	Dayak Nonguh	—	0369 1
	Dayak	Dayak Nyadupm	—	0370 5
	Dayak	Dayak Oruung da'an	—	0371 0
	Dayak	Dayak Pampang	—	0373 4
	Dayak	Dayak Pandu	—	0374 6
	Dayak	Dayak Pangin	—	0375 1
	Dayak	Dayak Pangkodan	—	0376 3
	Dayak	Dayak Pengkedang	—	0376 3
	Dayak	Dayak Pantu	—	0377 5
	Dayak	Dayak Panu	—	0378 0
	Dayak	Dayak Papak	—	0379 2
	Dayak	Dayak Pasir	—	0380 6
	Dayak	Dayak Paus	—	0381 1
	Dayak	Dayak Pawan	—	0382 3
	Dayak	Dayak Pawatn	—	0383 5
	Dayak	Dayak Paya'	—	0384 0
	Dayak	Dayak Penihing	—	0385 2

No.	Ethnic Group	Sub-ethnic	Alias	Code
	Dayak	Dayak Penihing	Penihing	0538 4
	Dayak	Dayak Penihing	Pinihing	0785 4
	Dayak	Dayak Peruan	—	0386 4
	Dayak	Dayak Pompakng	—	0387 6
	Dayak	Dayak Pompang	—	0388 1
	Dayak	Dayak Ponan/Dayak Punan/ Dayak Punang	—	0389 3
	Dayak	Punan Badeng	—	0787 1
	Dayak	Dayak Ponti/Dayak Punti	—	0390 0
	Dayak	Dayak Pos	—	0391 2
	Dayak	Dayak Pruna'	—	0392 4
	Dayak	Dayak Pruwan	—	0393 6
	Dayak	Dayak Putuk	—	0394 1
	Dayak	Dayak Putuk	Putuk	0788 3
	Dayak	Dayak Randu'	—	0395 3
	Dayak	Dayak Randuk/Dayak Ronduk	—	0396 5
	Dayak	Dayak Ransa	—	0397 0
	Dayak	Dayak Rantawan	—	0398 2
	Dayak	Dayak Raut	—	0399 4
	Dayak	Dayak Rembay	—	0400 2
	Dayak	Dayak Ribun	—	0401 4
	Dayak	Dayak Salako/Dayak Salako Badamea-Gajekng/Dayak Salako Garantukng Sakawokng	—	0402 6
	Dayak	Dayak Sambas	—	0403 1
	Dayak	Dayak Sami	—	0404 3
	Dayak	Dayak Samihin	—	0405 5
	Dayak	Dayak Samihin	Samihim	0510 0
	Dayak	Dayak Sampit	—	0406 0
	Dayak	Arkais/Dayak Bakumpai/Kota Waringin Barat/Sampit	—	0495 0
	Dayak	Dayak Bakumpai	—	0471 4
	Dayak	Dayak Sane	—	0407 2
	Dayak	Dayak Sanggau	—	0408 4
	Dayak	Dayak Sangku'	—	0409 6
	Dayak	Dayak Sapatoi	—	0410 3
	Dayak	Dayak Sawai	—	0411 5

No.	Ethnic Group	Sub-ethnic	Alias	Code
	Dayak	Dayak Sawe	—	0412 0
	Dayak	Dayak Sebaruk	—	0413 2
	Dayak	Dayak Seberuang	—	0414 4
	Dayak	Dayak Segai	—	0415 6
	Dayak	Dayak Sekajang	—	0416 1
	Dayak	Dayak Sekubang	—	0417 3
	Dayak	Dayak Sekujam	—	0418 5
	Dayak	Dayak Selawe	—	0419 0
	Dayak	Dayak Selayang	—	0420 4
	Dayak	Dayak Selibong	—	0421 6
	Dayak	Dayak Selimpat	—	0422 1
	Dayak	Dayak Semayang	—	0423 3
	Dayak	Dayak Sengkunang	—	0424 5
	Dayak	Dayak Seritok	—	0425 0
	Dayak	Dayak Seru/Dayak Skrang/ Dayak Undup	—	0426 2
	Dayak	Dayak Seru/Dayak Skrang/ Dayak Undup	Undup	0598 3
	Dayak	Dayak Seru/Dayak Skrang/ Dayak Undup	Skrang	0589 4
	Dayak	Dayak Seru/Dayak Skrang/ Dayak Undup	Seru/Serul/ Srul	0588 2
	Dayak	Dayak Sikukng	—	0427 4
	Dayak	Dayak Silatn Muntak	—	0428 6
	Dayak	Dayak Sintang	—	0429 1
	Dayak	Dayak Sisang	—	0430 5
	Dayak	Dayak Sontas	—	0431 0
	Dayak	Dayak Suaid	—	0432 2
	Dayak	Dayak Suaid	Dayak Suhaid	0433 4
	Dayak	Dayak Sum/Dayak Sum Daruk	—	0434 6
	Dayak	Dayak Sungkung	—	0435 1
	Dayak	Dayak Suruh/Dayak Suruk	—	0436 3
	Dayak	Dayak Suti	—	0437 5
	Dayak	Dayak Taba	—	0438 0
	Dayak	Dayak Tabuas	—	0439 2
	Dayak	Dayak Tadietn	—	0440 6
	Dayak	Dayak Tagel	—	0441 1

No.	Ethnic Group	Sub-ethnic	Alias	Code
	Dayak	Tagel/Tagol	—	0542 0
	Dayak	Dayak Tagelan	—	0739 0
	Dayak	Dayak Tamambalo	—	0442 3
	Dayak	Dayak Taman	—	0443 5
	Dayak	Dayak Taman Sekado	—	0444 0
	Dayak	Dayak Tameng	—	0445 2
	Dayak	Dayak Tawaeq	—	0446 4
	Dayak	Dayak Tebang	—	0447 6
	Dayak	Dayak Tebidah	—	0448 1
	Dayak	Dayak Tenggalan	—	0449 3
	Dayak	Dayak Tengon	—	0450 0
	Dayak	Dayak Tingging	—	0451 2
	Dayak	Dayak Tingui	—	0452 4
	Dayak	Dayak Tinying	—	0453 6
	Dayak	Dayak Tobak	—	0454 1
	Dayak	Dayak Tola'	—	0455 3
	Dayak	Dayak Tulak	—	0456 5
	Dayak	Dayak Tunjung	—	0457 0
	Dayak	Dayak Tunjung	Tunjung	0545 6
	Dayak	Dayak Turije'ne	—	0458 2
	Dayak	Dayak Uheng Kereho	—	0459 4
	Dayak	Dayak Aoheng	—	0469 5
	Dayak	Dayak Aoheng	Auheng	0553 3
	Dayak	Dayak Aoheng	Ohong	0536 0
	Dayak	Dayak Aoheng	Oheng	0575 2
	Dayak	Dayak Ulu Ai'/Dayak Ulu Air	—	0460 1
	Dayak	Dayak Ulu Sekadau	—	0461 3
	Dayak	Dayak Undak Sanang	—	0463 0
	Dayak	Dayak Undau	—	0464 2
	Dayak	Dayak Urang Da'an	—	0465 4
	Dayak	Dayak Ot Danum	—	0372 2
	Dayak	Dayak Uud Danum	—	0466 6
	Dayak	Dayak Uud Danum Cihie	—	0467 1
	Dayak	Dayak Uud Danum Dohoi	—	0468 3
	Dayak	Dayak Badang	—	0470 2
	Dayak	Empran	—	0473 1
	Dayak	Empran	Ulu Batang Ali	0511 2

No.	Ethnic Group	Sub-ethnic	Alias	Code
	Dayak	Gaat	—	0474 3
	Dayak	Harakit	—	0505 2
	Dayak	Huang Tering	—	0529 5
	Dayak	Hulu Banyu	—	0506 4
	Dayak	Kanowit	—	0475 5
	Dayak	Katibas	—	0565 1
	Dayak	Katingan/Ngaju	—	0476 0
	Dayak	Kendayan	—	0477 2
	Dayak	Dayak Jalan/Dayak Ka-Lepo Ka	—	0283 1
	Dayak	Lepo Bakung/Lepo Jalan/Lepo Tukung/LepoTepu	—	0479 6
	Dayak	Lapo Bakung/Lapo Bem/Lapo Ke/Lapo Kulit/Lapo Maut/ Lapo Ngibun/Lapo Timai/ Lapo Tukung	—	0531 4
	Dayak	Lepo Mant	—	0568 0
	Dayak	Lepo Tau	—	0569 2
	Dayak	Tukung	—	0595 4
	Dayak	Long Paka	—	0570 6
	Dayak	Long Gelat/Paka	—	0532 6
	Dayak	Lundayeh	—	0533 1
	Dayak	Malang	—	0571 1
	Dayak	Mangku Anam/Nyumit/Pauk/ Purui/Singa Rasi/Tungku	—	0534 3
	Dayak	Menui	—	1333 2
	Dayak	Merab	—	0535 5
	Dayak	Murung	—	0486 1
	Dayak	Oloh Kantu'	—	0576 4
	Dayak	Oloh masih	—	0577 6
	Dayak	Paku	—	0579 3
	Dayak	Pitap	—	0509 3
	Dayak	Sagai	—	0583 6
	Dayak	Sani	—	0584 1
	Dayak	Sarbas/Saribas/Sebayau	—	0488 5
	Dayak	Segayi	—	0539 6
	Dayak	Sekadau	—	0489 0
	Dayak	Seputan	—	0540 3

No.	Ethnic Group	Sub-ethnic	Alias	Code
	Dayak	Siak Murung/Siang Murung	—	0490 4
	Dayak	Siang	—	0491 6
	Dayak	Sekayang	—	0586 5
	Dayak	Senunang	—	0587 0
	Dayak	Sului	—	0541 5
	Dayak	Suntung	—	0590 1
	Dayak	Tabuyan	—	0492 1
	Dayak	Tamuan	—	0493 3
	Dayak	Timai	—	0593 0
	Dayak	Tomun	—	0494 5
	Dayak	Touk	—	0543 2
	Dayak	Tou	—	0594 2
	Dayak	Tumbit	—	0544 4
	Dayak	Tungui	—	0596 6
	Dayak	Umaq Alim/Umaq Baka/ Umaq Bakaq/Umaq Baqaq/ Umaq Jalan/Umaq Lasan/ Umaq Pramuka/Umaq Suling/ Umaq Tau	—	0546 1
	Dayak	Umaq Badang/Umaq Kulit/ Umaq Lokan	—	0547 3
	Dayak	Umaq Lasung/Umaq Leken/ Umaq Naving/Umaq Paku/ Umaq Pliau/Umaq PugungPuh	—	0548 5
	Dayak	Undang Sanang	—	0597 1
	Dayak	Warukin	—	0512 4
3	Pasir	Pasir	—	0537 2
	Pasir	Pasir Adang	—	0775 3
	Pasir	Pasir Balik	—	0776 5
	Pasir	Pasir Burat Mato	—	0777 0
	Pasir	Pasir Keteban	—	0778 2
	Pasir	Pasir Misi	—	0779 4
	Pasir	Pasir Pematang	—	0780 1
	Pasir	Pasir Pembesi	—	0781 3
	Pasir	Pasir Saing Bewei	—	0782 5
	Pasir	Pasir Tajur	—	0783 0
	Pasir	Pasir Telake	—	0784 2
	Pasir	Pasir Laburan	—	0711 3

No.	Ethnic Group	Sub-ethnic	Alias	Code
	Pasir	Pasir Tanjung Aru	—	no code
	Pasir	Pasir Kendilo	—	no code
4	Kutai	Kutai	—	0530 2
5	Saqi	Saqi	—	0585 3
6	Telaga	Telaga	—	0592 5
7		Others in Kalimantan	—	6000 5

Sulawesi

No.	Ethnic Group	Sub-ethnic	Sub-sub-ethnic	Alias	Code
1	Ampana	—	—	—	0621 0
2	Anak Suku Seko	—	—	—	0689 1
3	Atinggola	—	—	—	0806 2
4	Babongko	—	—	Bobangko	0622 2
	Babongko	Masama	—	—	0654 2
5	Bada	—	—	Lore	0623 4
	Bada	—	—	Napu	0623 4
	Bada	—	—	To Bada	0671 5
	Bada	—	—	Tobada	0718 3
	Bada	—	—	Besoa	0632 3
6	Bajao	—	—	Bajo	0624 6
	Bajao	—	—	Bayo	0624 6
	Bajao	—	—	Wajo	0624 6
7	Balantak	—	—	—	0626 3
	Balantak	Dale-dale	—	—	0637 6
	Balantak	Tanoturan	—	—	0791 4
	Balantak	Tanoturan	—	Tanutor	0626 3
	Balantak	—	—	Mian Balantak	no code
8	Balesang	—	—	—	0627 5
9	Banggai	Mian Banggai	—	—	0630 6
	Banggai	Mian Sea-Sea	—	—	0630 6
	Banggai	Mian Sea-Sea	—	Mian/Sea-sea	0655 4
10	Baras	—	—	—	0690 5
11	Benggaulu	—	—	—	0691 0
12	Bentong	—	—	—	0692 2
13	Bingi	—	—	—	0693 4
	Bingi	—	—	Dunggu	0696 3

No.	Ethnic Group	Sub-ethnic		Alias	Code
	Bingi	—	—	Toribinggi	0696 3
	Bingi	—	—	Tribinggi	0816 3
14	Bonao	—	—	—	0735 6
15	Bonerate	—	—	—	0694 6
16	Bubis	—	—	—	0736 1
17	Bungku	—	—	Tobungku	0634 0
18	Buol	—	—	—	0635 2
19	Buginese	—	—	—	0695 1
	Buginese	—	—	Ugi	0732 0
	Buginese	Bugis Pagatan	—	—	0502 3
	Buginese	Bugis Pagatan	—	Pagatan	0508 1
	Buginese	Amatoa	—	Ammatowa	0688 6
	Buginese	Amatoa	—	Orang Kajang	0688 6
	Buginese	Tolotang	—	—	0723 1
20	Buton	—	—	Butong	0738 5
	Buton	—	—	Butung	0738 5
	Buton	Wolio	—	—	0804 5
21	Cika	—	—		0560 5
22	Duri	—	—	—	0697 5
	Duri	—	—	Masen Rempulu	0708 2
23	Ereke	—	—	—	0740 4
24	Galumpang	—	—	Kalumpang	0698 0
25	Gamkonora	—	—	—	0741 6
26	Gorontalo	—	—	—	0807 4
	Gorontalo	Polahi	—	—	0786 6
27	Kahumamahon	—	—	—	0642 4
28	Kaili	—	—	Palu	0660 2
	Kaili	—	—	Parigi	0660 2
	Kaili	—	—	Sigi	0660 2
	Kaili	Tamungkolowi	—		0660 2
	Kaili	—	—	Tokaili	0660 2
	Kaili	—	—	Toraja Barat	0660 2
	Kaili	—	—	Tosigi	0633 5
	Kaili	Rai	—	—	0189 2
	Kaili	Balinggi	—	—	0628 0

No.	Ethnic Group	Sub-ethnic	Sub-sub-ethnic	Alias	Code
	Kaili	Baluase	—	—	0628 0
	Kaili	Bangga	—	—	0628 0
	Kaili	Banggakoro	—	—	0628 0
	Kaili	Kulawi	—	—	0628 0
	Kaili	Susu	—	—	0628 0
	Kaili	Binimaru	—	—	0633 5
	Kaili	Lindu	—	—	0633 5
	Kaili	Dolo	—	Todolo	0639 3
	Kaili	Dolo	—	Toridolo	0800 4
	Kaili	Kaliki	—	—	0644 1
	Kaili	Raranggonau	—	—	0665 5
	Kaili	Sibalaya	—	—	0665 5
	Kaili	Sidondo	—	—	0665 5
	Kaili	Binimaru	—	Birumaru	0734 4
	Kaili	Binimaru	—	Tobirumaru	0734 4
	Kaili	Ledo	—	—	0651 3
	Kaili	Baku	—	—	no code
	Kaili	Dolago	—	—	no code
	Kaili	Pakuli	—	—	no code
	Kaili	Petimpe	—	—	no code
29	Kaladeng	—	—	—	0699 2
30	Kalaotoa	—	—	—	0700 0
31	Kalowo	—	—	—	0701 2
32	Kamarian	—	—	—	0743 3
33	Karey	—	—	—	0744 5
34	Kayeli	—	—	—	0745 0
35	Koba	—	—	—	0747 4
36	Kola	—	—	—	0702 4
37	Kompane	—	—	—	0703 6
38	Kumapu	—	—	—	0748 6
39	Laba	—	—	—	0749 1
40	Labbu	—	—	—	0750 5
41	Laha	—	—	—	0752 2
42	Lauje	—	—	—	0650 1
43	Limakatina	—	—	—	0756 3
44	Lola	—	—	—	0757 5

No.	Ethnic Group	Sub-ethnic	Sub-sub-ethnic	Alias	Code
45	Lo'on	—	—	Loun	0608 5
	Lo'on	—	—	—	0758 0
46	Lorang	—	—	—	0704 1
47	Luang	—	—	—	0759 2
48	Luhu	—	—	—	0760 6
49	Luwu	—	—	—	0705 3
50	Mamasa	—	—	—	0809 1
51	Mamuju	—	—	—	0810 5
52	Mandar	—	—	—	0513 6
53	Manusela	—	—	—	0762 3
54	Makassarese	—	—	—	0706 5
55	Manombai	—	—	—	0707 0
56	Mariri	—	—	Molio	0805 0
	Mariri	—	—	Mori Atas	0805 0
	Mariri	—	—	Mori Bawah	0805 0
57	Masahan	—	—	—	0764 0
58	Masela	—	—	—	0765 2
59	Masiwang	—	—	—	0766 4
60	Memale	—	—	—	0768 1
61	Minahasa	Borgo	—	—	0605 6
	Minahasa	Minahasa	—	—	0609 0
	Minahasa	Babontehu	—	—	0599 5
	Minahasa	Bantik	—	—	0600 3
	Minahasa	Pasan	—	Ratahan	0610 4
	Minahasa	Ponosakan	—	—	0611 6
	Minahasa	Tombulu	—	—	0614 5
	Minahasa	Tonsawang	—	—	0615 0
	Minahasa	Tonsea	—	Tonseas	0616 2
	Minahasa	Totemboan	—	Tonteboan	0617 4
	Minahasa	Totemboan	—	Totembuan	0618 6
	Minahasa	Toulour	—	—	0619 1
62	Mongondow	Bintauna	—	—	0601 5
	Mongondow	Bolaang Itang	—	Itang	0602 0
	Mongondow	Bolaang Mongondow	—	—	0603 2
	Mongondow	Bolaang Uki	—	—	0604 4
	Mongondow	Kaidipang	—	—	0606 1

No.	Ethnic Group	Sub-ethnic	Sub-sub-ethnic	Alias	Code
	Mongondow	Kaidipang	—	Kodipiang	0607 3
63	Moronene	—	—	—	0771 2
64	Muna	—	—	—	0773 6
65	Mungku	—	—	—	0774 1
66	Nerekang	—	—	—	0656 6
67	Ngusumbatu	—	—	—	0657 1
68	Pado'e	—	—	—	0710 1
69	Pamona	Pamona	—	—	0661 4
	Pamona	Pamona	—	Bare'e	0631 1
	Pamona	Pamona	—	Tojo	0676 1
	Pamona	Lalaleo	—	—	0647 0
	Pamona	Lalaleo	—	Tolalaeo	0677 3
	Pamona	Poso	—	—	0663 1
	Pamona	Rau	—	—	0666 0
	Pamona	Wana	—	—	0686 2
	Pamona	Bancea	—	—	0629 2
	Pamona	Buyu	—	—	0636 4
	Pamona	Kadambuku	—	—	0641 2
	Pamona	Lage	—	Tolage	0646 5
	Pamona	Lamusa/ Lembo	—	—	0649 4
	Pamona	Longkea	—	—	0652 5
	Pamona	Payapi	—	—	0659 5
	Pamona	Pebato	—	—	0659 5
	Pamona	Pu'umboto	—	—	0664 3
	Pamona	Pu'umboto	—	Puumbato	0664 3
	Pamona	Unda'e	—	—	0666 0
	Pamona	Unda'e	—	Ondae	0658 3
	Pamona	Wotu	—	—	0687 4
	Pamona	Kalae	—	—	0643 6
	Pamona	Pada	—	Topada	0726 0
	Pamona	Pada	—	—	0659 5
	Pamona	Pakambia	—	—	0659 5
	Pamona	Palende	—	—	0659 5
	Pamona	Pu'umnana	—	—	0664 3
	Pamona	Tanandoa	—	—	0666 0
	Pamona	Laiwonu	—	—	0753 4

No.	Ethnic Group	Sub-ethnic	Sub-sub-ethnic	Alias	Code
	Pamona	Lampu	—	Tolampu	0648 2
	Pamona	Tawi	—	—	0666 0
70	Pattae	—	—	—	0811 0
71	Rongkong	—	—	—	0712 5
72	Saluan	—	—	—	0667 2
73	Sangir	—	—	—	0612 1
74	Sangsangluang	—	—	—	0713 0
75	Sariung	—	—	—	0789 5
76	Selayar	—	—	—	0714 2
77	Silaton	—	—	—	0715 4
78	Suwawa	—	—	—	0808 6
	Suwawa	—	—	Bune	0737 3
79	Ta'a	—	—	—	0668 4
80	Talaud	—	—	—	0613 3
81	Tana'	—	—	—	0591 3
82	Tialo	—	—	—	0670 3
83	To Ala	—	—	—	0716 6
	To Ala	To Ala Walenrang	—	—	0717 1
	To Ala	To Ala Sekko	—	—	0792 6
	To Ala	To Ala Tanomanae	—	—	0793 1
84	Tobalo'e	—	—	—	0719 5
85	Tobana	—	—	—	0720 2
86	Tofuti	—	—	—	0794 3
87	Togian	—	—	—	0674 4
88	Toimpo	—	—	—	0675 6
89	Tokalompi	—	—	—	0721 4
90	Tolaa	—	—	—	0795 5
91	Tolaki	Tolaki Mekongga	—	Mekongga/ Tolaki	0767 6
	Tolaki	Tolaki Mekongga	—	Wiwirano	0767 6
	Tolaki	Tolaki Mekongga	—	—	0796 0
	Tolaki	—	—	Laki-laki	0754 6
	Tolaki	—	—	Lolaki	0754 6
	Tolaki	—	—	Toke	0754 6

No.	Ethnic Group	Sub-ethnic	Sub-sub-ethnic	Alias	Code
	Tolaki	Aserawanua	—	—	0733 2
	Tolaki	Labeau	—	—	0751 0
	Tolaki	Mowewe	—	—	0772 4
	Tolaki	Tamboki	—	—	0790 2
	Tolaki	Tolaki Konawe	—	—	no code
	Tolaki	Wawonii	—	—	0803 3
92	Tolampung	—	—	—	0722 6
93	Tolidu	—	—	—	0679 0
94	Tomapung	—	—	—	0724 3
95	Tomatabaho	—	—	—	0797 2
96	Tombelala	—	—	—	0798 4
97	Tomia	—	—	—	0799 6
98	Tomini	Balaesang	—	—	0625 1
	Tomini	Dampelas	—	—	0638 1
	Tomini	Dondo	—	—	0640 0
	Tomini	Kasimbar	—	—	0645 3
	Tomini	Moutong	—	—	0645 3
	Tomini	Patapa	—	—	0645 3
	Tomini	Tinombo	—	—	0645 3
	Tomini	Kasimbar	—	Tajio/Ta'jio	0669 6
	Tomini	Toli Toli	—	—	0678 5
	Tomini	—	—	Tomenui	0680 4
	Tomini	Umalasa	—	—	0684 5
	Tomini	Mautong	—	—	0709 4
	Tomini	Boano	—	Buano	0898 1
99	Tomobahono	—	—	—	0681 6
100	Tomoiki	—	—	—	0682 1
101	To Molioa	—	—	—	0672 0
102	To Molongkuni	—	—	—	0673 2
103	Tonandoa	—	—	—	0683 3
104	Topakkalotong	—	—	—	0727 2
105	Topembuni	—	—	Tominbun	0725 5
	Topembuni	—	—	Tomembuni	0725 5
	Topembuni	—	—	Totembuni	0730 3
106	Toraja	—	—	—	0665 5
	Toraja	Pipikoro	—	—	0662 6
107	Torampi	—	—	—	0728 4

No.	Ethnic Group	Sub-ethnic	Sub-sub-ethnic	Alias	Code
108	Toroda	—	—	—	0801 6
109	Tosumunya	—	—	—	0729 6
110	Totaramanu	—	—	—	0812 2
111	Towala-wala	—	—	—	0813 4
112	Towara	—	—	—	0814 6
113	Towatu	—	—	—	0815 1
114	Towotu	—	—	—	0731 5
115	Una-una	—	—	—	0685 0
116	Wakatobi		—	—	0802 1
117	Wang Saq	—	—	—	0817 5
118	Others in Sulawesi	—	—	—	7000 0

Maluku

No.	Ethnic Group	Sub-ethnic	Sub-sub-ethnic	Alias	Code
1	Amahai	—	—	—	0820 6
2	Ambelau	—	—	—	0821 1
3	Ambon	—	—	—	0822 3
4	Ange	—	—	—	0900 1
5	Aputai	—	—	—	0823 5
6	Aru	—	—	—	0824 0
7	Asilulu	—	—	—	0825 2
8	Babar	—	—	—	0826 4
9	Bacan	—	—	—	0901 3
10	Banda	—	—	—	0827 6
	Banda	—	—	Eli Elat	0841 3
11	Barakai	—	—	—	0828 1
12	Bati	—	—	—	0829 3
13	Batuley	—	—	—	0830 0
14	Benggoi	—	—	—	0831 2
15	Biyoli	—	—	Waioli	0902 5
	Biyoli	—	—	Waoli	0902 5
16	Bobot	—	—	—	0832 4
17	Buli	—	—	—	0903 0
18	Buru	—	—	—	0833 6
19	Dai	—	—	—	0835 3

No.	Ethnic Group	Sub-ethnic	Sub-sub-ethnic	Alias	Code
20	Damar	—	—	—	0836 5
21	Dawelor	—	—	—	0837 0
22	Dawera	—	—	—	0838 2
23	Desite	—	—	—	0839 4
24	Dobel	—	—	—	0840 1
25	Emplawas	—	—	—	0842 5
26	Erai	—	—	—	0843 0
27	Fordata	—	—	—	0845 4
28	Galela	—	—	—	0904 2
29	Gamkonoro	—	—	—	0905 4
30	Gane	—	—	Gani	0906 6
31	Geser-Gorom	—	—	—	0846 6
32	Halmahera	—	—	—	0908 3
33	Haruku	—	—	—	0847 1
	Haruku	Pelauw	—	—	0874 5
34	Hitu	—	—	—	0848 3
35	Hoti	—	—	—	0849 5
36	Hulung	—	—	—	0851 4
37	Iliun	—	—	—	0852 6
38	Imroing	—	—	—	0853 1
39	Jailolo	—	—	—	0854 3
40	Kadai	—	—	—	0910 2
41	Kaibobo	—	—	—	0855 5
42	Kau	—	—	Kao	0911 4
	Kau	—	—	Kayoa	0912 6
43	Kei	—	—	—	0856 0
	Kei	—	—	Evav	0844 2
44	Kisar	—	—	—	0857 2
45	Laloda	—	—	Loloda*	0755 1
46	Larike-Wakasihu	—	—	—	0858 4
47	Leti	—	—	—	0860 3
48	Lisabata-Nuniali	—	—	—	0861 5
49	Maba	—	—	—	0913 1
50	Mafa	—	—	—	0864 4
51	Makian	—	—	—	0761 1
	Makian	Makian Barat	—	—	0914 3

No.	Ethnic Group	Sub-ethnic	Sub-sub-ethnic	Alias	Code
	Makian	Makian Barat	—	Jitine	0742 1
	Makian	Makian Timur	—	—	0915 5
	Makian	Makian Timur	—	Tabayama	0924 4
52	Mangole	—	—	—	0916 0
53	Manipa	—	—	—	0917 2
54	Mare*	—	—	—	0763 5
55	Moa*	—	—	—	0769 3
56	Modole*	—	—	—	0770 0
57	Module	—	—	—	0918 4
58	Morotai	—	—	—	0919 6
59	Naibobo	—	—	—	0865 6
60	Nakaela	—	—	—	0866 1
61	Nila	—	—	—	0869 0
62	Nusalaut	—	—	—	0870 4
63	Oirata	—	—	—	0871 6
64	Pagu	—	—	—	0872 1
65	Patani	—	—	—	0920 3
66	Paulohi	—	—	—	0873 3
67	Perai	—	—	—	0875 0
68	Piru	—	—	—	0876 2
69	Pugu	—	—	—	0921 5
70	Rana	—	—	—	0877 4
71	Roma	—	—	—	0878 6
	Roma	—	—	Romang	0878 6
	Roma	—	—	Ruma	0878 6
72	Sahu	—	—	Sa'u	0922 0
73	Salas Gunung	—	—	—	0879 1
74	Saleman	—	—	—	0880 5
75	Saparua	—	—	—	0881 0
76	Seith-Kaitetu	—	—	—	0882 2
77	Selaru	—	—	—	0883 4
78	Seluwasan	—	—	—	0884 6
79	Sepa	—	—	—	0885 1
80	Seram	—	—	—	0886 3
	Seram	—	—	Alfuru	0818 0

No.	Ethnic Group	Sub-ethnic	Sub-sub-ethnic	Alias	Code
	Seram	—	—	Ibu	0909 5
	Seram	Alune	—	—	0819 2
	Seram	Lumoli	—	—	0863 2
	Seram	Nuaulu	—	Naulu	0867 3
	Seram	Nuaulu	—	Nuahunai	0867 3
	Seram	Nuaulu	—	Huaulu	0850 2
	Seram	Wemale			0895 2
81	Serili	—	—	—	0887 5
82	Serua	—	—	—	0888 0
83	Seti-Liana	—	—	—	0889 2
84	Siboyo	—	—	—	0923 2
85	Sula	—	—	—	0899 3
86	Taliabu	—	—	—	0925 6
87	Tanimbar	Laru-Tomata Laru	—	—	0859 6
	Tanimbar	Nember	—	Orang Timur Laut	0868 5
	Tanimbar	—	—	—	0891 1
	Tanimbar	Yamdena	—	—	0897 6
88	Talur	—	—	—	0890 6
89	Tarangan	—	—	—	0892 3
90	Ternate	—	—	—	0926 1
91	Tidore	—	—	—	0927 3
92	Tobaru	—	—	—	0928 5
93	Tobelo	—	—	—	0929 0
94	Tugutil	—	—	—	0620 5
95	Wai Loa	—	—	—	0893 5
96	Wai Apu		—		0862 0
97	Watubela	—	—	—	0894 0
98	Weda	—	—	—	0930 4
99	Yalahatan	—	—	—	0896 4
100	Others in Maluku	—	—	—	8000 2

Note: * Laloda/Loloda, Mare, Moa and Modole are the misplaced cases. They were initially grouped under Sulawesi.

Papua

No.	Ethnic Group	Sub-ethnic	Sub-sub-ethnic	Alias	Code
1	Abau	—	—	—	0931 6
2	Abra	—	—	—	0932 1
3	Aikwakai	—	—	—	0934 5
	Aikwakai	—	—	Araikurioko	1001 4
	Aikwakai	—	—	Eritai	1055 3
	Aikwakai	—	—	Sikari	1232 3
	Aikwakai	—	—	Tori	1260 2
4	Air Mati	—	—	Kwerba	0991 5
	Air Mati	—	—	Nabuk	0991 5
5	Airoran	—	—	—	0994 4
	Airoran	—	—	Adora	0933 3
	Airoran	—	—	Iriemkena	1073 1
	Airoran	—	—	Sasawa	1215 0
6	Airo Sumaghaghe	—	—	Airo	0992 0
	Airo Sumaghaghe	—	—	—	0993 2
7	Amanab	—	—	—	0937 4
8	Ambai	—	—	—	0995 6
9	Amabai	—	—	—	0936 2
10	Amberbaken	—	—	—	0938 6
11	Amungme	—	—	—	0997 3
	Amungme	—	—	Amung	0996 1
	Amungme	—	—	Hamung	0996 1
	Amungme	—	—	Amui	no code
12	Anate	—	—	—	0998 5
13	Anu	—	—	Anus	1000 2
14	Arandai	—	—	—	0939 1
	Arandai	—	—	Yaban	1299 2
15	Aero	—	—	—	0988 4
16	Arfak	—	—	—	1002 6
	Arfak* (see note)	—	—	—	1002 6

No.	Ethnic Group	Sub-ethnic	Sub-sub-ethnic	Alias	Code
	Arfak	Atam	—	Hatam	0942 2
	Arfak	Atam	—	Hattam	0951 1
	Arfak	Atam	—	Tinam	0983 1
	Arfak	Atam	—	Mire	1161 0
	Arfak	Manikion	—	—	0966 5
	Arfak	Manikion	—	Sough	0978 3
	Arfak	Meiyakh	—	—	1154 5
	Arfak	Meiyakh	—	Meyah	0970 1
	Arfak	Meiyakh	—	Meyak	0970 1
	Arfak	Moire	—	—	1163 4
17	Arguni	—	—	—	0940 5
18	Asmat	Betch-Mbup	—	—	1004 3
	Asmat	Brazza	—	—	1034 6
	Asmat	Cicak	—	Citak Mitak	1034 6
	Asmat	—	—	Kaunak**	1101 1
	Asmat	Bismam	—	—	1028 6
	Asmat	Emari Ducur	—	—	1053 6
	Asmat	Joerat	—	—	1081 5
	Asmat	Kaimo	—	—	1085 6
	Asmat	Safan	—	—	1209 0
	Asmat	Simai	—	—	1234 0
	Asmat	Unisiarau	—	—	1267 2
	Asmat	Sawi	—	—	1221 0
	Asmat	Sawi	—	Sawuy	1223 4
	Asmat	Auyu	—	—	1007 2
	Asmat	Oser	—	—	1196 6
	Asmat	Pisa	—	—	1204 4
	Asmat	Awyu	—	Away	1008 4
	Asmat	Kayagar	—	Kaigir	1084 4
	Asmat	Kayagar	—	Kayigi	1084 4
	Asmat	Kayagar	—	Kaygir	1104 0
	Asmat	Keenok	—	—	no code
	Asmat	Batia	—	—	no code

No.	Ethnic Group	Sub-ethnic	Sub-sub-ethnic	Alias	Code
19	Atogoim	—	—	Autohwaim	1005 5
	Atogoim	—	—	Kaugat	1100 6
20	Ayfat* (see note)	—	—	Mey Brat	1158 6
	Ayfat	—	—	Meibarat	0967 0
	Ayfat	—	—	Ayamaru	1010 3
21	Awye	—	—	Awyi	1009 6
22	Babe	—	—	—	1011 5
23	Babirua	—	—	Baburiwa	1012 0
	Babirua	—	—	Baburua	1012 0
24	Bagusa	—	—	—	1013 2
25	Baham	—	—	—	0944 6
	Baham	—	—	Patimuni	1202 0
26	Banlol	—	—	—	0945 1
27	Bapu	—	—	—	1014 4
28	Barau	—	—	—	0946 3
29	Baso	—	—	—	1015 6
30	Bauzi	—	—	Baudi	1016 1
	Bauzi	—	—	Bauji	1016 1
	Bauzi	—	—	Bauri	1016 1
	Bauzi	—	—	Bazi	1016 1
	Bauzi	—	—	Bausi	1017 3
	Bauzi	—	—	Bauwi	1018 5
	Bauzi	—	—	Bauzi	1019 0
31	Bedoanas	—	—	—	0947 5
32	Biksi	—	—	—	1025 0
33	Berik	—	—	—	1020 4
34	Betaf	—	—	—	1021 6
35	Bgu	—	—	Bonggo	1022 1
36	Biak-Numfor	—	—	Mafoorsch	1023 3
	Biak-Numfor	—	—	Noefor	1023 3
37	Bipim	—	—	Biplim	1026 2
38	Bira	—	—	—	1027 4
39	Bonefa	—	—	—	1029 1

No.	Ethnic Group	Sub-ethnic	Sub-sub-ethnic	Alias	Code
40	Boneraf	—	—	—	1030 5
	Boneraf	—	—	Bonerif	1031 0
41	Borapasi	—	—	—	1032 2
42	Borto	—	—	—	1033 4
43	Bresi	—	—	—	1035 1
44	Bunru	—	—	—	1036 3
45	Burate	—	—	—	1037 5
46	Buruwai	—	—	Asienara	0941 0
	Buruwai	—	—	Buruwai	0949 2
	Buruwai	—	—	Karufa	0949 2
	Buruwai	—	—	Madidwana	1137 2
47	Dabra	—	—	—	1038 0
48	Damal	—	—	—	1039 2
49	Dani	—	—	Ndani	1040 6
	Dani	—	—	Lani	1130 2
	Dani	Lani Barat	—	—	1131 4
	Dani	Lani Lembah	—	—	1132 6
50	Dauwa	—	—	Nduga	1041 1
	Dauwa	—	—	Ndugwa	1041 1
	Dauwa	Pesekhem	—	—	1203 2
	Dauwa	Pesekhem	—	Dawa	no code
	Dauwa	Pesekhem	—	Pesegem	no code
51	Dem	—	—	Lem	1042 3
52	Demba	—	—	—	1043 5
53	Demta	—	—	—	1045 2
54	Demisa	—	—	—	1044 0
55	Dera	—	—	—	1046 4
56	Dosobou	—	—	Dou	1048 1
	Dosobou	—	—	Doufou	1048 1
57	Dubu	—	—	—	1049 3
58	Edopi	—	—	—	1050 0
59	Ekagi	—	—	Auwye	1006 0
	Ekagi	—	—	Ekari	1006 0

No.	Ethnic Group	Sub-ethnic	Sub-sub-ethnic	Alias	Code
	Ekagi	—	—	Kapauku	1006 0
	Ekagi	—	—	Me Mana	1006 0
	Ekagi	—	—	Simori	1006 0
	Ekagi	—	—	Tapiro	1006 0
	Ekagi	—	—	Yabi	1006 0
	Ekagi	Mee	—	—	1153 3
60	Emumu	—	—	—	1054 1
	Emumu	—	—	Imimkal	1068 3
	Emumu	—	—	Kiamorep	1111 2
61	Faoau	—	—	—	1056 5
	Faoau	—	—	Foau	1059 4
62	Faranyao	—	—	—	1057 0
	Faranyao	—	—	Kaniran	1089 0
	Faranyao	—	—	Mairasi	0965 3
63	Foya	—	—	—	1060 1
64	Fayu	—	—	—	1058 2
65	Gebe	—	—	—	1061 3
	Gebe	—	—	Gebi	0907 1
66	Gressi	—	—	Gressik	1062 5
67	Hambai	—	—	—	1063 0
68	Hugula	—	—	—	1065 4
69	Humboldt	—	—	—	1066 6
70	Hupla	—	—	—	1067 1
71	Iha	—	—	Kapaur	0952 3
	Iha	—	—	Lha	1134 3
72	Ina	—	—	—	1069 5
73	Inanwatan	—	—	—	0953 5
74	Inlom	—	—	—	1070 2
75	Irahutu	—	—	Irarutu	0954 0
76	Iresim	—	—	—	1071 4
77	Iri	—	—	—	1072 6
78	Itik	—	—	—	1075 5
79	Iwur	—	—	—	1076 0

No.	Ethnic Group	Sub-ethnic	Sub-sub-ethnic	Alias	Code
80	Isirawa	—	—	Okwasar	1074 3
81	Jaban	—	—	—	1077 2
82	Jair	—	—	—	1078 4
	Jair	—	—	Aghu	0989 6
	Jair	—	—	Aghul	0990 3
83	Janggu	—	—	—	1079 6
	Janggu	—	—	Morwap	1171 1
	Janggu	—	—	Sawa	1219 1
	Janggu	—	—	Tabu	1247 0
84	Jinak	—	—	Zinak	1080 3
85	Kabera	—	—	—	1082 0
86	Kaeti	—	—	—	1083 2
87	Kalabra	—	—	—	1086 1
88	Kaladar	—	—	Kimagama	1087 3
89	Kamberau	—	—	Kambrau	0956 4
	Kamberau	—	—	Lambrau	0956 4
90	Kaowor	—	—	Kauwol	1092 1
91	Kapauri	—	—	Kapori	1093 3
92	Karas	—	—	—	0957 6
93	Karema	—	—	—	1096 2
94	Karfasia	—	—	—	1097 4
95	Karon	—	—	—	0958 1
96	Kasueri	—	—	—	1098 6
97	Katik	—	—	—	1099 1
98	Kaureh	—	—	—	1102 3
99	Kawamsu	—	—	—	1103 5
100	Kawe	—	—	—	0959 3
101	Kayu Batu	—	—	Kayu Pulau	1105 2
102	Keburi	—	—	—	0960 0
103	Keder	—	—	—	1106 4
104	Kembrano	—	—	—	0961 2
105	Kemtuik	—	—	Kemtuk	1315 4
106	Kendate	—	—	—	1107 6

No.	Ethnic Group	Sub-ethnic	Sub-sub-ethnic	Alias	Code
107	Kerom	—	—	—	1108 1
	Kerom	—	—	Keron	1109 3
	Kerom	Walsa	—	—	1281 6
108	Ketengban	—	—	—	1110 0
	Ketengban	—	—	Hmanggona	1064 2
	Ketengban	—	—	Hmonono	1064 2
	Ketengban	—	—	Kimnyal	1064 2
	Ketengban	—	—	Nalca	1064 2
	Ketengban	—	—	Kimyal	1113 6
	Ketengban	—	—	Kupel	1125 4
	Ketengban	—	—	Kupol	1125 4
	Ketengban	—	—	Eipomek	1051 2
	Ketengban	—	—	Eiponek	1052 4
109	Kimbai	—	—	—	1112 4
110	Kiri-kiri	—	—	—	1114 1
111	Kofei	—	—	—	1115 3
112	Koiwai	—	—	Aiduma	1314 2
	Koiwai	—	—	Kaiwai	1314 2
	Koiwai	—	—	Kayumerah	1314 2
	Koiwai	—	—	Koiwai	1314 2
	Koiwai	—	—	Namatota	1314 2
	Koiwai	—	—	Namatote	1180 0
113	Kokoda	—	—	—	0962 4
114	Kombai	—	—	—	1117 0
115	Koneraw	—	—	—	1118 2
116	Korapu	—	—	Korupun	1119 4
117	Korowai	—	—	—	1120 1
	Korowai	—	—	Korufa	1121 3
118	Kosare	—	—	—	1122 5
119	Kotogut	—	—	—	1123 0
120	Kurudu	—	—	—	1126 6
121	Kuangsu	—	—	—	1124 2
122	Kwerisa	—	—	—	1127 1

No.	Ethnic Group	Sub-ethnic	Sub-sub-ethnic	Alias	Code
123	Kwesten	—	—	—	1128 3
124	Lairawa	—	—	—	1129 5
125	Liki	—	—	—	1135 5
126	Madik	—	—	—	0964 1
127	Maden	—	—	—	1136 0
	Maden	—	—	Sapran	1213 3
128	Mander	—	—	—	1139 6
129	Mandobo	—	—	—	1140 3
	Mandobo	—	—	Wambon	1282 1
	Mandobo	—	—	Wandub Wambon	1285 0
130	Maniwa	—	—	—	1142 0
131	Manem	—	—	—	1141 5
	Manem	—	—	Yeti	1312 5
	Manem	—	—	Skofro	1236 4
	Manem	—	—	Wembi	1294 6
132	Mansim	—	—	—	1143 2
133	Mapi	—	—	—	1145 6
134	Marind Anim	—	—	—	1149 0
	Marind Anim	Kanum	—	—	1090 4
	Marind Anim	Marin	—	—	1148 5
	Marind Anim	Yey	—	—	1313 0
	Marind Anim	Yey	—	Yei Anim	no code
	Marind Anim	Yey	—	Yei Nan	no code
	Marind Anim	Yab-Anim	—	—	no code
	Marind Anim	Maklew	—	—	1138 4
	Marind Anim	Kurkari	—	—	no code
	Marind Anim	Bian Marind	—	—	1024 5
135	Marembori	—	—	—	1146 1
136	Maremgi	—	—	Marengge	1147 3
137	Masimasi	—	—	—	1150 4
138	Massep	—	—	—	1151 6
139	Mawes	—	—	Mawesi	1152 1

No.	Ethnic Group	Sub-ethnic	Sub-sub-ethnic	Alias	Code
140	Memana	—	—	—	1156 2
141	Meninggo	—	—	—	1157 4
142	Meoswar	—	—	—	0968 2
143	Mer	—	—	—	0969 4
	Mer	—	—	Muri	1176 4
144	Mimika	—	—	—	1159 1
	Mimika	Sempan	—	—	1227 5
	Mimika	Sempan	—	Nararafi	1182 4
	Mimika	—	—	Nefarpi	1185 3
	Mimika	—	—	Mukamuga	1174 0
	Mimika	—	—	Kamoro	1088 5
	Mimika	—	—	Kaokonau	1091 6
	Mimika	—	—	Komora	1091 6
	Mimika	—	—	Lakahia	1091 6
	Mimika	—	—	Maswena	1091 6
	Mimika	—	—	Nagramadu	1091 6
	Mimika	—	—	Neferipi	1091 6
	Mimika	—	—	Umari	1091 6
	Mimika	—	—	Kokonau	1116 5
145	Mintamani	—	—	—	1160 5
	Mintamani	—	—	Aiso	0935 0
	Mintamani	—	—	Kais	0955 2
	Mintamani	—	—	Atori	0943 4
146	Moni	—	—	—	1167 5
147	Molof	—	—	—	1164 6
148	Mombum	—	—	—	1165 1
149	Mor	—	—	—	1168 0
150	Moraid	—	—	—	1169 2
151	Moraori	—	—	—	1170 6
152	Moi	—	—	—	0971 3
	Moi	—	—	Mooi	0971 3
	Moi	—	—	Mosena	1173 5
	Moi	—	—	Mosana	1172 3

No.	Ethnic Group	Sub-ethnic	Sub-sub-ethnic	Alias	Code
	Moi	—	—	Mekwai	1155 0
	Moi	—	—	Mekwei	1155 0
153	Momuna	—	—	—	1166 3
154	Momuna	—	—	Somage	1239 3
155	Murop	—	—	—	1177 6
156	Muyu	—	—	—	1178 1
157	Nabi	—	—	—	0972 5
	Nabi	—	—	Modan	1162 2
	Nabi	—	—	Kuri	0963 6
158	Nafri	—	—	—	1179 3
159	Nambrung	—	—	Nimboran	1181 2
160	Narau	—	—	—	1183 6
161	Ndom	—	—	—	1184 1
162	Ngalik	—	—	Yali	1187 0
	Ngalik	—	—	Yalik	1187 0
	Ngalik	—	—	Yaly	1304 1
	Ngalik	—	—	Silimo	1233 5
163	Ngalum	—	—	—	1188 2
164	Ninggerum	—	—	—	1189 4
165	Nisa	—	—	—	1191 3
166	Nipsan	—	—	—	1190 1
167	Nopuk	—	—	—	1192 5
168	Onin	—	—	—	0973 0
169	Okparimen	—	—	—	1193 0
170	Oria	—	—	Uria	1194 2
	Oria	—	—	Saweh	1220 5
171	Ormu	—	—	—	1195 4
172	Otodema	—	—	—	1197 1
173	Palata	—	—	—	1199 5
174	Papasena	—	—	—	1200 3
175	Podena	—	—	—	1205 6
176	Pyu	—	—	—	1207 3
177	Roon	—	—	—	0974 2

No.	Ethnic Group	Sub-ethnic	Sub-sub-ethnic	Alias	Code
178	Riantana	—	—	—	1208 5
179	Sailolof	—	—	—	1210 4
	Sailolof	Palamul	—	—	1198 3
180	Samarokena	—	—	—	1211 6
181	Sangke	—	—	—	1212 1
182	Sarmi	—	—	—	1214 5
183	Sauri	—	—	—	1216 2
184	Sause	—	—	—	1217 4
	Sause	—	—	Sauso	1218 6
185	Sawung	—	—	—	1222 2
186	Sedasi	—	—	—	1224 6
187	Seget	—	—	—	0975 4
188	Seka	—	—	Seko	1225 1
	Seka	—	—	Sko	1225 1
189	Sekar	—	—	—	0976 6
190	Sela	—	—	—	1226 3
191	Semini	—	—	—	0977 1
192	Senggi	—	—	—	1228 0
193	Sentani	—	—	—	1229 2
194	Siagha-Yenimu	—	—	Siagha	1230 6
	Siagha-Yenimu	—	—	Yenimu	1230 6
	Siagh-Yenimu	—	—	Syiaga-Yenimu	1245 3
195	Siamai	—	—	—	1231 1
196	Siromi	—	—	—	1235 2
197	Skouw	—	—	—	1237 6
198	Sobei	—	—	Biga	0948 0
	Sobei	—	—	—	1238 1
199	Sota	—	—	—	1240 0
200	Sowei	—	—	—	1241 2
201	Suabau	—	—	Suabo	0979 5
202	Sukubatong	—	—	—	1242 4
203	Tabati	—	—	Sumaghaghe Tabati	1243 6

No.	Ethnic Group	Sub-ethnic	Sub-sub-ethnic	Alias	Code
	Tabati	—	—	—	1246 5
204	Tabla	—	—	—	0980 2
205	Tafaro	—	—	—	1248 2
206	Taikat	—	—	—	1249 4
207	Tamagario	—	—	—	1250 1
208	Tamnim	—	—	—	1251 3
209	Tandia	—	—	—	0981 4
210	Taori	—	—	—	1252 5
211	Tapuma	—	—	—	1253 0
212	Tarfia	—	—	Tarpia	1254 2
	Tarfia	—	—	Surai	1244 1
	Tarfia	—	—	Kapitiauw	1094 5
	Tarfia	—	—	Kaptiau	1095 0
213	Taurap	—	—	Tauraf	1255 4
	Taurap	—	—	—	1256 6
214	Tause	—	—	—	1257 1
215	Tehit	—	—	Tehid	0982 6
	Tehit	—	—	Tehiyit	0982 6
216	Timorini	—	—	—	1258 3
217	Tofamna	—	—	—	1259 5
218	Towarta	—	—	—	1261 4
219	Tunggare	—	—	—	1262 6
220	Turui	—	—	—	1264 3
221	Tyu	—	—	—	1265 5
222	Una	—	—	—	1266 0
223	Unurum	—	—	—	1268 4
224	Urangmirin	—	—	—	1269 6
225	Urundi	—	—	Lau	1133 1
	Urundi	—	—	Turu	1263 1
	Urundi	—	—	—	1270 3
	Urundi	—	—	Ururi	1271 5
	Urundi	—	—	Foi	no code
	Urundi	—	—	Voi	1274 4

No.	Ethnic Group	Sub-ethnic	Sub-sub-ethnic	Alias	Code
226	Uruway	—	—	—	1272 0
227	Usku	—	—	—	1273 2
228	Wandamen	—	—	—	0985 5
229	Wanggom	—	—	Wanggo	1286 2
230	Waina	—	—	—	1275 6
231	Waigeo	—	—	—	0984 3
232	Waipam	—	—	—	1276 1
233	Waipu	—	—	—	1277 3
234	Wairata	—	—	—	1278 5
235	Wakde	—	—	—	1279 0
236	Walak	—	—	—	1280 4
237	Wamesa	—	—	—	1283 3
238	Wanam	—	—	—	1284 5
239	Wano	—	—	—	1287 4
240	Warkai	—	—	—	1291 0
241	Warembori	—	—	—	1288 6
242	Waris	—	—	Wares	1289 1
	Waris	—	—	—	1290 5
243	Waropen	—	—	Worpen	1292 2
244	Warotai	—	—	—	1293 4
245	Wiri	—	—	—	0986 0
	Wiri* (see note)	—	—	Dive*	1047 6
	Wiri	—	—	Dulve	1047 6
246	Woda	—	—	Wodani	1295 1
	Woda	—	—	Wolani	1295 1
247	Wodam	—	—	—	1296 3
248	Woi	—	—	—	1297 5
249	Woriasi	—	—	—	1298 0
250	Yafi	—	—	—	1300 0
251	Yaghay	—	—	—	1301 2
252	Yahadian	—	—	—	0987 2
	Yahadian	—	—	Nerigo	1186 5
253	Yahrai	—	—	Yahray	1302 4

No.	Ethnic Group	Sub-ethnic	Sub-sub-ethnic	Alias	Code
254	Yair	—	—	—	1303 6
255	Yamna	—	—	—	1305 3
256	Yanggon	—	—	—	1306 5
257	Yaninu	—	—	—	1307 0
258	Yansu	—	—	—	1308 2
259	Yapen	Busami	—	—	0950 6
	Yapen	Ansus	—	—	0999 0
	Yapen	Arui	—	Serui	1003 1
	Yapen	Arui	—	Serui Laut	1003 1
	Yapen	Munggui	—	—	1175 2
	Yapen	Papuma	—	—	1201 5
	Yapen	Pom	—	—	1206 1
	Yapen	—	—	—	1309 4
260	Yarsun	—	—	—	1310 1
261	Yaur	—	—	—	1311 3
262	Others in Papua	—	—	—	8000 4
263	Other tribes	—	—	—	9000 4

Note: * Wiri, as mentioned by Hidayah (1995), include the Duve/Duvle, but the census recorded them as Dive/Dulve. The number of Arfak may be overestimated, as some Afyat may have been included under "Arfak", as Arfak and Ayfat were put under the same code (1002). Similarly, the number of people in "Ayfat/Mey Brat/Ayamuru" may have been underestimated as some Ayfat may have been recorded under Arfak.
** Kaunak is an alias of Citak Mitak and Cicak.

Foreign Origins

No.	Ethnic Group	Sub-ethnic	Sub-sub-ethnic	Alias	Code
1	Arab	Arab	—	—	1317/9110
2	Chinese	Cina	—	—	1319/9121
		Cina PRC	—	—	1320/9122
		Cina Taiwan	—	—	1321/9123
3	Timor-Leste origins:				
	Belu	—	—	—	0140 1
	Belu	—	—	Tetun	no code

No.	Ethnic Group	Sub-ethnic	Sub-sub-ethnic	Alias	Code
	Idate	—	—	—	0200 1
	Ilimano	—	—	—	0201 3
	Makasai	—	—	—	0204 2
	Mambai	—	—	—	0206 6
	Na Ueti	—	—	—	0183 4
	Tokodede	—	—	—	0196 4
4	Other foreign origins				
	American	—	—	—	1316/9100
	Australian	—	—	—	1318
	Indian	—	—	—	1322/9130
	British	—	—	—	1323/9140
	Japanese	—	—	—	1324/9150
	Korean	—	—	—	1325/9160
	Malaysian	—	—	—	1326/9170
	Pakistani	—	—	—	1327/9180
	Filipino	—	—	—	1328/9190
	Singaporean	—	—	—	1329
	Thai	—	—	—	1330/9200
	Dutch	—	—	—	1331/9210

Note: Except for those with Timor-Leste origins, other foreign origins have two codes. The ones beginning with "13" are the codes used by the BPS, while the codes starting with "9" are the codes given by the IPUMS (Integrated Public Use Microdata Series) International.

APPENDIX 2

The Classification of the Twenty Languages Spoken Daily at Home: Indonesia, 2010

No.	Language	Sub-Language	Alias/Same Code	Code
1	Javanese	—	—	0088
		Tengger	—	0093
		Banyuwangi	Osing	0090
		Samin	—	0089
2	Indonesia	—	—	1167
3	Sundanese	—	—	0086
		—	Priangan	0086
4	Malay	—	—	0030
		—	Bahasa Melayu	0030
		Melayu Ambon	—	0649
		Melayu Baca	—	0754
		Melayu Bacan	Batjan	0662
		Melayu Bali	—	0098
		Melayu Banda	—	0012
		Melayu Bengkulu	—	0063
		Melayu Berau	—	0459
		Melayu Dayak	—	0410
		Melayu Ende	Melayu Larantuka	0115
		Melayu Jambi	Djambi	0041
		Melayu Kota Bangun Kutai	—	0460
		Melayu Makassar	—	0568
		Melayu Manado	—	0490
		Melayu Minahasa	—	0569
		Melayu Palembang	—	0051
		Palembang	Sekayu	0052
			Musi	0052

No.	Language	Sub-Language	Alias/Same Code	Code
		Melayu Papua	—	1060
		Melayu Riau	—	0036
		Melayu Tengah	—	0045
		Melayu Tenggarong Kutai	—	0461
		Melayu Ternate	Melayu Utara Moluccan	0755
		Melayu Selimbau	—	1176
		Melayu Putusibau-Semitau-Nanga Suhaid		1177
		Melayu Nanga Bunut	—	1178
		Melayu Boyan	—	1179
		Melayu Embau	—	1180
		Melayu Ulu Gurung	—	1181
		Melayu Ulu Silat	—	1182
		Melayu Semangut	—	1183
		Melayu Pinoh	—	1184
		Melayu Sokan	—	1185
		Melayu Kota Baru	—	1186
		Melayu Sayan	—	1187
		Melayu Ela Hilir	—	1188
		Melayu Sintang	—	1189
		Melayu Sekadau	—	1190
		Melayu Sanggau	—	1191
		Melayu Meliau	—	1192
		Melayu Tayan	—	1193
		Melayu Landak	—	1194
		Melayu Sambas	—	1195
		Melayu Merabuan	—	1196
		Melayu Ketapang	—	1197
		Melayu Cali	—	1198
		Melayu Tumbang Titi	—	1199
		Melayu Pebihingan	—	1200
		Melayu Simpang Dua	—	1201
		Melayu Balai berkuak	—	1202
		Melayu Pontianak	—	1203
		Banyu Asin	—	0043
		Kikim	—	0048
		Lematang	—	0050

No.	Language	Sub-Language	Alias/Same Code	Code
		Lintang	Pasemah	0045
		—	Semendo	0045
		Bengkulu	—	0045
		Semende	—	0058
		Serawai	—	0068
		Enim	—	0047
		Sindang	—	0046
		Cul	—	0046
		Col	—	0046
		Kerinci	Kinchai	0026
		Lubu	—	0035
		Komering	Kumoring	0049
		Belitung	—	0075
		Sakai	—	0037
		Duano	—	0033
		Kubu	—	0040
		Siak Sri Indrapura	—	0038
		Talang Mamak	—	0039
		Anak Dalam	Orang Hutan	0040
		—	Orang Rimba	0040
		Aji	Haji	0042
		Belido	—	0044
		Bilide	—	0044
		Bintuhan	Ka'ur	0059
		—	Kaur	0059
		—	Mulak	0059
		Lambak	Lembak	0062
		Bangka	—	0074
		Belitong	Belitung	0075
		Lonchong	Loncong	0077
		Seka	Sekah	0077
		Sekak	—	0079
		Bukit	Melayu Bukit	0434
		—	Meratus	0434
		Tamiang	—	0014
5	Madurese	—	Madhura	0091
		—	Madure	0091

No.	Language	Sub-Language	Alias/Same Code	Code
		—	Basa Mathura	0091
		—	Kangean	0092
6	Minangkabau	—	Minang	0028
		—	Padang	0028
7	Banjarese	—	Labuhan	0385
		—	Melayu Banjar	0385
8	Buginese	—	Bugi	0554
		—	De'	0554
		—	Rappang Bugi	0554
		—	Ugi	0554
		Campalagian	Tallumpanuae	0627
		—	Tasing	0627
		—	Tjampalagian	0627
9	Balinese	—	—	0096
10	Batak	Batak Alas-Kluet	Alas-Kluet Batak	0015
		Batak Angkola	Anakola	0016
		—	Angkola	0016
		Batak Dairi	Dairi	0017
		—	Pakpak	0017
		—	Pakpak Dairi	0017
		Batak Karo	Karo Batak	0018
		Batak Mandailing	Mandailing Batak	0019
		Batak Pak-Pak	—	0020
		Batak Pesisir	—	0021
		Batak Samosir	—	0022
		Batak Simalungun	Simelungan Timur	0023
		Batak Toba	Toba Batak	0024
		—	Batta	0024
11	Cirebonese	—	—	0084
		Dermayon	—	0085
		Indramayu	—	0085
12	Lombok	—	—	0164
		—	Sasak	0164
13	Acehnese	—	Aceh	0001
		—	Acheh	0001
		—	Achi	0001
		Aceh Aneuk	—	0002

No.	Language	Sub-Language	Alias/Same Code	Code
		Aceh Hulu Singkil	—	0003
		Aceh Jamac	—	0004
		Aceh Kluet	—	0005
		Aceh Pulau Banyak	—	0006
		Aceh Simeleu Barat	—	0007
		Aceh Simeleu Tengah	—	0008
14	Betawi	—	Batavi	0082
		—	Batawi	0082
		—	Melayu Betawi	0082
		—	Melayu Jakarta	0082
		—	Melayu Jakarte	0082
15	Dayak	Dayak Ahe	—	0480
		Dayak Bakau	—	0439
		Dayak Bara Injey	—	0391
		Dayak Darat	Dayak Klemautan	0440
		Dayak Dohoi	—	0392
		Dayak Dusun	—	0393
		Dayak Kaninjal	Kaninjal Dayak	0246
		—	Kaninjal	0246
		—	Keninjal	0246
		Dayak Katingan	—	0394
		Dayak Kenyah	Bahau	0428
		Dayak Laut	Heban	0247
		Dayak Manyan	—	0395
		Dayak Murut	—	0441
		Dayak Ngaju	—	0396
		Dayak Punan	—	0442
		Kendayan Dayak	Kendayan-Ambawang	0210
		—	Kendayan	0210
		—	Baicit	0210
		—	Damea	0210
		Maanyak Dayak	Ma'anjan	0483
		—	Ma'anyan	0483
		Ngaju Dayak	Ngadju	0387
		—	Ngaja	0387
		—	Barito Barat Daya	0387

No.	Language	Sub-Language	Alias/Same Code	Code
		—	Biadju	0387
		Sea Dayak	—	0340
		Tawoyan Dayak	Tawoyan	0418
		—	Tewoyan	0418
		—	Tabojan	0418
		—	Tabojan Tongka	0418
		—	Tabuyan	0418
		Taman Dayak	Taman	0248
		—	Dayak Taman	0248
		Tunjung Dayak	Tunjung	0475
		Kubitn	—	0199
		Air Durian	—	0200
		Air Upas	—	0201
		Kelabit	—	0202
		Banana'	—	0203
		Rantawan	—	0204
		Baaje'	—	0205
		Banyuke	—	0206
		Badamea	—	0207
		Bubung	—	0209
		Bakambai	Bakumpai	0211
		Bakati'	—	0212
		Bakati' Rara	—	0213
		Bakati' Sara	—	0214
		Balangitn	—	0215
		Balantiatn	—	0217
		Selibong	Bamak	0218
		Bangae' Moro	—	0219
		Banyadu'	—	0220
		Banyur	—	0221
		Barai	—	0222
		Batu Entawa'	—	0223
		Batu Payung	—	0224
		Batu Tajam	—	0225
		Baya	—	0226
		Beabon-abon	—	0227

No.	Language	Sub-Language	Alias/Same Code	Code
		Beapay-apay	—	0228
		Beape-ape	Ella	0229
		Beginci	—	0230
		Keneles	—	0231
		Belaban	—	0232
		Benadai	—	0233
		Iban	—	0234
		Benatu	—	0235
		Benawas	—	0236
		Cempede	—	0237
		Bi Somu	—	0238
		Jagoi	—	0239
		Bihak	—	0240
		Buket	—	0242
		Butok	—	0243
		Cihie	—	0244
		Daro'	—	0245
		Desa	—	0249
		Dohoi	—	0250
		Ensilat	—	0253
		Gerai	—	0255
		Gerunggang	—	0256
		Golik	—	0257
		Gun	—	0258
		Hibun	—	0259
		Punan Bungan	—	0260
		Inggar Silat	—	0261
		Jangkang	—	0262
		Jawatn	—	0263
		Kalis	—	0264
		Kancikng	—	0265
		Kantu'	—	0266
		Kayaan	—	0268
		Kayong	—	0270
		Kebuai	—	0271
		Kekura'	—	0272

No.	Language	Sub-Language	Alias/Same Code	Code
		Keluas	—	0273
		Kengkubang	—	0274
		Kenyilu	—	0275
		Kepuas	—	0276
		Kerabat	—	0277
		Keramay	—	0278
		Ketior	—	0279
		Ketungau Sesae'	—	0280
		Kodatn	—	0281
		Koman	—	0282
		Kowotn	—	0283
		Krio	—	0284
		Kualatn	—	0285
		Lamantawa	—	0286
		Lau'	—	0287
		Laur	—	0288
		Laya	—	0289
		Lemandau	—	0290
		Liboy	—	0291
		Limbai	—	0292
		Linoh	—	0293
		Mahap	—	0294
		Mali	—	0295
		Mayan	—	0296
		Mayau	—	0297
		Melahoi	—	0298
		Membulu'	—	0299
		Menggaling	—	0300
		Mentebah	—	0301
		Menterap Kabut	—	0302
		Menterap Sekado	—	0303
		Mentuka'	—	0304
		Mualang	—	0305
		Muara	—	0306
		Mudu'	—	0307
		Nado	Nto	0308

No.	Language	Sub-Language	Alias/Same Code	Code
		Nahaya'	—	0309
		Oruung Da'an	—	0310
		Pangin	—	0311
		Pangkalan Suka	—	0312
		Panu	—	0314
		Paus	—	0315
		Pawatn	—	0316
		Pelanjau	—	0317
		Penyarang	—	0318
		Perigi	—	0319
		Pesaguan Hulu	—	0320
		Pesaguan Kanan	—	0321
		Pompakng	—	0322
		Pringkunyit	—	0323
		Pruwan	—	0324
		Punan	—	0325
		Punti	—	0326
		Randau Joka'	—	0327
		Randu'	—	0328
		Ransa	—	0329
		Rembay	—	0330
		Riam	—	0331
		Sajan	—	0333
		Salako	—	0334
		Sami	—	0335
		Sane	—	0336
		Sanggau	—	0337
		Sangku'	—	0338
		Sapatoi	—	0339
		Sebaru'	—	0341
		Seberuang	—	0342
		Sekajang	—	0343
		Sekakai	—	0344
		Sekapat	—	0345
		Sekubang	—	0346
		Sekujam	—	0347

No.	Language	Sub-Language	Alias/Same Code	Code
		Selawe	—	0348
		Semanakng	—	0349
		Sempadian	—	0350
		Senangkatn	—	0351
		Senduruhan	—	0352
		Sepauhan	—	0353
		Sikukng	—	0354
		Silatn Muntak	—	0355
		Sisang	—	0356
		Sontas	—	0357
		Suaid	—	0358
		Suka Maju	—	0359
		Sum	—	0360
		Sumanjawat	—	0361
		Suru' Ilir	—	0362
		Suru' Ulu	—	0363
		Suruh	—	0364
		Suti Bamayo	—	0365
		Taba	—	0366
		Tadietn	—	0367
		Talaga-Ngabukit	—	0368
		Tamambalo	—	0369
		Taman Sekado	—	0370
		Tameng	—	0371
		Tanjung	—	0372
		Tawaeq	—	0373
		Tebang	Tobak	0374
		Tembiruhan	—	0375
		Tengon	—	0376
		Tinying	—	0377
		Tola'	—	0378
		Ulu sekado	—	0379
		Undau	—	0380
		Paku	—	0382
		Barito	—	0386
		Ngaju Dayak	—	0387
		Lawangan	—	0388

No.	Language	Sub-Language	Alias/Same Code	Code
		Siang	—	0392
		Ot Danum	Uud Danum	0407
		—	Uut Danum	0407
		Manyan	—	0408
		Punan Merap	—	0414
		Rejang Baram	—	0415
		Sampit	—	0417
		Tawoyan Dayak	—	0418
		Aoheng	Penihing	0425
		Punan Aput	—	0426
		Berau	—	0431
		Burusu	—	0432
		Bulungan	—	0435
		Busang	—	0436
		Kayan	—	0445
		Kenyah	Usun Apau kenyah	0450
		kenyah Barat	Uma' Lasan	0451
		Kenyah Wahau	—	0452
		Lun Bawang	Lun Daya	0457
		—	Lun Dayah	0457
		—	Lun Daye	0457
		—	Lun Dayoh	0457
		—	Lundaya Putuk	0457
		Lundayeh	—	0458
		Merau	—	0463
		Modang	—	0465
		Uma' Lung	—	0467
		Punan Tubu	—	0468
		Putuk	Putoh	0469
		Sembakung Murut	—	0472
		Tagol	—	0473
		Tidung	—	0474
		Uheng Kereho	—	0476
		Bidayuh Biatah	—	0478
		Bidayuh Bukar-Sadong	Bideyu	0479
		Maloh	Embaloh	0481
		—	Malo	0481

No.	Language	Sub-Language	Alias/Same Code	Code
		Tagal Murut	—	0485
		Uma	—	0529
		Sawai	—	0772
		Entebang	—	0860
		Marau	—	1051
16	Makassarese	—	Makasar	0557
		—	Makassa	0557
		—	Mengkasara	0557
		—	Mangasara	0557
		—	Taena	0557
		—	Tena	0557
		—	Goa	0557
		Bentong	Dentong	0552
		Konjo	—	0559
		Konjo Pantai	—	0561
		Konjo Pegunungan	—	0562
		Konjo Pesisir	—	0560
		Konjo Tanah Tinggi	Konyo	0562
		Salayar	Salayer	0578
		—	Saleier	0578
		—	Selayar	0578
		—	Siladja	0578
		—	Silajara	0578
		—	Salajar	0578
17	Bantenese	Indramayu	—	0095
18	Nias	—	Batu	0025
		Sikule	Sikhule	0013
		—	Sichule	0013
		—	Wali Banuah	0013
19	Bangka	—	—	0074
20	Chinese	China Hakka	—	1161
		China Mandarin	—	1162
		China Min Dong	—	1163
		China Min Nan	—	1164
		China Hokian	—	1175
		China Yue	—	1165

Index

ABOUT THE AUTHORS

Aris Ananta was a Senior Research Fellow at the Institute of Southeast Asian Studies (ISEAS), Singapore. Currently, he is Professor at the Faculty of Economics and Business, University of Indonesia (UI), Depok, West Java, Indonesia.

Evi Nurvidya Arifin was a Visiting Research Fellow at the Institute of Southeast Asian Studies, Singapore. Currently, she is a demographer at the Centre for Ageing Studies, University of Indonesia (UI), Depok, West Java, Indonesia.

Nur Budi Handayani is a Statistician and Head of Planning Section in Sub-Directorate Education and Social Welfare, Directorate Statistics on People's Welfare, Statistics-Indonesia (BPS), Jakarta, Indonesia.

M. Sairi Hasbullah is a Statistician and Head of Statistics-Indonesia (BPS) — East Java, Surabaya, East Java, Indonesia.

Agus Pramono is a Statistician at Statistics-Indonesia (BPS), Jakarta, Indonesia.

www.ingramcontent.com/pod-product-compliance
Lightning Source LLC
Chambersburg PA
CBHW072043020426
42334CB00017B/1374